THE SYLLABLE IN SPEECH PRODUCTION

THE STRUCTURE OF SERIAL PRODUCTION

THE SYLLABLE IN SPEECH PRODUCTION

Barbara L. Davis • Krisztina Zajdó

LEA Lawrence Erlbaum Associates
Taylor & Francis Group

New York   London

Lawrence Erlbaum Associates
Taylor & Francis Group
270 Madison Avenue
New York, NY 10016

Lawrence Erlbaum Associates
Taylor & Francis Group
2 Park Square
Milton Park, Abingdon
Oxon OX14 4RN

© 2008 by Taylor & Francis Group, LLC
Lawrence Erlbaum Associates is an imprint of Taylor & Francis Group, an Informa business

Printed in the United States of America on acid-free paper
10 9 8 7 6 5 4 3 2 1

International Standard Book Number-13: 978-0-8058-5480-0 (Softcover) 978-0-8058-5479-4 (Hardcover)

Visit the Taylor & Francis Web site at
http://www.taylorandfrancis.com

and the LEA and Routledge Web site at
http://www.routledge.com

Contents

Foreword

Björn Lindblom

Stockholm University

and

The University of Texas at Austin

There are no absolute explanations in science, only broader and deeper accounts. Every academic discipline chooses its own starting points and proceeds from there to investigate its chosen fragment of the universe. In this sense, any scientific explanation rests on a (set of) preliminary, and vulnerable, claim(s). Progress takes place when scientists succeed in broadening and deepening their understanding of reality.

The syllable is a linguistic primitive, a unit found in all languages. It is made up of vowels and consonants which are similarly ubiquitous in the world's languages. These entities are part of the "starting points" of linguistic and phonetic inquiry. On the basis of their status as "universals without exceptions," they are not questioned. They are axiomatically postulated and serve as building blocks in the phonetician's and phonologist's attempts to explain speech and sound structure.

"Axiomatically postulated" means that they are indeed primitives. They are a prioris to be taken for granted. Hence, the question of where they come from becomes a non-issue. The descriptive convenience of having them outweighs any urge to dig deeper and get below their axiomatic surface.

Enter Peter MacNeilage who refuses to treat syllables and phonetic segments as givens maintaining that their existence *both should and can* be explained, provided of course that we adopt a biological style of inquiry!

To a true Darwinian biologist, that approach means asking four questions when studying any phenomenon in living organisms. Originally proposed by Niko Tinbergen they are: The question of mechanism: "How does it work?"; the question of function: "What does it do for the organism?"; and two questions of origin: "How did it get that way?" both in ontogeny and phylogeny. The basic mechanism of change is taken to be "descent with modification" driven by natural selection promoting successful use.

Here are some short samples of the evidence that Peter has put forward. The most detailed treatment of his position is found in his new book: *The Invisible Miracle: A Darwinian Theory of Speech* [henceforth IM]. Through the topics touched upon below runs the common theme of the open-close movement of the mandible.

In adult speech production, vowels are open articulations whereas consonants are closed. Note that the degree of openness does not refer to how constricted the vocal tract is. For while it is true that consonants are more constricted than vowels, a much better correlate of openness is the position of the mandible. This is a preferable choice as shown by a number of facts. For instance, consider the vowel [a] which is made with a narrow constriction in the posterior part of the vocal tract. Nonetheless, it is classified as an open vowel because of its wide mandible opening. It follows that a sequence of syllables will exhibit several cycles of an open-close alternation of the mandible. This is a fact about the syllabic organization of adult speech, a fundamental one that lacks an explanation so far but that certainly calls for one.

Adult jaw movement has a parallel in early speech development. From six months on, all normal children produce vocalizations called reduplicated *babbling* resembling [ba ba ba]. The preceding transcription incorrectly implies that the production of such output is organized in terms of discrete segments. There is no evidence to justify such a conclusion. Rather the pseudo-syllabic and pseudo segmental character of these utterances can be assumed to be the fortuitous consequence of the child combining phonation with an open-close alternation of the mandible, the main articulatory activity in this behavior.

Another curious parallel to the motion of the jaw in speech is presented by facio-visual communication in primates: Rhythmically repeated up-and-down movement of the mandible is found in certain facial gestures used as communicative signals by primates. The most common example is the *lipsmack* often combined with phonation and typically occurring during grooming and ingestion of whatever happens to be discovered during that process.

Why is jaw movement in speech restricted to an up-down motion (cf. the "degrees of freedom problem" discussed below)? Peter notes that a large number of animal movements are oscillatory. Consider breathing, scratching, digging, tail wagging, different forms of locomotion (walking, running, swimming, flapping of wings). Mammal feeding behavior (mastication, sucking and licking) presents other examples particularly relevant to speech. Chewing movements show a strong mandibular component.

Looking at brain mechanisms Peter observes that the lateral frontal lobe is the main site of cortical feeding control in mammals and that a continuous steady electrical current applied to motor regions of the brain can produce rhythmic movements. For instance, stimulation of the premotor cortex evokes activity resembling normal chewing both in animals and humans.

Stimulation of the SMA (Supplementary Motor Area) can produce rhythmic repetitions of a syllable like nonsense speech. Lesions to the same area have been reported to result in utterances such as [la, la, la, la] and [da, da, da, da].

Striking support for Peter's account comes from work on mirror neurons in monkeys. In an area lateral to a region linked to manual movements—and considered to be homologous with part of Broca's area—neurons associated with mouth movements have been identified. Exploration of these mouth-related neurons revealed that they are involved in both ingestion and making visuo-facial lipsmacks.

So where do syllables come from? The short answer, according to the Frame/Content theory, is that the origin of the syllable goes back to prehistoric times when the biomechanics and neural structures evolved in mammals for feeding. A second major landmark is the use of these structures in the communicative behavior of primates (lipsmacks). A third evolutionary way station is the co-opting of the mechanism for speech purposes and the emergence of the Frame.

Before the F/C theory, thinking about the jaw in speech we might at first have considered the syllable as an epiphenomenon arising from the alternation of open vowels and closed consonants. But then one could quickly dismiss that line of thought because it raises the question of where vowels and consonants come from in the first place.

We might also have taken the same road as many phoneticians have done (myself included) modeling articulators as damped spring-mass systems. This approach treats the mandible as an oscillator and derives speech jaw motions as free vibrations. Again there would be reasons for second thoughts since the jaw is clearly not such an oscillator. In response to an instantaneous force, it would not, like a tuning fork, sustain its vibration because, biomechanically, it is an over damped system. To make it go up and down a series of opposite and alternating forces would need to be applied.

Such considerations make us realize that mandibular oscillation cannot be explained in terms of simple metaphors borrowed from physics. It is evidently driven by neural machinery that has been set up to deliver patterns of alternating opening and closing forces.

Where does that mechanism come from? We are led to say with Peter that mandibular oscillation must have been shaped by an evolutionary development, namely the borrowing from pre-existing neural circuits (pattern generators) whose main job was to do "ingestive cyclicities."

Another point we should make to fully appreciate the implications of Peter's synthesis is to look at jaw movement in speech in terms of the degrees of freedom problem. This is the problem of selecting a unique movement path from a very rich set of possible motions. While phoneticians see jaw movement as mainly one-dimensional, those investigating mastication are used to dealing with a complex set of anterior-posterior, inferior-superior and transversal movements. In other words, the lower jaw is capable of much more complex movement than open-close alternations.

Thinking about the mandible in that way we can say that Peter's contribution helps solve the degrees of freedom problem. From there we can return to biomechanics and compare the jaw to an oscillator, this time a virtual one that includes the reciprocal innervation and other structures. We may then begin to see how 3-D chewing could turn into (primarily) 1-D speech movements. To deal with that transition my personal preference would be to invoke an evolutionarily plausible constraint: the minimization of physiological energy. Albeit compatible with the F/C theory, that suggestion requires another story.

Let me comment on another of Peter's major contributions, his strong criticism of Noam Chomsky's work.

In the eighties Chomsky wrote: "In my view …. natural selection in itself does not provide anywhere near enough structure to account for what happens in evolution." (Knowledge of language).

At about the same time David Premack remarked: "Human language is an embarrassment for evolutionary theory because it is vastly more powerful than one can account for in terms of selective fitness."

If we were to ask Peter today: "Didn't both Chomsky and Premack get it backwards? It is Chomsky's theory that becomes embarrassing when examined in the context of evolution, isn't it?," –he would without hesitation say: "Yes, absolutely!"

So what's wrong with the classical structure of Chomskyan linguistic theory? In short, Peter faults Chomsky for treating language as a *de novo* development and for leaving out the developmental and evolutionary time dimension. Peter states: "*Novel forms or behaviors don't suddenly appear out of nowhere. They are always modifications of pre-existing forms or behaviors. And these novel forms or behaviors evolve as a result of successful use."* (IM chapter 1). Contrast that statement with Chomsky's *"You can't just assume that because something's there, it is functional, or has been adapted for. . . . It could be just there."* (interview in the *New Yorker* with MacFarquhar 2003).

Peter's Frame/Content theory offers an action-based explanation of where syllables and vowels and consonants come from. It differs radically from Chomsky's Universal Grammar which either has to remain silent on where syllables and phonetic segments come from, or must resort to pre-specification in Universal Grammar (=declare syllables and phonetic segments innate). Peter's account, on the other hand, is in perfect line with both Roger Sperry's idea of *"embodiment"* (deriving mind from body) and Karl Lashley's view that the principles underlying *serial organization* have motor origins.

We often hear of the Chomskyan "revolution" which is odd since there *never was* a genuine revolution in the sense of a true intellectual paradigm shift. Admittedly Chomsky's impact on linguistics and related fields has been spectacular in a sociological sense. But it is important to note that by endorsing the Saussurean distinction between "langue" and "parole" and introducing his own parallel distinction between "competence" and "performance," he made a life-long commitment to structuralism: *"It seems natural to suppose that the study of actual linguistic performance can be seriously pursued only to the extent that we have a good understanding of the generative grammars that are acquired by the learner and put to use by the speaker or hearer. The classical Saussurean assumption of the logical priority of the study of langue (and the generative grammars that describe it) seems quite inescapable."* Chomsky has in fact come to symbolize structuralism.

What's wrong with structuralism? Why does it still represent the ruling paradigm? Why is it still popular? I presume that, with respect to the preceding quote, Peter would say that Chomsky got it backwards again and that the *"logical priority of the study of langue"* is not at all *"inescapable."* Instead we should say that it is *"the study of"* "langue" that *"can be seriously pursued only to the extent that we have a good understanding of"* its acquisition *"by the learner"* and its *"use by the speaker or hearer."*

Rather than put words in Peter's mouth, let me share with you one of my own reasons for wishing that structuralism would go away.

Many of the triumphs of the descriptive linguistics of the past century derive from splitting the study of speech sounds into phonology dealing with sound structure (the hierarchical and serial organization of timeless, discrete units such as syllables, segments, features) and phonetics describing continuous time-varying movements and audible signals. I often return to the following quote always noting the tone of relief and gratitude in Stephen Andersen's description of how Saussure commendably split away phonetics from phonology. He states that one of Ferdinand de Saussure's main contributions was: *".... to focus the attention of the linguist on the system of regularities and relations which support the differences among signs, rather than on the details of individual sound and meaning in and of themselves.....For Saussure, the detailed information accumulated by phoneticians is of only limited utility for the linguist, since he is primarily interested in the ways in which sound images differ, and thus does not need to know everything the phonetician can tell him. .... By this move, then, linguists could be emancipated from their growing obsession with phonetic detail."* (sic!).

After a century of structuralism, phonology, a component of grammatical competence (the linguist's concern), still relegates phonetics to performance (the experimentalist's concern). However, linguists have begun to demand more than observational and descriptive adequacy. The question of explanation has been raised. This ambition creates a huge problem for the phonologist since, in seeking explanations, it is necessary to refer back to the phonetic substance (the *explanans knowledge*) that was discarded in the process of defining the discrete units and the structure (the *explananda*).

Can this problem be solved? The answer is that, since it is trapped in the conceptual prison of the form/substance distinction, structuralist linguistics has come up against a definitive roadblock. There is no way this problem can be solved within existing frameworks. Linguistics is currently paying the price of having gone structuralist and thereby sawing off the explanatory branch it was sitting on.

My recommendation to fellow phonologists would be this: Completely reject the phonetics/phonology split. Deduce sound structure from language use. Anchor theory construction in the universal conditions under which all speech communication must take place. Start from "first principles' and not circularly from the data to be explained (cf. *"markedness"*). At the level of the individual user, model phonological structure, not as autonomous form, but as an emergent organization of phonetic substance acquired by each native speaker in the context of socially shared, ambient knowledge. At the population level, model this knowledge as a use- and user-dependent process that undergoes change along the historical time scale. Here is the key step: *Make the "intrinsic phonetic content" an integral part of the theory from scratch.* Treat intrinsic content as the source that helps generate discrete structure and that constrains both synchronic and diachronic phonological patterning.

How should such an undertaking be implemented? Ultimately by responding to Tinbergen's four questions: How does it work? What does it do for the organism? How did it get that way in development and evolution?

Chomsky's view focusing on syntax differs drastically from the above picture. Unfortunately it has been allowed to dominate linguistic theory construction: We have been told that linguistic form is totally arbitrary and idiosyncratic. Hence finding functional explanations are regarded as a futile pursuit.

Why do phoneticians and syntacticians see the situation so differently?

To comment on that question I will make two observations. The first is that we are all prone to fall victim of Bishop Paley's fallacy (see below). The second concerns the fact that, in the world of learning engaged in the noble pursuit of truth, academic programs are not only controlled by their scientific content but also by their survival niches as shaped by various market forces (student background, enrollment, availability of jobs, etc.). Combining these two points we will realize that there is more to overthrowing a paradigm such as structuralism than just the purely scientific issues.

Here is my first point.

In the *Blind Watchmaker* Richard Dawkins tells us about Bishop William Paley who lived in the 18th century and wrote *Natural Theology —or Evidences of the Existence and Attributes of the Deity Collected from the Appearances of Nature*. Paley was fascinated with the complex beauty of Nature. He compared the eye with the telescope and concluded that "there is precisely the same proof that the eye was made for vision, as there is that the telescope was made for assisting it." Consequently, he argued, the eye must also have had a designer. Let us call this analogy Paley's fallacy.

Dawkins notes that human beings seem predisposed to reason as Paley did. He suggests that it is "as if the human brain were specifically designed to misunderstand Darwinism and to find it hard to believe. ...Our brains are built to deal with events on radically different timescales from those that characterize evolutionary change. We are equipped to appreciate processes that take seconds, minutes, years or, at most, decades to complete. Darwinism is a theory of cumulative processes so slow that they take between thousands and millions of decades to complete. All our intuitive judgments of what is probable turn out to be wrong by many orders of magnitude."

This inability to do the mental arithmetic required in picturing cumulative evolutionary change is what underlies Paley's fallacy and makes it tempting for critics of Darwinism to say: "Just because something is there, does not mean that natural selection had anything to do with it. It could just be there!" (cf. Chomksy quote above).

To make my second point I will frame it in terms of a hypothetical conversation with a close friend and colleague.

Let us suppose that this friend was originally in linguistics but became a successful sociology professor later on. We shall also make him a university administrator who frequently says that he would like to see some more action in the area of Liberal Arts.

One day I look him up with the following proposition:

— "Here is the deal," I say. "We are going to rewrite linguistics on Darwinian principles. Make it part of evolutionary biology. Massively multi-disciplinary and experimental. Really high-powered stuff. Look at the reviews. All from top-notch people representing science at the cutting edge of the major fields. They just love it. What do you think?"

—"Lindblom my friend, you are such an idiot. I have read your proposal and it just won't fly. Don't you realize that the study of human language has always been part of the humanities and that's the way it's going to be. The backbone of linguistics is structuralism. Saussure is our man. Bless his soul. Structuralism puts the focus on language structure, not language behavior. That means *autonomy*. A key strategic word my friend. Autonomy helps you keep linguistics within the Liberal Arts. It discourages interaction with other fields. In other words, gets rid of all the interdisciplinary stuff. Spoken language is vast and complex. Never mind. Put emphasis on syntax. Tag on a bit of phonology. Ignore how people actually speak. Deal only with what they 'know.' The mental stuff."

— "You are beginning to sound like Chomsky."

— "Sure. Why not? His paradigm is perfectly adapted to the autonomy niche. Whether linguists agree with him or not, that's where they survive academically."

— "Spoken language can be studied as a physical, physiological, psychological, social, cultural ....."

— "Let's not mess with all that. Performance is not part of the program. No need for experiments and laboratory work. Have students study the grammars of specific languages. Assign simple and doable stuff like trying to figure out how sentences are generated, how vowels and consonants are used in words, etc. Write rules and develop rule systems and theories to account for observed data."

— "What about phonetics?"

— "Well, all that is needed from you guys is a list of the world's speech sounds. That will be used for the phonological component. Let the real linguists take it from there. Recall Trubetzkoy's statement in *Grundzüge der Phonologie*: "*Um einen treffende Vergleich Roman Jakobsons zu wiederholen, verhält sich die Phonologie zur Phonetik wie die Nationalökonomie zur Warenkunde oder die Finanzwissenschaft zur Numismatik.*"

— "Wait a minute. If linguists just limit their work to formal descriptions of syntactic and phonological patterns, in what sense are their descriptions real? Don't such descriptions have to explain something? What you are advocating seems like mere curve fitting to me."

— "The beauty of the scheme is that the phenomena to be investigated are so complex and idiosyncratic that coming up with functional explanations for them is utterly remote."

— "How do kids learn then?"

—"The genetic component makes a strong contribution. Native language experience serves to fine tune the process. Mostly innate."

— "That is pure Chomsky! May I dare to ask: What if this is all wrong?"

— "Unfortunately for naïve idealists like yourself, academic programs are not shaped by the noble pursuit of scientific truth alone. Chomsky's tale of human language as an autonomous mechanism has created a stronger, more autonomous linguistics. His brilliance and charisma help convey the impression that he got it right. He has worked out lots of answers to deal with the opposition thereby effectively blocking the roads to and from other disciplines that deal with performance, evolution and development etc. Admittedly a gamble, but a fairly safe one, since language structure is so idiosyncratic and complex that it will be a while before alternative approaches catch up. Do phoneticians and linguists agree with him or not? That is, my friend, totally irrelevant. Chomsky has made their survival niche stronger and more prestigious and kept it within the Liberal Arts. If you touch structuralism and accuse Chomsky for upgrading and consolidating it, you will be perceived as a threat and you will once more see the relevance of the old saying "entrenched beliefs tend not to be altered by the facts."

My hope is that these concluding remarks have indicated that Peter's problem with Chomskyan linguistics is not only his, but everybody's problem. It translates into a battle between two powerful paradigms. The Chomskyan school of thought exemplifies a flaw in traditional humanistic thinking, namely the view of *man as separate from nature*.

The neo-Darwinian approach sees *man as part of nature* and maintains that human nature can only be understood in terms of its full biological context. We are greatly indebted to Peter for conveying that message to us.

Preface

Barbara L. Davis

Department of Communication Sciences and Disorders

The University of Texas at Austin

Austin, Texas, USA

and

Krisztina Zajdó

Division of Communication Disorders

University of Wyoming

Laramie, Wyoming, USA

The original impetus for this tribute volume emerged from an international conference held in honor of Peter MacNeilage. The first steps toward this idea were initiated by Dr. Zajdó as well as lab members working with the Speech Production Lab at The University of Texas at Austin. We felt strongly that we needed to properly celebrate Peter's prolonged and substantial contributions to the discipline of phonetic sciences. The resulting conference was held as a satellite meeting associated with the 15th International Congress of Phonetic Sciences in Barcelona, Spain on August 1st and 2nd, 2003. As we began asking people to participate in this conference tribute to Peter, we found that everyone we contacted was pleased to be included in such an event. We had positive responses from 36 different scientists representing 12 countries. The result was an exciting two day meeting packed with talks and discussion as well as food and congeniality; a fitting tribute both to Peter's scholarly contributions and to his dry New Zealand wit.

As a testament to the scope of Peter's scholarly work across his 40 year career, conference participants represented a wide variety of focus areas for scientific inquiry. Fittingly, participant contributions spanned a broad spectrum of the seminal issues addressed by phonetic and evolutionary science over a number of years. Approaches to the problems raised by attempting to understand these fundamental topics were illustrated, as well, in the broad diversity of paradigms represented at the conference. This diversity forms a major type of tribute to the applicability of scholarly questions pursued by MacNeilage across his career.

Subsequent to that meeting, we contacted participants about involvement in this tribute volume. Again, we were overwhelmed with their positive response. Indeed, we were faced with the difficult task of considering how many chapters we could conceivably fit into one volume, as our first pass through conference attendees who were potential authors resulted in the possibility of two volumes. The present work, *The Syllable in Speech Production*, represents the outcome of this outpouring of respect for Peter MacNeilage and his contributions to scientific inquiry into the nature and ultimate causes of speech production patterns in ontogeny and in phylogeny.

Chapters are arranged around five thematic areas. Two themes, *Evolutionary Perspectives on Speech Production* and *Acquisition of Speech*, reflect the major thrust of Peter's scholarly career over the past 25 years. The other three themes reflect the broad implications of Peter's work for scholars who focus on diverse scientific domains cogent to the broad questions about speech production and its origins that Peter has posed across his career. These sections include chapters on *Perception-Action Relationships* and *Modeling and Movement*, as well as *Alternative Perspectives on the Syllable*. These paradigms for considering speech production reflect seminal dimensions of Peter's approach to the problem of understanding the underlying nature of the output system for language more fully. The structure of the volume around these themes also constitutes a look at the diverse status of research into the nature and ultimate causes of speech production patterns in modern languages.

Chapter 1 opens this dialog with an introduction by Peter of the major claims and supportive data for the Frame/Content theory. His chapter provides a general level of focus for many of the contribution in this volume. In particular, Peter summarizes the precise evolutionary hypothesis of the Frame/Content theory as well as the large body of speech acquisition studies employed to test this hypothesis over the past 20 years. He argues that data on ontogeny illustrates that the syllable as a functionally separate organizational unit in modern languages emerged as a result of a step-like developmental process during evolution. In short, in considering potential explanations for the origin of modern language structure, ontogeny provides a robust and valid mirror into probable early steps of the phylogenetic sequence toward use of a vocal communication channel. In addition to the body of work on acquisition, MacNeilage reviews an integrative scenario encompassing understanding of the underlying neurology of the speech production process whereby at the neurological level, control of the frame and content components has evolved within two motor control subsystems—an intrinsic system involving medial pre-motor cortex (SMA) for frame control, and an extrinsic system involving ventral pre-motor control (Broca's area) for content control.

The subsequent section, *Evolutionary Perspectives on Speech Production*, contains four chapters addressing the ultimate origins and causes of the nature of modern speech production patterning. In Chapter 2, Oller and Griebel employ cross species comparisons to consider aspects crucial to the emergence of language syllabification. In particular, the authors argue that the complex temporal organization of modern language required special adaptations of syllable structure to allow rapid transmission of richly coded, flexible information. Temporal organization of high complexity implies the existence of minimal rhythmic units that can be sequenced and recombined. The researchers note that the term "syllable" is typically used to characterize these minimal units. The Frame/Content proposal is considered by the authors to be one approach to underlie a key aspect of the logic of the necessary adaptation to rhythmic structure in cases of high complexity. Oller and Griebel further emphasize the necessity to incorporate the phonatory component along with the strong emphasis on the articulatory component embodied in the claims of the Frame/Content Theory.

In Chapter 3, Boë and colleagues consider the language origin question by evaluating a language typology paradigm. The researchers employ rigorous statistical analyses to examine Merritt Ruhlen's conclusions on genetic typology. The authors argue that the similarities observed in Ruhlen's data are not due to the fact that all the languages spoken in the world today originate from the same mother tongue. Instead, the authors suggest the alternative hypothesis that these similarities emerge from the fact that modern speakers use the same vocal tract and hearing system to differentiate phonological shapes of lexical items and that a common set of vowels and consonants are used across all the world's languages. The researchers conclude that the Frame/Content theory has useful explanatory power for elucidating universal tendencies observed in syllables structures. Demolin's narrative is focused on considering emergence of consonants in sound systems and their status within the frame/content theory of speech evolution. Using cross species comparisons of palatal dimensions, his argument is that an important observation can be made about consonant distribution: the vast majority of consonants in the world's languages are produced with a closure or a constriction between the lips and the velum because consonants articulated in this part of the vocal tract require some proprioceptive control between the tongue and the upper palate. Demolin proposes that this fact is a likely consequence of the phylogenetic evolution of the vocal tract shape during late evolution of hominoids. Foreshortening of the face, mandible and maxilla played a crucial role in the enlargement of the supralaryngeal vocal tract allowing the tongue to play a more extensive role in reshaping the cavity during phonation enabling a much wider range of sounds for speech. The conjoint set of sounds and sound patterns favored in babbling and in the world's languages may constitute in effect the fossil record of contemporary speech patterns. In Chapter 5, Locke theorizes about the relationship between the evolution of social gestures and speech, by emphasizing the importance of an ethological framework. The author asserts that in evolution, the mandibular action supporting speech may have manifested earlier in the form of primate lipsmacking. If so, preexisting social functions of this behavior may have been preserved along with its biomechanical action. According to Locke, this action complex would have given hominids a means of relating that was both affiliative in function and syllabic in form, constituting an optimal context for the evolution of human language.

Two chapters in the second section focus on *Neurobiological Aspects of Speech Production*. In Chapter 6, Fogassi and Ferrari propose that mirror neurons underlie the capacity to understand actions and gestures and could have constituted a neural basis for language evolution. In the researchers' view, one function in which such a matching system could be involved is inter-individual communication. Recent results about neural activity patterns in the most lateral part of area F5 during monkeys' execution of mouth actions suggest that in this sector of F5 neurons responding to both observation and execution of mouth actions (mouth mirror neurons) are found. The authors propose that the properties of mouth mirror neurons suggest a possible evolution of the communicative system from a neural substrate involved in ingestive behaviors. In the final chapter in this section, Schiller examines the role of syllables in psycholinguistic theory. The author notes that, for a long time, there was hope that syllables would also play a prominent role in psycholinguistics. However, after initial euphoria in both speech comprehension and speech production, conceptions pertaining to the status of syllables in phonological encoding changed when better-controlled new experiments failed to replicate old results. New evidence from Schiller's lab suggests that syllabic effects can be obtained under certain experimental conditions. This position is in line with a theoretical standpoint that conceives of syllables as being created on the fly instead of being retrieved from a repository of syllabic frames, which are filled with phonemic content. However, Schiller points out that the assumption of syllables being created on the fly does not go against the idea of a basic syllable, it only questions the claim of stored metrical frames.

Perception/Action Relationships are the focus of the subsequent four chapters. Ohala presents an alternative view of syllable production from the Frame/Content theory. In his view, there are sufficient differences between chewing and speech to make MacNeilage & Davis's evolutionary scenario of speech production suspect. He argues that the function of speech originally (and still) is the production of a sequence of sufficiently differentiated sounds. Modulations in the speech "carrier" may be made in several acoustic dimensions: amplitude, periodicity, spectrum, and fundamental frequency. Each of these acoustic parameters may be varied within a physically and physiologically constrained range. Syllables may be viewed as stretches of sequential modulations exhibiting local maxima separated by local minima within the range of possible modulations of the carrier signal. Thus, syllables are epiphenomenal and not basic elements of speech. Schauwers and colleagues describe recent findings on babbling development in congenitally deaf children who received cochlear implantation and children wearing conventional hearing aids. Their results indicate that the development of children with cochlear implants resembled that of the normally hearing children, while the development of the deaf children showed a serious delay. In the authors' view, this discrepancy emphasizes the role of hearing in vocal development in the first year of life. In Chapter 10, Moore reviews findings about syllable acquisition in children with cochlear implants. She examines patterns of consonant-vowel sequences of syllables in babbling and first words in over 40 children receiving cochlear implants in light of the Frame/Content theory, as well as age of implantation and type of speech processing strategy. Although previous findings suggest that variability of performance is common in this population, results indicate that children implanted under the age of 2 years of age show syllable shapes consistent with the Frame/Content theory. Older children with longer periods of deafness, age-appropriate sign language and cognition, show patterns of syllable development which deviate from the expected consonant-vowel co-occurrence patterns. van Beinum explores questions including why deaf infants often do not start babbling in their first year of life, the necessity for deaf children after cochlear implantation to start babbling before acquiring speech, and ways that babbling can be stimulated for speech development in these atypically developing infants.

The third section focuses on *Acquisition of Speech*, a major focus of work in the Speech Production Laboratory at UT-Austin over the past 20 years. Van der Stelt considers the role of dentition in speech acquisition. The author hypothesizes that eruption of teeth may be an important biological factor in the development of articulated speech. Christine Matyear summarizes her findings, in Chapter 13, pertaining to the acoustical structure of consonant-vowel sequences in babbling of infants raised in American English-speaking families. The author reports on the relationship between the acoustic properties of the consonants and vowels of lingual-plosive/vowel sequences in the babbling output of four typically developing infants reared in a monolingual American English environment. Analysis of second formant values at vowel onset compared to those at vowel mid-point in plosive-vowel sequences indicates a strong one-to-one correlation between the two values. The author interprets her findings to indicate that, during CV sequences produced during babbling, the tongue is not often making independent articulatory movements between consonant and vowel production. Stoel-Gammon and Peter analyze early words acquired by American children using data from the *MacArthur Communicative Development Inventories* (M-CDI). Their analyses reveal that words beginning with the labial stop /b/ accounted for 22% of the first 100 words acquired. Other labial consonants did not occur more frequently than expected. This finding is not easily explained by the influence of prelinguistic babble, because as the coronal stop [d] is more frequent than [b] in consonant-vowel babble. The influence of input (i.e., child-directed speech) cannot fully account for the finding either. Preferential use of /b/-initial words is examined in light of the frame-content theory proposed by MacNeilage and Davis, as well as other possible articulatory and linguistic factors. Validly, the authors point out that no single factor fully accounts for the observed pattern.

In the section on *Modeling and Movement*, two chapters are devoted to considering the power of modeling approaches to the understanding of speech production patterning in acquisition and in languages. In Chapter 15, Lindblom explores issues related to speech behaviors through the introduction of SPIDER, a simple learning algorithm. Though clearly limited by it's own primitive structure, SPIDER can "speak," "listen," "imitate," "remember" and "learn." Lindblom proposes that SPIDER's behavior is determined by two major characteristics: storing phonetic experience in a dynamic "memory" and biomechanical constraints on articulatory output. The author considers whether SPIDER's utterances exhibit Frame/Content properties and concludes that the relevance of the Frame/Content paradigm is reinforced via SPIDER. Redford and van Donkelaar review current phonetic and phonological data related to the asymmetric nature of the jaw cycle. They argue that an asymmetric jaw cycle has influenced the phonetic realization and phonological character of syllable-final consonants, and formed the basis for an iterative principle of syllable structure, where languages add to syllable onsets before they add to syllable offsets in an iterative fashion. Evidence is presented to show that the jaw opens more slowly than it closes, and in what order segmental gestures are planned for execution. Jaw cycle asymmetry is suggested as one possible explanation for the expansion of syllable inventories in a language over time.

In the final section, two chapters are devoted to considering *Alternative Perspectives on the Syllable*. Sandler reviews current knowledge about the phonology of spoken and signed languages, in order to identify ways to understanding of these unique systems. The author argues that the main difference between modalities is that while both have some serial organization at the sub-lexical level, the time patterning is close-grained and complex in speech, but minimal in sign, leading to the characterization of the modalities as sequential and simultaneous respectively. Like the feature, the syllable also has an analog in signed languages, and can be characterized separately from morpheme and word. However, the phonetic and the phonological structure of this unit are each significantly different in each modality. In particular, the notion that there might be a cross-modality commonality in sonority seems untenable. Sandler concludes that, while the similarities between spoken and signed languages are sufficiently important to have profound implications for the evolution of the mind in relation to language, the differences are so wide as to render the suggestion that the two modalities share a single phonological component of Universal Grammar devoid of explanatory power. In Chapter 18, Abry and colleagues put forward a proposal for interfacing the syllable and word within the metrical foot in speech and in gesture acquisition. Their hypothesis is that the 3 Hz mode is used by the speech frame and that the 1.5 Hz is used by the sign frame.

This tribute volume reflects the diverse scholarly applications of Peter MacNeilage's body of work across the course of a 40 year career. The variety of perspectives and paradigms considering the nature and ultimate explanation of speech production patterning presented here and at the tribute conference form the highest possible tribute to Peter's stature as a scholar. His sustained productivity across his long career has raised issues addressed both directly and indirectly by these scholars who focus on understanding the complex system embodied in the speech production. We express thanks to all the authors for sharing their time and work with a wide audience in appreciation of Peter.

List of Contributors

Christian Abry
Institut de la Communication Parlée
Université Stendhal
Grenoble, France
and
Institut National Polytechnique de Grenoble
Grenoble, France

Nicolas Audibert
Institut de la Communication Parlée
Université Stendhal
Grenoble, France
and
Institut National Polytechnique de Grenoble
Grenoble, France

Florien J. van Beinum
Institute of Phonetic Sciences
Universiteit van Amsterdam
Amsterdam, The Netherlands
and
Amsterdam Center for Language and Communication
Amsterdam, The Netherlands

Pierre Bessière
Informatique Graphique, Vision, Robotique (GRAVIR)
Grenoble, France

Louis-Jean Boë
Institut de la Communication Parlée
Université Stendhal,
Grenoble, France
and
Institut National Polytechnique de Grenoble
Grenoble, France

Barbara L. Davis
Department of Communication Sciences and Disorders
The University of Texas at Austin
Austin, Texas, USA

Didier Demolin
Universidade de São Paulo
Sao Paulo, Brazil
and
Université Libre de Bruxelles
Bruxelles, Belgium

Paul van Donkelaar
Department of Human Physiology
The University of Oregon
Eugene, Oregon, USA

Virginie Ducey
Institut de la Communication Parlée
Université Stendhal
Grenoble, France
and
Institut National Polytechnique de Grenoble
Grenoble, France

Pier Francesco Ferrari
Dipartimento di Neuroscienze
Università di Parma
Parma, Italy
and
Dipartimento di Psicologia
Università di Parma
Parma, Italy

Leonardo Fogassi
Dipartimento di Neuroscienze
Università di Parma
Parma, Italy
and
Dipartimento di Psicologia
Università di Parma, Borgo
Parma, Italy

Steven Gillis
Department of Linguistics
University of Antwerp
Antwerp-Wilrijk, Belgium

Paul J. Govaerts
Department of Linguistics, University of Antwerp
Antwerp-Wilrijk, Belgium
and
The Eargroup
Antwerp-Deurne, Belgium

Ulrike Griebel
Department of Biology
The University of Memphis
Memphis, Tennessee, USA
and
Konrad Lorenz Institute for Evolution and Cognition Research
Altenberg, Austria

Nadia Ladjili
Institut de la Communication Parlée
Université Stendhal
Grenoble, France
and
Institut National Polytechnique de Grenoble
Grenoble, France

Claire Lalevèe
Institut de la Communication Parlée
Université Stendhal
Grenoble, France
and
Institut National Polytechnique de Grenoble
Grenoble, France

Björn Lindblom
Department of Linguistics
Stockholm University
Stockholm, Sweden
and
Department of Linguistics
The University of Texas at Austin
Austin, Texas, USA

John L. Locke
Department of Speech–Language–Hearing Sciences
Lehman College
City University of New York
Bronx, New York, USA

Peter F. MacNeilage
Department of Psychology
The University of Texas at Austin
Austin, Texas, USA

Christine L. Matyear
Department of Communication Sciences and Disorders
The University of Texas at Austin
Austin, Texas, USA

Jan Allison Moore
Department of Communication Sciences and Disorders
The University of Texas at Austin
Austin, Texas, USA

John J. Ohala
Department of Linguistics
University of California at Berkeley
Berkeley, California, USA

D. Kimbrough Oller
School of Audiology and Speech-Language Pathology
The University of Memphis
Memphis, Tennessee, USA
and
Konrad Lorenz Institute for Evolution and Cognition Research
Altenberg, Austria

Beate Peter
Department of Speech & Hearing Sciences
University of Washington
Seattle, Washington, USA

Melissa A. Redford
Department of Linguistics
The University of Oregon
Eugene, Oregon, USA

Wendy Sandler
Department of English Language and Literature
The University of Haifa
Haifa, Israel

Karen Schauwers
Department of Linguistics
University of Antwerp
Antwerp-Wilrijk, Belgium
and
The Eargroup
Antwerp-Deurne, Belgium

Niels O. Schiller
Department of Cognitive Neuroscience
Maastricht University
Maastricht, The Netherlands

Jeannette M. van der Stelt
Institute of Phonetic Sciences
Universiteit van Amsterdam
Amsterdam, The Netherlands
and
Amsterdam Center for Language and Communication
Amsterdam, The Netherlands

Carol Stoel-Gammon
Department of Speech & Hearing Sciences
University of Washington
Seattle, Washington, USA

Anne Vilain
Institut de la Communication Parlée
Université Stendhal
Grenoble, France
and
Institut National Polytechnique de Grenoble
Grenoble, France

Krisztina Zajdó
Division of Communication Disorders
University of Wyoming
Laramie, Wyoming, USA

1

The Frame/Content Theory

Peter F. MacNeilage

Department of Psychology

The University of Texas at Austin

Austin, Texas, USA

The Frame/Content (F/C) theory (MacNeilage, 1998a) attempts to explain the evolution and acquisition of speech. It says, in brief, that speech was made possible by our evolving the capacity to program syllabic "Frames" with consonantal and vocalic "Content" elements, and that the acquisition of that capacity in infants is the key window into how this happened. This theory owes much to four perspectives.

The most important perspective is given in the title of a paper by Dobzhansky: "Nothing in Biology Makes Sense Except in the Light of Evolution" (Dobzhansky, 1973). According to Darwin (1859), evolution occurred by natural selection, resulting in a process of descent with modification, which eventually gave us the entire tree of life. And as Lindblom has often pointed out, most notably in a paper entitled "Can the models of evolutionary biology be applied to phonetic problems?" (1984), this makes it necessary to derive language in general and speech in particular from nonlinguistic phenomena including nonlinguistic precursors. The Frame/Content theory (1998a) is a phylogenetic response to this advocacy in which the initial form of speech is attributed to classic Darwinian natural selection acting on pre-existing, non-speech capacities. However, the elaboration of speech into its modern form with more than 6,000 variants is deemed more attributable to *cultural* selection.

One aspect of this perspective that apparently cannot be emphasized enough (literally, since some people never get it) is the importance of the time domain. To try to understand the origin of speech simply on the basis of its present form is likely to be an unrewarding enterprise. Speech must have evolved across time, and this must have been a matter of going from simple to more complex forms. So instead of attacking modern speech head-on, it might be more profitable to try to reconstruct the phylogenetically early simple forms, and then try to explain how and why the present-day complexities arose from them. The basic contention here is that the early simple forms probably resembled the early forms of modern infants.

This perspective is in stark contrast to the modern generative linguistic approach to speech, which is based on Platonic Essentialism. For Plato, the world consisted of a number of essences—fixed and unchanging forms (See Toulmin & Goodfield, 1965, p. 40). Perhaps surprisingly to many readers, this idealized view of reality has been almost universally accepted by Western philosophers, most notably Descartes, and, more surprising still, has persisted even after Darwin made Essentialism scientifically obsolete. Chomsky, a modern-day Platonist (and vocal anti-Darwinist), has proposed an innate Universal Grammar that is basically a set of fixed and unchanging forms. He specifies no plausible origin for them and no process of change. Chomsky obviously had language in mind when he said: "You can't just assume that just because something's there it is functional, or has been adapted for. . . . It could be just there" (Chomsky, cited by MacFarquhar, 2003, p. 71). (A detailed comparison between the F/C and the Chomskyian generative approaches to the evolution of speech can be found both in an article by MacNeilage and Davis, 2005a, and in a book by MacNeilage, 2008.)

A second major perspective bears on the question of how Darwinism might apply to the understanding of mental activity in particular. This perspective, increasingly important in modern cognitive science, is called

"Embodiment" (Clark, 1997;   see also Davis & MacNeilage, 2000). The embodiment perspective holds that mental activity, and the brain activity underlying it, cannot be ultimately explained outside of the context of bodily actions. This makes embodiment a variant of Darwinism, because natural selection is fundamentally based on modifications of successful *actions*. Roger Sperry, anticipating many years ago the emphasis of the embodiment perspective on action, said that "the entire output of the nervous system consists of nothing but patterns of motor coordination" (Sperry, 1951, pp. 297-298). The F/C theory is driven, both conceptually and methodologically, by Sperry's suggestion that the best way to understand the mind is to begin with patterns of motor coordination and derive the underlying mental structures from them. According to the F/C theory, the mental structures underlying speech arose from motor structures phylogenetically, and these structures arise from motor structures ontogenetically.

A third important perspective, which led to the particular form of the F/C theory, was laid out by Karl Lashley in a classic 1951 paper entitled "The Problem of Serial Order in Behavior." That problem, which Lashley considered "the most neglected problem in cerebral physiology" (p. 114), is simply this: How does an organism put together any time-extended action pattern? Speech, of course, is serial organization par excellence. Lashley's belief that serial-ordering errors in speech were crucial to its understanding was what first got me interested in speech almost half a century ago. For me, solving the serial-ordering problem for speech will allow us to best understand its evolution.

The fourth perspective comes from the discipline of Ethology, the study of naturally occurring animal behavior. Tinbergen (1963) has posed a set of four questions, and has asserted that "a comprehensive, coherent science of Ethology has to give equal attention to all of them and to their integration" (p. 412). These questions were later adopted by Hauser (1996) in his monograph on "The Evolution of Communication." He asserted that "These perspectives . . . provide the only fully encompassing and explanatory approach to communication in the animal kingdom including human language" (p. 2). Here are these questions, as presented elsewhere (MacNeilage & Davis, 2005a) with some additions to Hauser's description. The term "trait" here refers to any enduring behavior characteristic of a species: 1. Mechanistic: *"How does it work?"* That is, what are the mechanisms (neural, physiological, psychological, etc.) underlying the expression of a trait? 2. Functional: *"What does it do for the organism?"* That is, what effects does the trait have on survival and reproduction? (This is the central Evolutionary Psychology issue of adaptation), 3. Ontogenetic: *"How does it get that way in development?"* That is, what genetic and environmental factors guide the development of a trait? 4. Phylogenetic: *"How did it get that way in evolution?"* That is, how does the evolutionary history of the species help us understand the structure of the trait in light of ancestral features?

These perspectives have one thing in common—the focus on *action*. Darwinian natural selection occurs on the basis of successful *use*. Embodiment involves bodily *movement*. Lashley was concerned with serial organization of *output*. Ethology focuses on *behavior*.

The main empirical base for the theory as it has developed over the last 15 years or so has come to be an ever-increasing set of speech macro patterns— statistical regularities in serial organization within and across syllables, some of them found wherever there is speech like activity, but others present in only some speech domains. This mix of universals and non-universals makes it possible to triangulate in on a particular speech phenomenon. The connotation of the triangulation metaphor is that we can best understand a particular phenomenon by noting the extent to which it occurs at the intersection of various speech genres, or, put more simply, by noting the pattern of its occurrence and non-occurrence. My colleague Barbara Davis has been a partner in this work.

The Theory

Modern Adult Speech Organization and its Phylogenetic Roots

A theory of the evolution of speech must *begin* with a conception of what it is like now, even though it cannot end there. Lashley's basic insight was that speech errors in which one or more parts of a speech utterance are accidentally displaced in an otherwise correct sequence tell you both about what the functional units of speech are and how they are serially organized. The main organizational principle that emerged from work on speech errors at the phonological level is summarized by the Frame/Content metaphor (e.g. Levelt, W. J. M. 1992). Consonant and vowel "content" elements are placed into syllable structure "frames." The basic pattern is that misplaced consonant elements get put into consonantal positions in syllable structure and misplaced vowel elements get put into vowel positions. This is best illustrated by spoonerisms such as "pain mattern" for "main pattern" and "who nine" for "high noon." Most importantly, consonants and vowels play mutually exclusive roles in on-line syllable organization. Vowels are syllable nuclei, and consonants occupy syllable margins. They cannot exchange with each other as in "no" -> "own."

How did this F/C mode of organization arise? A basic observation lying behind Frame/Content theory is that the *movements* of the only articulator that is always involved in both consonants and vowels—the mandible—must have always been mutually exclusive for the two forms. Consonants involve mandibular elevation (mouth closing) and vowels involve mandibular depression (mouth opening). If this close-open alternation was the basic articulatory pattern of the simple initial phases of speech, before consonants and vowels evolved a separable mental superstructure derived from this peripheral action pattern, then there may never have been an opportunity for vowels and consonants to get mixed up with each other in the evolution of the control program.

Where did this mandibular oscillation come from? One possibility was that the pattern was exapted from a basic mandibular cyclicity that evolved in the earliest mammals in conjunction with new capacities for oral ingestion and processing of food—chewing, sucking and licking. The cycle may then have gone through an intermediate stage of visual communicative cyclicities—lipsmacks, tonguesmacks, teeth chatters—cyclicities widespread in other modern primates (Redican, 1985), before being systematically paired with phonation to form protosyllables.

Selection pressure for mandibular cyclicities with phonation may have been exerted in the prespeech context of the evolution of "vocal grooming" as a substitute for actual hands-on grooming when ancestral troop sizes got too large for the latter to remain effective, as suggested by Dunbar (1996). More generally, the ability to do these motor frames, and importantly to imitate them, may have been just one aspect of the evolution of a general-purpose mimetic ability as suggested by Donald (1991). There are good reasons to accept Donald's contention that a quantum jump in mimetic capability preceded the evolution of language and therefore speech.

Speech Ontogeny and its Implications for Phylogeny

The contention that the mandibular cycle is evolutionarily basic to speech is supported by the relatively fully formed emergence of the cycle with phonation at the advent of babbling in present day 7-month-old infants. Infants don't gradually and haltingly put together the close-open cycle in utterances such as "bababa." These events are perceptibly rhythmic from the beginning, as befits a phylogenetically old function.

One particular fact, beyond the cyclical character of these early vocal patterns made them seem relevant to the earliest speech of hominids. It is that the dominant alternation pattern was in fact a close-open one rather than the reverse. The close-open alternation also underlies the only universal syllable pattern in languages—the Consonant-vowel (close-open) syllable. Even profoundly deaf infants, if they produce syllable-like behavior at all, tend to favor this CV pattern (McCaffrey, Davis & MacNeilage, 2000). This suggests that it is a basic motor pattern, as these infants are unlikely to have derived *it* rather than its VC mirror image from the input.

During the babbling stage, from roughly 7 to 12 months of age, and the so-called 50 word stage, from 12 to 18 months, a vocal output episode consists primarily of a single CV or a series of repetitions of the same CV. The latter is called reduplicative babbling. Consonants are primarily labial (lip) or coronal (tongue front) stop consonants and nasals, and vowels are primarily in the quadrant of the vowel space that contains mid and low, front and central vowels.

Our approach to speech acquisition (MacNeilage & Davis, 1990), again motivated by Lashley, was to look more closely at serial organization patterns in babbling and early speech, both within and across CV alternations. In this work we focused on stop consonants and nasals. We used a simple classification of consonantal place of articulation into labial, coronal and dorsal and a simple 3 × 3 division of the vowel space into a height dimension—high, mid, low—and a front-back dimension—front, central, back.

The main thing we discovered at the CV level was a set of favored consonant-vowel co-occurrence patterns. Coronal (front) consonants tended to occur with front vowels, and dorsal (back consonants) tended to occur with higher back vowels, though dorsals and back vowels both tended to be rare. Thus for these forms, the tongue apparently tends to stay in either a front or a back position in the mouth during the CV alternation.

The third pattern we found was for labial (lip) consonants to co-occur with central vowels. This result suggests that even where the tongue is not involved in the consonant it still tends to occupy the same position in the mouth throughout the CV alternation, in this case, presumably its rest position. One can therefore conclude that in these early stages of speech acquisition there is a minimum of active articulation produced by the tongue. We have now found these three patterns numerous times and they have also been found by a number of other investigators (see Davis & MacNeilage, 2002 for a summary).

There is evidence that the same lack of active change holds for the other two major articulators, the lips and the soft palate. Munhall and Jones, J. A. (1998) found evidence that the lips were passive in babbling. The soft palate tends either to stay in its rest position, resulting in an utterance with nasal consonants and nasalized vowels (Matyear, et al., 1996) or is elevated before the CV alternation begins and left in that position resulting in oral consonants and non-nasalized vowels. The overall pattern is one of "Frame Dominance" (Davis & MacNeilage, 1995). Articulators other than the mandible primarily show inertia during an utterance.

This characterization seems to apply not only to single CVs but to sequences of them, too. As already mentioned, babbling tends to be reduplicative. Accordingly, we have found that the three CV co-occurrences involving the tongue front-back dimension are also present in utterance-internal VC sequences; that is front vowel-coronal, back vowel-dorsal and central vowel-labial. In addition, we have found that when successive CV alternations show variegation in babbling and early words (that is, there is a different second vowel or second consonant or both) most of the changes are either in amount of consonant constriction or in vowel height, both of which can be attributed to variation in mandible height (e.g., Davis, MacNeilage & Matyear, 2002). In other words, variegation may be mainly attributable to frame variation, much of which may not be intentional, not to active changes in other articulators.

Our response to this highly impoverished initial infant output pattern was to ask why the vocal output of the first speakers would be any different. We believe that the protosyllabic mode was primarily one of "Pure frames"— alternations between labials and central vowels with minimal independent tongue movement, and only perhaps an option of producing a nasalized or an oral utterance.

To better understand the significance of these patterns, we asked whether they are also present in modern *languages*. Some earlier work by John Locke (1983) and Tore Janson (1986) suggested that languages might have some favored CV patterns. We looked for both CV and VC co-occurrences in dictionary counts of 10 diverse languages. The languages were English, Estonian, French, German, Hebrew, Japanese, New Zealand Maori, Quichua, Spanish and Swahili. Focusing again on stops and nasals, we looked at CVC words, CVCV words and words that began with a CVC... sequence (i.e., CVC...). Pooling the results from the CVC, CVCV and CVC... forms we found the coronal-front, dorsal-back and labial-central CV patterns in about 75% of cases. Eight out of the 10 languages had the dorsal-back pattern and 7 out of 10 languages had the coronal-front and labial-central patterns (MacNeilage, Davis, Kinney & Matyear, 2000).

The finding that the three CV co-occurrence patterns are characteristic of languages provides further evidence that they may have been present in the first words. Because of their strongly inertial nature, they must have been present in vocal output as long as the close-open alternation has been present, and we believe that the alternation might even have been a pre-speech pattern. That is, it might have been present before concepts and sound patterns were paired to form the first words. The presence of the labial-central pattern in languages is especially remarkable because it suggests that the role of tongue inertia is sufficiently fundamental to have remained present throughout language history even when the tongue is free from the requirement of participating in the production of the previous consonant.

But although the three CV co-occurrence patterns may be characteristic of languages, the VC patterns may not be, at least under certain circumstances. When pooling data from CVC, CVCV and CVCV... forms we could find no definite trend towards three VC co-occurrences corresponding to the CV co-occurrences (MacNeilage et al, 2000). In contrast, Rousset (2003) found three VC co-occurrences in her data, which was obtained by pooling all VC sequences in entire words regardless of their structure. In a subsequent analysis (unpublished observations) we found that while there was no trend towards three VC co-occurrences in CVCV and CVC... forms in our set of 10 languages, there was such a trend in CVC forms. As a syllable boundary occurs between V and C in CVCV and CVCV forms it appears that there is a tendency for the three VC co-occurrences to be absent when the V and the C are part of different syllables.

More information is necessary to resolve the apparent differences between the results of the MacNeilage et al. study (2000) and the Rousset (2003) study. One possibility is that the VC co-occurrences are strongly present at the ends of words, which were included in the Rousset sample but not the MacNeilage et al. sample, except for CVC and CVCV words. They could also be present if the C is the first element in a consonant cluster. We did not include words with consonant clusters in our analysis. However, our results from CVCV and CVCV... forms raise the possibility that inertial effects on VC sequences, which may have been present early in the history of speech, judging by their presence in infant patterns, have been superseded across syllable boundaries in the evolution of modern languages.   The significance of this finding can be better appreciated if we step back for a moment and consider the overall task of speech development. Infants, as we have said, favor repeating the same syllable. But languages strongly disfavor this repetition. For instance, in our analysis of 10 languages the same major place of consonantal articulation was repeated in a CVC sequence only 67%, as often as was expected by chance. Rousset (2003) also found that two consonants in CVC sequences were more often different in place of articulation than the same. This dislike of repetition is so obvious in languages that linguists have given it the status of a principle—the Obligatory Contour Principle (Kenstowicz, 1994). It seems clear that the same forces that have made languages favor intersyllabic variegation have led to the evolution of the syllable as a separate organizational unit. They are probably culturally mediated forces towards increase in the size of the communicable message set, rather than direct reflections of anything inherent in the basic speech production capability.

If speech started out favoring syllable reduplication, how did it proceed towards evolving variegation as the favored pattern? Let us begin by asking how infants begin to make their output variegated. A well known step in this direction in infants is to begin a word with a labial consonant and follow it, after the vowel, with a coronal consonant (Ingram, 1974). In our study of the first words of 10 infants (MacNeilage, Davis, Matyear & Kinney, 2000), nine showed this tendency. The mean ratio of preference of LC over CL patterns was 2.55:1.

We have argued that this labial-coronal or LC effect is a self-organizational consequence of the simultaneous operation of three factors in first word production (MacNeilage & Davis, 2000). First, frames with labial consonants and central vowels may be easier to produce than frames with coronals and front vowels because the latter involves the addition of a tongue fronting movement, while the former only involves pure frame production. Second, an addition to the functional load associated with vocalization in the babbling stage occurs at the first word stage when an infant has to interface a vocal episode with a lexical concept rather than simply producing an output episode. This produces a generalized bias towards increasing use of pure frames, with their labial-central pattern in first words. Several studies have shown a tendency for use of more labial than coronal consonants in first words (MacNeilage & Davis, 2002). Third, the initiation of action is a separable functional role of motor systems (Gazzaniga & Heatherton, 2003), and initiation may become more difficult, the more complex the output pattern is. As a consequence of these three factors, a tendency may arise, in instances in which infants are simulating an adult word with intercyclical variegation, to begin the simulation with the easier pure frame pattern and then add a tongue movement to the next frame.

As with the CV and VC patterns, in order to fully understand the LC pattern, it is necessary to know whether it is also favored in languages. We studied the occurrence of stops and nasals in CVC words, CVCV words and words beginning with a CVCV sequence in 10 languages (MacNeilage et al., 2000). The LC preference was found in every language except Japanese. The mean ratio of LC to CL patterns was a remarkably high 2.3:1, a ratio almost as high as found infants. Rousset (2003) has also shown that this pattern is predominant in her 14 language sample. Our conclusion is that the same factors that may produce the LC effect in a self-organizational manner in infants may have been at work in earlier hominids, except for the fact that modern infants have a language model to copy, while hominids had to invent it.

The Emergence of the Word

What were the first words like? Here we have to concern ourselves with links between phonetics and semantics because we need to understand how certain simple sound patterns available at the time the first words were formed got linked to meanings. I think that we have to assume that some particular sound patterns were *naturally* linked to some concepts. That is, the linkage must have fallen out of spontaneously occurring behavior. This must have involved *particular* sound patterns and *particular* concepts, and the involvement of particular sound patterns rather than others is very much a phonetic issue. This line of thought moves into very speculative territory. But I am spending some time on the question because I share a common belief (see Jackendoff, 2002) that the advent of the word was the most significant single event in hominid evolution, and the first words were probably *spoken* words (see MacNeilage & Davis, 2005b, for arguments against the first language being a signed language).

A number of phonetically relevant suggestions have been made about the sound patterns of the first words. One of them is that they were onomatopoeic: the sound properties of the word corresponded to the sounds made by the entity that the sound stood for. An example is the word "hiss" linked to entities such as snakes that emit sounds having a particular range of broadband noise. Another more specific suggestion, also onomatopoeic, has been dubbed the Size Principle. Words for larger things have sounds with lower spectral centers of gravity in the vocalic portion. For example, "huge" versus "tiny."

Without denying the possible relevance of these two possible forms of concept-sound linkage to the early stages of speech, it is possible that the very *first* words were parental terms originating within the parent-infant communicative dyad. The anthropologist Murdock (1959) pointed out a long time ago that there is a certain orderliness in the sounds used for kinship terms—

in particular, terms for mother and father. In a study of kinship terms in 474 languages he found that 78% of the words for mother began with a nasal while only 34% of the words for father began with an oral consonant. This pattern seems to have originated in the linguistically marginal genre of baby talk, which involves use of a set of word forms shared by parents and infants which are not in the language proper. A study of baby talk words in six diverse languages by Ferguson (Arabic, Comanche, English, Gilyak, Marathi and Spanish) provides evidence for this possibility (Ferguson, 1966). All the baby talk words for mother in these 6 languages had a nasal consonant in them and none of the words for father did.

A number of people (most recently Falk, 2004) have suggested that the word may have originated in the baby talk mode. The adult-infant communicative dyad, within which baby talk occurs, must have long had an intimate, repetitive, interactive structure conducive to endowing certain vocalizations with meaning. Baby talk seems to be a critical aspect of dyadic interaction because it provides what Fernald (1992) has called "emotional communication" between participants, a process carrying profound adaptive consequences. We have found, as one might expect, that baby talk words have the same serial organization patterns as babbling and infant's first words— patterns that we believe characterized hominid's first words (MacNeilage & Davis, 2004). The CV alternation is the dominant suprasegmental structure. In an analysis of a corpus of 80 CVCV words from Ferguson's corpus, we found the three CV co-occurrence constraints, the three VC co-occurrence constraints, and a tendency to reduplicate CVs which was as strong in babbling, i.e., a given CV syllable was followed by another instance of the same one about 50% of the time. As in the first word period, there were more LC sequences than CL sequences, even though variegated sequences were relatively rare.

In short, according to the Frame/Content theory, baby talk words may have been the first words because the serial organization patterns of baby talk words are exactly those that the first words would be expected to have. And of course the first syllables of the kinship terms, upon which Murdoch focused have the 3 CV co-occurrence patterns (MacNeilage & Davis, 2004).

But how did nasal consonants get associated with the female parent and orals with the male parent?   Roman Jakobson claimed many years ago (1960) that infants have a tendency to make nasal sounds while suckling, while the oral airway is occupied. Goldman (2001) has recently reported a widespread tendency for infants to make an alternation between a labial nasal sound and a vocalic sound as means of getting the attention of the mother, between the ages of 2 and 6 months. McCune et al. (1996) identified a class of "nasal grunts" important in infant-parent communication in the first year. An earlier hominid mother's cognitive response to such nasal sounds may have been one of "This sound stands for me." If, as we would argue, this hominid mother was already exercising her ability to pair mandibular oscillation with phonation in vocal grooming situations, she may have imitated the infant by producing her own equivalent of this nasal vocalization in the form of [mama], as it would be produced today. Then, perhaps in the first step towards a linguistic system, the male parent may have become labeled with a contrasting form—a form like [papa] with oral rather than nasal consonants. Conscious reflection on these pairings might have eventually led to the "naming insight"—the insight that things could be given names (McShane, 1979).

The baby talk genre with its parental terms has probably been around for as long as we have had words. As Trask (2003) shows, these terms, like other words, have been subject to change in the history of languages. They even sometimes drop out, but are sometimes subsequently replaced by the same or very similar terms. I suggest that, despite this bumpy history, baby talk parental terms are *living fossils*, in the sense that forms of them similar to the relatively ancient original forms continue to appear to this day in many languages. These terms may be the *missing link* between prelinguistic and linguistic hominids. With the coinage of this pair of contrastive terms, hominids may have begun to systematically produce phonetically contrastive words, using the structural template necessary for the subsequent combinatorial level of phonological organization of language—the frame. Whether spoken language first evolved once, or evolved separately several times, this may be the way that it got started, if we take combinatorial phonology to be a definitional property of language, which I argue that we must.

Universals of Serial Organization of Speech: Implications for Generative Linguistics

On the basis of the comparisons we have made between infants and languages, it becomes possible, as a response to Lashley's (1951) question, to formulate some general statements regarding putative universal properties of serial organization of speech. Table 1.1 is a summary of these properties. As Table 1.1 indicates, we believe that there is only one universal of serial organization in the sense that it is always present in any domain in which speech occurs. It is the CV form— the close-open alternation or frame. We believe it will *always* be the predominant form found in groups of infants, and while not necessarily predominant in a particular language, it is apparently always present as a syllabic form (Bell & Hooper, 1978). Moreover, there are other serial organization properties that can be regarded as domain-specific universals— universals unique to infants or to languages. Two of these involve the internal organization of strings of CV alternations. We believe that in infants' first words, reduplication will always be the predominant intercyclic form, whereas variegation will always be the favored intercyclical form for adults. As already mentioned, this dichotomy of non-inclusive universals seems to have to do with the evolution of the syllable as a unit of adult language function in response to evolutionary pressures towards an increase in phonetically distinctive messages. Information relevant to the development of the syllable as a discrete functional unit during the life span is carried intergenerationally by memory units that Dawkins (1976) has called "memes." This information takes the form of a tendency towards an absence of the three infant VC co-occurrence patterns in the structure of words of the language (see also Blackmore, 1999). This tendency allows infants to construct separate syllabic units during the early part

Table 1.1.
Proposed Universals of Serial Organization According to the Frame/Content Theory.

	Universal	Infant Universal	Language Universal
Mandibular Oscillation	CV form	Reduplication (Frame)	Variegation (Syllabification)
Specific Patterns	3 CV Co-ccurrences	3 CVCV Co-occurrences	LC Effect

of their lifespan, as hominids must have done during the course of evolution of speech. In our view, the parental terms of baby talk were the first of these memes.

Three universals are specific to infants: the three CV co-occurrence patterns which are also usually seen in languages, with some exceptions; the three VC co-occurrence patterns which may usually be absent in languages in CVCV sequences though often present in CVC forms; the LC effect, which is also usually present in languages, with some exceptions. All three of these infant universals are considered to have also been universals in the earliest hominid speech, but have sometimes been superceded in the history of an individual language in the case of the CV co-occurrence patterns and the LC effect, and usually been superceded in the case of the VC co-occurrence patterns.

This framework is obviously incompatible with the scenario for the origin of speech that comes from generative linguistics. According to the generative perspective, anything that is truly universal can be attributed to an innate universal grammar. But there is no provision in this scenario for different universals in the two different domains of speech considered here—infant and adult—and it is quite unthinkable that there be opposite universals such as reduplication versus variegation in the two domains. Even Optimality Theory, the most versatile version of universal grammar when it comes to *accounting for* contradictory findings, in the typical parlance of the phonologist, would not be comfortable postulating two opposite universal constraints.

The Neurobiology of Speech Evolution

The F/C theory also includes a conception of how control of the frame and content components of speech evolved in the brain. (I have also formulated a theory of evolution of the left hemisphere specialization for speech [MacNeilage, 1998b]). Space only allows a brief summary of this component of the F/C theory here (see MacNeilage, 1998a; MacNeilage, 2008; MacNeilage & Davis, 2001; MacNeilage & Davis, 2005c, for detailed expositions).

The cortical control of mandibular cyclicity underlying the frame may have evolved primarily in the mammalian homolog of Broca's area because that region is the main cortical locus of control of ingestive processes in mammals. However, higher order control of frames for speech may have eventually shifted to an area of medial pre-motor cortex consisting of the Supplementary Motor Area (SMA) and the Pre-SMA, judging by the involuntary production of speech automatisms consisting of strings of reduplicated syllables (e.g. "babababababa") in 3 different types of patient with abnormal SMA-Pre-SMA function under certain conditions (MacNeilage & Davis, 2001). Thus, today, on-line production of speech as an action involves generation of frames in the SMA-Pre-SMA and content elements in and around Broca's area. These two regions have more general roles in action control, as components of intrinsic (self-generated) and extrinsic (externally controllable) subsystems respectively (Goldberg, 1985). The latter system is the repository of "mirror neurons" (Rizzolatti & Arbib, 1998). These are units which discharge when a monkey (and presumably a human) makes a particular action, and when the same animal sees another performing this action. They provide a possible basis for the learning of the phonological content of whichever of the several thousand human languages an infant is exposed to.

The speech automatisms are, in effect, repetitions of a single cycle of a CV Frame. How can their existence be explained? They may reveal the presence of a component of the mental-motor interface for speech production that evolved and develops from the motor frame in the course of establishing a mental superstructure for speech.

Consider first the ontogenetic situation. In an infant, the motor frame first appears at the onset of babbling before the infant can be said to even have a word. A short time after the infant begins to acquire words (at about 1 year) a general-purpose superstructure for their mental representation begins to crystalize out by means of self organization. Adult speech errors show us that this mental representation eventually includes independent segmental and syllable structure components. The close-open alternation is a constant part of the developmental process, and it consequently acquires a separate abstract representational status, somewhat independent of the actual close-open movements for individual words, but also somewhat independent of both the segmental entities in words and the detailed syllable structure of words. The derivation of this structure from early speech behaviors allows us to understand why adult patients produce such a childlike form, so superficially unrelated to their premorbid speech behavior.

As befits its intermediate status between detailed movements and abstract mental structures for words, this frame is best described as a cognitive-motor entity. It is cognitive enough to allow elaborate modulations for particular syllables, which in English, for example, might involve not one but several consonants. The role of this frame in the ordering of sounds in syllables is pre-motor in that it must be laid down before the movements needed to proceed from one segment to the next within each frame are computed. At the same time it is motor enough to have its own basic rhythmic figure, resulting in a characteristic movement rate which would vary in individuals with different speaking rates.

The phylogenetic derivation of this cognitive-motor frame was presumably similar to its ontogenetic derivation. The first words may have been produced with motor frames which lacked separate mental representations. But as words continued to accumulate, a general-purpose superstructure for their mental representation must have begun to crystalize out, and the cognitive-motor frame played a role in this as part of the mental-motor interface necessary for producing individual speech events.

Finally, recent findings make it necessary to add to the conventional conception of the extrinsic system for speech which has traditionally been confined to Wernicke's area and Broca's area and the temporofrontal pathway that connects them—the arcuate fasciculus. As Aboitiz and Garcia (1997) have pointed out, brain imaging evidence of the importance of the inferior parietal lobe in the phonological loop of working memory makes it necessary to include this region in the conception of the extrinsic system, perhaps involving spatial targets as part of the control process (MacNeilage, 1970). Catani, Jones, and Fytche (2005) have shown, capitalizing on recent developments in white-matter imaging, the existence of the temporo-parietal and parieto-frontal pathways called for by this revised conception.

Speech and Birdsong: Convergent Evolution of the Frame/Content Mode

It has become clear in recent years that what have been called syllables in birdsong are analogous to syllables in speech in that each one involves a beak open-close cycle (e.g., Podos, Southall, and Rossi-Santos, 2004). These "frames," typically produced in rhythmic series, are programmed with acoustic "content" primarily under syringeal control. It has also been found, in analogy to the production of rhythmic frame sequences with electrical stimulation of the SMA in humans (MacNeilage & Davis, 2001), that stimulation of the forebrain vocal control nucleus (HVC) and robustus arachistriatalis (RC) in zebra finches and canaries results in the production of rhythmic syllable sequences (Vicario & Simpson, 1995). Overall, there appears to be convergent evolution of the Frame/Content mode, in the sense that relatively unrelated taxonomic groups independently produce the same adaptation, thus suggesting its general utility in the particular problem space involved.

Conclusions and Implications

Let us now evaluate the F/C from the standpoint of the four perspectives with which we began.

The Neodarwinian Perspective. The F/C is a theory of evolution by natural selection in the traditional Neodarwinian mould. It centers on descent by modification. The basic element of the theory, the Frame, is considered to have evolved by means of a series of exaptations (use of earlier adaptations for new purposes), from ingestive cyclicities to visuofacial communicative cyclicities, and from there to becoming paired with phonation and being selected as the vehicle for the first spoken words. The original protosyllabic forms of the frame stage are considered to be a result of biological adaptation. However, the initial pairing of concepts with frames to form words is regarded as an invention, and the subsequent elaboration of the system is considered to have involved sociocultural selection of additional sounds and patterns for words within the boundaries of the frame (memes), in response to selection pressures for increase in the number of distinguishable messages.

The Embodiment Perspective. A response to Sperry's advocacy to derive mental patterns from motor patterns is the concept of the cognitive-motor frame, controlled primarily by the Supplementary Motor Area and Pre-SMA as part of a necessary mental-motor interface for speech production. Again it is a matter of conservation co-existing with modification. A merit of this proposal is that it makes sense of an otherwise anomalous infant-like output pattern in adult neurological patients in which this frame component is involuntarily elicited in isolation.

The Problem of Serial Order. The F/C theory offers a solution to Lashley's problem of serial order for speech. What has evolved is the capability of programming frames. In effect we have order within order. The frame calls for one or more instances of the fundamental consonant-vowel alternation—a fixed order. But within the frame, which serves as a carrier, numerous detailed ordering possibilities for segmental combinations develop. It is of interest to also note, particularly in the context of the common Frame/Content modes of speech and birdsong, that Lashley (1951) believed what he called rhythm generators would be found to play a very important role in serial ordering of behavior. The frame is one such rhythm generator.

Tinbergen's Four Questions. The theory is an integrated answer to these four questions.

1. How does it work? Speech has a frame/content mode of organization whereby segmental content elements are programmed into syllable structure frames.

2. What does it do for the organism? It allows elements of a large message set to be distinguishable from each other.

3. How does it get that way in development? Frames develop first and then content.

4. How did it get that way in evolution? Frames evolved from pre-existing mandibular oscillations, and content evolved in response to selection pressures for a larger message set.

Finally, I want to again emphasize the importance of recognizing that speech has evolved across the time domain. According to the Frame/Content theory, there have been two stages in the deep time frame of speech evolution that are paralleled today in the shallow time frame of acquisition. It is crucial to understand that while the second stage was built on the first, it is quite radically different from it. The lack of a time domain in generative linguistics has the result that there is only one set of basic principles that apply to all contemporary language. As noted earlier, generative phonologists have formulated one particular principle relevant to the general properties of serial organization. It is the Obligatory Contour Principle (which bars successive identical consonant or vowel segments in CVCV utterances). The principle—considered explanatory, but actually tautologous—is derived from the fact that successive syllables tend to be variegated in languages. Like all universals in generative linguistics, this principle must be innate. But if so, how is it that a principle exactly opposite to this (also universal and therefore necessarily innate) operates in infant speech, where recurrence of the same consonantal or vowel segment in successive cycles is originally favored. This problem arises for any approach which simply takes the present-day end point of evolution (in this case adult speech) and puts it in the beginning. It cannot handle functional reversals. The present thesis is that if you recognize that the time domain is central to the understanding of speech and acknowledge, the possibility of two successive stages in speech phylogeny as well as ontogeny, this insuperable problem for current generative linguistics goes away.

Acknowledgments

This paper was prepared with the support of grant HD 27733-12 from the Public Health Service. I thank John Trimble for help in preparing the manuscript.

References

Aboitiz, F., & Garcia, V. (1977). The evolutionary origin of the language areas in the human brain: A neuroanatomical perspective. *Brain Research Reviews, 25,* 381–396.

Bell, A., & Hooper, J. B. (1978). *Syllables and segments.* Amsterdam: North–Holland.

Blackmore, S. (1999). *The meme machine.* Oxford: Oxford University Press.

Catani, M., Jones, D. K., & Fytche, D.H. (2005) Perisylvian networks of the human brain. *Annals of Neurology, 57,* 8–16.

Clark, A. (1997). *Being there: Putting brain, body and world together again.* Cambridge, MA: MIT Press.

Darwin, C. (1859) *The origin of species.* London: John Murray.

Davis, B. L., & MacNeilage, P. F. (1995). The articulatory basis of babbling. *Journal of Speech and Hearing Research, 38,* 1199–1211.

Davis, B. L., & MacNeilage, P. F. (2000). An embodiment perspective on the acquisition of speech perception. *Phonetica, 57,* 229–241.

Davis, B. L., & MacNeilage, P. F. (2002). The internal structure of the syllable. In T. Givon & B.F. Malle (Eds.), *The evolution of language out of prelanguage* (pp. 135–154). Amsterdam: John Benjamins.

Davis, B. L., MacNeilage, P. F., & Matyear, C. L. (2002). Acquisition of serial complexity in speech production: A comparison of phonetic and phonological approaches. *Phonetica, 59,* 75–107.

Dohzhansky, T. (1973). Nothing in biology makes sense except in the light of evolution. *The American Biology Teacher, 35,* 125–129.

Dawkins, R. (1976). *The selfish gene.* Oxford: Oxford University Press.

Donald, M. (1991). *Origin of the modern mind*. Cambridge, MA: Harvard University Press.

Dunbar, R. I. M. (1996). *Grooming, gossip and the evolution of language*. London: Faber and Faber.

Falk, D. (2004). Prelinguistic evolution in early hominins: Whence motherese. *Behavioral and Brain Sciences, 27*, 491–503.

Fernald, A. (1992). Human maternal vocalizations to infants as biological relevant signals: An evolutionary perspective (pp. 391–428). In J. H. Barkow, L. Cosmides & J. Tooby (Eds.), *The adaptive mind*. Oxford: Oxford University Press.

Gazzaniga, M. S., & Heatherton, T. F. (2003). *Psychological science*. New York: Norton.

Goldberg, G. (1985). Supplementary motor area structure and function: Review and hypothesis. *Behavioral and Brain Sciences, 8*, 567–616.

Goldman, H. I. (2001). Parental reports of "MAMA" sounds in infants: An exploratory study. *Journal of Child Language, 28*, 497–506.

Hauser, M. D. (1996). *The evolution of communication*. Cambridge, MA: MIT Press.

Ingram, D. (1974). Fronting in infant phonology. *Journal of Child Language, 1*, 233–241.

Jackendoff, R. (2002). *Foundations of language: brain, meaning, grammar, evolution*. Oxford: Oxford University Press.

Jakobson, R. (1960). Why "Mama" and "Papa." In B. Caplan & S. Wapner (Eds.), *Essays in honor of Heinz Werner* (pp. 124–134). New York: International Universities Press.

Janson, T. (1986). Cross-linguistic trends in the frequency of CV sequences. *Phonology Yearbook 3*, 179–195.

Kenstowicz, M. (1994). *Phonology in generative grammar*. Oxford: Blackwell.

Lashley, K. S. (1951). The problem of serial order in behavior. In L. A. Jeffress (Ed.), *Cerebral mechanisms in behavior* (pp. 112–136). New York: Wiley.

Levelt, W. J. M. (1992). Accessing words in speech production: Stages, processes and representations. *Cognition, 42*, 1–22.

Lindblom, B. (1984). Can the models of evolutionary biology be applied to phonetic problems? In A. Cohen & M. van den Broecke (Eds.), *Proceedings of the 10th International Congress of Phonetic Sciences, Vol. II*, pp. 67–82.

Locke, J. L. (1983). *Phonological acquisition and change*. New York: Academic Press.

MacFarquhar, L. (2003). The Devil's accountant. *The New Yorker*, March 31, 64–79.

MacNeilage, P. F. (1970). Motor control of serial ordering of speech. *Psychological Review, 77*, 182–196.

MacNeilage, P. F. (1998a). The frame/content theory of evolution of speech production. *Behavioral and Brain Sciences, 21*, 499–546.

MacNeilage, P. F. (1998b). Towards a unified view of cerebral specializations in vertebrates. In A. D. Milner (Ed.), *Comparative Neuropsychology* (pp. 167–183). Oxford: Oxford University Press.

MacNeilage, P. F. (2008). *The invisible miracle: A Darwinian Theory of Speech.* Oxford: Oxford University Press.

MacNeilage, P. F., & Davis, B. L. (1990). Acquisition of speech production: Frames, then content. In Jeannerod, M. (Ed.), *Attention and performance XIII: motor representation and control* (pp. 452–468). Hillsdale, N.J: Erlbaum.

MacNeilage, P. F., & Davis, B. L. (2000). Origin of the internal structure of word forms. *Science, 288,* 527–531.

MacNeilage, P. F., & Davis, B. L. (2001). Motor mechanisms in speech ontogeny: Phylogenetic, neurobiological and linguistic implications. *Current Opinion in Neurobiology, 11,* 696–700.

MacNeilage, P. F., & Davis, B. L. (2002). On the origins of intersyllabic complexity. In T. Givon & B. F. Malle (Eds.), *The evolution of language out of prelanguage* (pp. 155–170). Amsterdam: John Benjamins.

MacNeilage, P. F., & Davis, B. L. (2004). Baby talk and the emergence of first words. *Behavioral and Brain Sciences, 27,* 517–518.

MacNeilage, P. F., & Davis, B. L. (2004). Baby talk and the origin of the word. Paper presented at the Fifth International Conference on the Evolution of Language, Leipzig, Germany, April, 2004.

MacNeilage, P. F., & Davis, B. L. (2005a). Evolution of language. In D. Buss (Ed.), *Handbook of Evolutionary Psychology* (pp. 698–723). New York: Wiley.

MacNeilage, P. F., & Davis, B. L. (2005b). A cognitive-motor frame for speech production: Evidence from neuropathology. In W. J. Hardcastle & J. MacKenzie Beck (Eds.), *A figure of speech: A festschrift for John Laver.* Mahwah N.J.: Erlbaum.

MacNeilage, P. F., & Davis, B. L. (2005c). The frame/content theory of evolution of speech: A comparison with a gestural-origins alternative. *Interaction Studies, 6,* 173–199.

MacNeilage, P. F., Davis, B. L., Matyear, C. L., & Kinney, A. (2000). Origin of speech output complexity in infants and in languages. *Psychological Science, 10,* 459–460.

MacNeilage, P. F., Davis, B. L., Kinney, A. & Matyear, C. L. (2000). The motor core of speech: A comparison of serial organization patterns in infants and languages. *Child Development, 71,* 153–163.

Matyear, C. L., MacNeilage, P. F., & Davis B. L. (1998). Nasalization of vowels in nasal environments in babbling: Evidence for frame dominance. *Phonetica, 55,* 1–17.

McCaffrey, H. A., Davis, B. L., & MacNeilage, P. F. (1999). Effects of multichannel cochlear implantation on the organization of early speech. *Volta Review, 101,* 5–28.

McCune, L., Vihman, M. M., Roug Hellichius, L., Bordenave, & Gogate, L. (1996). Grunt communication in human infants (*Homo sapiens*). *Journal of Comparative Psychology, 110*, 27–36.

McShane, J. (1979). The development of naming. *Linguistics, 17*, 879–905.

Munhall, K. G., & Jones, J. A. (1998). Articulatory evidence for syllable structure. *Behavioral and Brain Sciences, 21*, 524–525.

Murdock, G. P. (1959). Cross-language parallels in parental kin terms. *Anthropological Linguistics, 1*, 1–5.

Podos, J., Southall, J. A., & Rossi-Santos, M. R. (2004). Vocal mechanics in Darwin's finches: Correlation of beak gape and song frequency. *Journal of Experimental Biology, 207*, 607–619.

Redican, W. K. (1975). Facial expressions in nonhuman primates. In L. A. Rosenblum (Ed.), *Primate behavior: Developments in field and laboratory research, Vol. 4*, 103–194. New York: Academic Press.

Rizzolatti, G., & Arbib, M. A. (1998). Language within our grasp. *Trends in Neurosciences, 21*, 188–194.

Rousett, I. (2003). From lexical to syllabic organization: Favored and disfavored co-occurrences. In M. J. Solé, D. Rescasens & J. Romero (Eds.), *Proceedings of the 15th International Congress of Phonetics*, Barcelona, August, 2003, Vol. 1, 715–718.

Sperry, R. (1951). Neurology and the mind-brain problem. *American Scientist, 39*, 291–312.

Tinbergen, N. (1963). On aims and methods of Ethology. *Zeitschrift für Tierpsychologie, 20*, 410–433.

Toulmin, S. E., & Goodfield, J. (1965). *The discovery of time, 40.*. New York: Harper & Row.

Trask, R. L. (2003). Where do mama/papa words come from? http://www.sussex.ac.uk/linguistics/documents/where_do_mama2.pdf

Vicario, D. S., & Simpson, H. B. (1995). Electrical stimulation in forebrain nuclei elicits learned vocal patterns in songbirds. *Journal of Neurophysiology, 73*, 2602–2607.

I: Evolutionary Perspectives on Speech Development

2

The Origins of Syllabification in Human Infancy and in Human Evolution

D. Kimbrough Oller [1,2]

and

Ulrike Griebel [1,2]

[1] *School of Audiology and Speech-Language Pathology*

The University of Memphis

Memphis, Tennessee, USA

[2] *Konrad Lorenz Institute for Evolution and Cognition Research*

Altenburg, Austria

What were the early changes that created differentiation between the communication abilities of hominids and their primate relatives? In recent years, much has been written about the obvious difference between humans and non-humans in the ability to manipulate the syntax of language, producing creative, complex sentences from a rich repertoire of lexical material (e.g., Pinker & Bloom, P., 1990). Further scholarship has been devoted to the origins of lexical items themselves (e.g., Deacon, 1997; Gärdenfors, 2004; Sinha, 2004). Peter MacNeilage, to whom this volume is dedicated, has focused on the fact that the rich developments of syntax and even of lexicon, depend upon a logically prior ability to produce controlled, well-formed syllables (MacNeilage, 1998; MacNeilage & Davis, 1990a, 1990b; MacNeilage, Davis, & Matyear, 1997).

Well-formed syllable control clearly differentiates humans from non-humans. In the evolution of hominids, then, the appearance of syllables obeying modern human principles of well-formedness must have corresponded to substantial vocal differentiation of hominids from the primate background, and in important regards, must have preceded evolution of lexical/syntactic abilities. MacNeilage's thesis on this point is solid.

In this chapter we suggest an addition to, and perhaps a fundamental revision in, MacNeilage's framework. We posit that before ancient hominids differentiated from other primates by producing well-formed syllables, they had already evolved more fundamental vocal capabilities new to the primate lineage (Oller & Griebel, 2005). In our view, the ability to produce well-formed syllables is the culmination of a series of evolutionary steps unique in humans among the primates. Our proposition is based partly on theoretical considerations and is supported by results of studies from human development and primate vocalization, results that suggest evolution in hominids of voluntary control over phonation preceded evolution of the syllabic articulatory control that is the focus of MacNeilage's proposal.

Natural Logic of Vocal Development and Evolution

Our theoretical considerations include a natural logic of steps that could be naturally selected, yielding a communicative system of increasing elaborateness and consequent utility (Oller, 2000; Oller & Eilers, 1992; Oller & Griebel, 2005). The term "natural logic" is intended to specifically contrast with any sort of logic that might fail to take into account forces of natural selection, and might thus posit steps of evolution or development that could occur in machine simulation, but would be unlikely to evolve in living systems. In our view, natural logic implies that evolving and developing voluntary phonatory control has priority over evolving and developing syllabic articulatory control.

The empirical evidence of the natural logic originally came from human infants across the first half-year of life. Infants develop capabilities for vocalization in an ordered fashion that appears to be universal and that appears to lay necessary foundations for speech. The outline of these developments, wherein phonatory control precedes syllabic articulatory control, has been in place for some time (Koopmans-van Beinum & van der Stelt, 1986; Oller, 1978, 1980; Stark, 1981; Stark, 1980). Further, comparison of the results on human infants with descriptions of vocal capabilities in non-human primates (Elowson, Snowdon, & Lazaro-Perea, 1998; Hauser, 1996; Jürgens, 1995; Marler, 1976; Seyfarth & Cheney, 1997) suggests that by five months, human infants have surpassed vocal capabilities of non-human primates at any age (Oller, 2000). Our chapter presents evidence from human infants and clarifies why it suggests steps of vocal evolution that must have preceded well-formed syllabification.

MacNeilage and colleagues have sought an enhanced perspective on how the human brain evolved for syllabic production (MacNeilage & Davis, 1990a, 1993). His proposals on this point have encountered a complex review, largely positive on the general goal of laying out a neuroscientific model of syllable evolution, but less positive on the specific brain mechanisms that he posited to instantiate the model (e.g., Abry, Boë, & Laboissière, 1998; Andrew, 1998; Ghazanfar & Katz, 1998; Sessle, 1998). Our opinion is that precursor steps to syllables need to be taken into account, since they correspond to neurological foundations that have not been considered in MacNeilage's effort.

Descent with Modification

Still there is much to agree about at the level of paradigm. Like MacNeilage, we assume "descent with modification" (Darwin, 1859, p. 420). Generally speaking, large steps of evolution do not occur in short time periods, but instead, new capabilities are built by modifying earlier ones, and large changes typically require many generations. This view contrasts with a popular claim that human language may have evolved in a single massive leap (Chomsky, 1968, 1986). The popular view is preformationist, assuming innate language capabilities for which no evolutionary account is provided, beyond the vague reference to "a mutation." This verbiage has had primarily negative effects on research, leaving the question of origins in darkness. A recent collaborative paper (Hauser,

Chomsky, & Fitch, 2003) muddies these waters a bit, because Chomsky co-wrote this paper with evolutionary scientists, and appears to have shifted his point of view, at least somewhat, in the process.

MacNeilage has persuasively assailed the popular Chomskyan view, arguing that language must have emerged from elaboration of primitive abilities for motoric control of the vocal apparatus (MacNeilage, 1998). He has posited that the syllabification in humans may have been tinkered into existence from prior capabilities. In particular, he focuses on the possibility that syllabification is based on ingestion-related (particularly mastication-related) neural substructures. Further, he has posited the existence of a fundamental distinction between "frame" and "content," where syllable frames are the product of oscillatory jaw movement founded in mastication substructures, and where segmental content is generated through modulation supraglottal articulatory movements superimposed upon the syllabic frames. The notion of "frame dominance," as presented by MacNeilage and colleagues, suggests that emergence of primitive syllables (without independent segmental content) precedes the emergence of more advanced syllables with freely recombinable segmental content in both evolution and development.

MacNeilage's claim that "frames" precede "content" in development and evolution has been widely accepted (for dissent see Ohala, this volume, and Ohala, 1998). The frame/content distinction corresponds to a naturally logical distinction (syllabification/segmentation, Oller, 2000), but this particular difference from MacNeilage's portrayal is merely terminological. MacNeilage's frame/content terminology is also compatible with other alternatives that have been introduced in support of models that presuppose a developmental precedence of whole syllables over segmented consonant-vowel syllables (e.g., Vihman, 1996).

In addition, we side with MacNeilage in taking the view that each posited step of evolution needs to be explicated in terms of natural selection pressures. Lindblom amplified the point in a commentary on the MacNeilage hypothesis (Lindblom, 1998), emphasizing that the evolutionary tinkering that produced a speech capability could hardly have been random, but must have been guided by selection pressures at each step; otherwise, the notion of tinkering could be misdirected to support non-Darwinian speculations about the origin of speech, yielding "an alibi for the Chomskyan paradigm" (p. 521). We need to specify, then, not only what the logical steps were, but how they could have been selected for. That is, what circumstances of physical environment, reproduction, and/or sociality could have made each step adaptive? The importance of this question is highlighted by the fact that there exist about 200 primate species and there existed many more during the past 5 million years (Martin, R. D., 1990), but only one controls well-formed syllables. What was special about hominid circumstances that favored this adaptation? Since the evolution of well-formed syllable structures was clearly adaptive in the human case, what circumstances prevented other primates from capitalizing on the same advantages? Furthermore, what circumstances have favored the evolution of elaborate vocal capabilities in many species of birds, marine mammals, and land carnivores, capabilities that substantially surpass those of non-human primates? While human-like well-formed syllabification is not present in any of these animals, other foundational features of vocal control that are absent in non-human primates are present in many species, and (at least primitively) syllable-like control features are seen in a large number. What analogies can be drawn between vocal abilities (and the circumstances that favored their evolution) in other animals and in humans to explicate origins of vocal control and well-formed syllabification?

The evidence does not support the idea that natural selection could have yielded well-formed syllabification in hominids by directly tinkering ingestion-related abilities to cyclically modulate movements of the supraglottal articulatory apparatus (although the evidence is consistent with a more indirect relation between ingestion cyclicities and speech cyclicities). Prior steps seem necessary because modern non-human primates (and by implication, the primates from which hominids descended) have only minimal voluntary control of vocalization itself (i. e., the production of periodic vocal energy generated by the glottal/respiratory system). Without vocalization controlled at will, sounds generated by voluntary articulatory movements of the supraglottal apparatus are limited to a relatively small class of voiceless clicks, bursts and/or friction sounds, most of which are inherently low in amplitude by comparison with vocalized sounds and thus offer a weak basis for audition-based communication. Articulation yielding such limited communicative value would present a poor target for selective tinkering.

Indeed, natural languages that utilize voiceless clicks, bursts and friction sounds (English, for example, utilizes the latter two), always use them in syllables where the nuclear element is a vowel, that is, a voiced element. The perceptual advantages to the human auditory system of syllabic articulation that includes *voiced* transitions between vowels and consonants (the latter can be voiced or unvoiced) have been extensively documented (Delattre, Liberman, A. M., & Cooper, 1955; Liberman, A. M., Cooper, Shankweiler, & Studdert-Kennedy, 1967; Liberman, A. M., Delattre, Cooper, & Gerstman, 1954; Studdert-Kennedy, 1980). We hear and recognize speech articulation with precision because these articulations are performed *with vocalization*, which yields trackable formant transitions providing robust cues to both consonant and vowel characteristics. In order for articulatory movements to form an optimal target for natural selection, we reason they need to be produced in the context of vocalization where articulatory movements accompanying vocalization can be easily discerned and interpreted to adaptive advantage. Consequently, we argue, evolution of control over the vocal production (respiratory and glottal) apparatus that produces acoustic energy has naturally logical priority over specialized control of the articulatory apparatus in the evolution of hominid vocal communication.

To cast the point in terms of the source/filter theory of speech acoustics (Fant, 1960), there is a naturally logical precedence of source-control development over filter-control development, because filter-control is of relatively limited value in the evolvable world of communication without a flexible source of energy to modulate. Our view of the naturally selective tinkering that must have occurred to yield well-formed syllables in humans focuses, then, on the likelihood that syllable control could only have been selected after vocal/phonatory control had been more substantially evolved than it has been in any of the non-human primates.

The argument that phonatory control holds logical priority over articulatory control does not in any way diminish the importance of articulation in mature speech. Without articulation, a vocal communication system would be enormously more limited in power and efficiency than speech is, and natural spoken languages in their mature form always include both vocalization and articulation. In contrast to the numbers of discrete communicative signaling units that can be effectively constructed based on phonatory control alone (perhaps a dozen or so), articulation in the context of vocalization vastly expands the variety of communicative units (to thousands of syllable types). The point of the argument that vocalization holds logical priority is simply that if an organism is unable to produce vocalization voluntarily, its articulatory capability will be to no substantial avail (because it is hard to hear the effects of articulation alone). Vocalization affords articulation its audibility and transmission power. So it makes sense that a primate, evolving toward speech, would need to evolve vocal control as a foundation upon which to build articulated vocalization. We take seriously the fact that every human infant we have ever observed in longitudinal research (well over a hundred infants by now) has always gained control over well-formed or normal phonation first, and well-formed articulation in syllables later.

This chapter is organized around: 1) a survey of vocal development stages in human infants that precede well-formed syllables; 2) an outline of naturally logical requirements that appear to guide the sequence of development along with reasons that the naturally logical steps (formulated at a suitably abstract level) should be expected to occur in both development and evolution; and 3) a summary perspective on signal production and syllabification in other species, a perspective that posits selection forces that tend to yield flexible communication, and one that raises doubts regarding too direct a role for capabilities controlling mastication in the evolution of speech.

Stages of Vocal Development in the Human Infant

An Ethologically and Theoretically-Enriched Approach to the Study of Vocal Development

Beginning in the 1970s there has been much research illustrating stages of vocal development in human infancy. It was crucial, in order for the stages to be discerned, that the researchers abandoned the prior approach of phonetic transcription as a means of characterizing infant sounds. Instead the researchers adopted a more general ethologically-oriented descriptive approach that does not attempt to force infant sound characterization prematurely into well-formed syllabic or segmental categories (Oller, 1976, 1980; Stark, 1978; Stark, Rose, & McLagen, 1975; Zlatin-Laufer & Horii, 1977; Zlatin, 1975b). The more modern approach described infant sound production as an ethologist would describe the sounds of another species in field work. The question posed by the researchers on hearing a particular vocalization from a young infants was not thus "what speech sound is this?" Instead the investigators asked: "What are the acoustic characteristics of this sound? Does this sound pertain to a category of sounds that occurs systematically in this infant? How is this sound utilized to social or other effect?"

This approach has revealed steps of vocal development preceding well-formed syllables. Some of these steps reveal structural foundations of well-formed syllables. The work led to formulation of the concept "canonical syllable" (Oller, 1978), and the definition proposed for the term includes components that correspond to naturally logical steps of development in well-formed syllabification. To summarize the standard definition, a canonical syllable consists of 1) continuous normal phonation (without articulation), 2) minimal articulatory movement of the supraglottal tract during the occurrence of normal phonation, 3) a salient distinction during articulatory movement of a more closed margin (or consonant-like portion) and a more open vocal tract posturing (the vowel-like portion) where the supraglottal tract is not at rest and where a transition between closure and opening is likewise clearly present, and 4) a crisp timing of the articulatory transition, nominally < 120 ms. Succinctly, a canonical syllable consists of a normally phonated nucleus (or vowel) adjacent to at least one consonant-like closure, with salient differentiation between the nucleus and the margin, and a rapid transition between the two.

The definition was formulated for two purposes. First to provide a summary of the properties of syllables as they occur in natural languages all over the world, and second, to offer perspective on steps of development that had been observed in longitudinal research on human infant vocalization conducted by both the first author and his colleagues (Oller, 1980; Oller & Eilers, 1992; Oller, Eilers, & Basinger, 2001), and by other investigators in two independent laboratories in the USA (Stark, 1980; Zlatin, 1975b). European longitudinal studies having begun at around the same time (1970s through early 1980s), also adopted an ethologically-oriented approach and provided additional support for the basic stages (Holmgren, Lindblom, Aurelius, Jalling, & Zetterström, 1986; Koopmans-van Beinum & van der Stelt, 1986; Roug, Landberg, & Lundberg, 1989). Briefly, there are three important stages that precede canonical syllabification and for which there is substantial consensus in the various longitudinal studies.

Stages in Human Vocal Development

In the "phonation stage" (0-2 months) infants produce unarticulated vocalizations that are neither fixed signals (crying, laughter, moaning, shrieking, etc.) nor vegetative sounds (coughs, sneezes, hiccoughs, etc.). These unarticulated vocalizations show normal phonation, the kind of phonation that occurs in speech. The supraglottal tract is typically at rest during these "quasivowel" productions, which begin in the first days of life as brief sounds that seem to be tied to the breathing cycle, with quasivowels occurring on egress. Across this initial stage, phonatory control of the infant over quasivowels increases, in that the tie to the breathing cycle begins to be broken in two important ways. First the length of sounds increases as the infant varies the breathing pattern to accommodate long and short vocalized egresses (Netsell, 1981). Second, glottal interrupts occur between sounds, yielding primitive, irregular, syllable-like units, without supraglottal articulation (Koopmans-van Beinum, Clement, & van den Dikkenberg-Pot, 2001; Koopmans-van Beinum & van der Stelt, 1986).

In the "primitive articulation stage" (1-4 months) infants produce minimal movements of the supraglottal apparatus during normal phonation. The most salient form of this articulation occurs in "gooing," a pattern of vocalization where infants produce an astonishing array of non-stereotyped sounds, often in face-to-face playful interaction (Oller, 1980; Stark et al., 1975; Tronick, Als, & Brazelton, 1980; Tronick, 1982), a pattern of affiliative vocal interaction that has not been reported to occur in any non-human primate. The term "gooing' invokes the fact that the dorsum of the tongue appears to be involved in many of the articulations. However, the supraglottal articulations of gooing are often, if not usually, accompanied by only slight openings of the vocal tract, so that a salient contrast between closure and opening is absent. Gooing yields only minimal articulatory movement.

Further, there is substantial variation in how gooing sounds are produced and vocalized moment-to-moment, variation that yields an impression of wandering vocal exploration rather than repetitive systematic articulatory control. To be sure, there is a kind of control manifest in gooing: The infant proves with these highly variable sounds that an enormous amount of "raw material" of vocalization and potential speech-like contrastive sound material is available for development. But in the raw material of gooing, the lack of systematic and repetitive occurrence of predictably timed closure-opening sequences highlights the limited nature of the control over articulation. Gooing provides a preliminary view of the systematic syllabification of the later canonical stage when the infant produces repetitive, clearly articulated syllables with much more predictable and clearly differentiated open-closing cycles.

Other research on motor development also suggests that exploratory movements are routinely precursors to well-timed repetitive movements as infants gain motoric control (Thelen, 1981; Thelen, 1995).

Infants occasionally produce sounds that are, physically speaking, fully canonical during the primitive articulation stage. The wandering and exploration of sound production that typifies the primitive articulation stage results in a vast array of amorphous material, viewed from the perspective of controlled canonical babbling. But occasionally, that wandering produces a seemingly accidental canonical syllable.

In the "expansion stage" (3-8 months) infants appear to explore and play with sounds that are highly contrastive (Oller, 1980; Zlatin, 1975a). They produce sequences of sounds that possess a particular characteristic, e.g., high pitch (squealing), and then switch to contrasting sounds with very low pitch (growling). Or they contrast high pitch sequences with vowel-like sounds in the mid-range of pitch within the same recording session, sometimes repeating each type within a few seconds. Lag sequential analysis provides evidence that such sequences are systematically alternating and non-random (Oller, Buder, & Nathani, 2003), confirming the auditory impression that infants in the stage are forming primitive vocal categories. The same sort of exploratory vocalization shows manipulation of amplitude in playful yelling and whispering. Infants also appear to explore the range of vowel-like sounds (where the vocal tract is open) and to contrast these with various closed sounds, the most salient of which is surely the raspberry sound, so common in expansion stage infants. In "marginal babbling," also a common vocalization type of the expansion stage, infants produce single utterances consisting of a wide array of closed sounds such as raspberries, fricative-like or nasal sounds adjacent to open vowel-like sounds, also of many sorts.

Neither marginal babbling nor any of the other sounds of the expansion stage include systematic repetitive articulatory sequences, but tend instead to consist of a rather unpredictable articulatory meandering, illustrating rich raw material, not yet clearly prepared for presentation as the stuff of potential words.

Vocalization in the expansion stage is more elaborate than in the primitive articulation stage, and individual articulatory movements have greater range, but regular, well-timed syllabification is still absent. Notably, marginal babbles are unlike speech in that the transitions between closures and openings tend to be irregular and long, exceeding the 120 ms limit.

As with gooing, however, marginal babbling also shows variability such that occasionally a canonical syllable occurs as a product of the exploration. The lack of repetition of particular marginal babble structures, however, suggests lack of control, and parents react accordingly, and do not treat marginal babbles as words.

In the "canonical stage" (5-10 months) infants produce normally phonated full-vowels, articulated with consonant-like margins, and the consonant-like and vowel-like parts are connected by rapid transitions. The syllables thus produced have all the characteristics of well-formed syllables and could serve as exemplars of words in any language that happens to have words that share the form of those syllables. Such syllables are not just well-formed as individual utterances; they also occur in repetitive sequences, alerting parents to the fact that the sounds are no longer merely raw material, but "negotiable phonological product." Parents react intuitively to the occurrence of these repetitive canonical syllables and begin to "bargain" opportunistically with the child over possible meanings (Papoušek, M., 1994). If the baby says [ba], [ba], [ba], the parent may react, "Do you mean ball (or bottle, etc.)?"

Variety and Repetitiveness

The distinction between raw material and negotiable phonological product is indispensable in making sense of infant vocal development, in understanding how parents react to infant sounds, and consequently in understanding how the infant sounds can be molded in social interaction toward a speech system. It is easy to imagine that the infant has hundreds of phonetic contrasts if we investigate infant sounds out of context, one by one, as acoustic raw material. The baby produces an amazing variety of sounds throughout the first year of life, but repetition by the baby suggests only a few contrastive types are under control in the early canonical stage.

Repetitiveness provides an anchor, indicating emerging control by the infant, and indicating to the parent that a particular sound or syllable could be produced again by the infant at will, and thus could come to be used as a word. These indications set off in the parent an intuitive pattern of interaction with the infant over these negotiable phonological products of babbling, a pattern that involves shaping, imitation, scaffolding, and direct lexical instruction. But none of that begins until the infant has gone through three stages of development that form foundations for repetitive syllable production, stages that build a capacity for vocal control in systematic increments.

Naturally Logical Requirements of Canonical Syllable Development and Evolution

How the Stages of Vocal Development Reveal Foundations for Canonical Syllables and for Speech

We contend that the three stages of development seen in the human infant before the emergence of canonical syllables are all necessary. This contention implies that there must be neurological foundations developed to produce sounds at each of the stages, and that the neurological capabilities associated with the later stages are built upon those of the earlier ones. The contention also depends upon clarity regarding what is implied by the notion "voluntary control of canonical syllables." Control implies more than the mere ability to produce an occasional sound that meets the definitional requirements. Even a gelada baboon may occasionally produce a moderately acceptable syllable (Andrew, 1976), and certainly human infants do it, sometimes at the end of crying bouts in the first month of life, and sometimes in gooing. Control of canonical syllables, however, implies more than accidental occurrence. It implies that syllables can be produced at will, with precision, so that one syllable type can be efficiently contrasted with another rapidly and in succession.

The Logical Primacy of Phonatory Control in Speech Evolution

An unavoidable necessity to begin the process of development for this sort of control is that the individual must come to be able to phonate at will. It is unclear that any non-human primate has a capability to phonate at will that matches that of the human infant by the first four months of life. In general, vocalization occurs in non-human primates in specific circumstances and for specific purposes, such as greeting, threat, warning, or courtship (see review in Hauser, 1996). In the absence of appropriate releasing circumstances (internal or external stimuli), it proves difficult or impossible for non-human primates to produce vocalizations. Learning of vocalization by non-human primates is clearly difficult when compared with human learning of vocalization. Instrumental conditioning of sounds in non-human primates proves demanding, and only limited kinds of sounds can be conditioned (Myers, 1976; Sutton, 1979; Sutton, Larson, Taylor, & Lindeman, 1973). Even the existence of direct cortical connection to laryngeal moto-neurons is doubted by key researchers of non-human primates (Jürgens, 1992; Jürgens, 1995).

The best example of vocal control in non-human primates may be that of infant or juvenile pygmy marmosets who sometimes produce repetitive sequences of sounds (Elowson et al., 1998; Snowdon, 2004). But even in this "pygmy marmoset babbling," the vocalization categories produced are not primarily innovations. Rather, the great majority are infantile versions of sounds drawn from the adult repertoire. Further, pygmy marmoset babbling has been reported to occur only in social circumstances, not when the animal is alone. The human infant, in contrast, shows vocalization at will during both periods of aloneness and periods of interaction. Importantly, the sounds thus produced in human infants often do not pertain to vegetative or fixed signal categories, nor to speech, and do not thus pertain to elements of an adult repertoire. The human infant sounds appear to consist of innovations of the infant, the product of vocal exploration.

The earliest human sounds that are not fixed signals or vegetative sounds are quasivowels, occurring by the time of the phonation stage, produced often with no sign of distress, when the infant is alone, feeding, or in face-to-face interaction (Oller, 2000; Oller et al., 2003). And across the first two months of life, the infant seems clearly to gain control over *how* quasivowels are produced, first continuously on egress and in the breathing cycle (with consequent short duration), and later with or without glottal interrupts and with extended breathing patterns that suggest control over breathing and over the consequent vocalization, which can be over three seconds in duration (Koopmans-van Beinum & van der Stelt, 1986; Netsell, 1981; van der Stelt, 1993). None of these key developments of the phonation stage involves supraglottal articulation. The initial development is focused on laryngeal control.

In the human infant "contextual freedom" (Oller, 2000) or "contextual flexibility" over normal phonation appears in the phonation stage long before that ability is applied to production of canonical syllables. Notably, no other primate species seems to have laryngeal control to match the human infant. Controlled canonical syllables are impossible without controlled phonation; so it makes sense that phonation has to be producible under control, before it can be controlled in coordination with supraglottal modulations that must occur during well-formed syllables.

On Emergence of Articulatory Modulations

Supraglottal articulation during normal phonation is a more complex action than normal phonation alone, and so we reason that the latter takes logical precedence in development and should be expected to have taken precedence in evolution. In addition the extent of supraglottal articulation during phonation in the primitive articulation stage, while notably elaborate, is less elaborate than articulations in the subsequent expansion stage; further sounds of the primitive articulation stage lack the systematic contrastivity obvious by the expansion stage. The greater elaborateness of vocalization in the expansion stage is seen in wider vocalic explorations (wider and more varied openings of the mouth, greater variety of lip posturing, etc.) and more diverse friction and trilling sounds produced at various points in the vocal tract as well as more elaborate sequences of both vocalic elements and friction and trilling sounds produced both within utterances and within clusters of utterances. The greater contrastivity of the expansion stage is seen in playful sequences of sounds that systematically alternate from one grossly identifiable type to another. But the primary developments of contrastive capability seen in systematic alternation of sounds through the expansion stage are not articulatory, but phonatory.

The keystone of articulatory development in the first year is canonical babbling. Here articulatory control is consolidated in repetitive movements coordinated with normal phonation, forming the syllables without which human language would be impossible. The advantage of commanding canonical syllables lies in their crisp rhythmic organization and in the high contrastivity of potential different syllables that can be produced and perceived with extreme ease and speed. But these advantages are clearly dependent on logically prior abilities to control phonation, and coordinate phonation with supraglottal movements, and create systematic contrasts among these articulated phonations.

Parental and Sexual Selection in Early Stages of Vocal Evolution

As a first step away from the primate background, ancient hominid infants may have been selected to produce sounds resembling those that occur in the earliest phases of modern human infancy. An adaptive function for such sounds in ancient hominids may have been solicitation of parental investment in infant caretaking. Such sounds certainly elicit attention and caretaking in modern human infants (Locke, 2006). No non-human primate infant has been reported to be as altricial as the human, and the prolonged helpless period seems to have been a characteristic of the hominid line in very ancient time (Bogin, 1990; Bogin & Smith, 1996). The altriciality of hominids may have created a special pressure among them (greater than in other primates) favoring vocal displays by infants that could serve as fitness indicators to parents whose caregiving investment could then be differentially applied to infants of differing vocal capabilities.

An initial enhancement of contextual flexibility in vocalization could have been selected in this way and then could have been elaborated as the evolving neurological infrastructure for vocalization provided a progressively more solid foundation for expansion and a continuing target for selection. After progress in evolution of more elaborate vocalization, ancient hominid infants may have soon gained the ability to produce primitively articulated sounds that were coordinated with vocalization. In modern infants in the second stage of vocal development, such sounds often occur in face-to-face interactions, with variable articulations of the supraglottal tract during phonation. These sound sequences show little if any crisp internal categorization (that is, little repetition of elements), but they include plenty of raw material for contrastive sounds. Such elaborate sounds provide substantial evidence to the modern parent of the rich vocal potential that the infant possesses, and may thus provide an important fitness indicator, eliciting investment in caregiving. The same sort of force may have driven a continuing enhancement and elaboration of vocal control in ancient hominid infants.

The effects of enhanced infant vocal abilities may have also been manifest in mate selection circumstances in ancient hominids. Vocal display capabilities early in life persist in modern humans, and may have persisted in ancient hominids, yielding reproductive advantages to the more vocally capable. Miller (2000) advocates the idea that mate selection played a central role in the evolution of language. He notes that elaborate fitness-indicating displays are widespread as mate selection behaviors across many species. He suggests that mate selection may have driven vocal language development in humans to an even greater extent than parental selection.

Breath Control as Another Function that may have Facilitated Vocal Control

Enhanced voluntary control over breathing may also have laid foundations for vocal control in ancient hominids. The larynx plays a critical role, not only in protection of the airway, but also in modulation of breathing in complex circumstances. An obvious possible circumstance that requires conscious control of breathing is in swimming. Ancient hominids are known to have been protein eaters (see review in Martin, R. D., 1990), and while much attention has been given to the role of hunting and meat-eating in this context (see review in Leakey, 1994), fishing and diving for fish and other aquatic animals also played important roles in ancient hominid diets. Hominids clearly lived by lakeshores commonly, if not preferentially. Humans appear to be particularly water-adapted among the primates, learning to swim relatively easily and possessing a fat layer and relative hairlessness (Morris, 1967), both suggesting an adaptation to a water environment, perhaps even a specific aquatic phase in ancient hominids (Hardy, 1960; Morgan, 1997; Westenhoefer, 1942) with protein acquired fishing and diving in addition to hunting. The aquatic adaptability of humans suggests there could have been an early period during which the ability of hominids to control breathing was highly adaptive. An incidental result may have been a greater ability to vocalize at will. That ability could have come under subsequent selection pressure having to do with either courtship communication or communication designed to elicit parental investment by the presumably altricial ancient hominid infant. In concert, selective forces related to breath control, parental investment, and mate selection may have provided the impetus to differentiate the hominid line from that of the other primates in the domain of vocalization.

PERSPECTIVES FROM OTHER SPECIES

Signal Repertoires and Fixed Signals in Animal Communication

Having reviewed the argument that well-formed syllabification is built on contextual flexibility of vocalization, we will review information on the evolution of contextual flexibility and on the extent to which syllabification of any sort appears in any species. The focus here is on circumstances where contextual flexibility occurs in evolution of communication in general and on the specific circumstances that may have been relevant in the human case. Thus we survey non-human species showing some degree of contextual flexibility in signaling. Numerous animals have evolved a variety of signals. Some have open-ended repertoires.

Still, animal signals typically consist of a small number of "fixed signals" (Huxley, 1914; Lorenz, 1951; Lorenz, 1978; Tinbergen, 1951), where each has one form and one function (e.g., Threat displays are used for one function, and alarm calls for another.). A fixed signal is stereotyped in form so that it can be easily recognized, conspicuous and unambiguous. Signal and function can be said to be coupled such that a particular signal cannot be used for any function other than the evolved one (the threat display cannot be used as an alarm, for example). The typical fixed signal repertoire in primates includes 5 to 7 types with gradations to express intensity and arousal levels and to allow some flexibility in situations of use. The functions (or "illocutionary forces," see Austin, 1962) can be roughly summarized in a typical system as expressing aggression, greeting, appeasement, contact and affiliation, warning, courtship, distress and comfort/pleasure. While some vocal learning appears to occur in the early years of non-human primates (see review in Cheney & Seyfarth, 1996), the outcome of learning is relatively fixed; the same relatively small repertoire of signals and functions is available to all members of the species. The primate may learn precisely when to use particular calls (for example, appropriate use of alarm calls may require learning which animals are predators), but does not learn sounds outside the limited repertoire nor new functions for the sounds. The result of learning is a coupled system of signals and functions with only minor exceptions.

Signal/Function Decoupling

In the human infant, as suggested by the descriptions above, signals and functions are decoupled early. Already in the first few months of life, both the initially fixed signal of crying and the pre-speech sounds are used flexibly. For example, squealing can be used in a variety of ways by four months of age: in a surprise context, with positive affect to express delight, in negative states to express complaint, or in circumstances that involve no obvious affect, and no function other than vocal play. Even crying, which always has a negative connotation, comes to be used flexibly. In the newborn, crying seems fully reflexive, while the four-month-old uses cry to attract attention or intentionally solicit caregiving (Bell & Ainsworth, 1972; Green, Gustafson, & McGhie, 1998; Gustafson & Green, 1991; Papoušek, H. & Papoušek, M., 1984).

As noted above, this sort of contextual flexibility is a logical precursor to production of well-formed syllables. Later, when infants start to speak, they learn to use those syllables to name a vast number of objects and states. They also learn to use names to express a wide variety of social functions (illocutionary forces). The same word can be used to request, to deny, to name, to criticize and so on. Using words in these ways requires vocal flexibility. It requires that the system of signals and functions be decoupled.

A hallmark of ritualized fixed signals is their stereotyped form. Primate ecology must have generally included a tendency to favor ritualization and stereotypy, but the hominid line clearly experienced pressures favoring variability of signal. To assess these pressures we address animal models. Fortunately, many such models are available, since variability of communicative action is fairly common outside the primates.

Deception

One pressure that can favor variability is related to deceptive use of signals. In many species there are examples of signals the either portray the environment or the state or identity of the sender falsely. For example, fixed coloration patterns that make a harmless animal look like a poisonous one are deceptive in this sense. However, deception can have additional adaptive advantages when it can be produced flexibly. Variability of deceptive signals is widely found, and even some invertebrates show it. For example, fireflies produce light pulses that vary across a variety of parameters and differ across species. Generally, in courtship a male flashes and a female of the species flashes back with a species-specific pattern. In such cases, selection favors distinctiveness and stereotypy. But in some species variability can occur. In the genus Photuris, the predatory females may respond with signals outside their species specific pattern to mating flashes from males of other Photuris species. The females deceptively lure the males of other species and then eat them (Eisner, Goetz, Hill, Smedley, & Meinwald, 1997). The female luring flash is learned; female fireflies also acquire man-made flash patterns not in any firefly repertoire (Lloyd, 1986). The firefly evidence suggests that an originally fixed signal capacity evolved for the function of courtship was apparently adapted by means of a learning program for a variable, deceptive predatory function.

Camouflage and Other Functions of the Cephalopod Chromatophore System

Camouflage can be particularly adaptive if it is variable. Cephalopods show a sophisticated chromatophore system in their skin allowing them to match their body surface to surroundings for camouflage. This very flexible system produces instantaneous changes in coloration and patterning (Hanlon & Messenger, 1996). But the chromatophores are used for other purposes as well in some species. For example, the Caribbean reef squid *Sepioteuthis sepioidea* shows a patterns used both for camouflage and social communication (courtship, aggression) (Moynihan & Rodaniche, 1982). Sometimes variable patterns are used in "protean behavior" to confuse and startle predators with false eye spots or unpredictable combinations of patterns and colors (Hanlon & Messenger, 1996; Driver & Humphries, 1988).

Cephalopod variable signaling is also used in courtship. Male Cuttlefish may use a female pattern while to approach and copulate with a female guarded by another male (Hanlon, Naud, Shaw, & Havenhand, 2005). In the Caribbean reef squid, a female pattern may be assumed by a male to avoid a conflict (a "formal contest") with another male (Griebel, Mather, & Oller, 2004, May). The squid signal system also shows variability in simultaneous "multiple signaling." Thus for example some species can display a courtship signal on one side of the body to a potential mate and an aggression signal to a sexual competitor on the other (Griebel et al., 2004, May). Cephalopods thus show a remarkable degree of variability and flexibility in production of signals on the skin.

Sexual Selection

Perhaps the most prominent force favoring variability is found in sexual selection which has produced complex mating songs and territorial displays in many species. Songbirds and humpback whales provide excellent examples (Hausberger, 1997; Kroodsma, 1999; Marler, 1999; Nooteboom, 1999; Payne, R. B. & Payne, L. L., 1997; Payne, R. S. & McVay, 1971; Tyack, P. L. & Sayigh, 1997). Mating and territorial songs often show rhythmic structure with notable similarity to language. Minimal rhythmic units within songs are sometimes called notes or syllables (Marler & Slabbekorn, 2004). The parallelism with human syllables is seen in the repeatability of units with relatively standard durations in songbird and humpback songs. At the same time animal syllables do not obey human well-formedness conditions for syllables such as margin-nucleus differentiation and constrained transition-timing as described above, and it is not clear that any animal syllables have internal organization and recombinability of syllable-internal elements as occurs with human syllables. In songbirds and humpback whales, the number of syllable and song types (which can be huge) provide a key indicator of the degree of variability. Another indicator of variability is the large number of transitions that can occur between individual syllables and songs within some animals (Tyack, P. L., 1999; Verner, 1975). Learning clearly occurs in songbirds and humpbacks with much change in repertoires over the years (Baptista & Petrinovich, 1986; Nottebohm, 1981; Payne, R. B. & Payne, L. L., 1997; West, King, & Freeberg, 1997). Male mating songs are sometimes shaped by intrasexual and intersexual selection at the same time (Kroodsma, 1999). The European starling differentiates male-male territorial competition song and courtship song (Hausberger, 1997). Thus both inter- and intrasexual selection forces can produce variable signaling that includes a several-to-several mapping of signal to function.

Social Cohesion as a Force Favoring Vocal Flexibility

Evolution also sometimes produces variety of signaling in cases where socialization is particularly prominent. When activities need to be coordinated flexibly, varied signaling is favored. Sounds functioning to produce coordination and societal stability can be thought of as social cohesion calls. The long-term stable groups of killer whales provide examples of social cohesion calls that often include variability (Bigg, Ellis, Ford, & Balcomb, 1987; Ford, 1991). Stable, discrete calls are also common in killer whales when they are traveling or foraging. But when groups are in social interaction, variable sounds are common, especially whistles and variable pulsed calls. In dolphins, fixed "calls" for specific functions, for example, courtship, aggression or warning, have not yet been clearly shown to exist. The various whistle types that are used seem to appear variably in many contexts. Thus dolphin communication appears to consist of a many-to-many mapping of signals and functions naturally selected as social cohesion devices.

Social cohesion as a selecting force also occurs in the circumstance of parental care, especially in species where parent-offspring bonding has particularly high priority. Pup recognition calls are important for example in crowded rookeries of pinnipeds (Schusterman, Hanggi, & Gisiner, 1992). Such calls need to be stereotyped because otherwise they might fail to yield unambiguous recognition. But in other social species, variability in social signaling by the offspring seems to have advantages. Notably variable vocalization occurs in at least some New World monkeys. Marmosets are cooperative breeders, and it has been reasoned that the very vocal offspring of marmosets elicit nurturance from their parents (Snowdon, 2004; Snowdon, Elowson, & Rousch, 1997). The sounds of these young marmosets have even been called "babbling." Since many sounds of marmoset babbling are used to achieve the attention getting function, it appears that parental attention has played a role in natural selection of a many-to-one mapping of signal to function.

Parental selection (Locke, 2006) could have played a key role in the emergence of contextual flexibility in hominid vocalizations. The altriciality and long period of dependency of the human infant (much greater than in other primates) creates a premium on a close bond between infant and caretaker. Variable vocalizations may have elicited attention, provided a fitness indicator to parents, and helped them make intelligent decisions about investment in infant welfare. The same capability for variability in vocalization could have been used later in life for coalition formation and the attraction of mates. Thus many social forces, including parental investment allocation, coalition formation and both inter- and intrasexual forces could have played significant roles in selecting for variability of vocalization in the large social groups of ancient hominids (Dunbar, 1996; Dunbar, 2004).

We are captivated by the possibility that hominid vocal evolution away from the primate background could have been initiated through a small step, perhaps suggested by the vocal capabilities of the cooperatively breeding and very social pygmy marmoset group. As noted above, infant and juvenile pygmy marmosets produce sounds more flexibly than has been observed in other non-human primates. Still, that variability is limited. They produce sounds in sequences repeating and alternating among types of sounds from the species repertoire. These patterns occur only in social circumstances, suggesting that they are fitness indicating displays, wherein the individual sounds are decoupled from their normal functions of affiliation, courtship and so on, for the purposes of display. Published descriptions thus far (Elowson et al., 1998; Snowdon, 2004) suggest that these displays fall far short of the variability and learning sensitivity seen in many songbirds as well as the degree of flexibility in sound types that is seen in human infants even in the first five months of life. In the cases of songbirds and human infants the variable sounds are truly innovative and learned, and present an enormous number of vocal types that are not precursors to a fixed adult repertoire. The pygmy marmoset vocal flexibility also falls far short of producing well-formed syllabification of the sort that is seen in human infants by the second half of the first year of life. It appears that in the marmosets a somewhat more flexible vocalization capability than in other non-human primates has been selected as a fitness indicator, and that in humans that sort of flexibility has expanded much further in a circumstance of even more intense pressures of sociality and infant altriciality. The premium may have been higher on variability in the hominid case than in the marmoset case precisely because the social and infant care demands were higher.

In our view, then, there is considerable evidence of natural selection forces that can break the coupling of signal and function usually seen in non-human primates. Our contention is that ancient hominids must have gone through stages that resemble stages of decoupling that are seen in many other species, with marmosets, songbirds, and cetaceans offering hints at the forces that may have produced the initial steps in hominids. None of the animals with variable vocalization produce well-formed syllabification. Instead they produce sounds indicating a foundational flexible capability to control vocalization itself. It seems likely that humans followed the same path before evolving supraglottal articulatory control.

Ingestion-Related Movements and Vocalization

MacNeilage's suggestion that lipsmacking gestures of non-human primates engaged in grooming may reveal a primate foundation for human syllables is intriguing. He also contends that rhythmic foundations for repetitive syllabification may be found in mastication. These behaviors suggest a central rhythmic generation system that could be brought to the service of repetitive syllable production. Critics have pointed out, however, that systems with feedback control (such as motoric systems) naturally and readily self-assemble oscillatory capabilities (Ghazanfar & Katz, 1998). This capacity perhaps obviate the need for a central rhythmic system of ancient evolutionary origin.

Further, lipsmacking and mastication do not entail vocalization, and it is voluntary control of the laryngeal vocalization capability that seems to constitute the key sticking point in getting the process of language evolution off the ground. In addition the mastication hypothesis has been criticized because the time frames seen in mastication in humans are about three times slower than the speed of syllable production (Greenberg, 1998; Jürgens, 1998).

In other species, mastication need not be involved in order for vocal flexibility to emerge. Several groups of animals seem to have evolved complex signaling repertoires without the involvement of mastication movements. Cetaceans, for example, either sieve their prey with a specialized baleen apparatus (mystecetes) and swallow the trapped prey whole, or they catch prey with either suction or teeth and also swallow their prey whole. Both processes seem to be completely independent of the production of vocalizations, which involve special apparatuses (not larynges) in the nasal passages (the only partially understood "monkey lips," see Cranford, 2000; Cranford & Amundin, 2006). The sounds occur mostly with the mouth closed. In birds it also seems implausible to tie beak movement in sound production to feeding-related movements which are usually quite different from mastication movements found in many mammals. We are not aware of a description of any connection between mastication and vocalization in birds. Yet both birds and cetaceans have in many cases evolved the capability to use vocalization flexibly, and have developed at least primitive abilities to syllabify (by rhythmic repetition of repeatable elements) their complex outputs.

In order for a vocal communication system to become particularly useful it must, we suggest, begin by being evolved to include a flexible source of sound with substantial power capabilities. The larynx in mammals, the syrinx in songbirds, and nasal passage structures in cetaceans are all adapted to make a wide range of loud and soft sounds possible, and those mechanisms are very widely involved in communication in those species. As we see it, syllabification can only be selected after a flexible sound source control capability is already in place. Human infant development suggests that hominid vocal evolution may have begun with flexible vocalization, and proceeded later to evolution of rhythmic utilization of that sound source to produce syllables. Thus we argue that the frame/content hypothesis needs to address precursors to syllabification that are seen in contextual flexibility of vocalization.

Acknowledgment

This work was supported by the National Institutes of Deafness and other Communication Disorders (R01DC006099-01, D. K. Oller PI and Eugene Buder Co-PI), and by the Konrad Lorenz Institute for Evolution and Cognition Research, and by the Plough Foundation.

References

Abry, C., Boë, L. J., & Laboissière, R. (1998). A new puzzle for the evolution of speech? A commentary on P. F. MacNeilage's The frame/content theory of evolution of speech production. *Behavioral & Brain Sciences, 21*, 513–514.

Andrew, R. J. (1976). Use of formants in the grunts of baboons and other nonhuman primates. In S. Harnad, H. Steklis & J. Lancaster (Eds.), *The origins and evolution of language, 280*, 673–693.

Andrew, R. J. (1998). Cyclicity in speech derived from call repetition rather than from intrinsic cyclicity of ingestion: A commentary on P. F. MacNeilage's The frame/content theory of evolution of speech production. *Behavioral & Brain Sciences, 21*, 513–514.

Austin, J. L. (1962). *How to do things with words.* London: Oxford.

Baptista, L. F., & Petrinovich, L. (1986). Song development in the White-crowned sparrow: Social factors and sex differences. *Animal Behavior, 34*, 1359–1371.

Bell, S., & Ainsworth, M. D. S. (1972). Infant crying and maternal responsiveness. *Child Development, 43*, 1171–1190.

Bigg, M. A., Ellis, G. M., Ford, J. K. B., & Balcomb, K. C. (1987). *Killer whales – a study of their identification, genealogy and natural history in British Columbia and Washington State.* Nanaimo, B.C.: Phantom Press.

Bogin, B. (1990). The evolution of human childhood. *BioScience, 40.*

Bogin, B., & Smith, B. H. (1996). Evolution of the human life cycle. *American Journal of Human Biology, 8*, 703–716.

Caldwell, M. C., & Caldwell, D. K. (1965). Individualized whistle contours in bottlenose dolphins (Tursiops truncatus). *Science, 207*, 434–435.

Caldwell, M. C., Caldwell, D. K., & Tyack, P. L. (1990). A review of the signature whistle hypothesis for the Atlantic bottlenose dolphin, Tursiops truncatus. In S. Leatherwood & R. Reeves (Eds.), *The Bottlenose dolphin: Recent progress in research* (pp. 199–243). San Diego, CA: Academic Press.

Cheney, D. L., & Seyfarth, R. M. (1996). Function and intention in the calls of non-human primates. *Proceedings of the British Academy, 88*, 59–76.

Chomsky, N. (1968). *Language and mind.* New York: Harcourt.

Chomsky, N. (1986). *Knowledge of language: Its nature, origin, and use.* New York: Praeger.

Cranford, T. W. (2000). In search of impulse sound sources in Odontocetes. In W. W. L. Au, A. N. Popper & R. R. Fay (Eds.), *Hearing by whales and dolphins.* New York: Springer Verlag.

Cranford, T. W., & Amundin, M. E. (2003). Biosonar pulse production in Odontocetes: The state of our knowledge in the Year 2000. In J. Thomas, C. Moss & M. Vater (Eds.), *Advances in the Study of Echolocation.* Chicago, IL: The University of Chicago Press.

Darwin, C. (1859). *The origin of species.* Cambridge, MA: Harvard Press.

Deacon, T. W. (1997). *The symbolic species.* New York: W. W. Norton & Co. Ltd.

Delattre, P. C., Liberman, A. M., & Cooper, F. S. (1955). Acoustic loci and transitional cues for consonants. *Journal of the Acoustical Society of America, 27*, 769–773.

Driver, P. M., & Humphries, N. (1988). *Protean behavior: The biology of unpredictability.* Oxford: Oxford University Press.

Dunbar, R. (1996). *Gossiping, grooming and the evolution of language.* Cambridge, MA: Harvard University Press.

Dunbar, R. I. M. (2004). Language, music and laughter in evolutionary perspective. In D. K. Oller & U. Griebel (Eds.), *The evolution of communication systems: A comparative approach* (pp. 257–274): MIT Press.

Eisner, T., Goetz, M. A., Hill, D. E., Smedley, S. R., & Meinwald, J. (1997). Firefly "femmes fatales" acquire defensive steroids (lucibufagins) from their firefly prey. *Proceedings of the National Academy of Sciences, 94*, 9723–9728.

Elowson, A. M., Snowdon, C. T., & Lazaro-Perea, C. (1998). "Babbling" and social context in infant monkeys: Parallels to human infants. *Trends in Cognitive Sciences, 2*(1), 31–37.

Fant, G. (1960). *Acoustic theory of speech production*. Gravenhage: Mouton.

Ford, J. K. B. (1991). Vocal traditions among resident killer whales (Orcinus orca) in coastal waters of British Columbia. *Canadian Journal of Zoology, 69*, 1454–1483.

Gärdenfors, P. (2004). Cooperation and the evolution of symbolic communication. In D. K. Oller & U. Griebel (Eds.), *The evolution of communication systems: A comparative approach* (pp. 237–256): MIT Press.

Ghazanfar, A. A., & Katz, D. B. (1998). Distributed neural substrates and the evolution of speech production: Commentary on P. F. MacNeilage's The frame/content theory of evolution of speech production. *Behavioral & Brain Sciences, 21*, 516–517.

Green, J. A., Gustafson, G. E., & McGhie, A. C. (1998). Changes in infants' cries as a function of time in a cry bout. *Child Development, 69*(2), 271–279.

Greenberg, S. (1998). A syllable-centric framework for the evolution of spoken language: Commentary on P. F. MacNeilage's The frame/content theory of evolution of speech production. *Behavioral & Brain Sciences, 21*, 518.

Griebel, U., Mather, J. A., & Oller, D. K. (2004, May). *Double signaling in the Caribbean reef squid Sepioteuthis sepioidea*. Memphis, TN: 65th Annual Conference of the Association of Southeastern Biologists.

Gustafson, G. E., & Green, J. A. (1991). Developmental coordination of cry sounds with visual regard and gestures. *Infant Behavior and Development, 14*, 51–57.

Hanlon, R. T., & Messenger, J. B. (1996). *Cephalopod behaviour*. Cambridge, England: Cambridge University Press.

Hanlon, R. T., Naud, M.-J., Shaw, P. W., & Havenhand, J. N. (2005). Transient sexual mimicry leads to fertilization. *Nature, 433*, 212.

Hardy, A. (1960). Was man more aquatic in the past? *New Scientist, 5*, 642–645.

Hausberger, M. (1997). Song acquisition and sharing in the starling. In C. T. Snowdon & M. Hausberger (Eds.), *Social influences on vocal development* (pp. 57–84). Cambridge, UK: Cambridge University Press.

Hauser, M. (1996). *The evolution of communication*. Cambridge, MA: MIT Press.

Hauser, M., Chomsky, N., & Fitch, W. T. (2003). The faculty of language: What is it, who has it, and how did it evolve? *Science, 298*, 1569–1579.

Holmgren, K., Lindblom, B., Aurelius, G., Jalling, B., & Zetterström, R. (1986). On the phonetics of infant vocalization. In B. Lindblom & R. Zetterström (Eds.), *Precursors of early speech* (pp. 51–63). New York: Stockton Press.

Huxley, J. S. (1914). The courtship-habits of the Great Crested Grebe (Podiceps cristatus); with an addition to the theory of sexual selection. *Proceedings of the Zoological Society of London, 35*, 491–562.

Jürgens, U. (1992). On the neurobiology of vocal communication. In H. Papoušek, U. Jürgens & M. Papoušek (Eds.), *Nonverbal vocal communication* (pp. 31–42). New York: Cambridge University Press.

Jürgens, U. (1995). Neuronal control of vocal production in non-human and human primates. In E. Zimmerman, J. D. Newman & U. Jürgens (Eds.), *Current topics in primate vocal communication* (pp. 199–206). New York: Plenum Press.

Jürgens, U. (1998). Speech evolved from vocalization, not mastication: A commentary on P. F. MacNeilage's' The frame/content theory of evolution of speech production. *Behavioral & Brain Sciences, 21*, 519–520.

Koopmans-van Beinum, F. J., Clement, C. J., & van den Dikkenberg-Pot, I. (2001). Babbling and the lack of auditory speech perception: A matter of coordination? *Developmental Science, 4*(1), 61–70.

Koopmans-van Beinum, F. J., & van der Stelt, J. M. (1986). Early stages in the development of speech movements. In B. Lindblom & R. Zetterström (Eds.), *Precursors of early speech* (pp. 37–50). New York: Stockton Press.

Kroodsma, D. E. (1999). Making ecological sense of song development. In M. D. Hauser & M. Konishi (Eds.), *The design of animal communication* (pp. 319–342). Cambridge, MA: MIT Press.

Leakey, R. (1994). *The origin of humankind.* New York: Basic Books.

Liberman, A. M., Cooper, F. S., Shankweiler, D. P., & Studdert-Kennedy, M. (1967). Perception of the speech code. *Psychological Review, 74*, 431–461.

Liberman, A. M., Delattre, P. C., Cooper, F. S., & Gerstman, L. J. (1954). The role of consonant-vowel transitions in the perception of the stop and nasal consonants. *Psychological Monographs, 68*, 127–137.

Lindblom, B. (1998). A curiously ubiquitous articulatory movement: A commentary on P. F. MacNeilage's The frame/content theory of evolution of speech production. *Behavioral & Brain Sciences, 21*, 521–522.

Lloyd, J. E. (1986). Oh, what a tangled web. In R. W. Mitchell & N. S. Thompson (Eds.), *Deceptions: Perspective on human and nonhuman deceit* (pp. 113–128). Albany, NY: SUNY Press.

Locke, J. L. (2006). Parental selection of vocal behavior: Crying, cooing, babbling, and the evolution of language. *Human Nature, 17(2)*, 155-168.

Lorenz, K. (1951). Ausdrucksbewegungen höherer Tiere. *Naturwissenschaften, 38*, 113–116.

Lorenz, K. (1978). *Vergleichende Verhaltensforschung: Grundlagen der Ethologie.* Wien/New York: Springer.

MacNeilage, P. F. (1998). The frame/content theory of evolution of speech production. *Behavioral & Brain Sciences, 21*(4), 499–546.

MacNeilage, P. F., & Davis, B. L. (1990a). Acquisition of speech production: Frames then content. In M. Jeannerod (Ed.), *Attention and performance XIII: Motor representation and control* (pp. 453–476). Hillsdale, NJ: Lawrence Erlbaum.

MacNeilage, P. F., & Davis, B. L. (1990b). Acquisition of speech production: The achievement of segmental independence. In W. J. Hardcastle & A. Marchal (Eds.), *Speech production and speech modeling* (pp. 55–68). Dordrecht, Kluwer.

MacNeilage, P. F., & Davis, B. L. (1993). Motor explanations of babbling and early speech patterns. In B. de Boysson-Bardies, S. Schonen, P. Jusczyk, and P. F. MacNeilage & J. Morton (Eds.), *Changes in speech and face processing in infancy: A glimpse at developmental mechanisms of cognition* (pp. 341–352). Dordrecht, Kluwer Academic Publishers.

MacNeilage, P. F., Davis, B. L., & Matyear, C. L. (1997). Babbling and first words: Phonetic similarities and differences. *Speech Communication, 22* (2–3), 269–277.

Marler, P. (1976). Social organization, communication and graded signals: The chimpanzee and the gorilla. In P. P. G. Bateson & R. A. Hinde (Eds.), *Growing points in ethology* (pp. 239–280). Cambridge, UK: Cambridge University Press.

Marler, P. (1999). On innateness: Are sparrow songs "learned" or "innate"? In M. D. Hauser & M. Konishi (Eds.), *The design of animal communication* (pp. 293–318). Cambridge, MA: MIT Press.

Marler, P., & Slabbekorn, H. (2004). *Nature's music: The science of birdsong.* Amsterdam: Elsevier Academic Press.

Martin, R. D. (1990). *Primate origins and evolution: A Phylogenetic reconstruction.* Princeton: Princeton University Press.

McCowan, B., & Reiss, D. (1995). Quantitative comparison of whistle repertoires from captive adult bottlenose dolphins (Delphinidae, Tursiops truncatus): A re-evaluation of the signature whistle hypothesis. *Ethology, 100,* 193–209.

McCowan, B., & Reiss, D. (1997). Vocal learning in captive bottlenose dolphins: A comparison with humans and nonhuman animals. In C. T. Snowdon & M. Hausberger (Eds.), *Social influences on vocal development* (pp. 178–207). New York: Cambridge University Press.

Miller, G. (2000). *The mating mind: How sexual choice shaped the evolution of human nature.* New York: Doubleday.

Morgan, E. (1997). *The aquatic ape hypothesis.* London: Souvenir Press Ltd.

Morris, D. (1967). *The naked ape.* New York: Dell.

Moynihan, M. H., & Rodaniche, A. F. (1982). The behaviour and natural history of the Caribbean reef squid Sepioteuthis sepioidea with a consideration of social, signal and defensive patterns for difficult and dangerous environments. *Advances in Ethology, 125,* 1–150.

Myers, R. E. (1976). Comparative neurology of vocalization and speech: Proof of a dichotomy. In S. Harnad, H. Steklis & J. Lancaster (Eds.), *The origins and evolution of language and speech, 280,* 745–757.

Netsell, R. (1981). The acquisition of speech motor control: A perspective with directions for research. In R. Stark (Ed.), *Language behavior in infancy and early childhood* (pp.127–156). Amsterdam: Elsevier North Holland.

Nooteboom, S. G. (1999). Anatomy and timing of vocal learning in birds. In M. D. Hauser & M. Konishi (Eds.), *The design of animal communication* (pp. 63–110). Cambridge, MA: MIT Press.

Nottebohm, F. (1981). A brain for all seasons: Cyclical anatomical changes in song control nuclei of the canary brain. *Science, 214,* 1368–1370.

Ohala, J. (1998). Content first, frame later: A commentary on P. F. MacNeilage's The frame/content theory of evolution of speech production. *Behavioral & Brain Sciences, 21*, 513–514.

Oller, D. K. (1976). *Analysis of infant vocalizations: A linguistic and speech scientific perspective.* Houston, TX: Mini-seminar presented at the Convention of the American Speech and Hearing Association.

Oller, D. K. (1978). Infant vocalization and the development of speech. *Allied Health and Behavioral Sciences, 1*, 523–549.

Oller, D. K. (1980). The emergence of the sounds of speech in infancy. In G. Yeni-Komshian, J. Kavanagh & C. Ferguson (Eds.), *Child phonology, Volume 1, Production* (pp. 93–112). New York: Academic Press.

Oller, D. K. (2000). *The emergence of the speech capacity.* Mahwah, NJ: Lawrence Erlbaum Associates.

Oller, D. K., Buder, E. H., & Nathani, S. (2003). *Origins of speech: How infant vocalizations provide a foundation.* Chicago: Miniseminar for the American Speech-Language Hearing Association Convention.

Oller, D. K., & Eilers, R. E. (1992). Development of vocal signaling in human infants: Toward a methodology for cross-species vocalization comparisons. In Papoušek, H., Jürgens, U. & Papoušek, M. (Eds.), *Nonverbal vocal communication* (pp. 174–191). New York: Cambridge University Press.

Oller, D. K., Eilers, R. E., & Basinger, D. (2001). Intuitive identification of infant vocal sounds by parents. *Developmental Science, 4*(1), 49–60.

Oller, D. K., & Griebel, U. (2005). Contextual freedom in human infant vocalization and the evolution of language. In R. Burgess & K. MacDonald (Eds.), *Evolutionary perspectives on human development* (pp. 135–166). Thousand Oaks, CA: Sage Publications.

Papoušek, H., & Papoušek, M. (1984). Qualitative transitions during the first trimester of human postpartum life. In H. F. R. Prechtl (Ed.), *Continuity of neural functions from prenatal to postnatal life* (pp. 220–244). London: Spastics International Medical Publications.

Papoušek, M. (1994). *Vom ersten Schrei zum ersten Wort: Anfänge der Sprachentwickelung in der vorsprachlichen Kommunikation.* Bern: Verlag Hans Huber.

Payne, R. B., & Payne, L. L. (1997). Field observations, experimental design, and the time and place of learning bird songs. In C. T. Snowdon & M. Hausberger (Eds.), *Social influences on vocal development* (pp. 57–84). Cambridge, UK: Cambridge University Press.

Payne, R. S., & McVay, S. (1971). Songs of the humpback whale. *Science, 173*, 583–597.

Pinker, S., & Bloom, P. (1990). Natural language and natural selection. *Behavioral & Brain Sciences, 13*, 707–784.

Roug, L., Landberg, I., & Lundberg, L.-J. (1989). Phonetic development in early infancy: A study of four Swedish children during the first eighteen months of life. *Journal of Child Language, 16*, 19–40.

Sayigh, L. S., Tyack, R. S., Wells, R. S., & Scott, M. D. (1990). Signature whistle of free-ranging bottlenose dolphins, Tursiops truncatus: Stability and mother-offspring comparisons. *Behavioral Ecology and Sociobiology, 26*, 247–260.

Schusterman, R. J., Hanggi, E. B., & Gisiner, R. (1992). Acoustic signaling in mother-pup reunions, interspecies bonding, and affiliation by kinship in California sea lions (Zalophus califonianus). In J. Thomas, R. A. Kastelein & A. Y. Supin (Eds.), *Marine mammal sensory systems* (pp. 533–551). New York: Plenum Press.

Sessle, B. J. (1998). Recent evidence of the involvement of lateral frontal cortex in primate cyclic ingestive movements: Commentary on P. F. MacNeilage's The frame/content theory of evolution of speech production. *Behavioral & Brain Sciences, 21*, 529–530.

Seyfarth, R. M., & Cheney, D. L. (1997). Some general features of vocal development in nonhuman primates. In C. T. Snowdon & M. Hausberger (Eds.), *Social influences on vocal development* (pp. 249–273). New York, NY: Cambridge University Press.

Sinha, C. (2004). The evolution of language: From signals to symbols to system. In D. K. Oller & U. Griebel (Eds.), *The evolution of communication systems: A comparative approach* (pp. 217–235): MIT Press.

Snowdon, C. (2004). Social processes in the evolution of complex cognition and communication. In D. K. Oller & U. Griebel (Eds.), *Evolution of communication systems: A comparative approach* (pp. 131–150). Cambridge, MA: MIT Press.

Snowdon, C. T., Elowson, A. M., & Rousch, R. S. (1997). Social influences on vocal development in New World primates. In C. T. Snowdon & M. Hausberger (Eds.), *Social influences on vocal development* (pp. 234–248). New York: Cambridge University Press.

Stark, R. (1981). Infant vocalization: A comprehensive view. *Infant Medical Health Journal, 2*(2), 118–128.

Stark, R. E. (1978). Features of infant sounds: The emergence of cooing. *Journal of Child Language, 5*, 379–390.

Stark, R. E. (1980). Stages of speech development in the first year of life. In G. Y. Komshian, J. Kavanagh & C. Ferguson (Eds.), *Child phonology, vol. 1* (pp. 73–90). New York: Academic Press.

Stark, R. E., Rose, S. N., & McLagen, M. (1975). Features of infant sounds: The first eight weeks of life. *Journal of Child Language, 2*, 205–222.

Studdert-Kennedy, M. (1980). Speech perception. *Language and Speech, 23*, 45–66.

Sutton, D. (1979). Mechanisms underlying learned vocal control in primates. In H. D. Steklis & M. J. Raleigh (Eds.), *Neurobiology of social communication in primates: An evolutionary perspective* (pp. 45–67). New York: Academic Press.

Sutton, D., Larson, C., Taylor, E. M., & Lindeman, R. C. (1973). Vocalization in rhesus monkeys: Conditionability. *Brain Research, 52*, 225–231.

Thelen, E. (1981). Rhythmical behavior in infancy: An ethological perspective. *Developmental Psychology, 17*, 237–257.

Thelen, E. (1995). Motor development: A new synthesis. *American Psychologist, 50*(2), 79–95.

Tinbergen, N. (1951). *The study of instinct.* Oxford: Oxford University Press.

Tronick, E. D., Als, H., & Brazelton, T. B. (1980). Monadic phases: A structural descriptive analysis of infant-mother face to face interaction. *Merrill-Palmer Quarterly, 26*, 3–24.

Tronick, E. Z. (1982). *Social interchange in infancy.* Baltimore: University Park Press.

Tyack, P. L. (1999). Communication and cognition. In J. E. Reynolds & S. A. Rommel (Eds.), *Biology of marine mammals* (pp. 287–323). Washington, DC: Smithsonian Institution Press.

Tyack, P. L., & Sayigh, L. (1997). Vocal learning in cetaceans. In C. T. Snowdon & M. Hausberger (Eds.), *Social influences on vocal development* (pp. 208–233). New York: Cambridge University Press.

van der Stelt, J. M. (1993). *Finally a word: A sensori-motor approach of the mother-infant system in its development towards speech.* Amsterdam, the Netherlands: Uitgave IFOTT.

Verner, J. (1975). Complex song repertoire of male long-billed marsh wrens in Eastern Washington. *The Living Bird, 14*, 263–300.

Vihman, M. M. (1996). *Phonological development: The origins of language in the child.* Cambridge, MA: Blackwell Publishers.

West, M. J., King, A. P., & Freeberg, T. M. (1997). Building a social agenda for the study of bird song. In C. T. Snowdon & M. Hausberger (Eds.), *Social influences on vocal development* (pp. 41–56). Cambridge, England UK: Cambridge University Press.

Westenhoefer, M. (1942). *Der Eigenweg des Menschen.* Berlin: Mannstaedt & Co.

Zlatin-Laufer, M. A., & Horii, Y. (1977). Fundamental frequency characteristics of infant non-distress vocalization during the first 24 weeks. *Journal of Child Language, 4*, 171–184.

Zlatin, M. (1975b). *Preliminary descriptive model of infant vocalization during the first 24 weeks: Primitive syllabification and phonetic exploratory behavior* (Final Report, Project No 3–4014, NE–G–00–3–0077): National Institutes of Health Research Grants.

3

Simple Combinatorial Considerations
Challenge Ruhlen's Mother Tongue Theory

Louis-Jean Boë [1]

Pierre Bessière [2]

Nadia Ladjili [1]

and

Nicolas Audibert [1]

[1] *Institut de la Communication Parlée*

Université Stendhal, INPG

Grenoble, France

[2] *Informatique Graphique, Vision, Robotique*

Grenoble, France

In their proposal for the origin of internal structure of word forms, Peter MacNeilage and Barbara Davis (2000) asked whether patterns they observed in infants were relevant for historical linguistics. They tested this hypothesis on the list of the 27 Proto-World roots or Global Etymologies (henceforth GEs), proposed in 1994 by Merritt Ruhlen and John D. Bengtson (henceforth R&B). These GEs are presumed to derive from a common source, an ancestor language spoken 50,000 years ago. MacNeilage and Davis observe:

"This study shows that a corpus of proto-word forms shares four sequential sound patterns with words of modern languages and the first words of infants. Three of the patterns involve intrasyllabic consonant-vowel (CV) co-occurrence: labial (lip) consonants with central vowels, coronal (tongue front) consonants with front vowels, and dorsal (tongue back) consonants with back vowels. The fourth pattern is an intersyllabic preference for initiating words with a labial consonant-vowel-coronal consonant sequence (LC) … Remarkably, all three CV co-occurrence patterns favored by infants and languages are strongly favored, even in this extremely small protolanguage corpus [of GEs]. And the LC sequence is much more frequent than the CL sequence as well." (MacNeilage & Davis, 2000, pp. 527, 529).

And MacNeilage and Davis concluded from these observations: "If the finding of not only the three CV co-occurrence patterns but also the LC effect in infant, language, and proto-language corpora means that these patterns are indeed basic to the origin of speech, then the controversial method of multilateral comparison, pioneered by Greenberg, J. H. (1963, 1987) and used by Bengtson and Ruhlen to construct their proto-language corpus, gains validity." (MacNeilage & Davis, 2000, pp. 529-530).

In this paper we (1) review certain key points in the debate and issues at stake with respect to the existence of a single mother tongue for all the world's spoken languages, (2) review methodology and linguistics choices, both lexical and phonological, made by Ruhlen and Bengtson in order to arrive at the 27 Global Etymologies, and (3) propose a combinatorial evaluation of lexical similarities observed by R&B between the lexicons of different languages distributed among different families. Are these similarities or are they not due to chance? We note that the world's sign languages do not share a common origin with the world's spoken languages. The well-documented history of the emergence of Nicaraguan Sign Language in the 1970s makes this clear. In other words, can we reject the null hypothesis and demonstrate that similarities observed between lexicons of different languages of the world reflect constraints on speech production and perception common to the human species and do not prove the existence of an original language.

Origin of Languages and Origin of Man

For centuries, theories addressing the origin of man and the origin of languages have been closely linked. In the 17th century, an earliest interest in the origin of language and the identity of mankind was rekindled and became a dominant subject of discussion. In the orthodox view, the Bible was still the main source of information about the earliest history of the earth and mankind. It was believed that the Earth, mankind and human language along with mankind, were no older than about six thousand years. By the turn of the 19th century, with the simultaneous developments of comparative philology and anthropology, the question of the origin of man and language had been revisited with new perspectives. In Germany (see E. Haeckel and A. Schleicher) and in France (see P. Broca and A. de Quatrefages) the relationship between linguistics and anthropology had always been very close. More generally, a circular argumentation was already appearing. On the one hand, linguists used anthropological hypotheses to validate their assumption of monogenesis for language. On the other hand, anthropologists referred to the hypothesis of the mother tongue to corroborate the assumption of monogenesis for mankind. Thus, in the 19th century, de Quatrefages (1888), a "fixist" anthropologist, took the theory of linguistic monogenesis and used it to support that of the uniqueness of the human species.

And a century later, Ruhlen (1994) considered that his claim of a unique origin of languages was corroborated by certain work in population genetics (Cavalli Sforza et al., 1988; Cavalli Sforza, 1991). We believe that the debate will be made clearer if the questions of the origin of man and the origin of languages are dissociated. Even if we hypothesize the unique origin of modern man, it is entirely possible that language appeared later in different populations. As Broca (1861-1862) emphasized, more than a century ago, the central question joining anthropology and linguistics is not the origin of languages, but that of the language faculty and its cerebral localization. If there is a unique point, it is that the language faculty is specific to man; whether there is a unique origin for languages is separate problem.

In our current state of knowledge, both the question of the origins of man and of the origin of languages seem to be "ill-posed" problems in the mathematical sense of the term (as proposed by Hadamard in 1923). A problem is well-posed if a solution exists, the solution is unique, and the solution depends continuously on the initial data (stability property). A problem is ill-posed if it fails to satisfy at least one of the conditions. However, theories on the origin of man are not stable; they rely too much on the discovery of new fossils. Each new discovery casts doubt on previous theories, as recently occurred with the discoveries of the Abel fossil (Chad, 1995), Toumaï (Chad, 2001), and the Man of Flores (Indonesia, 2003). With the origin of language, the problem is complicated by the fact that there is no fossilized word, no recording, and no trace of writing dating to tens of thousands, much less hundreds of thousands, of years ago. And we know very well that the phonetic form of a modern word cannot reliably tell us about its phonetic form centuries ago. From a chronological point of view, 5,000 years is a possible leap back into the past for Indo-European constructions, but it is impossible to go back 50,000 years to reunite the languages of the peoples then in Australia, and it is impossible to go back 500,000 years to classify populations by DNA.

Multilateral or Mass Comparison

In the traditional comparative approach of historical linguistics, a relationship between two languages is revealed by finding words with different regular diachronic phonological correspondences and demonstrable affiliations in meaning. This principle of the *regularity of sound correspondences* it is basic to the sciences of etymology and comparative linguistics.

Greenberg's work uses a radically different approach. Greenberg's first major work was the genetic typology of the languages of Africa, published in the *Southwestern Journal of Anthropology* in 1949-50. The first principle (Greenberg, J. H. 1949:79-83), is the exclusion of typological features (phonological, grammatical or semantic patterns) from genetic classification. Instead, "the arbitrary pairings of form and meaning, in both morphology and lexicon, provide the best evidence for genetic classification." His second principle is the exclusion of nonlinguistic evidence from the establishment of linguistic genetic families (Greenberg, J. H. 1950a: 57, 58).

After African language classification, Greenberg applied his methodology to the study of the languages of the Americas. In Australia, he identified one widespread family, which he called *General Australian* and a large number of small families. These classifications were severely criticized. In response, he formulated a third principle, the simultaneous comparison of the full range of languages or *mass comparison*, later *multilateral comparison* (Greenberg, J. H. 1954a: 406-8). Contrary to the traditional comparative approach, the *multilateral approach* consists of looking at many languages across a few words rather than at a few languages across many words. This technique excludes historical linguistic history.

In fact, this method is neither original, nor recent, and it is not a revolution. In the 19th century, Antonio Balbi used linguistics in compiling his *Ethnographic atlas of the globe or classification of the modern and ancient peoples according to their languages*. For his classifications, he used 26 roots: *sun, moon, day, earth, water, fire, father, mother, eye, head, nose, mouth, tongue, tooth, hand, foot,* and the numbers from *one* to *ten*. As a by-product of his classifications, he uncovered similarities among words that did not seem to be due to chance, but which nevertheless did not allow him to consider that the words belonged to a single language family.

"In this parallel between geographic boundaries and ethnographic [linguistic] boundaries, we have always abstracted from these analogies of form and of roots that one encounters more or less in almost all the languages of the globe, analogies which are too numerous to be reasonably attributed to chance, whereas they are not numerous enough, in other respects, to allow the

ethnographer to classify all the languages he discovers in the same family."
(Balbi, 1826; *our translation*).

In 1952, before Greenberg had proposed his multilateral comparison method, Swadesh had developed his glottochronology using word lists as a tool for identifying linguistic "stocks" worldwide (see Appendix) Using a single criterion of relatedness, that is the percentage of shared cognates, Swadesh proposed a classification of the languages of the Americas (1959) and also of the languages of the world (1962, 1971). Greenberg's classificatory work is in the same vein as that of Swadesh: he applied a single criterion of relatedness, a much looser version of Swadesh's criteria (measure of resemblance in core vocabulary), to a whole hemisphere.

Megalocomparisons

Following a suggestion from Dyen (1987) to provide evidence for the mother tongue, Ruhlen accepts that Greenberg's method of mass comparison of all the world's languages at once is valid without limitation:

"Although the reduction of the world's roughly 5,000 languages to a mere 17 families would be considered a radical step by a good number of contemporary linguists, there are indications that even further consolidation is not only possible, but necessary. (…) In seeking a more comprehensive classification, one must avoid the trap of binary comparison, which at level of research seems so tempting. Rather, one should adopt a global approach, taking into account *all* of the world's languages, as Dyen (1959:546) suggested." (Ruhlen, 1987, p. 258).

Ruhlen's attempt can be considered to be a megalocomparison. MICROCOMPARISON can be practiced on close-knit families like Romance, a time-depth of no more than 2000 years. MACROCOMPARISON is appropriate for far-flung but demonstrably valid groupings like Indo-European, with time-depth of up to about 6000 years. MEGALOCOMPARISON takes on any more remote relationship, where sound-correspondences are not regular and putative cognates are few, so that chance rivals genetic relationship as the explanation for perceived similarities (Matisoff, 1990, p. 108).

The Global Etymologies of Ruhlen and Bengtson

R&B's thesis (Bengtson and Ruhlen 1994a, 1994b, Ruhlen 1987, 1994a, 1994b, 1997) states that all the world's spoken languages come from a universal language spoken by a pre-proto sapiens 50,000 years ago. This theory is backed up by a methodology which enables them to look for and find phonological and semantic equivalencies between words of different languages. In the end, these equivalencies enable them to make comparisons from a set of 32 families and 1,316 languages and proto-languages (on average 41 languages per family). Finally they propose 27 GEs and, for each of them, the most general meaning and the phonological shape (Table 3.1). We note that almost all of the GEs are taken from Swadesh lists. The GEs 6 and 20 on the one hand, and 22 and 25 on the other, differ only in their phonological form. GEs have been presented as evidence for "proto-world." The results are listed in a data base (Ruhlen, 1994a, 1997).

Although they do not note this fact, R&B use a subset of words from Swadesh lists in the Global Etymologies they propose (21 GEs out of 27 are from Swadesh lists). These lists are available for more than a thousand languages and we have compiled a data base for 361 languages from five families (Ladjili, 2005) using data from two websites. The lists are available for 95 Indo-European languages (see Dyen et al., 1992). In addition, over 1200 languages are listed in the Rosetta Project. The RosettaProject is a global collaboration of language specialists and native speakers working to develop a contemporary version of the historic Rosetta Stone (http://www.rosettaproject.org).

Table 3.1.
Global Etymologies with Most General Meanings and Phonological Shapes. We note that almost all of the GEs are taken from Swadish lists. The GEs 6 and 20 on the one hand, and 22 and 25 on the other, differ only in their phonological form.

1. *mother* *older female* AJA	2. *knee* *to bend* BU(N)KA	3. *ashes* *dust* BUR	4. *nose* *to smell* ćUN(G)A
5. *hold* *(in the hand)* KAMA	6. *arm* KANO	7. *bone* KATI	8. *hole* K'OLO
9. *dog* KUAN	10. *who?* KU(N)	11. *woman* KUNA	12. *child* MAKO
13. *to suck* *Nurse, Breast;* MALIQ'A	14. *to stay* *(in a place)* MANA	15. *man* MANO	16. *to think* *(about)* MENA
17. *what?* MI(N)	18. *two* PAL	19. *to fly* PAR	20. *arm* POKO
21. *vulva* PUTI	22. *leg* *Foot* TEKU	23. *finger* *one* TIK	24. *earth* TIKA
25. *leg* *Foot* TSAKU	26. *hair* TSUMA	27. *water* AQ'WA	

Ruhlen's and Bengston's Criteria

To provide evidence for their Global Etymologies, R&B must use a set of semantic and phonological correspondences.

Semantic Equivalence

Eco (1993) coined the expression "la furia dell'etimologia" for this frantic etymological hunting. The search for phonological similarities led R&B to extend the meaning of each root they used, with an average of 24 semantic correspondences per Global Etymology. Thus, the first GE *mother, older female* is associated with the equivalent etymologies: *aunt, bitch = female dog, male dog, daughter, father, father's sister, female, girl, grandmother, husband's younger sister, father's mother, woman, woman's sister, wife*. The GE *hole* (number 8), is associated with: *anus, armpit, back, back part, breast, buttock(s), cave, crack, elbow= arm hole, fissure, grave, hiding place, hip, hole in the tree, hollow, incision, loins, nostrils, posterior, quiver, ravine, rear of army, river, shoulder, scoop out, to tickle, tickle a tired pig to make it go, tickling, valley*. And the GE *to think (about)* (number 16), is associated with: *abuse, admonish, appreciate, assume, be hungry, bewitch, brains, I can, command, conjecture, conjure, count, curse, desire, do you love me?, dream, folk song, guess, have friendly feelings, know, like, love, melody, memory, mind, name, order, possessed (applied to somnambulism), prayer, prefer, remember, remind, request, say, scold, seek, speak, story, summon, tale, talk, test, think, thought, try, understand, warn, wish, word*. We do not intend to challenge the validity of these semantic equivalences (for critiques, see Bender, 1993; Salmon, 1992), but it is important to note that increasing the number of semantic equivalences increases the chances of "discovering" GEs. Nevertheless, we would expect Ruhlen to have selected world roots without any semantic overlap. It is therefore surprising to note that the list contains two pairs of identical roots (numbers 6 and 20, and 22 and 25), with the same general meanings *arm* and *leg, foot*, different phonological shapes **KANO-POKO** and **TEKU-TSAKU,** and sharing five same meanings: *ankle, hip, hoof, thigh, upper leg*. We have questioned Ruhlen about this. He replied: "One of the deciding factors (though not necessarily correct) was that there seemed to be a consistent difference between a stop and an affricate, though clearly the affricate could easily derive from the stop. Another factor was that in some families both roots seem to exist. For example, in Afro-Asiatic we find both *tak- "walk" and saka "leg," and both roots seem to appear in Proto-Caucasian. In no way do I exclude the possibility

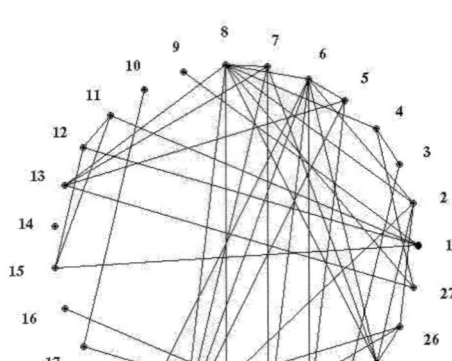

Figure 3.1.
Connections between roots sharing at least one meaning (an average of three).

that these two roots are really just one." (Ruhlen, personal communication, 2003).

The root numbers 10 KU(N) who? and 17 MI(N) what? share eleven meanings: do what, how many, what, what kind, what sort, when, where, who, who(ever), why.

More generally, Figure 3.1 presents semantic connections between the 27 GEs. Each link indicates that the two roots have at least one meaning in common. According to our calculations, 118 meanings are shared by two or more roots, and on average, a root shares a meaning with three other roots. If we put together the roots which share one or more meanings we obtain four semantic groups: (1) GEs 1, 9, 11, 12, 15; (2) GE 14; (3) GEs 18; (4) GEs 2-8, 10, 13, 16, 17, 19-27. The first group refers to people: *mother, woman (and bitch), man, child.* The second and third correspond to an action (*to stay*) and a number (*two*), and the last is a hodgepodge due to the "etymological fit of rage."

Phonological Choices and Equivalences

To detect phonological similarities, Ruhlen uses well-known rules proposed by Indo-Europeanists of the 19th century, without taking chronology into account. All of the GEs (with the exception of GE 13) present a CVCV word structure. Ruhlen does not use complex rules to authenticate similarities between phonological shapes. Concerning consonant similarities he writes: "You don't need a Ph.D. in linguistics ... just common sense" (1994a, p. 18). He proposes main classes of similarities (1994a, p. 40) and we have systematically listed the equivalences used by R&B in their database (*On the Origin of Languages*, 1994, pp. 277-330; *L'origine des langues*, 1997, pp. 238-271). For consonants, they use ten macroclasses, with the following equivalences. (We will see later on that for R&B all vowels are equivalent.)

1. /P B/ p p^h $p\!f$ ph pj pjw pp pk pr $p\!?$

b bb bh br bw

$_+$ $ß$ cb $ć$ $\!f\!f\!f^h$ $\!fl$ fr h hmb k kp lb m mb mp rf rp t $t\!f$ th v w $?b$ $?$ l $?mb$ $?p$ $?ph$

For example, for **POKO** *boko faxa va ha spõka mbake*

PAL   *ḥmbar pjeel wi ʌrre*

PAR   *p? floḍ fri har*

PUTI *ʃapsi*

2. /M/ m $m\|$ mb md mg mj mk ml mlq mlq^w mm mn mnj mnw mp

mst mt mx

b bm $\!fm$ g hm j jm $ʉm$ $ŋ$ $ŋk$ $nk\|$ s sm t w xm zm $?m$ $?mq$ $n?$

3. /T D/ t $t\!\|t^h$ t' $t'\|$ $t\!\dashv td$ tg th tk tl $t^ß$ $t^{ß\|}$ $t^ß kh$ tn tr ts tt tx tz

d $ð$ $ʒ$ dh d^h dr $d^ß$ dz

c $č$ $\!f\!f\!ft$ $ğ$ gts h hs jt k kl ks $ʉ$ $lk\|$ nd $nǰ$ nt r $ř$ rr rt s $s\|$ $s\|k$ ss st $st^ß$ xts z $?$ $?t$

4. /TS/ *tˢ tˢ' tˢk t ts tsh dtˢ' dˢ̵*

ʃ ʃ' ʃʰ ʃm ʃq' g h j js ks kts ntˢ ŋs s stˢ z? ?z

5. /N/ *n ñ n˥ ñj ñn ñt nb nc nʃ nʃ nd ng ngg ngk nh n' nj*

njg nk" nkx nl nm nn ns nt nt˫ nts ntj nw nz n?x

b c ʃ ʃt ʃ˫ d dn g h hh hm j jd jjn jn k k˫ k" kn kt l m mn ŋ ŋg ŋk
p q r rn s sk t t˥ ts tsw tt w x z ? ?n ?t

6. /K G (N)K (N)G/ *k k' kb kʃ kʰ kh khs kj kkh kk kkw kl kl' km kⁿ kn*
kp kr ks kt kth kts kv k" kw k'w kx nk ŋk nk' ŋkw

g gb gg gh gl gn gr gt g" gw gw? ng ngg ngk nğ njg ŋ ŋg

b bs c cl ʃ ʃb ʃk ʃp ʃml ff d ɣ ɣ' ɤŋ ɤw h hk hw jj jk k? l lk lp m
mlj n nc nd nj nn ns nt nw p pp pk q qq q' qk qn qs q"' q" qw r
rs s sh skw sp sq t tʰ tk t˥ tˢk tˢkw ts v w wğ wɤ wh wkʰ x xb xj xk
xl xn xp xs xt xtˢ x" z ž zk ?g ?k ?p ?tks ?ts ?w !k

7. /Q' Q'W/ *q q˫ q" q qv*

ʃ ʃʃ ʃ˫ ʃ˫ʃ˫ ʃt d g ğ g" h hqʰ hw hk k kk k˫ k˫k˫˫ kʰ kh kˢ k˫˫˫w kk kl ks
k" kw̥ q˫ rk⁻" st w x xk xvb x" x"? žt ? ?k?k

8. /L/ *l l' lh l˥ lk ll lqm lst*

gl j kr n ng r rd rn rr rs

9. /R/ *r rb rc rd rf rɤ rɤw rk rp rr rs rt rx*

b b?d d dr l n nn sk wr

10. /J/ *j h k kw l n ng r ts*

We note that R&B do not hesitate to use equivalences even among these macroclasses. We have listed these equivalences and present them in Figure 3.2. For vowels, it is well known, for example in Indo-European, that vowel quality can change over time, by the processes of umlaut, metaphony or inflection. It is therefore not surprising that R&B do not take vowels into account and rather consider them all to be similar. Thus, for the /A/ of the GE PAL, R&B propose in addition to /α/, the vowels i e E × o u / as in firi, pilia, wi, prin, peele, peia, ferfir, pEle, w×r, pol, poya, von, pula, brue, huave, bu, bur.

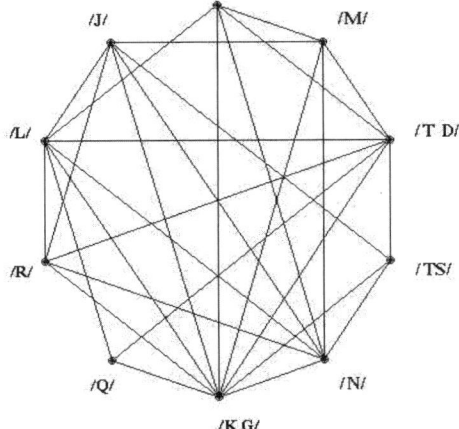

Figure 3.2.
Similarities between phonemes sharing at least one confusion (for example, /P B/ can be confused with /M/ or with /T D/ or with /N/, even though they are different phonemes).

For the GE TIK, R&B considers the following phonological shapes as equivalent: *atgu, ʃiʃ, зeœ, digitu, dlianŋ, зɥkku, itygin, iʃaki, motook, otejji, řak, sik, taihwo, tʌ́gu, tku, tsˈliœʷ, sakwe, zekatikkuagpaa.*

The vowel /I/ of this GE is judged to be equivalent to nine other vowel phonemes as indicated in Table 3.2. Such strong phonological similarities for consonants and vowels lead to only 242 different possible (C)VC(V) phonological shapes, if we allow the presence or absence of the first consonant and of the final vowel (11 x 11 x 2).

Criteria for the Emergence of a GE

To support the existence of 27 GEs, R&B (Ruhlen, 1994 :277–328 ; Ruhlen, 1997 : 233–271) indicate that: the 27 world roots ... are represented in at least six of these families, but a root is represented on average in 12 families, and the most widespread one, KU(N), "who," is represented in 23 or 24 families (Ruhlen, 1997: 234) (our translation).

Table 3.2.
Vowel phonemes and % occurrences corresponding to phoneme /I/ of the
Global Etymology **TIK.**

i	e	ɛ	a	y
38%	20%	1%	15%	1%
j̇	ʎ	u	o	ɥ
1%	1%	8%	13%	1%

Figure 3.3 presents a schematization of this criteria: to belong to same GE, at least six equivalent phonological forms out of 24 synonyms must be present in at least six languages from six different families. Is this conclusive proof of the existence of a mother tongue or could it be the result of mere chance, or of lexical constraints?

TESTING THE NULL HYPOTHESIS

There is currently a considerable literature detailing how criteria for determining both a semantic and a phonological match are almost entirely lacking, and there are numerous publications arguing against multilateral comparisons (Campbell, L., 1988, 1998a, 1998b, 1999; Guy, 1995; Matisoff, 1990; McMahon, A. and McMahon, S., 1995; Nichols, 1996; Rankin, 1992; Ringe, 1992, 1995, 1996, 1998, 1999; Trask, 1996). Aitchison provides an excellent summary of the problems, which we discuss further below:

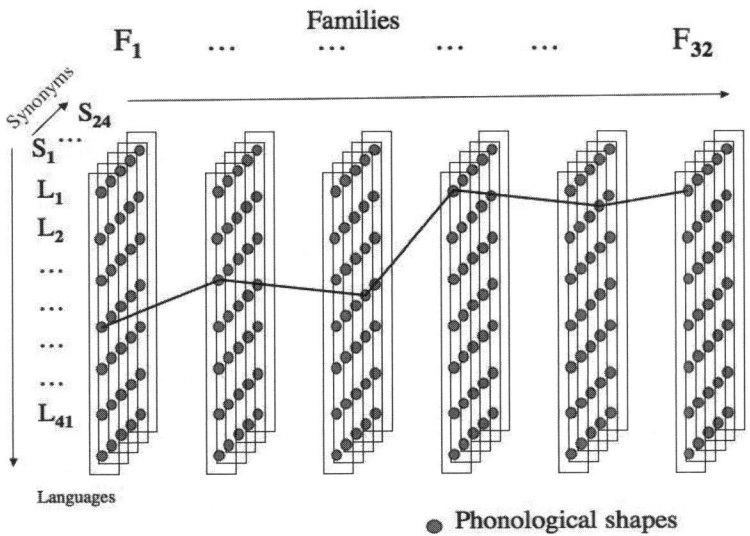

Figure 3.3.
Ruhlen and Bengtson's criteria: for each Global Etymology find the same phonological form + meaning, including 24 synonyms (S), in six languages (L) belonging to 6 different families (F).

Chance resemblances are easy to find among different languages if only vague likenesses among shorter words are selected. Sounds change radically over the centuries. Words which existed so long ago are unlikely to have survived in anything like their original state. Taboo is a further problem. The "lucky dip" approach does not make any attempt to eliminate accidental correspondences, nor does it control for phonetic probability or taboo. Meanings tend to be reduced to fairly simple, straightforward items, with a limited number of phonetic shapes. In these circumstances, chance similarities are likely to play a worryingly high role, and this "mass comparison" method is unlikely to stand the test of time (Aitchison, 1996: 173).

In more damning critiques, many linguists even consider that the Global Etymologies "cannot teach us anything about the origins of human languages" (Bender, 1993; Hock, 1993; McWhorter, 2001; Picard, 1998; Rosenfelder, 1999;

Salmon1992a, 1992b, 1997). In fact, any demonstration of a relationship between languages depends largely on finding words of similar phonological shape and roughly equivalent meaning in the languages considered. However it must be shown that the similarities observed could not have arisen by chance. Unfortunately Ruhlen does not take this precaution. We must therefore determine whether the observed similarities give us reason to reject the null hypothesis that the similarities are merely a product of chance factors. As Hurford puts it:

"As linguists like Larry Trask, Don Ringe and Lyle Campbell, L., to name but a few, loudly insist, no good answer has yet been given to the charge that the correspondences noted by the long-range reconstructionists are not above the chance level. In other words, no effort has been put into rejecting the null hypothesis." (Hurford, 2003, p203).

Lexical Homogeneity/heterogeneity of Families

The number of different phonetic forms for the same root (*Ndiff*) in a given family seems to us to be an essential lexical parameter. This number gives us an idea of the cohesiveness and existence of families. The value of *Ndiff* must of course be greater than 1; otherwise there would only be a single language per family. But on the other hand, *Ndiff* cannot be as great as the number of languages in the same family; otherwise, the existence of the family would be called into question. *Ndiff* is therefore an important piece of information about linguistic typology that has led the experts to classify languages by family. It represents a compromise between the homogeneity of the family and the existence of different languages for the same family. The value of *Ndiff* can only be evaluated using counts realized with data bases. We have performed database counts using Swadesh lists for the following five families: Afro-Asiatic, Andamanese, East Papuan, Austronesian and Indo-European, and have found a different number of languages per family. Figure 3.4 presents the average value for the GEs proposed by R&B.

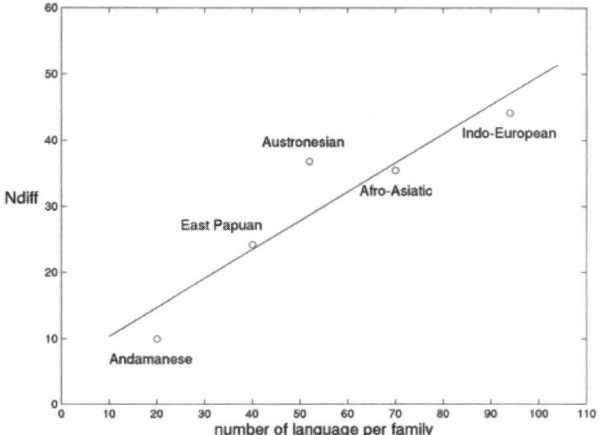

Figure 3.4.
Mean values for different phonological shapes Ndiff for Ruhlen's 19 GEs in five families related to the number of languages per family.

The mean values for N_{diff} by family vary between 9 for Andamanese and 45 for Indo-European, and we observe a significant correlation (R = 0.92 ; p = 0.022) with the number of languages per family. In choosing a great number of languages per family, we proportionally increase the chance of finding similarities. Ruhlen worked with 41 languages per family, which corresponds to an N_{diff} of approximately 15. This number increases with the number of synonyms. To illustrate this, we take the case of the GE *who,* for which R & B use synonyms like *what, when, where, how,* and *if.* These synonyms are also found in the Swadesh lists. For the five families, we have thus calculated the N_{diff} values for the GE *who* after the addition of 1 to 5 of these synonyms. We note that N_{diff} increases and tends towards a different asymptote for each family, as shown in Figure 3.5 between values of 45 and 180. With 24 synonyms and 41 languages per family, R&B have an N_{diff} of at least 60. Ndiff increases with the number of semantic correspondences and depends on the number of languages per family that we analyzed for this GE. Afro-Asiatic is the most homogeneous family, and Austronesian the least homogeneous.

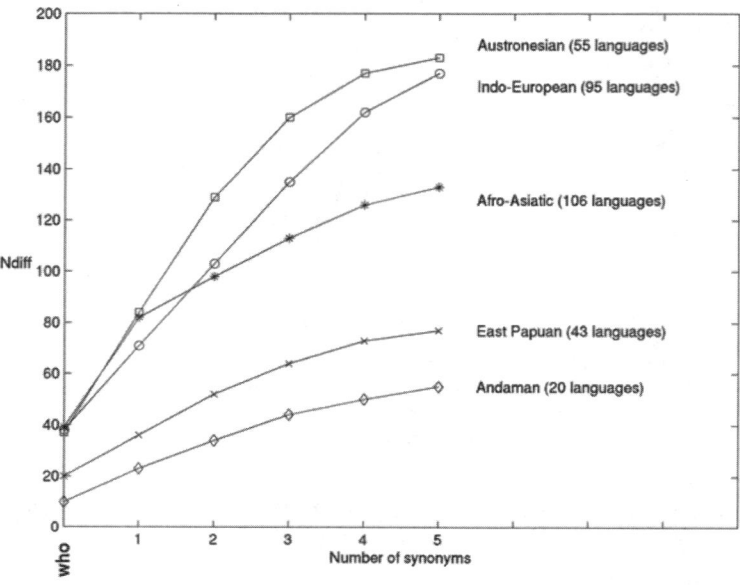

Figure 3.5.
Values of Ndiff for the GE **who** after the addition of synonyms (results for five families).

The GEs *water, mother* and *dog* have the lowest *Ndiff* values and *man, woman*, and *child* the highest values. These tendencies should be confirmed with a greater number of families. But we are not surprised to find *mother* among the GEs with low values. It has been well-known for centuries that nursery forms (like mama, nana, papa, dada, kaka) are similar across the world's languages. Murdock (1959) listed 531 terms for *mother* in different languages and concluded that the data [c]onfirm the hypothesis [of] a striking convergence in the structure of these parental kin terms throughout historically unrelated languages (Murdock, 1959).

And Jakobson in his paper "Why « *MAMA* » and « *PAPA* » ? " proposed the following explanation:

Since the mother is, in Grégoire parlance, *la grande dispensatrice*, most of the infant's longings are addressed to her, gradually turn the nasal interjection into a parental term, and adapt its expressive make-up to their regular phonemic pattern (Jakobson, 1962:543).

Definition, Notation and Calculation

R&B find that for each GE, similar phonetic forms are found in at least six families. Is this a conclusive evidence of the existence of a mother tongue or could it be the result of mere chance? To answer this question we propose a very simple combinatorial computation:

Let N_{ge} be the number of GEs taken into account in the reasoning. Let N_m be the mean number of meanings per GE. In R&B's study, $Nm = 24$. Let N_{diff} be the number of different phonological shapes associated with a given GE in a given family. Of course, the bigger N_m is, the bigger N_{diff} is. According to our thorough analysis, N_{diff} is at least 10 (see Figure 3.5). Let N_{ph} be the total number of different possible phonological shapes. With Ruhlen's phonological similarity rules, for a CVCV structure, $N_{ph} = 182$ (see § 3). Let N_f be the total number of considered language families; In Ruhlen's demonstration $N_f = 32$. Finally, let f be the minimum number of families that contain for a given GE at least one phonological shape in common with another family.

In the following calculations, we assume that there are neither semantic equivalences between the 27 roots nor phonological equivalences between the 10 macroclasses.

For our demonstration, let us construct a table in which each column corresponds to a language family and each row to a possible phonological shape. Such a table has N_f columns and N_{ph} rows. For a given *GE*, let us enter 1 in each of the $N_f \times N_{ph}$ cells when a phonological shape appears in a given family associated with this *GE*. If the phonological shape does not appear, let us enter 0.

A small instance of such a table can be produced for $N_f = 10$, $N_{ph} = 25$ and $N_{diff} = 5$ (all the columns contain five cells containing a 1).

We can permute the position of two columns without changing the association between the phonological forms and the families. The same is true if we permute two rows. Thus, we can group on the left all the columns corresponding to families that share a phonological shape with another family. Let us imagine that we have ϕ such families. This leads to a table where $\phi = 7$. All the column on the right contain n cells containing a 1, and there are $N_f - \phi$ such columns.

Afterwards, we can group at the top all the rows of these ϕ families which contain at least one 1. Let us imagine that we have ξ such rows. We then obtain a table where $\xi = 7$. All the rows underneath should, because of how we have constructed the table, contain at most one cell with a 1. There are $Nph - \xi$ such rows.

We necessarily obtain the following inequality:

$$(N_f - \phi)N_{diff} \leq N_{ph} - \xi$$

Obviously, $\xi \geq N_{diff}$ so we obtain:

$$(N_f - \phi)N_{diff} \leq N_{ph} - N_{diff}$$

The formula is also true for the minimum possible value of ϕ: f. This leads to:

$$(N_f - f)N_{diff} \leq N_{ph} - N_{diff}$$

And we finally derive:

$(if..f < 0..f = 0)$

$$f = \frac{N_f - N_{diff}}{N_{diff}}$$

Figure 3.6 plots this minimum value of f. It reveals that for any given GE, as soon as N_{diff} exceeds 10 there are at least 14 families that share similar phonologic shapes (with $N_{ph} = 200$). It is plotted as a function of Ndiff, the number of different phonological shapes for a given family and a given GE, and for different values of N_{ph}.

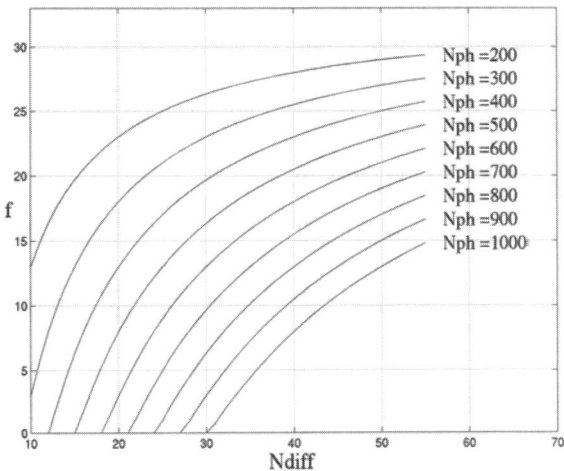

Figure 3.6.
The minimum number of families f, that share similar phonclogic forms.

With 24 synonyms, or a minimum value of N_{diff} = 60, R&B have a 100% chance of finding similarities among a couple dozen families. Even if they increase the number N_{ph}, assuming a couple dozen consonant categories (Nph on the order of 1000), they would find similarities in at least six families.

The null hypothesis cannot be rejected: R & B used too many equivalent meanings for each GE, and too many phonological equivalences for a too small number of different phonological shapes.

In effect, by using the data base that we have compiled using Swadesh lists and by adopting Ruhlen's criteria of emergence (*find the same phonological shape + meaning including 24 synonyms, in at least six languages belonging to 6 different families*), we were able to find for the GE **mother** two other phonological forms (number 1) different from AJA: **MAMA** for the Sino-Tibetan, Afro-Asiatic, Niger-Congo, Indo-European, Austronesian, Indo-Pacific (Adamanese and East Papuan) and Amerind families ; **ANA** for Indo-Hitite, Ouralian, Turk, Sino-Tibetan, Niger-Congo, Afro-Asiatic, Austronesian, and Indo-Pacific. Similarly for the GE **who** (number 10), we find for the Basque,

Niger-Congo, Afro-Asiatic, Daic, Indo-European, Japanese-Ryukyuen, Na-Dene, Sino-Tibetan families the phonological form **TA**, which is different from the form **KU(N)** proposed by R&B. We can therefore conclude that by applying the methods of R&B, we provide evidence for several mother languages.

Why So Many PHONOLOGICAL Similarities?

During almost half a century, the dominant theories in the field of language science (structuralism and generativism) have imposed an "inescapable hypothesis." From Saussure to Chomsky, the study of speech (*parole*) was relegated to a position of secondary importance, subordinate to the study of the language system (*langue*). Only at the beginning of the 1970s did a new approach (Lijencrants and Lindblom, 1972; Stevens, 1972) arise which places speech at the origin of the structuring of the phonological systems of the world's languages—at least their great trends—and which suggests a first modeling in this domain. We shall say that "substance," that is the speech production and perception processes, "informs" the phonological systems of the world's languages.

These processes are at the origin of the organization of these structures, other (biological, sociological) processes being, of course, likely to intervene as well. A series of studies of this "substance based" phonology, in which Davis and MacNeilage participate for ontogeny, has shown that the general tendencies of consonant and vowel systems can be explained and modeled by production and perception constraints (see Schwartz, J. L. et al., 1977b; Boë et al., 2005). Analysis of typologies of the phonological systems of the world's languages (Troubetzkoy, 1939; Crothers, 1978; Vallée, 1994; Schwartz, J. L. et al., 1997a) revealed that languages use relatively limited choices among all the possibilities determined by simple combinatory rules. The UPSID (Maddieson, 1986; Maddieson and Precoda, 1989) (UCLA Phonological Segment Inventory Database) (317 then 451 languages and now 566) gathers phonological systems of the world's languages, sampling more or less uniformly all language families. Among all the available consonants, phonological systems use only a very small

Table 3.3.
Percentages for places of articulation x manner of articulation for the 451 languages of UPSID (Boë et al., 2000).

	Bilabial	Coronal	Post alveolar	Palatal	Velar	Uvular	Pharyngeal	Glottal
STOPS	99*	100*	6	16	99*	13	1	48
NASALS	95*	96*	10	31	53	0	0	0
FRICATIVES	58	85	43	8	29	11	4	62
AFFRICATES	0	85*	49	4	1	1	0	0
APPROXIMANTS	79	78*	3	85 *	75	0	0	0

combination, although the possible combinations offered by the many categories of manner and place of articulation are quite large. Three places of articulation are the most common: bilabial, coronal, and velar (Table 3.3). The three or four places of articulation for each manner of articulation are in bold. Coronal place includes dental, alveodental, alveolar. The * marks the macroclasses adopted by R & B.

R&B's choice of 10 macroclasses of consonants corresponds almost exactly to the most common categories (with the exception of /Q/). It is therefore not surprising that this choice favors the phonological similarities of the GEs. Nor is the fact that MacNeilage and Davis observe that three CV co-occurrence patterns favored by infants and languages are strongly favored in data of R&B surprising. These main tendencies reveal that all the speakers have the same vocal tract, the same auditory system, and the same principles of control, but it is not a proof of the existence of a unique mother tongue.

Conclusion

We have demonstrated by simple combinatorial considerations that the Global Etymologies proposed for a proto-sapiens language in *The Origin of Languages* can be explained by random chance: The null hypothesis cannot be rejected. With the methodology used, R & B had a 100% chance of finding 27 Global

Etymologies common to the 32 families and validating their mother tongue hypothesis. They used too few Global Etymologies, too many equivalent meanings, too many languages per family, and too many phonological equivalences for too small number a of different phonological shapes.

Our demonstration is not proof that the hypothesis of monogenesis for spoken languages can be rejected, simply that the procedure adopted by R & B has no combinatorial validity. The method used to reconstruct proto-languages is one of the weakest points of this "New Synthesis" promoted by L. Cavalli-Sforza, C. Renfrew and M. Ruhlen which brings together genetic, archeological and linguistic data in the reconstruction of human evolution.

Is it really possible to prove the existence of a mother tongue spoken 50,000 years ago with a simple comparison of phonological forms of modern spoken words? The MacNeilage and Davis program, which seeks to find universal sensorimotor principles, seems to us more well founded, more promising in terms of development and results for the origin of speech. Furthermore, this program has the advantage of being independent of the question of the existence of a unique mother tongue.

Acknowledgments

This research was conceived in the Representation and Diffusion of Scientific Ideas in Speech and Language Sciences project (managed by Louis-Jean Boë and Christian Abry, ICP, since 1999) and funded by the Maison des Sciences de l'Homme-Alpes. It was a part of research in the Congruence project (managed by Pierre Darlu, INSERM, since 2001), being part of the Origine de l'Homme du Langage et des Langues project (managed by Jean-Marie Hombert) funded by the CNRS. Thanks to Christian Abry, Paul Boersma, Lyle Campbell, Rob McMahon, James Mattisoff, Manu Mazer, Boyd Michailovsky, Diverson Mzemba, Don Ringe, and Pauline Welby for their assistance and helpful criticisms.

References

Aitchison, J. (1996). *The seeds of speech: language origin and evolution.* Cambridge: Cambridge University Press.

Bender, M. L. (1993). Are Global Etymologies Valid? *General Linguistics 33*,191–219.

Bengtson, J. D., Ruhlen, M. (1994). Another look at *TIK 'Finger, One'. *California Linguistics Newsletter*, *24*(2):9–11.

Boë, L. J. (1997). Sciences phonétiques et relations forme/substance : 1. Un siècle de ruptures, négociations et réorganisations. 2. Du poids de la substance sur la forme aux réarticulations scientifiques. *Histoire Epistémologie de la Linguistique, HEL* XIX, *1*, 5–41, *2*, 5–25.

Boë, L. J., Abry, C., Cathiard, M., Schwartz, J. L., Vallée, N., Badin, P. (2005). Comment les exceptions des handicaps révèlent les universaux phonologiques: contraintes visuelles et auditives des systèmes consonantiques des langues du monde. *Faits de langues*, 25 (Special issue «L'exception entre les théories linguistiques et l'expérience » ed. by I. Vilkou-Poustovaïa), 175–190.

Boë, L. J., Schwartz, J. L., Vallée, N. (1994) The prediction of vowel systems: Perceptual contrast and stability. In *"Fundamentals of speech synthesis and speech rRecognition*, 185–213. Ed. by E. Keller. Chichester: John Wiley.

Boë L. J., Vallée N., Badin P., Schwartz J. L., Abry C. (2000). Tendencies in phonological structures: the influence of substance on form. *Bulletin de la Communication Parlée*, *5*, 35–55.

Boë, L. J., Vallée N., Schwartz J. L., Abry C. (2002). The nature of vowel structure *Acoustical Science and Technology*, *23*, 4, 221–228.

Broca P. (1861). Perte de la parole, ramollissement chronique et destruction partielle du lobe antérieur gauche du cerveau. *Bulletins de la Société d'Anthropologie de Paris*, *2*, 235–238.

Broca, P. (1862). La linguistique et l'anthropologie. *Bulletins de la Société d'Anthropologie de Paris*, *III*, 264–319.

Campbell, L. (1988). Review of Language in the Americas, by Joseph Greenberg. *Language, 64*, 591–615.

Campbell, L. (1998a). *Historical linguistics.* Edinburgh: Edinburgh University Press. (1999, American edition: Historical linguistics. Cambridge, MA: MIT Press.)

Campbell, L. (1998b). *Nostratic: a personal assessment. Nostratic: sifting the evidence*, ed. by Brian Joseph and Joe Salmons, 107–152. Amsterdam: John Benjamins.

Campbell, L. (1999). *Nostratic and linguistic palaeontology in methodological perspective. Nostratic: Evaluating a Linguistic Macrofamily*, ed. by Colin Renfrew and Daniel Nettle, 179–230. Cambridge: The McDonald Institute for Archaeological Research.

Cavalli-Sforza, L. L. Piazza, A. Menozzi, P. Mountain, J. (1988). Reconstruction of Human Evolution: Bringing together Genetic, Archeological and Linguistic Data, *Proc. Nat. Acad. Sciences*, 85, 6002–6006, 1988.

Crothers, J. (1978). Typology and Universals of Vowel Systems. In *Universals of Human Language*. J. H. Greenberg (Ed.), 93–152, Stanford Univ. Press.

Dyen 1992, http://www.ntu.edu.au/education/langs/ielex/IE-DATA1.

Dyen, I. (1959). Review of *Essay in Linguistics*, by Joseph Greenberg. *Language 37*, 527–552.

Dyen, I. Kruskal, J. B, Black, P. (1992). An Indoeuropean Classification: A Lexicostatistical Experiment. *Transactions of the American Philosophical Society*, 82, 5. http://www.ntu.edu.au/education/langs/ielex/IE-DATA1

Eco, U. (1993). La ricerca della lingua perfetta nella cultura europa, Roma-Bari: Laterza.

Greenberg, J. H. (1949). Studies in African linguistic classification: I. Introduction, Niger-Congo family. *Southwestern Journal of Anthropology 5*,79–100.

Greenberg, J. H. (1950a). Studies in African linguistic classification: IV. Hamito-Semitic. *Southwestern J. Anthropology 6*, 47–63.

Greenberg, J. H. (1950b). The patterning of root morphemes in Semitic. *Word* 6.162–81.

Greenberg, J. H. (1953). Historical linguistics and unwritten languages. *Anthropology today*, ed. A. L. Kroeber, 265–86. Chicago: University of Chicago Press. (Reprinted in Greenberg 1971b, 11–48.)

Greenberg, J. H. (1954). Studies in African linguistic classification VIII. Further remarks on method; revisions and corrections. *Southwestern Journal of Anthropology 10*, 405–15.

Greenberg, J. H. (1955). *Studies in African linguistic classification*. New Haven: Compass Press.

Greenberg, J. H. (1963). *The languages of Africa*. Bloomington: Indiana University Press.

Greenberg, J. H. (1987). *Language in the Americas*. Cambridge: Cambridge University Press.

Greenberg, J. H. (1988). Language in the Americas. *Language, 64*, 591–615.

Grégoire, A. (1937). *L'apprentissage du langage*. Bibliothèque de la Faculté de Philosophie et de Lettres de l'Univ. de Liège, 73.

Guy, J. (1995). Merritt Ruhlen: On the Origin of Languages, book review. *Anthropos: revue internationale d'ethnologie et de linguistique, 90*, 638–639.

Hock, H. H. (1993). SWALLOW TALES: chance and the "world etymology" MALIQ'A 'swallow, throat'. *Chicago Linguistic Society* 29.215–9.

Hurford, J. R. (2003). Review of Michael C. Corballis, *From Hand to Mouth: the origins of language*, Princeton: Princeton University Press, 2002. *Journal of Linguistics*, 39, 201–216. Cambridge University Press.

Jakobson, R. (1929). Remarques sur l'évolution phonologique du russe comparée à celle des autres langues slaves. Travaux du Cercle Linguistique de Prague, 2. [Reprinted in Selected writings of Roman Jakobson, volume 1: Phonological studies, 538–545. The Hague: Mouton, 1962, first edition.]

Jakobson, R. (1962) 'Why "mama" and "papa"? In Jakobson, R. *Selected Writings, Vol. I: Phonological Studies*, pp. 538–545. The Hague: Mouton.

Ladjili, N. (2005). Constitution d'une base de données de listes lexicales de Swadesh. Les différences phonétiques intrafamille. Master Industrie de la Langue. Université Stendhal, Grenoble.

Liljencrants, J., Lindblom, B. (1972). Numerical simulations of vowel quality systems: The role of perceptual contrast. *Language,* 48, 839–862.

MacNeilage, P. F. (1998). The frame/content theory of evolution of speech production. *Behavioral and Brain Sciences*, 21, 499–511.

MacNeilage, P. F. and Davis, B. L. (2000). On the origin of internal structure of word forms. *Science, 288*, 527–531.

Maddieson, I. (1986). *Patterns of sounds*. Cambridge: Cambridge University Press. 2nd ed.

Maddieson, I., Precoda, K. (1989). *Updating UPSID*. UCLA Working Papers in Phonetics 74, 104–111.

Matisoff, J. A. (1990). On megalo-comparison: a discussion note. *Language, 66*, 106–20.

McMahon, A., McMahon, S. (1995). Linguistics, genetics and archaeology: internal and external evidence in the Amerind controversy. *Transactions of the Philological Society, 93*, 125–225.

McWhorter, J. (2001). *The power of Babel: a natural history of language*. New York: Time Books.

Murdock, G. P. (1957). Cross-language parallels in parental kin terms. *Anthropological Linguistics* 1 (9), 1–5, 1957.

Nichols, J. (1996). *The comparative method as heuristic. The comparative method revised*, ed. by Mark Durie and Malcolm Ross, 39–71. Oxford: Oxford University Press.

Picard, M. (1998). The Case against Global Etymologies: Evidence from Algonquian. *International Journal of American Linguistics* 64, 141–7. [Published also 1995, On the nature of the Algonquian evidence for global etymologies. *Mother Tongue, 24*. 50–54.]

Rankin, R. L. (1992). Review of Language in the Americas, by J. H. Greenberg. *International Journal of American Linguistics, 58*, 324–51.

Renfrew, C. (1987). *Archaeology and language : The puzzle of indo-european origins*, London: Jonathan Cape, 1987.

Ringe, D. A. (1992). On calculating the factor of chance in language comparison. *Transactions of the American Philosophical Society, 82*, 1, 1–110, 1992.

Ringe, D. A. (1995). Nostratic and the factor of change. *Diachronica 12*, 55–74.

Ringe, D. A. (1996). The mathematics of 'Amerind'. *Diachronica, 13*, 135–54.

Ringe, D. A. (1998). *Probabilistic evidence for Indo-Uralic. Nostratic: sifting the evidence*, ed. by Brian Joseph and Joe Salmons, 153–97. Amsterdam: John Benjamins.

Ringe, D. A. (1999). How hard is to match CVC-roots? *Transactions of the Philological Society, 97*, 213–244.

Rosenfelder, M. (1999). Deriving Proto-World with tools you probably have at home. http://www.zompist.com/proto.html

Ruhlen, M. (1987). *A guide to the world's languages, volume 1: classification.* Stanford: Stanford University Press.

Ruhlen, M. (1994a). *The origin of language. Tracing the evolution of the mother tongue*, New York: John Wiley & Sons, Inc.

Ruhlen, M. (1994b). *On the origin of languages. Studies in linguistic taxonomy*, Stanford: Stanford University Press.

Ruhlen, M. (1997). *L'origine des langues.* Paris: Belin.

Salmons, J. (1992a). A look at the data for a global etymology: *tik 'finger'. Explanation in Historical Linguistics*, ed. by Garry W. Davis and Gregory K. Iverson, 208–28. Amsterdam: John Benjamins.

Salmons, J. (1992b). Theory and practice of global etymology. *Proceedings of the 15th International Congress of Linguists, 1*, 153–155.

Salmons, J. (1997). 'Global etymology' as pre-Copernican linguistics. *California Linguistic Notes, 25*, 1, 5–7.

Schwartz, J. L., Boë, L. J.,Vallée, N., Abry, C. (1997a). Major Trends in Vowel System Inventories. *J. of Phonetics, 25*, 3, 233–253.

Schwartz, J. L., L. J. Boë, L. J., N. Vallée, N., Abry, C. (1997b). The Dispersion-Focalization Theory of Vowel Systems. *J. of Phonetics 25*, 3, 255–286.

Stevens, K. N. (1972). The quantal nature of speech: Evidence from articulatory-acoustic data, *In Human Communication: A unified view.* 51–66. Ed. by E. E. Davis & P. B. Denes, Mc Graw-Hill, New-York .

Swadesh, M. (1952). Lexicostatistic dating of prehistoric ethnic contacts. *Proceedings of the American Philosophical Society, 96*, 452–463.

Trask, R. L. (1996). *Historical Linguistics*, London: Arnold.

Troubetzkoy, N.S. (1939). Grundzüge der Phonologie. *Travaux du Cercle Linguistique de Prague* 7. [French translation by J. Cantineau *Principes de phonologie*. 1949, 1970, Paris : Klincksieck.]

Vallée, N. (1994). *Systèmes vocaliques : de la typologie aux prédictions.* Thèse de Doctorat en Sciences du Langage, Université Stendhal, Grenoble.

Appendix

200-word Swadesh list is in lower case letters. The Global Etymologies of Ruhlen and Bengtson are in bold upper case letters.				
all	fall	I	right	sun
and	far	ice	river	swell
animal	fat	if	road	swim
ASHES	father	in	root	tail
at	feather	kill	rope	that
back	hair	knee	rotten	there
bad	few	know	round	they
bark	fight	lake	rub	thick
because	fingernail	laugh	salt	thin
belly	fire	leaf	sand	woman
big	fish	left	say	think
bird	five	leg	sing	this
bite	float	lie	scratch	thou
black	flow	live	sea	three
blood	flower	liver	see	throw
blow	fly	long	seed	tie
BONE	fog	louse	sew	tongue
breast	foot	man	sharp	tooth
breathe	forest	many	short	tree
burn	four	meat	sit	turn
CHILD	freeze	moon	skin	two
cloud	fruit	mother	sky	vomit
cold	full	mountain	sleep	walk
come	give	mouth	small	warm

correct	good	name	smell	wash
count	grass	narrow	fear	water
cut	green	near	smoke	we
day	guts	neck	smooth	wet
die	hand	new	snake	what
dig	he	night	snow	when
dirty	head	nose	some	where
DOG	hear	not	spit	white
drink	heart	old	split	who
dry	heavy	one	squeeze	wide
dull	here	other	stab	wife
dust	hit	person	stand	wind
ear	**HOLD**	play	star	wing
EARTH	horn	pull	stick	wipe
eat	how	push	stone	with
egg	hunt	rain	straight	worm
eye	husband	red	suck	year
				yellow

4

The Frame/Content Theory and the Emergence of Consonants

Didier Demolin

Department of Linguistics

Universidade de São Paulo

São Paulo, Brazil

Phonology Laboratory

Université Libre de Bruxelles

Brussels, Belgium

The Frame/Content theory of the evolution of speech production (MacNeilage, 1998) predicts that only modern humans superimpose a continual rhythmic alternation between an open and a closed mouth—defined as a Frame—on the sound production process. MacNeilage emphasizes that the question of skill development in speech production requires some background. An important issue to note in this perspective is that most work on sound preferences in babbling and in early words has been done on consonants. But the question of the emergence and control of these sounds has not been developed as explicitly as for vowels. Since Lindblom (1986), principles explaining the emergence of vowels in sound systems of human languages are better understood. Lindblom and Maddieson (1988) suggested a consonant classification in three levels of difficulty in terms of the number of separate active subcomponents required. This does not explain how the "simple" consonants of this classification emerge.

For MacNeilage there is heuristic value in asking what sound structures were present in the first words. He has proposed that the conjoint set of sounds and sound patterns favored in babbling and in the phonological systems of the world's languages constitute, in effect, the fossil record of true speech (MacNeilage, 1994), likely the consequence of the phylogenetic evolution of the vocal tract shape that was seriously modified in the late evolution of hominoids. More specifically, the foreshortening of the face, mandible, and maxilla played a crucial role in the enlargement of the supralaryngeal vocal tract. This enlargement allowed the tongue to play a more extensive role in reshaping the cavity during phonation, with the result that a much wider range of sounds became available for speech. Particularly, length reduction of the maxilla favored lateral movements and short sustained contacts of the tongue with the upper palate. Also, the tongue shape of the late Homo and modern humans provides a better control of place of articulation, lateral movements and lateral contacts facilitating coarticulation. These morphological changes have important effects on tongue activity due to the change in mandibular position. Thus this modification of vocal tract shape combined with the alternation between open and closed vocal tract (the "frame") likely led to a better control of tongue positions and other movements necessary to produce consonants. This chapter examines some of the possible motivations for the emergence of consonants in sound systems within the Frame/Content theory of speech evolution.

The Emergence of Consonants

The importance of consonants in the acquisition of speech has been emphasized by, e.g., Locke (1983), Boysson Bardies (1993) and Vihman (1996). However, little has been done to understand the constraints acting on the growth of these sounds. According to a widely accepted definition (e.g., *Handbook of the IPA*, 1999), consonants involve a narrowing or a "stricture" at an identifiable place in the vocal tract. The mandibular movement required for consonants is an elevation implying some closure of the mouth. For most consonants, an increase of pressure behind the constriction leads to a clearly identifiable acoustic event when the constriction is released. This is an important constraint because it requires a specific contact of some part of the tongue with the upper maxillary bone.

When one looks at the distribution of consonants in the world's languages, another important observation can be made in relation to the stricture constraint mentioned above. The vast majority of consonants are produced with a closure or a constriction between the lips and velum (Schwartz, J. L. et al., 2000). Since the production of consonants implies, in the majority of cases, the existence of a contact between the tongue and the palate, this place of contact becomes essential. Based on these findings, we assume that most consonants articulated in this part of the vocal tract require some proprioceptive control between the tongue and the upper palate. In this view, it is necessary to understand the nature and the possible evolution of palatal contact to explain the emergence of consonants in the phylogeny and ontogeny of speech.

Phylogeny

When examining speech from an evolutionary perspective, one important thing is to determine when the anatomical components of speech (the respiratory system, the position of the larynx and the shape of the vocal tract) for modern humans appear to be in operation. To have full language or speech capacity also implies that such features are coordinated by the brain. When one looks at the evolution of speech, substantial evidence supports the appearance of the modern human capacities for respiration in hominids about 1,500,000 years ago (Frayer & Nicolay 2000, p. 228). The authors show that at such an early stage chests were already barrel-shaped and noses were projecting from the face. Barrel-shaped chests are important because this feature allows generation and control of the rather constant subglottal pressure observed during the production of speech (Ohala, 1990). Noses projecting from the face indicate an enlargement of the nasal cavities that might already have played a role in the production of sounds in hominids. Those features are not typical of the early form of hominids and are not present in living apes like chimpanzees, bonobos, gorillas and orangutans. Even though having a barrel-shaped chest and a projected nose does not imply the ability to speak, it suggests that the anatomical features necessary for respiration and the nasal resonating chambers typical of language in modern humans were present (Frayer & Nicolay, 2000, p. 228). The enlargement of the nasal cavities has a debatable role as evidence in relation to speech, given what we know of nasal resonances in modern human spoken language. Nasal resonances depend on coupling between the nasal and oral cavities; a consequence of another anatomical movement, velum lowering. Even if the external nose projection looked alike in modern humans and hominoids from 1,500,000 BP, it does not demonstrate that the resonating chambers were similar, since their size greatly depended on the reduction of the longitudinal dimension of the face, a change attained much later.

Chest shape and size of the nasal cavities alone are not enough to guarantee full speech capacities. As emphasized by Duchin (1990), palate dimensions are important indicators of speech and sound-production capacity. The inability of chimpanzees to produce consonants is related to their long, flat and narrow palates because this prevents accurate thin tongue contacts with the upper palate and flexible tongue movements in the oral cavity. Frayer and Nicolay (2000, p, 231) when comparing the upper palate dimension of modern humans with various hominids and chimpanzees conclude that most specimens older than roughly 250,000 years do not differ from the chimpanzees. Figure 4.1 that compares palate dimensions in humans, chimpanzees and various hominoids at the level of the third molars.

Figure 4.1 shows that in humans the length of the palate is just slightly greater than the breadth, while for chimpanzees the dimensions show that the length of the palate is about twice the breadth (Frayer & Nicolay, 2000, p. 229). This feature is common to all species of living apes as one can see from the cast of a gorilla palate given in Figure 4.2. This conclusion is important since it suggests that early members of our genus were probably capable of language.

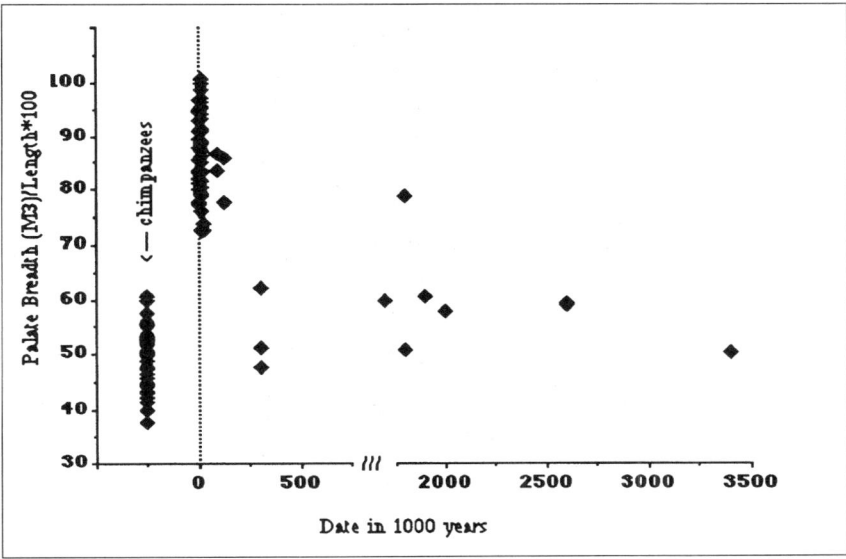

Figure 4.1.
Palate proportions at M3 for humans and chimpanzees aver the past 3.5 million years. (From Frayer & Nicolay, 2000.)

This does not demonstrate that they actually had language, but that the full capacity to produce sounds in modern human languages was present. To have language would imply that the full neurological wiring was present and that brain expansion and organization of areas specific to language was achieved. Frayer and Nicolay (2000, p. 217) claim that the latter was acquired early in the hominid lineage, but this does not demonstrate the association between speech capacity and language. The most important point implied from Frayer and Nicolay's claims is that the full capacity to produce frames could have been present about 250,000 years ago. This goes in the direction of what MacNeilage et al. (2000, p. 158) say when they claim that syllables themselves may also have been subject to phylogenetic progression.

Ontogeny

Once some characteristics of speech phylogeny are considered, it is important to know how the main anatomical features of the vocal tract are implemented in

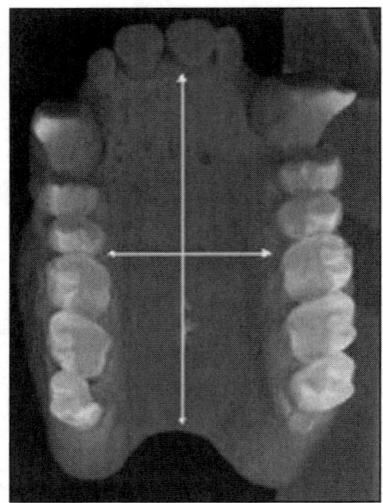

Figure 4.2.
Cast in epoxy of a gorilla palate showing the ratio between length and breath.

ontogeny. Claims about the recapitulation of phylogeny in ontogeny are frequent and have been discussed abundantly in the literature (e.g., Gould, 1977, 2002) so they will not be discussed here. However, it is still frequently claimed that babies are comparable to apes from the point of view of vocal tract growth. If it is indeed true that the larynx of babies is higher than that of young children who have full capacity for speech, this accounts for only part of what is involved in vocal tract growth. As will be seen below, other features of the vocal tract do not show the needed correlation between phylogeny and ontogeny.

In order to understand the shape of the upper maxillary bone during the embryo's growth, a number of palate prints have been collected, measured and compared with the data presented by Frayer and Nicolay (2000). Results presented in Table 4.1 and Figure 4.3 show that from the early stages of the embryo's growth to later stages, the shape of the upper maxillary bone is already proportioned like mature modern humans. Therefore since the shape of the front part of the vocal tract is typically human (i.e., that the ratio between the breadth and the length of the upper maxillary bone is comparable) this shows that there is no recapitulation of phylogeny in the ontogeny in the front part of the vocal

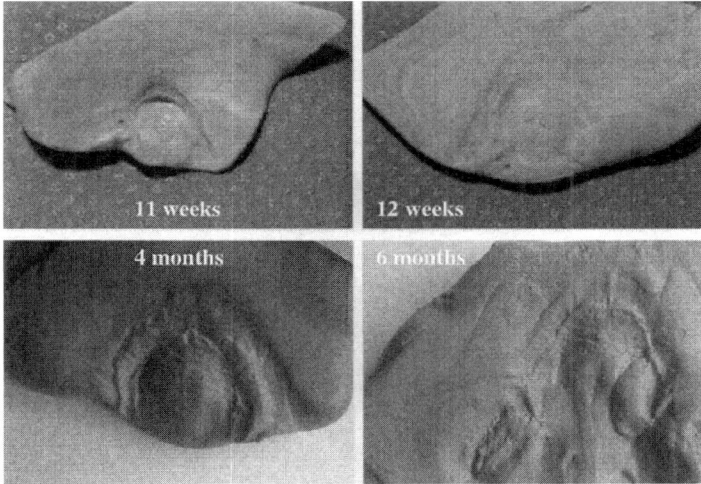

Figure 4.3.
Casts of embryos showing the development of the upper palate at different developmental stages that is typical of living apes.

tract. The shape of the palate, that is crucial in the production of consonants appears to be a typically modern human feature.

Tongue and Palate Contact

Emergence of consonants in relation to the Frame/Content theory should be examined. For a consonant, there must be a closure or constriction in the vocal tract, which requires contact between the tongue and palate. The importance of control for this contact is seen by looking at fricatives that require specific articulatory positions and aerodynamic conditions. The shape of the constriction for alveolar fricatives is well-known. This is illustrated by a comparison between the four voiceless fricatives of Amharic—singleton and geminated alveolar fricatives and singleton and geminated alveolar ejective fricatives [s, s:, s', s:'].

Table 4.1.
Dimensions of the palate on the embryo casts. The ratio is: breath taken at the end of the dental arch x length from this line to the prostion.

11 weeks	3 × 3 mm
12 weeks	5 × 5 mm
4 months	8 × 9 mm
6 months	10 × 11mm

Method

To study and compare the articulatory positions of the tongue for fricatives, EPG data were recorded with one Amharic speaker. These data were recorded with the Reading system, (see Fougeron et al., 2000, for details on the method). The speaker was recorded pronouncing the words given in Table 4.2. Data were processed with the Signal Explorer software. Figure 4.4 shows results comparing the tongue position at five moments during the production of the fricatives. The comparison between [s] and [s:], although the vocalic contexts are entirely similar, shows that the narrow constriction in the alveolar and post-alveolar regions is present from the beginning to the end for the geminated [s:] while it is set a little later for the singleton [s]. When alveolar ejective fricatives [s'] and [s:'] are compared, both show a wider tongue contact from the beginning. A very narrow constriction is made from the beginning of [s'] and is slightly increased towards the end. This corresponds to the time when the intensity of the noise is at its highest level. The geminated [s:'] has comparable tongue shape globally with the difference that there seems to be a quasi closure in the dental, alveolar and post-alveolar regions. The audio waveform reveals a leakage allowing air to escape through this quasi closure. It is only at the end that one can observe an elevation of the noise intensity that probably corresponds to the elevation of the larynx produced to generate the fricative. The

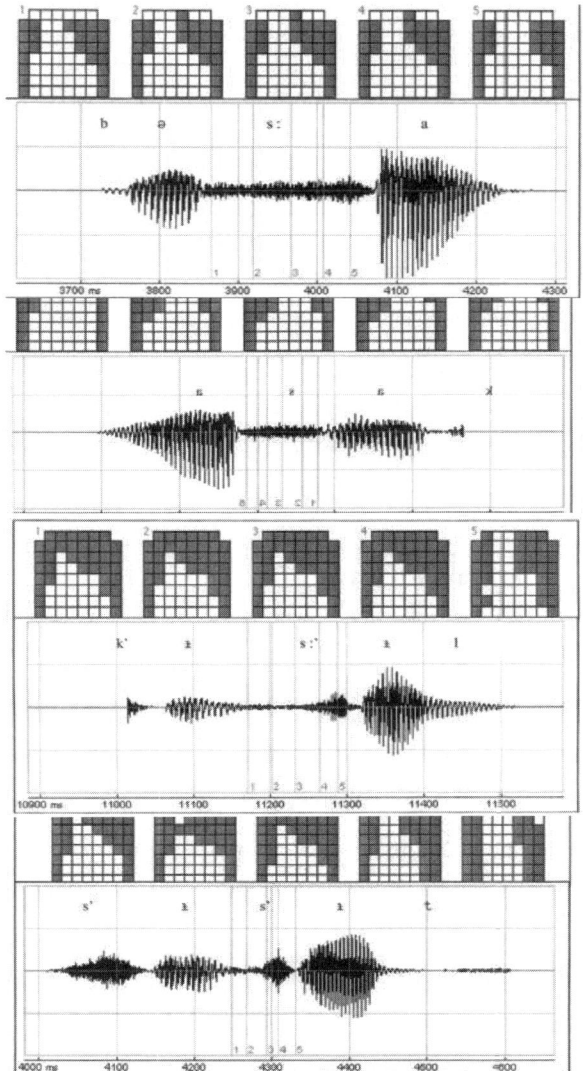

Figure 4.4.
EPG and audio waveform of the four Amharic words : kasa "Compensation,"
bɐ́ssa, "He pierced," s,'s'jt "Adjective," s,'s,'t "regret." EPG shows five moments
(1, 2, 3, 4, 5) during the fricatives' constriction. Each moment is labeled.

bi-phasic production of geminated ejective fricatives explains why such a highly

constrained sound in terms of aerodynamic requirement is possible (see Demolin,

Table 4.2.
Words of Amharic used in the EPG experiment

kasa	Compensation
bʌssa	He pierced
k'jss'jl	Adjective
s'js'jt	Regret

2002). These data suggest that that the subject controls the lateral size of the constriction in order to generate the correct acoustic output. Since the vocalic environments are comparable, it is difficult to claim that the difference in the tongue-palate contact is due to an elevation of the tongue. This suggests that constriction size is controlled by speakers to fit two aerodynamic requirements necessary to produce fricatives: the level of intraoral pressure (Po) and the volume velocity of the oral airflow.

In order to test the hypothesis that speakers can adapt the size of the constriction to the aerodynamic requirements of fricatives, a second experiment was devised. A recording of intraoral (Po) pressure was synchronized with a recording of the acoustic signal. Recordings were made at the O.R.L unit of the Hospital Erasme of the Université Libre de Bruxelles. Po was measured via a small plastic tube (ID 2mm) inserted through the nasal cavity into the oropharynx. It was connected to a Physiologia workstation (Teston & Galindo, 1990, 1995) consisting of a PC computer and an acquisition system equipped with various transducers and the signal editing and processing software "phonedit." A second tube (ID 5mm) was passed through the second nostril to create a perturbation during the production of sustained fricatives of a French speaker, in short expression such as [sɛtynnassēee] "C'est une nasse serrée." At random moments, one of the experimenters activated a void pump connected to the second and largest tube, to create a perturbation of Po in the oropharyngal cavity. In order to observe the contact between the tongue and the palate and the size of the constriction, the subject had a pseudo-palate connected and synchronized to the Physiologia workstation (see Fougeron et al., 2000, for details). The acoustic signal was recorded with a directional microphone connected to the Physiologia workstation. The signal was sampled at 16 kHz and processed with the software signal explorer.

Results of both experiments suggest that the lateral size of the constriction for fricatives can be adapted. Speakers have some control of the articulation as a function of change in aerodynamic conditions of production.

Frame/Content and Universal Tendencies

To the extent that the Frame/Content theory seems to fit both the tendencies in language acquisition and in the phonological systems of the world languages, it is interesting to see from rare or extreme cases whether the theory also fits the predictions. Some languages, such as !xóõ and Lendu ˻(aθa dialect) are particularly interesting in this respect. The former is a language with predominant CV syllables that can have very complex onsets and shows fewer front vowels in the most frequent syllabic types than back vowels (Traill, 1985; Rousset, 2004). The latter shows cases of syllables without apparent vocalic nucleus, (Demolin, 2002; Kutsch Lojenga, 1989). How can we account for these cases in the Frame/content framework?

The Khoisan language offers good example to test a number of assumptions of the Frame/content theory. First as shown by Rousset (2004), !xóõ is a language in which the prototypical syllable is CV. More than 80% of syllables are of this type (Rousset 2004: 116). This could look surprising in regard to the apparent complexity of syllables that one can encounter in !xóõ. In fact, since the vast majority of syllables are produced with a click in the onset, there are severe constraints in articulatory coordination. Every click is produced with a simultaneous double closure, one in the velar or uvular region and the other more front, i.e., palatal, alveolar dental or bilabial. The front closure is always released before the back. The gestures to make the two points of articulation and the temporal coordination necessary to produce a click can be accompanied by one or several other gestures that do not threaten the click itself.

Table 4.3.

Examples of !xóõ words from Ladefoged and Traill (1994).

kǎā̀	Wait for
ŋ̌àā	One's peer
ŋ̌aʔm	Evade an attack
ŋ̌ʰài	Fall
k̃ʔqʔáa	Spread out
k̃ˣáa	Go to a distance

For example clicks can be nasalized (voiced or voiceless) with an audible velar accompaniment and a fricative or an aspirated release in words (see Table 4.3). Those gestures are simply the coordination of laryngeal gestures, velum opening or closure with a specific type of release, aspiration or frication articulated with the click itself. Therefore nothing in this sometimes very complex coordination of gestures threatens the double contact of the front and back parts of the tongue with the upper palate that precedes the lowering of the mandible necessary to produce the following vowel. This leads to the second interesting finding made by Rousset (2004) showing that front vowels are strongly disfavored in !xóõ. This is likely due to the coordination of articulatory movements required to produce clicks that need the back closure to be released after the front closure to permit the generation of the noise characteristic of the click release. Indeed, the front part of the tongue is, in a way, inhibited by the requirement that the back closure cannot be released before any other significant movement of the tongue. As predicted by the Frame/Content theory, there is a significantly higher amount of association between low and back vowels with back consonants in !xóõ. Velar or uvular consonants that accompany clicks

(Ladefoged & Traill, 1994) favor vowels like [a, o, u] whatever the phonation type considered. However, it has to be noted that back vowels are also strongly associated with back consonants. This is likely due to a similar constraint that disfavors front vowels, because the late back closure release would favor the lowering of the tongue.

Lendu

The other interesting case to evaluate the Frame/Content theory in regard to consonants is Lendu. Mertens (1997), Kutsch Lojenga (1989) and Demolin (2002) have shown that voweless syllables occur with voiced and voiceless alveolar fricatives [s, z] and trills [r], which can be preceded by labial, alveolar and velar stops. The interesting case, that will be examined here, concerns sequences of CVCV syllables like [zźzz̀] "loss" and [z̀zzź] "drink" in which the segments bearing the tones are syllabic nuclei. Since there must be a cyclic lowering of the mandible to account for the Frame/Content theory, one can wonder how such words are articulated, given the constriction requirement on voiced fricatives. As shown in Demolin (2002), aerodynamic data allows us to infer that the syllable onset is made with a narrow constriction while the nucleus is likely produced with a larger constriction, which is sufficient to maintain some frication. One can assume that there is not much lowering of the mandible in this case, if at all. The lowering movement of the mandible necessary to make the vowel is accomplished by a lowering movement of the tongue body creating the resonances of a vowel whose timber oscillates between a centralized high front vowel or schwa-like vowel. When comparative data are examined, it can be seen that the so-called voweless syllables of the ₊aθa dialect of Lendu come from [-ATR] high front vowels of Ngiti, the other dialect of Lendu (see Demolin, 2002; Kutch Lojenga, 1989). The particular case of Lendu that is also observed in other languages of the world accounts for a case where there is a blending or a superposition of the closing and lowering mandibular movements. However, the sequence of non-syllabic [z] and syllabic [z] in Lendu generates a CV pattern, since the syllabic [z] that is accompanied by resonances accounts for a larger vocal tract that comes from a lowering movement of the tongue.

Berber Chleuh

Another language that is interesting to examine is Berber Chleuh that has the possibility to have any consonant, including voiceless stops, in the nucleus of a syllable, (Coleman, 2001; Dell, F. & Elmedlaoui, 1985, 1988, 2002; Louali & Puech, 1999a, 1999b; Ridouane, 2003). Ridouane (2003) claims there is no schwa or vocoid in the environment of syllabic consonants contrary to the analyses of Coleman, Louali, and Puech. Thus, this type of syllable presents a challenge to Frame/Content. Even if one shows the presence of small vocoids next to syllabic consonants, these are rather short and do not account for an important lowering of the jaw, if there is one. Words like those presented in Table 4.4 from Ridouane's data are enough to show the complexity of the problem. The way to account for these sequences of voiceless consonants in the Frame/Content theory might be simpler than it appears at first sight. Indeed, sequences of consonants, whether they are followed by a vowel or not, always require a succession of closure or constriction and a release if the consonants are to be identified. This corresponds to a requirement to produce any consonant: to have a closure or a constriction and an audible release that are the consequence of a contact between the tongue and the upper palate, in most cases. In Berber Chleuh, to produce the words in Table 4.4 there must be a succession of opening

Table 4.4.
Words of Berber Chleuh from Ridouane (2003)

fkt	Give it
tkʃt	She is dirty
kkst	Take her
tʃsχt	You cancelled

and lowering of the jaw. These words could be considered as made by frames that only have a consonant content.

Discussion

MacNeilage (1998) observed that in ordering errors in adult speech, consonants and vowels never occupy each other's position in syllables. Speech phylogeny and ontogeny are primarily a matter of giving an internal content to frames. Since consonants and vowels require diverging mandibular movements, they must be present in the origin of independent premotor programming. If the hypothesis that early speech patterns in infants are similar to early speech patterns in hominoids is true, syllables may also have been subject to a phylogenetic progression. The "pure frame" consisting of a labial consonant and an open vowel might account for this since the consonant and vowel in question do not require any contact between the tongue and the palate. The gradual differentiation of contacts in place and in manner of articulation that is observed in the speech of infants might reflect the phylogenetic evolution. The anatomical requirements to produce consonants seem to be a modern human feature that also results from a phylogenetic evolution. The modification of the shape of the upper palate and of the tongue allows for the fine contacts necessary for the production of diverse consonants. Neuromotor data is essential to demonstrate and explain the nature of these contacts, but is beyond the scope of the present study. The results of these experiments on the modification on the shape of the tongue for fricatives suggests that some peripheral feedback control might be exerted to adjust the lateral size of the constriction.

Data from !xóõ support Frame/Content predictions about the serial ordering of consonants and vowels, i.e., the tendency to associate back consonants with back vowels. Lendu and Berber show that even in the absence of apparent vowels, as in Lendu, or without any vowel at all, as in Berber, the basic cycle of oscillation between high and low mandible remains a robust parameter for describing syllables. Indeed Lendu and Berber can be considered as extreme cases in the content dimensions of syllables. Lendu blends C and V and Berber has a content with no V. Data discussed here only account for patterns in speech production and do not consider auditory aspects that play a crucial role in babbling and in early speech. However, mental representations cannot be understood without considering the constraints and the actions of the speech production mechanisms because it is on top of these constraints that representations are built.

Conclusion

Some of the possible reasons that explain the emergence and the importance of consonants in sound systems within the Frame/Content theory of the evolution of speech were examined. Data from phylogeny and ontogeny suggest that the capacity for speech appeared early in the evolution of hominids. Frames could have been present about 250,000 years ago. The capacity to make consonants, that require some proprioceptive contact between the tongue and the palate, and are absent in modern apes, may also have appeared at that time. The shape of the palate in modern humans is very different from living apes and appears to be a modern human feature. Experiments showed that speakers exert some control on the lateral size of the constriction of fricatives. Tendencies observed in some rare cases in the world's languages confirm predictions made by the frame/content theory about frame, the differentiation in the content, and the serial ordering of consonants and vowels.

Acknowledgments

I want to thank Stephane Louryan and Sergio Hassid for the help in collecting embryo data at the Hospital Erasme of the Université Libre de Bruxelles. Nathalie Vallée, Isabelle Rousset, Luc Bouchat, Linda van Elsaker, Kris d'Août and Moges Yigezu contributed to data collection. Bernard Teston, and the Laboratoire Parole et Langage of the Université de Provence made the EPG experiments possible. This research was supported by Jean-Marie Hombert in the frame of the ESF project: 'The origin of man language and languages'. A grant 'Evolution des langues, du langage et de la parole' and by the National Bank of Belgium. Discussions with Peter MacNeilage, Barbara Davis, Louis Goldstein, Jean-Luc Schwartz and Luciana Storto improved the paper.

References

Boysson-Bardies, B. (1993). Ontogeny of language-specific syllable production. In B.-Bardies, S, de Shonen, P. Juczyk, P. MacNeilage & J. Morton (eds.), *Developmental neurocognition: Speech and face processing in the first year of life*. Dordrecht, Kluwer Academic Press.

Coleman, J. (2001). The phonetics and phonology of Tashlhiyt Berber syllabic consonants. *Transactions of the Philological Society*, *99*: 29–64.

Davis, B. L., P. F. MacNeilage and C. L. Matyear (2002). Acquisition of serial complexity in speech production: a comparison of phonetic and phonological approaches to first word production. *Phonetica*, *59*: 75–107.

Dell, F. and M. Elmedlaoui (1985). Syllabic consonants and syllabification in Imdlawn Tashiliyt Berber, *Journal of African Languages and Linguistics*, 7: 105–130.

Dell, F. and M. Elmedlaoui (1985). Syllabic consonants in Berber: Some new evidence, *Journal of African Languages and Linguistics*, *10*: 1–17.

Dell, F. and M. Elmedlaoui (2002). *Syllables in Tashiliyt Berber and in Moroccan Arabic*, Dordrecht: Kluwer Academic Publications.

Demolin, D. (2002). The search for primitives in phonology and the explanation of sound patterns: the contribution of fieldwork studies, In C. Gussenhoven e N. Warner (eds.), *Papers in Laboratory Phonology 7*. Mouton de Gruyter, Berlin: 455–513.

Duchin, L. E. (1990). The evolution of articulate speech : comparative anatomy of the oral cavity in Pan and Homo. *Journal of Human Evolution*, 19 : 687–697.

Fougeron, C., Y. Menadier and D. Demolin. (2000). 62 vs. 96 electrodes: a comparative analysis of Reading and Kay Elemetrics EPG pseudo-palates, *Proceedings of the 5th Seminar on Speech Production*, Kloster, 309–312.

Frayer, D. W. and C. Nicolay (2000). Fossil evidence for the origin of speech. In N. L. Wallin, B. Merker and S. Brown (eds.) *The origin of Music*. Cambridge: MIT Press.

Gould, S. J. (1977). *Ontogeny and Phylogeny*, Cambridge: Harvard University Press.

Gould, S. J. (2002). *The structure of the evolutionary theory*, Cambridge: Harvard University Press.

International Phonetic Association (1999). *Handbook of the International Phonetic Association*. Cambridge : Cambridge University Press.

Kutsch Lojenga, C.K. (1989). The secret behind voweless syllables in Lendu. *Journal of African Languages and Linguistics*, II: 115–127.

Ladefoged, P. and Traill, A. (1994) Clicks and Their accompaniments, *Journal of Phonetics,* 22: 333–64.

Lindblom, B. (1986) Phonetic Universals in Vowel Systems. In *Experimental Phonology* (J. J. Ohala and J. J. Jaeger editors) pp. 13–44. Orlando. Academic Press.

Lindblom, B. and Maddieson, I. (1988) Phonetic universals in consonant systems. In *Language, Speech and Mind* (L. Hyman and C. Li editors), pp. 62–78. London. Routledge.

Locke, J. L. (1983). *Phonological acquisition and change.* New-York : Academic Press.

Louali, N. and G. Puech (1999a). La syllabification en berbère Tachelhit, In S. Wauquier-Gravelines et Ferré (eds.) *Syllabes: 2ème journées d'Etudes Linguistiques,* Nantes: Université de Nantes, 35–40.

Louali, N. and G. Puech (1999b). Syllabification in Berber, the case of Tashlhiyt, *Proceedings of the 14th International Congress of Phonetic Sciences,* 747–750.

MacNeilage, P. F. (1994) Prolegomena to a theory of the sound pattern of the first spoken language. *Phonetica,* 51, 184–194.

MacNeilage, P. F. (1998) The Frame/content theory of evolution of speech production, *Brain and Behavioral Sciences,* 21, 499–548.

MacNeilage, P. F., B. L. Davis, A. Kinney and C. L. Matyear (2000). The motor core of speech: a comparison of serial organization patterns in infants and languages. *Child Development,* 71, 1: 153–163.

Mertens, F. (1997) *Dictionnaire Bbadha-Swahili-Français,* Tervuren: Musée Royal de l'Afrique Centrale, Série Sciences Humaines et Sociales.

Ohala, J. J. (1990). Respiratory activity in speech, In W. J. Hardcastle and A. Martchal (Eds.) *Speech production and speech modeling.* Dordrecht: Kluwer Academic Publishers, 23–53.

Ridouane, R. (2003). *Suite de consonnes en Berbère Chleuh: phonétique et phonologie.* Thèse de doctorat, Université de Paris III.

Rousset, I. (2004). Structures syllabiques et lexicales des langues du monde: données, typologies, tendances universelles et contraintes substantielles. Thèse de doctorat, Université de Grenoble III.

Schwartz, J. L., Abry, C. Boë, L.-J. (2000). Phonology in a Theory of Perception-for-Action-Control. In *Phonology: from Phonetics to Cognition* J. Durand & B. Laks (Eds.), Oxford: Oxford University Press.

Teston, B. and B. Galindo (1995). A diagnostic and rehabilitation aid workstation for speech and voice pathologies, *Proceedings of Eurospeech 4,* European Speech Commmunication Association: Madrid.

Teston, B. and B. Galindo (1990). Design and development of a work station for speech production analysis, *Proceedings VERBA 90, International Conference on Speech Technologies*: Rome, 400–408.

Traill, A. (1985). *Phonetic and phonological studies in !xo@o Bushman.* Hamburg: Helmut Buske Verlag.

Vihman, M. M. (1996). *Phonological development : The origins of language in the child.* Oxford, Blackwell.

5

Lipsmacking and Babbling:
Syllables, Sociality, and Survival

John L. Locke

Department of Speech–Language–Hearing Sciences

Lehman College

City University of New York

Bronx, New York, USA

Just over forty years ago, Andrew (1963) suggested that language arose gradually "from an already well–developed and elaborate system of vocal displays modulated by the lips and tongue." (p. 94). To Andrew, the lip-smacking and grunting of baboons were prime examples of such displays. Later, MacNeilage appealed to lipsmacking as a possible origin of the syllabic frame, pointing to its biomechanical action and early vegetative origin (MacNeilage, 1986, 1998). I agree with MacNeilage that lipsmacking is relevant to linguistic evolution, so relevant that it seems strange when theorists say nothing about it.

Although he was aware that lipsmacking is a display, MacNeilage had less to say about its social functions, or the developmental and other processes whereby lip-smacking, as a signal, might have surrendered to syllabic vocalization. I begin here with a brief discussion of the form and functions of lipsmacking, including its development in infants, then turn my attention to grooming, the social behavior with which lipsmacking is intimately associated.

Next, I consider the possibility that if and when grooming went vocal, the new medium of socialization was not contact calls, as Dunbar (1993, 1996) suggested, but the mandibular oscillations of lipsmacking, set to phonation. This would have laid the groundwork for a linguistic modality that was vocal and a sound system that was syllabic. Finally, I ask about the role of lipsmacking–and any evolved approximations to vocal babbling–as these may have "trickled up" to influence the systems of social communication used by hominid adults.

Lipsmacking

Form

One of the first to comment on lipsmacking was Zuckerman, who undertook observations of a colony of Hamadryas baboons in 1929. Social and sexual encounters, he noted, were usually preceded by "quick lip, jaw, and tongue movements" (Zuckerman, 1932). Some years later, these movements were described by Anthoney (1968), who claimed that in lipsmacking "the moistened anterior dorsum of the tongue is laid flat against the backs of the upper incisors and anterior–most hard palate; then the contact between the lingual and dento–palatal surfaces is repeatedly broken and re–established by pulling the posterior part of the tongue rapidly back and forth (6–8 times per sec.). The mouth is kept slightly open," Anthoney's account continued, "and each time the tongue is pulled backward, the mandible is lowered a little, causing the mouth to open a bit more. The sound is actually produced each time the tongue is pulled away from the dento–palatal surface." (Anthoney, 1968, p. 360).

Clearly, this description raises questions about the term "lipsmacking," since it offers details about the action of the tongue but says nothing about the lips. In a similar report, Redican (1975) commented that at the same time the lips open and close slightly, "the tongue is brought forward and back between the teeth, so that the movements are usually quite audible . . . the actual smacking noise," he said, "appears to be made by the tongue breaking contact with the roof of the mouth and/or upper lip or row of teeth, rather than by the lips themselves parting. The tongue movements are often difficult to see, as the tongue rarely protrudes far beyond the lips." (Redican, 1975, p. 138). To the degree that human ears are a reliable measure, lipsmacking would thus appear to involve a series of mandibular oscillations with lingua–palatal if not bilabial points of closure, whose audibility is achieved through the rapid build–up and release of intraoral air pressure, not through phonation.

Function

As for function, Zuckerman thought that lipsmacking represented "an essential part of all friendly and sexual activities, both as a preliminary gesture and as an accompaniment." If two animals are sitting near each other, he noted, "their heads will turn, their eyes meet, and immediately they may begin to smack their lips. This social response may then be extended by the animals rising, and by one presenting to the other. Then follows more pronounced smacking of the lips, sometimes a rhythmical series of low deep grunts, and the animals will either groom each other or mount each other, or do both." (Zuckerman, 1932, p. 230).

To Anthoney, lipsmacking was linked to adult greeting and sexual behavior. Redican also noted a connection with grooming, copulation, and greeting. Although he occasionally saw lipsmacking in an antagonistic context, it is usually, he wrote, "a pacificatory, affiliative, or appeasement gesture." (Redican, 1975, p. 145). Others have also stressed the aggression–reducing or pacificatory function (DeVore, 1963; de Waal, 1989).

It is important to note here that lipsmacking may have emerged from infancy, according to Anthoney, when similar sounds are made in connection with nursing. In one study of rhesus monkeys, lipsmacking was present at birth, increasing in frequency over the succeeding month and declining thereafter (Kenney, Mason, & Hill, 1979). In another study, lipsmacking was infrequent in the first few months of life but increased sharply at seven months (Bernstein & Mason, 1962).

Primate infants are also the intended recipients of lipsmacking by their mothers, beginning at birth in free–ranging baboons and other primate groups

(DeVore, 1963). Terry (1970) called the presence of a newborn infant "the most important precipitate of grooming activity." (p. 131). At a week or two, mothers lipsmack to infants who are physically displaced by a few feet, seemingly in an effort to induce physical approach (Bolwig, 1980; Maestripieri & Call, 1996; Nakamichi & Yoshida, 1986). Frequently, the infants are responsive. That maternal lipsmacking excites infant attention and response is an issue we will return to later.

Control

If lipsmacking were an evolutionary precursor to the mandibular oscillations that are now associated with speech, the control centers for these activities would be similarly located in the brains of humans and other primates. In ventral premotor cortex (area F5) of macaques, motor neurons have been found that discharge selectively to the sight of lipsmacking—even when it is performed by a human—but not to other movements of the mouth (Ferrari, Gallese, Rizzolatti, & Fogassi, 2003). In the same species, electrical stimulation of an adjacent area (F6) has produced jaw movements (Petrides, Cadoret, & Mackey, 2005). These findings are significant in light of speculation that areas F5 and F6 are homologous to Broca's area, a region active in the control of speech (cf. Arbib, in 2005b; Heiser, Iacoboni, Maeda, Marcus, & Mazziotta, 2003).

Grooming

If lipsmacking were an evolutionary precursor to speech, it would be helpful to consider documented relationships between lipsmacking and grooming, especially since there are interesting parallels between grooming and social talking.

Form

There are two broad classes of grooming action. In *stroking*, an open, flattened palm is moved across the fur, revealing the parasites beneath, which are then removed with the fingers and ingested. In *picking,* the thumb and forefinger are used in a pincer-like grasp to pick parasites out of the fur. The two gestures are sometimes combined in a third, *pick–stroking* action. Various parts of the body are involved, some rich in fur and parasites, others not (Boccia, 1983, 1989).

Function

Grooming has two broadly different functions. One is hygienic or nutritional, as ectoparasites are transferred from the skin of the recipient to the mouth and stomach of the groomer. Ingestion was presumably the origin of lipsmacking, which later became ritualized into a signal that implies an intention to groom or acts as an independent social display. The other function of grooming, as I will discuss, is social. There appear to be interesting interactions between the two major forms of grooming, stroking and picking, and the two functions of grooming, nutrition and socialization.

In all hierarchically organized primate groups, grooming is a prominent means of servicing social relationships. Many studies indicate that dominant animals are groomed more often than subordinate ones, and are typically groomed by the lower-ranking animals (Cheney, 1977; Cheney & Seyfarth, 1990; Simpson, M. J. A., 1973). There also is evidence that females groom more frequently than males, whether baboons, bonnet macaques, rhesus macaques, Japanese macaques, or vervet monkeys (Walters, 1987).

I noted above that there appear to be interesting associations between the forms and functions of grooming. Research suggests that stroking is the more social of the two, picking the more nutritional. In a study of rhesus monkeys, for example, Boccia (1983) observed that high-ranking animals were stroked more often than picked, whereas low-ranking animals were more frequently the recipients of picking than stroking. Boccia also found that stroking exceeded picking when other animals were grooming each other, but picking exceeded stroking when animals were grooming themselves.

In two other studies, Boccia obtained evidence that stroking is more closely associated with tension reduction than is picking. In one study, Boccia and her colleagues measured the effect of grooming on the heart rate of a free–ranging pigtail macaque. They found that the monkey's heart rate dropped significantly when she was groomed by other monkeys, but there was no such decline when she groomed herself (Boccia, Reite, & Laudenslager, 1989; see Aureli, Preston, & de Waal, 1999 for similar findings). When the calming effect occurred, however, the animal was usually being stroked rather than picked. In the other study, Boccia (1989) observed pigtail macaques and bonnet macaques. Since pigtail macaques are naturally more aggressive and hierarchically structured than bonnets, it was assumed that they would have more need of relational and tension reducing maneuvers, whereas both primate groups would presumably stand to benefit from some level of hygienic function. Boccia found that the pigtails did more stroking than bonnets, as predicted, and that the bonnets did more picking and pick–stroking. Most directly relevant to functional differences, however, was the finding that the pigtail macaques issued a substantial number of affiliative displays, including lipsmacking, before grooming, with a sharp drop in such displays after grooming bouts were finished. The bonnets used few affiliative displays, too few to show much of a reduction after grooming. It thus appears that lipsmacking enjoys a relationship with stroking that it does not share with picking. In a moment, we will see what appears to be an analogous smacking–stroking–calming effect in the context of human interaction.

Human Grooming

Rank and Sex Effects

Although it is rarely recognized, humans groom too, and their grooming also appears to show sex and rank biases that parallel those reported in the other primates. In one village in 14th century France, all the grooming was done by women, who reserved this activity for men with whom they shared a romantic or familial relationship, and women of higher status (Le Roy Ladurie, 1978). In the early 20th century, manual grooming was performed as a preliminary to sexual intercourse in the Trobriand Islands of New Guinea. According to Malinowski's account, lovers "inspect each other's hair for lice and eat them–a practice disgusting to us and ill associated with love–making, but to the natives a natural and pleasant occupation between two who are fond of each other, and a favorite pastime with children." (Malinowski, 1929, p. 327).

Grooming has also been documented in the central Kalahari area of Botswana. According to data reported by Sugawara (1984, 1990), in about 80 percent of the adult grooming episodes the groomer was a female, as in 14th century France. Males participated in fewer than 15 percent of the episodes, and they never groomed females, though females occasionally groomed their husbands or unrelated adolescent males. Moreover, where the humans in grooming incidents were genetically unrelated, the groomer was the younger of the two parties in 70 percent of the cases, a finding not inconsistent with the status effect reported earlier.

In modern, fully clothed societies, grooming is rare but touching is commonplace. In Jones, S. E. and Yarbrough (1985), women did far more same-sex touching than men, and mothers touched their children more often than fathers did. Touching also varies with status. Hall (1996) found that high-status individuals tend to touch the arm or shoulder of their lower status colleagues–evidently as a form of affection or nurturance–but these lower status individuals tend to touch high-status colleagues by shaking hands with them, apparently in an attempt to express respect or to elevate their own status

If social talking did evolve from manual grooming, as Dunbar proposed, one might expect rhythmic movements of the hands and mandible to emerge at similar ages ontogenetically, and there is evidence that this is so (Ejiri, 1998; Locke, Bekken, McMinn–Larson, & Wein, 1995). There may also have been lingering effects of the hands in speech, and this is clearly true. Speech is often accompanied by gesticulation and gesture, even in congenitally blind children (Iverson & Goldin-Meadow, 1997, 1998). Experiments suggest that these hand movements may be an integral component of speech, and may even facilitate speech production (Krauss, 1998; Rimé, 1982). Recently, Arbib (2005a,b) has suggested that manual activity may have preceded, and laid the neural foundations for speech in evolution.

"Grooming Talking"

Some years ago, Morris introduced the term "grooming talking." What he had in mind was "the meaningless, polite chatter of social occasions, the 'nice weather we are having' or 'have you read any good books lately' form of talking." Grooming talking, Morris went on, "is not concerned with the exchange of important ideas or information, nor does it reveal the true mood of the speaker, nor is it aesthetically pleasing. Its function is to reinforce the greeting smile and to maintain the social togetherness. It is our substitute," he said, "for social grooming. By providing us with a non–aggressive social preoccupation, it enables us to expose ourselves communally to one another over comparatively long periods, in this way enabling valuable group bonds and friendships to grow and become strengthened." (Morris, 1967, p. 204).

One assumes that Dunbar liked Morris' concept of "grooming talking," for he argued that social grooming of the sort displayed by primates was, in fact, the evolutionary precursor to speech. Manual grooming, according to his proposal, was replaced by vocal grooming under the pressure of increasing group size and social competition, a step in the direction of languages that would be spoken (Dunbar, 1993, 1996).

Rank and Sex Effects in Speech

Considering the rank and sex biases of primate grooming, and of human grooming and touching, one might expect to find similar effects in social talking, and we do. Females are typically more voluble than males when speaking with a same-sex conversational partner of their choosing (Dabbs & Ruback, 1984; Ickes & Barnes, 1977), and from the early 1920s to the mid–1990s, at least eleven studies revealed that women, in various cultures, "out-gossiped" men (Bischoping, 1993). As for connections between status and speech, studies indicate that individuals of high status speak more often than those of low status, and also that people of high status get more attention than low status people, partly because speaking draws attention (Fisek & Ofshe, 1970; Kalma, 1991; Locke, 2000).

There are some physiological parallels between grooming and social talking, too. Earlier, we saw that primates groom by separate stroking and picking gestures, and that stroking seems to enjoy a stronger relationship to sociality than picking. Such findings bring to mind the terms "stroking" and "nit picking" in reference to flattering and critical forms of vocal grooming. In a study of neurotic women, verbal praise and reassurance by a psychiatrist significantly lowered heart rate and speech–muscle tension. Criticism and questioning, on the other hand, produced no such decrement, and occasionally caused sporadic increases in either or both measures (Malmo, Boag, & Smith, A. A., 1957).

It is unclear why Dunbar suggested that when grooming went vocal, social relationships were, from that point forward, serviced with *contact calls*. To be sure, contact calls are vocal and potentially loud, but they are relatively unmodulated by oral activity (with the exception of gelada calls) and unrelated to grooming. Lipsmacking, on the other hand, enjoys all the associations with social grooming that contact calls do not, being aspirate and relatively weak, but modulated by mandibular if not intraoral closures, and comprising an integral component of social grooming. That contact calls draw power from the lungs and larynx, and carry across great distances, would have made them useful in large group situations. But an appeal to such calls was probably unnecessary, for it has long been recognized that when behaviors are separated from their original context, as occurs in ritualization, they frequently become exaggerated (Huxley, 1966; Tinbergen, 1952). When manual grooming began to lose ground because of its inaudibility, it seems likely that a new role would have emerged for its already audible, socially adaptive companion–lipsmacking–and that when hand and finger movements faded away, efforts would have been made to amplify preexisting oral behaviors.

Since evolution is a tinker, and a miserly one at that, hominids could only have worked with preexisting behavioral materials. Several different types of social vocalizations, including girneys and coos (Blount, 1985; Green, S., 1975), would already have been available. It is possible that girneys are functionally related to manual grooming in primates and gossip in humans. Blount (1985) reported data to indicate that 90 percent of all the girneys in his study of captive Japanese Macaques were produced by females. If our hominid ancestors combined the laryngeal component of these sounds with the articulatory activity of lipsmacking, they might have been able to produce vocal pulses resembling syllables, possibly with contrasting points of oral closure. As we will see shortly, hominids may have had sufficient control to effect these changes.

Trickle up Phonetics

In the evolutionary account offered earlier, our concern was with the behavior of adults. In the construction of any new and more complex system of vocal communication the young would naturally have had a role to play (Locke & Bogin, 2006). Recently, I have suggested that when ancestral infants produced syllabic material, they may have elicited like responses in their adult caregivers. I call this "trickle up phonetics" (Locke, 2004).

If it seems odd that cultural change would originate with infants, one only need reflect on the fact that in monkeys, various behaviors–from bathing to food washing–have been displayed by infants before "catching on" with parents and other adults (Kawai, 1965; Kawamura, 1959). Infant transmitted behaviors are also common in humans, especially where vocalizations are concerned. In the case of syllabic activity, "trickle up" would have added an important new context to, and reinforced, the preexisting mandibular activity of parents and other caregivers, and may have nudged hominids a step closer to spoken language (Locke & Bogin, 2006).

What were the immediate benefits of "trickle up" to mothers and infants? I would suggest that there were at least two, one attentional, the other relational. We saw earlier that primate mothers occasionally attract their infants' attention by lipsmacking to them. Why this particular behavior draws attention is unknown, but one might speculate that the cause of primate mother lipsmacking is somehow linked to the fact that infants possess the same capability. In our own species, infant attention is easily achieved by adult imitation. This has been illustrated in a series of experiments by Meltzoff (1990), in which 14-month-olds attended to, and smiled at, an adult if he precisely replicated the infant's own actions, doing so far less frequently when the adult performed an unmatching action. In a group of 17- to 43-week-old infants, Pawlby (1977) found that over 90 percent of the phonetic imitation was attributable to mothers imitating their children. Pawlby commented, "babies do pay special attention (in that they laugh and smile and appear to be pleased) when the mothers themselves imitate an action which the child has just performed. The infant's action is thus 'highlighted' or 'marked out' as something special." (p. 220). Adding statistical support to Pawlby's impressions, Uzgiris and her colleagues found that throughout the first year, maternal imitation of infants' motor activities significantly exceeded infant's imitation of their mothers (Uzgiris, Benson, Kruper, & Vasek, 1989).

The presence of any shared behaviors—including lipsmacking or babbling—has implications for the relationship of mothers and infants. Dyads are made up of individuals who have, and continually look for, opportunities to reinforce existing points of attachment. Most beneficial are opportunities to respond in similar ways, and to do so in synchrony, and these are provided by syllabic vocalizations (Papoušek & Papoušek, 1989).

The idea that infants do not merely copy, but also originate, behaviors may violate orthodox conceptions of behavior transmission. Perhaps, one might suppose, parental accommodations of various sorts get attention, and pace or regulate behavior within a dyad, but fail to produce lasting effects. But the orthodoxy would be wrong, for "trickle up" phonetics does produce lasting effects. Decades ago, linguists began to report the use of specialized "baby words" by parents in a number of disparate cultures (Ferguson, 1964). Analysis revealed that these words were composed primarily of stops, nasals, and glides, frequently in CVCV patterns (e.g., "peepee," "wawa," "kaka"). The existence of these items, and such standard lexical items as "mommy," "daddy," "doggy" and "bye–bye," illustrate the strength of the tendency to incorporate infant sound patterns into languages (cf. Locke, 1983, 1985, 1990).

In evolution, there may have been intermediate stages between lipsmacking and vocal babbling. In this connection, it is interesting to note that around the time that babbling begins infants may be seen opening and closing the mouth repetitively. Sometimes this cyclic activity occurs in the context of chewing, where the movements have been heard as lingua–palatal "smacks" at 28 to 36 weeks (Gesell & Ilg, 1937). One student of vocal development also commented on the appearance of "lipsmacks" slightly before this interval (Stark, 1986). Meier and his colleagues have observed silent "jaw wags" and bilabial or alveolar smacks (with ingressive airflow) beginning at about 7 to 8 months (Meier, McGarvin, Zakia, & Willerman, 1997). In the Meier et al. study, wagging, smacking, and babbling appeared to be related inasmuch as infants occasionally shifted seamlessly from unphonated mandibular oscillations to audible syllables, and produced [mama]–like reduplications in response to parental lipsmacking. One notes, additionally, that when infants begin to babble, the most prominent closure is in the area of the alveolar ridge, and the manner is usually that of a stop (cf. Locke, 1983).

Parental Selection Hypothesis

Primate infants are able to lipsmack to their mothers, and if hominid infants had been able to perform similar actions with phonatory support, they could have interacted with their parents syllabically. Recently, I proposed a parental selection hypothesis, according to which infants who babble were more likely to receive preferential treatment, other things being equal, than infants who did not (Locke, 2006; Locke & Bogin, 2006). The hypothesis was argued, in part, on the basis of evidence that infants who are late to begin babbling may have a range of physical and cognitive abnormalities, and may also develop language slowly (Oller, Eilers, Neal, & Cobo–Lewis, 1998; Oller, Eilers, Neal, & Schwartz, H.

K., 1999). This being so, it is possible that hominid parents used vocal or phonetic criteria, among others, in making decisions about the investment of care. The plausibility of this hypothesis is affirmed, in part, by documentation of the sensitivity of primate parents to adult-like elements in the vocalizations of their infants (Elowson, Snowdon, & Lazaro-Perea, 1998a, 1998b; Snowdon, Elowson, & Roush, 1997), and the intuitive awareness of contemporary human parents to the existence of well-formed syllables in their infants' vocalizations (Oller, Eilers, Basinger, & Oller, 1991).

As for proximal effects, infants who produce a high rate of syllables per utterance appear more pleasant, friendly, and likeable than infants who vocalize less complexly (Bloom, K. & Lo, 1990; Bloom, K., D'Odorico, & Beaumont, 1993). If, in evolution, syllabic vocalization came to replace grooming–as an outgrowth of lipsmacking, a behavior that, on social grounds, is somewhat "synonymous" with grooming–one would expect parents to react positively to the cyclic sounds of their own infant's babbling.

Concluding Remarks

When Dunbar suggested that manual grooming went vocal, specifically in the form of contact calls, he offered an account for the *modality* of language, but missed an opportunity to account for its *structure*. The omission is paradoxical, for manual grooming was already accompanied by mandibular oscillations. These oscillations, as audible intention movements, had previously become ritualized as displays. All that had to be argued is that when manual activity was phased out, the remaining oral component of the display became more salient. The social value of grooming would have been "saved" by augmenting, through vocalization, the cyclicities that remained an integral part of the display.

It is difficult to account for the vocal flexibility of humans if one must take the context-bound calls and screams of primates as the point of departure. One recent solution has been to argue that at some time in evolutionary history the vocal tract became allied with the arms and hands–which enjoy a record of learning and flexibility, as well as a linked neural system of execution and representation–and that this conjunction facilitated the acquisition of vocal–motor control (Arbib, 2005a,b). But shrieks and cries were certainly not precursors to speech. A far more reasonable candidate is "close calls," including lipsmacks and girneys, which are issued quietly, typically by familiar individuals in relaxed and amicable conditions. The format is conversational (Hauser, 1992), and in some species the sounds may be quite variegated (Richman, 1987). If close calls were the forerunners of speech, it is not clear that a mediating system would be needed.

The other primates use regular or rhythmic mandibular oscillations, rendered audibly, to signal the desire to affiliate or act in a peaceful or conciliatory manner. Do such oscillations have a similar effect on humans? Do strings of syllables–without lexical content–calm and pacify people who are tense, frightened, or aggressive? Do babies babble to pacify themselves? In pursuit of answers, there would seem to be a role for listening experiments, ones that focus on adults' perceptual and physiological responses to repeating pulses or syllables, as well as the babbles and cries of infants. But it is essential that some basic studies of babbling be conducted, too, and these should be carried out within an ethological framework. For here, the central questions would include the social environment, and the reactions of family members, to infants when they are silent, when they vocalize, and when they babble.

References

Andrew, R. J. (1963). The origin of facial expressions. *Scientific American, 213*, 88–94.

Anthoney, T. R. (1968). The ontogeny of greeting, grooming and sexual motor patterns in captive baboons (superspecies *Papio cynocephalus*). *Behaviour, 31,* 358–372.

Arbib, M. A. (2005a). Interweaving protosign and protospeech: Further developments beyond the mirror. *Interaction Studies, 6,* 145–171.

Arbib, M. A. (2005b). From monkey-like action recognition to human language: An evolutionary framework for neurolinguistics. *Behavioral and Brain Sciences, 28,* 105–124.

Aureli, F., Preston, S. D., & de Waal, F. B. M. (1999). Heart rate responses to social interactions in free-moving rhesus macaques (*Macaca mulatta*): A pilot study. *Journal of Comparative Psychology, 113,* 59–65.

Bernstein, S., & Mason, W. A. (1962). The effects of age and stimulus conditions on the emotional responses of rhesus monkeys: Responses to complex stimuli. *Journal of Genetic Psychology, 101,* 279–298.

Bischoping, K. (1993). Gender differences in conversation topics, 1922–1990. *Sex Roles, 28,* 1–18.

Bloom, K., & Lo, E. (1990). Adult perceptions of vocalizing infants. *Infant Behavior and Development, 13,* 209–219.

Bloom, K., D'Odorico, L., & Beaumont, S. (1993). Adult preferences for syllabic vocalizations: Generalizations to parity and native language. *Infant Behavior and Development, 16,* 109–120.

Blount, B. G. (1985). "Girney" vocalizations among Japanese Macaque females: Context and function. *Primates, 26,* 424–435.

Boccia, M. L. (1983). A functional analysis of social grooming patterns through direct comparison with self-grooming in rhesus monkeys. *International Journal of Primatology, 4,* 399–418.

Boccia, M. L. (1989). Comparison of the physical characteristics of grooming in two species of macaques (*Macaca nemestrina* and *M. radiata*). *Journal of Comparative Psychology, 103,* 177–183.

Boccia, M. L., Reite, M., & Laudenslager, M. (1989). On the physiology of grooming in a pigtail macaque. *Physiology & Behavior, 45,* 667–670.

Bolwig, N. (1980). Early social development and emancipation of *Macaca nemestrina* and species of *Papio. Primates, 21,* 357–375.

Cheney, D. (1977). The acquisition of rank and the development of reciprocal alliances among free-ranging immature baboons. *Behavioral Ecology and Sociobiology, 2,* 303–318.

Cheney, D., & Seyfarth, R. M. (1990). *How monkeys see the world: Inside the mind of another species.* Chicago: University of Chicago Press.

Dabbs, J. M., & Ruback, R. B. (1984). Vocal patterns in male and female groups. *Personality and Social Psychology Bulletin, 10,* 518–525.

DeVore, I. (1963). Mother-infant relations in free-ranging baboons. In H.L. Rheingold (Ed.), *Maternal behavior in mammals* (pp. 305–355). New York: John Wiley.

de Waal, F. B. M. (1989). *Peacemaking among primates.* Cambridge, MA: Harvard University Press.

Dunbar, R. I. M. (1993). Coevolution of neocortical size, group size and language in humans. *Behavioral and Brain Sciences, 16,* 681–735.

Dunbar, R. I. M. (1996). *Grooming, gossip and the evolution of language.* London: Faber and Faber.

Ejiri, K. (1998). Relationship between rhythmic behavior and canonical babbling in infant vocal development. *Phonetica, 55,* 226–237.

Elowson, A. M., Snowdon, C. T., & Lazaro–Perea, C. (1998a). "Babbling" and social context in infant monkeys: Parallels to human infants. *Trends in Cognitive Sciences, 2,* 31–37.

Elowson, A. M., Snowdon, C. T., & Lazaro–Perea, C. (1998b). Infant "babbling" in a nonhuman primate: Complex vocal sequences with repeated call types. *Behaviour, 135,* 643–664.

Ferguson, C. A. (1964). Baby talk in six languages. *American Anthropologist, 66,* 103–114.

Ferrari, P. F., Gallese, V., Rizzolatti, G., & Fogassi, L. (2003). Mirror neurons responding to the observation of ingestive and communicative mouth actions in the monkey ventral premotor cortex. *European Journal of Neuroscience, 17,* 1703–1714.

Fisek, M. H., & Ofshe, R. (1970). The process of status evolution. *Sociometry, 33,* 327–346.

Gesell, A. L., & Ilg, F. L. (1937). Feeding behavior of infants: A pediatric approach to the mental hygiene of early life. Philadelphia: Lippincott.

Green, S. (1975). Variation of vocal pattern with social situation in the Japanese monkey (*Macaca fuscata*): A field study. In L. A. Rosenblum (Ed.), *Primate behavior: Developments in field and laboratory research* (pp. 1–102). New York: Academic Press.

Hall, J. A. (1996). Touch, status, and gender at professional meetings. *Journal of Nonverbal Behavior, 20,* 23–44.

Hauser, M. D. (1992). A mechanism guiding conversational turn-taking in vervet monkeys and rhesus macaques. In T. Nishida, F. B. M. de Waal, W. McGrew, P. Marler & M. Pickford (Eds.), *Topics in primatology. Volume 1. Human origins* (pp. 235–248). Tokyo: Tokyo University Press.

Heiser, M., Iacoboni, M., Maeda, F., Marcus, J., & Mazziotta, J. C. (2003). The essential role of Broca's area in imitation. *European Journal of Neuroscience, 17,* 1123–1128.

Huxley, J. (1966). Introduction. In Huxley, J. (Ed.), A discussion on ritualization of behaviour in animals and man. *Philosophical Transactions of the Royal Society of Britain, 251,* 249–271.

Ickes, W., & Barnes, R. D. (1977). The role of sex and self–monitoring in unstructured dyadic interactions. *Journal of Personality and Social Psychology, 35,* 315–330.

Iverson, J. M., & Goldin-Meadow, S. (1997). What's communication got to do with it? Gesture in children blind from birth. *Developmental Psychology, 33,* 453–467.

Iverson, J. M., & Goldin–Meadow, S. (1998). Why people gesture as they speak. *Nature, 396,* 228.

Jones, S. E., & Yarbrough, A. E. (1985). A naturalistic study of the meanings of touch. *Communication Monographs, 52,* 19–56.

Kalma, A. (1991). Hierarchisation and dominance assessment at first glance. *European Journal of Social Psychology, 21,* 165–181.

Kawai, M. (1965). Newly-acquired pre-cultural behavior of the natural troop of Japanese monkeys on Koshima islet. *Primates, 6,* 1–30.

Kawamura, S. (1959). The process of sub-culture propagation among Japanese macaques. *Primates, 2,* 43–60.

Kenney, M. D., Mason, W. A., & Hill, S. D. (1979). Effects of age, objects, and visual experience on affective responses of rhesus monkeys to strangers. *Developmental Psychology, 15,* 176–184.

Krauss, R. M. (1998). Why do we gesture when we speak? *Current Directions in Psychological Science, 7,* 54–59.

Le Roy Ladurie, E. (1978). Montaillou: Cathars and catholics in a French village 1294–1324. London: Scolar Press.

Locke, J. L. (1983). *Phonological acquisition and change.* New York: Academic Press.

Locke, J. L. (1985). The role of phonetic factors in parent reference. *Journal of Child Language, 12,* 215–220.

Locke, J. L. (1990). "Mama" and "papa" in child language: Parent reference or phonetic preference? In B. Metuzale-Kangere, & H.D. Rinholm, (Eds.), *Symposium Balticum: A Festschrift to honour Professor Velta Ruke–Dravina* (pp. 267–273). Hamburg: Helmut Buske Verlag.

Locke, J. L. (2000). Rank and relationships in the evolution of spoken language. *Journal of the Royal Anthropological Institute, 7,* 37–50.

Locke, J. L. (2004). Trickle up phonetics: A vocal role for the infant. *Behavioral and Brain Sciences, 27,* 516.

Locke, J. L. (2006). Parental selection of vocal behavior: Crying, cooing, babbling and the evolution of spoken language. *Human Nature 17(2)*, 155-168.

Locke, J. L., Bekken, K. E., McMinn-Larson, L., & Wein, D. (1995). Emergent control of manual and vocal-motor activity in relation to the development of speech. *Brain and Language, 51,* 498–508.

Locke, J. L., & Bogin, B. (2006). Language and life history: A new perspective on the evolution and development of linguistic communication. *Behavioral and Brain Sciences, 29,* 259-280.

MacNeilage, P. F. (1986). Bimanual coordination and the beginnings of speech. In B. Lindblom & R. Zetterström, (Eds.), *Precursors to early speech* (pp. 189–201). New York: Stockton Press.

MacNeilage, P. F. (1998). The frame/content theory of evolution of speech production. *Behavioral and Brain Sciences, 21,* 499–546.

Maestripieri, D., & Call, J. (1996). Mother–infant communication in primates. *Advances in the Study of Behavior, 25,* 613–642.

Malinowski, B. (1929). The sexual life of savages in North–Western Melanesia: An ethnographic account of courtship, marriage and family life among the natives of the Trobriand Islands, British New Guinea. New York: Halcyon House.

Malmo, R. B., Boag, T. J., & Smith, A. A. (1957). Physiological study of personal interaction. *Psychosomatic Medicine, 19,* 105–119.

Meier, R. P., McGarvin, L., Zakia, R. A. E., & Willerman, R. (1997). Silent mandibular oscillations in vocal babbling. *Phonetica, 54,* 153–171.

Meltzoff, A. N. (1990). Foundations for developing a concept of self: The role of imitation in relating self to other and the value of social mirroring, social modeling, and self practice in infancy. In D. Cicchetti & M. Beeghly (Eds.), *The self in transition: Infancy to childhood* (pp. 139–164). Chicago: University of Chicago Press.

128 Locke

Morris, D. (1967). *The naked ape: A zoologist's study of the human animal.* New York: McGraw-Hill.

Nakamichi, M., & Yoshida, A. (1986). Discrimination of mother by infant among Japanese macaques (*Macaca fuscata*). *International Journal of Primatology, 7,* 481–489.

Oller, D. K., Eilers, R. E., Basinger, D., & Oller, K. D. (1991). Intuitive identification of infant vocal sounds by parents. *Developmental Science, 4,* 49–60.

Oller, D. K., Eilers, R. E., Neal, A. R., & Cobo-Lewis, A. B. (1998). Late onset canonical babbling: A possible early marker of abnormal development. *American Journal on Mental Retardation, 103,* 249–263.

Oller, D. K., Eilers, R. E., Neal, A. R., & Schwartz, H. K. (1999). Precursors to speech in infancy: The prediction of speech and language disorders. *Journal of Communication Disorders, 32,* 223–245.

Papoušek, M., & Papoušek, H. (1989). Forms and functions of vocal matching in interactions between mothers and their precanonical infants. *First Language, 9,* 137–158.

Pawlby, S. J. (1977). Imitative interaction. In H. R. Schaffer (Ed.), *Studies in mother–infant interaction* (pp. 203–224). New York: Academic Press.

Petrides, M., Cadoret, G., & Mackey, S. (2005). Orofacial somatomotor responses in the macaque monkey homologue of Broca's area. *Nature, 435,* 1235–1238.

Redican, W. K. (1975). Facial expressions in nonhuman primates. In L. A. Rosenblum (Ed.), *Primate behavior: Developments in field and laboratory research* (pp. 104–194). New York: Academic Press.

Richman, B. (1987). Rhythm and melody in gelada vocal exchanges. *Primates, 28,* 199–223.

Rimé, B. (1982). The elimination of visible behaviour from social interactions: Effects on verbal, nonverbal and interpersonal variables. *European Journal of Social Psychology, 12,* 113–129.

Simpson, M. J. A. (1973). The social grooming of male chimpanzees. In R. P. Michael & J. H. Crook (Eds.), *Comparative ecology and behaviour of primates* (pp. 411–505). London: Academic Press.

Snowdon, C. T., Elowson, A. M., & Roush, R. S. (1997). Social influences on vocal development in New World primates. In C. Snowdon & M. Hausberger (Eds.), *Social influences on vocal development* (pp. 234–248). Cambridge: Cambridge University Press.

Stark, R. (1986). Prespeech segmental feature development. In P. Fletcher & M. Garman (Eds.), *Language acquisition* (pp. 149–173). Cambridge: Cambridge University Press.

Sugawara, K. (1984). Spatial proximity and bodily contact among the Central Kalahari San. *African Study Monographs, 3,* 1–43.

Sugawara, K. (1990). Interactional aspects of the body in co-presence: Observations on the Central Kalahari San. In M. Moerman & M. Nomura (Eds.), Culture embodied (pp. 79–122). *Senri Ethnological Studies 27.* Osaka, Japan: National Museum of Ethnology.

Terry, R. L. (1970). Primate grooming as a tension reduction mechanism. *Journal of Psychology, 76,* 129–136.

Uzgiris, I. C., Benson, J. B., Kruper, J. C., & Vasek, M. E. (1989). Contextual influences on imitative interactions between mothers and infants. In J. Lockman & N. Hazen (Eds.), *Action in a social context: Perspectives on early development* (pp. 103–127). New York: Plenum.

Walters, J. R. (1987). Transition to adulthood. In B. B. Smuts, D. L. Cheney, R. M. Seyfarth, R. W. Wrangham & T. T. Struhsaker (Eds.), *Primate societies* (pp. 358–369). Chicago: University of Chicago Press.

Zuckerman, S. (1932). *The social life of monkeys and apes.* New York: Harcourt, Brace & Company.

II: Neurobiological Aspects of Speech Production

6

Mirror Neurons and the Evolution of Communication and Language

Leonardo Fogassi [1,2]

and

Pier Francesco Ferrari [1,2]

[1] Dipartimento di Neuroscienze, Università di Parma

Parma, Italy

[2] Dipartimento di Psicologia, Università di Parma

Parma, Italy

There are different theories about language evolution. Some authors claim that language (and speech) evolved from monkey vocalization (Cheney & Seyfarth, 1990; Ghazanfar & Hauser, 1999; Hauser, 1996; MacLean, 1993). Others claim that language/communicative behavior stems from gestural communication (Armstrong et al., 1995; Corballis, 1992, 1999, 2002; Fogassi & Ferrari, 2004; Kimura, 1993; Paget, 1963; Rizzolatti & Arbib, 1998). Some even deny a direct evolution of language from some monkey precursor, considering the former as a completely new acquisition of the human species, with characteristics that are entirely different from any other animal cognitive function (Chomsky, 1986). Recently, this view has been partially modified. It has been suggested that the human faculty of language can be separated into a broad sense faculty (FLB) and a narrow sense faculty (FLN; Hauser et al., 2002). FLB includes a sensory-motor system, a conceptual-intentional system and an internal computational system (narrow syntax) for recursion that "takes a finite set of elements and yields a potential infinite array of discrete expressions" (i.e., FLN; pp. 1571). According to these authors, only the narrow sense faculty, that coincides with the abstract linguistic computational system alone, is uniquely human. An interesting aspect of this hypothesis is that, according to the authors, FLN was shaped by natural selection from preexisting structures evolved for reasons other than communication. The major merit of this new proposal is that it traces a possible evolutionary link between communicative systems in animals and humans. However, the hypothesis does not clarify how different forms of communication, such as gestural and vocal, did interact and contributed to the emergence of human language.

Although there is no direct evidence for the emergence of human language from nonhuman primate precursors, we argue that there are several empirical observations coming from different research fields (i.e., neuroscience, ethology, pycholinguistics, comparative anatomy) pointing to a commonality between nonhuman primate communication and the properties of human language. In this chapter, we will focus on the possible neurophysiological mechanisms and behavioral processes that might have formed the basis of the evolution of a vocal communicative system as complex as human speech.

Vocal Calls and Gestures in Nonhuman Primates: Comparing Two Forms of Communication in Relation to Language Evolution

Several studies have compared vocalizations of nonhuman primates with human speech (e.g., see Ghazanfar & Hauser, 1999) to find commonalities between the two forms of vocalizations. Pioneering work by Cheney and Seyfarth (1982) showed that different alarm-calls in vervet monkeys provide a listener conspecific with information about the type of predator approaching, such as a snake, a leopard or an eagle. These findings provided the first evidence of referential communication in a nonhuman primate species. Data regarding referential aspects of vocalization in other primate species have been documented in the last decade (see Ghazanfar & Hauser, 1999 for a review). Following the first enthusiasm for Cheney and Seyfarth's work, more recent re-evaluation and alternative interpretations have challenged the original proposal that this type of vocal referential communication in nonhuman primates has played an important role in evolution of language (see also Hauser et al., 2002).

Beyond the referential aspects of vocal calls there are several issues that weaken the role of primate vocal calls in the evolution of speech (see Hauser et al., 2002). For example, the repertoire of nonhuman primate calls is relatively small and is mainly restricted to indicating the presence of objects or events. This repertoire, once fully developed in the adult, shows poor combinatorial power and very little acoustic flexibility. In contrast, as we will document below, gestural communication provides a richer repertoire (see also Corballis, 2003; de Waal, 1982).

Another important feature that limits the communicative power of vocal calls is their relations with intense emotional states. The main function of these communicative signs is to signal urgent or imminent events. The major advantage of this manner of communication is that messages are clear and straightforward. On the other hand, the stereotyped patterns in which they are expressed do not allow a flexible use of vocalization in contexts of affiliative dyadic communication. In agreement with this interpretation, anatomical, electrical stimulation and neuroethological studies have shown that monkey vocal calls are under the neural control of the primitive limbic circuit known to be involved in emotional behavior (Jürgens, 1995, 2002). Both cortical and subcortical structures, such as mesial cortex (supplementary motor cortex and cingulate cortex), reticular formation and some brainstem nuclei, belong to or are involved in this circuit. This circuit seems to be responsible for the initiation and control of stereotyped utterances.

Unlike vocal calls, gestures are under the control of a voluntary neural circuit mainly present in the lateral cortex. A voluntary control of motor brachio-manual and oro-facial muscles allows for a more efficient utilization of the various degrees of freedom of these two systems. Note, in particular, that the brachio-manual system has reached in monkeys, and even more in apes, a sophisticated degree of control both in terms of execution of single joint movements and in terms of organization of movement sequences.

Historically, the issue of gestural communication was addressed by Darwin (1872), who compared facial expressions of animals with those of humans and studied their possible evolutionary link with emotions. In non-human primates, the evolution of facial communicative gestures has been largely investigated in the pioneering studies of van Hooff (1962, 1967) by comparing the functional role of each facial expression and its meaning in several species. Communication through brachio-manual gestures in apes have been documented only more recently (de Waal, 1982; Liebal et al., 2004; Maestripieri, 1997; Tanner & Byrne, 1996; Tomasello et al., 1997). Interestingly, it has been shown that chimpanzees use brachiomanual gestures extensively for the purpose of communicating with one another (Liebal et al., 2004). Overall, studies on gestural communication in monkeys and apes reveal that the production of most gestures, especially the brachiomanual ones, is probably not only a hard-wired phenomenon but can result from individual and social learning (Parr & Maestripieri, 2003; Tomasello et al., 1997). This latter aspect suggests that nonhuman primate gestures might reflect not only emotional states but also the achievement of a voluntary control that allows individuals to use these gestures in a wider and more flexible way.

In contrast to vocalizations, gestures are often displayed in social contexts such as grooming, playing, nursing and attracting a recipient's attention. Reports on spontaneous brachio-manual gestural communication in chimpanzees clearly indicate that this mode of communication shows a high degree of flexibility (Liebal et al., 2004; Tomasello et al., 1994; Tomasello et al., 1997). Thus, the same gestures can be used in different contexts, or different gestures can be applied in similar contexts interchangeably to achieve the same goal. The level of flexibility of hand gestures is also supported by other studies with captive chimpanzees showing that these animals often use hand gestures in association with sensory modalities such as visual, auditory and tactile (Hopkins & Leavens, 1998; Hostetter et al., 2001; Liebal et al., 2004). For example, chimpanzees are able to communicate to an experimenter the location of hidden food that is out of reach through a "request" made by arm and fingers extension (Leavens et al., 2004).

Identifying the different potentials of vocalization and gestures as possible tools for communication en route to language has been the focus of several investigations on language acquisition in apes. Early attempts to teach chimpanzees to produce human speech failed. The vocal production of sounds in chimpanzees was limited to very few "words," such as "ma ma" and "cup" (Hayes, K., & Hayes, C., 1951). Although anatomical constraints greatly limit the production of sounds, chimpanzees in these studies were also very limited in their comprehension of spoken English in the absence of specific contextual information (see Rumbaugh et al., 2003). In contrast, studies on sign language use in apes showed that it is much easier to train these animals to communicate with gestures (see Rumbaugh et al., 2003). Although the number of signs learned by chimpanzees was relatively limited, these studies revealed that chimpanzees who learned this mode of communication use gestures flexibly, combining them in different sequences and extending their communicative repertoire.

Neural Mechanisms for Action Execution and Action Perception in the Monkey Premotor Cortex

Unlike apes, communicative gestures in monkeys are limited to oro-facial and some types of body gesture, since brachio-manual repertoire in monkeys is very poor. However, what is important here is not simply the presence or absence of gestures in relation to communication. The neural mechanism that underpins inter-individual communication in monkeys needs identification. The comprehension of this mechanism could shed light on possible common neural control of gestures and vocalizations and thus on their relationships in the evolution of primate communication. Inter-individual communication requires the presence of two individuals, each of which can be both an emitter and a receiver. These two functions require anatomo-physiological structures that allow for producing, perceiving and understanding communicative behaviors. Our hypothesis is that at the basis of this executive/perceptual capacity is a neural mechanism represented by the mirror system (see Figure 1) that matches executed meaningful actions with similar observed meaningful actions. A deep understanding of this mechanism may elucidate the importance gestures have played in the evolution of sophisticated communicative systems.

Before proceeding to describe the main properties of the mirror system, we must briefly explain the concept of action and how actions are organized by the cerebral cortex. Using the word "action" implies the concept of motor control. The issue of motor control can be addressed both at a behavioral and a neurophysiological level. Behavioral investigation clearly shows that actions are goal-related movements (see Rizzolatti et al., 2001). In the past, the investigation of motor control at the neurophysiological level was mainly concentrated on the neural code of movement parameters, such as force, direction, amplitude. The basic idea underpinning this approach was that the main function of the motor cortex is to code movements, i.e., displacements around single joints. In contrast with this idea, a more modern view maintains that the main function of the motor cortex is to code goal directed actions (see Rizzolatti et al., 2000). Actions are coded at the single neuron level in several areas of the premotor cortex and in the parietal areas connected to it (see Fogassi et al., 2005; Gallese et al., 2002; Rizzolatti et al., 1988, 1998, 2000). The properties of action coding neurons were studied in more detail in the ventral premotor cortex of the macaque monkey, in particular in area F5. Single neuron recording experiments show that in F5 different types of hand and mouth actions are coded such as grasping, manipulating, holding, tearing. F5 motor neurons can code the action goal both at an abstract level (e.g., neurons discharging during grasping with the hand and the mouth) or more specifically (e.g., neurons discharging during a specific type of prehension; Rizzolatti et al., 1988).

Mirror Neurons and Gestural Communication

Besides motor neurons, there are also visuomotor neurons in area F5 that discharge both when the monkey *performs* hand actions and when it *observes* another individual (an experimenter or another monkey) performing a similar action (Fogassi & Gallese, 2002; Gallese et al., 1996; Rizzolatti et al., 1996). These neurons have been named "mirror neurons." The optimal visual stimulus for these neurons is the observation of a hand-object interaction, since the observation of either the hand mimicking the action without the object or of the object alone does not elicit a response. Recognizing the hand-object interaction means the recognition of the goal of a motor act. Further studies demonstrated that mirror neurons recognize the action goal even when the monkey observes an action in which the final part of the action is not visible, but the monkey knows that the object is present (Umiltà et al., 2001).

The most important property of mirror neurons is the congruence between the observed and the executed actions that are able to evoke their response. For example, a mirror neuron that responds during the observation of a grasping action will also be activated when the monkey executes grasping. However, the neuron will not be activated when the animal executes a different action, such as breaking. This matching between action observation and action execution allows for the understanding of actions made by others. The mechanism involved is hypothesized to be the following. When I execute an action, I also need to know the consequences of the action. Thus, my motor system contains not only an executive mechanism, but also the knowledge about the executed action. When I observe an action made by another individual, this "resonates" in my brain with the motor circuit representing that action and, in particular, the action knowledge, so that I can understand the action goal. This matching system, basically used for action understanding, can quite easily be employed for inter-individual gestural communication, without invoking a different type of mechanism for communication. Similar to the matching system used for hand actions, a communicative gesture made by an actor (the sender)

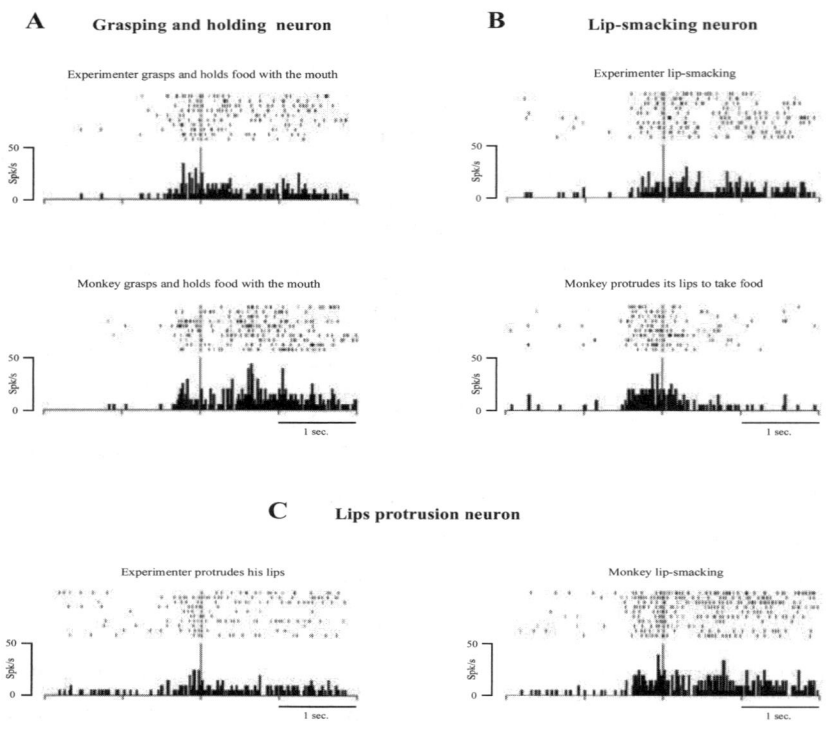

Figure 6.1.
Examples of mouth mirror neurons. In each panel the rasters and histograms represent neuron response during a single experimental condition. The histogram represents the average of ten trials. Rasters and histograms are aligned with the moment in which the mouth of the experimenter (observation of ingestive action condition) or of the monkey (motor ingestive conditions) touched the food. During observation of communicative actions the rasters and histograms alignment was made with the moment in which the action was fully expressed. Ordinates: spikes/sec; abscissae: time; bin width: 20 ms. A. Ingestive mouth mirror neuron. The experimenter approaches with his mouth the food held on a support, grasps it with the teeth and holds it. B. Communicative mouth mirror neuron. The experimenter makes a lip-smacking action looking at the monkey. C. Communicative mouth mirror neuron. The experimenter protrudes his lips looking at the monkey. During the experimenter lip protrusion the monkey responds almost simultaneously to the gesture by making a lip-smacking action.

retrieves in the observer (the receiver) the neural circuit encoding the motor representation of the same gesture. This 'matching' allows the receiver to *understand* the message of the observer and, perhaps, to begin a response (see Rizzolatti & Arbib, 1998; see also the *motor theory of speech perception,* Liberman & Mattingly, 1985).

The recent discovery of a new category of neurons (mouth mirror neurons; MMNs) could shed light on the above proposed link between the action observation/execution system and the communication system. MMNs constitute a category of mirror neurons that activate when a monkey observes and execute mouth actions (Ferrari et al., 2003).

Most MMNs respond to observation of ingestive actions such as biting, tearing with the teeth, sucking, licking, etc. An example of an "ingestive" MMN is shown in Figure 6.1. Similar to hand mirror neurons, these neurons do not respond to simple object presentation (food or 3D solids) or to observation of mouth actions mimicked without the object. Many ingestive MMNs respond during observation of a specific mouth action. Most ingestive MMNs show a very good congruence between the effective observed and executed actions. A smaller but significant percent of MMNs respond specifically to the observation of mouth communicative actions that belong to the monkey repertoire, such as lip-smacking, lip protrusion or tongue protrusion. Figure 6.1 shows an example of a "communicative" MMN. Communicative MMNs do not activate when the monkey observes ingestive actions. All actions found to be effective in triggering the visual response of communicative MMNs are affiliative actions endowed with low emotional content, and not threatening or aggressive gestures, normally endowed with more emotional content. The motor response of communicative MMNs is more complex. These neurons respond during communicative gestures produced by the monkey in response to experimenter gesture, but communicative MMNs also respond well when the monkey executes ingestive actions. Thus, the motor response seems to be less specific. However, when compared with the observed communicative actions, executed ingestive actions appear motorically similar to observed ones. For example, a neuron responding to the observation of lip-smacking also responds to the execution of sucking actions. In both cases, an alternation between lip protrusion and retraction and between jaw opening and closure is observed. This motoric activation of communicative MMNs for both communicative and ingestive actions appears to be very important. This finding suggests that in the ventral motor cortex there was a phylogenetic transition from the voluntary control of transitive actions involved in ingestive behavior and that of intransitive, meaningful actions that became important as signals for communication (see Ferrari et al., 2003). In support of the proposed transition, ethological studies show that it occurs through a process of ritualization where some communicative gestures such as lip smacking and pucker face very likely evolved from movements aimed to removing and eating particles such as skin parasites from the fur of group mates during grooming sessions. In several monkey species the beginning of a grooming session can be preceded or accompanied by a lip smacking action without ingestion (see Maestripieri, 1996; van Hooff, 1962, 1967). Interestingly enough, this latter lip-smacking produces a more pronounced sound than that associated with ingestion, as if underlining a different meaning. Thus, lip-smacking probably is derived from an ingestive action that lost its original behavioral meaning related to feeding and achieved communicative value. Taking a different approach, MacNeilage (1998) proposed a similar transition for explaining the evolution of syllable. In MacNeilage's view, the syllabic frame evolved in the ventral motor cortex from the cyclic mandibular open-close alternation typical of food ingestion. MacNeilage argued that the precursors of human syllables are monkey lip-smacks and tongue-smacks.

Mirror neurons present in the lateral sector of ventral premotor cortex are utilized for both ingestive actions and communicative gestures. This finding suggests that the mechanism at the basis of action understanding could have been exploited, during evolution, for building an oro-facial communicative system used in affiliative dyadic interactions devoid of strong emotional content. It is possible to hypothesize that originally this gestural communicative system probably evolved partially independently from the vocal-based communicative system, as it is evident to a large extent in monkeys. However, as we will illustrate in the next sections, the neurophysiological properties of the lateral motor cortex in monkeys provide a suitable substrate for the voluntary control of both gestures and articulated sound production. Apparently, this substrate is not accompanied by a parallel achievement of a sophisticated anatomical apparatus for sound emission and control.

Homology Between Ventral Premotor Area F5 and Broca's Area

Based on cytoarchitectonic data, several researchers (e.g., Petrides & Pandya 1994; von Bonin & Bailey, 1947) proposed that dysgranular area 44 (part of Broca's area) and area F5 can be considered homologues in humans (see Figure 6.2). This hypothesis has been corroborated by anatomo-functional data:

Both Broca's area and F5 are activated by mouth and hand movements. While the role of Broca's area in speech production is well known, brain imaging experiments have only recently demonstrated that it is also involved in hand movement tasks such as, for example, finger movements, mental imagery of grasping actions, hand mental rotation tasks and hand imitation tasks (Bonda et al., 1994; Buccino et al., 2004a; Chollet et al., 1991; Grafton et al., 1996; Iacoboni et al., 1999; Parsons et al., 1995). Similarly, area F5 contains motor neurons that discharge during the execution of both hand and mouth actions (Ferrari et al., 2003; Rizzolatti et al., 1988). Area F5 is endowed with a system for the control of laryngeal muscles and of oro-facial synergisms (Hast et al., 1974; Simonyan & Jürgens, 2003). It is interesting to note that electrical stimulation of a region very close to the inferior limb of the arcuate sulcus produces combined, indissociable movements of two laryngeal muscles. This result suggests that a higher functional role is assigned for this region in the control of this part of the phonatory apparatus (Hast et al., 1974). Several EEG, TMS, MEG and brain imaging experiments demonstrate that Broca's area is activated when subjects are required to observe goal-related hand and mouth actions made by another individual (for references, see Rizzolatti et al., 2001). In particular, recent fMRI (i.e., fast magnetic resonance imaging) experiments demonstrated that the inferior frontal gyrus is activated both when subjects observe biting action (Buccino et al., 2001, 2004b) and when they observe other

A

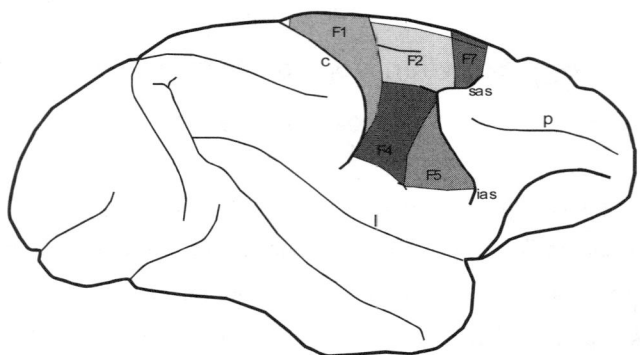

B

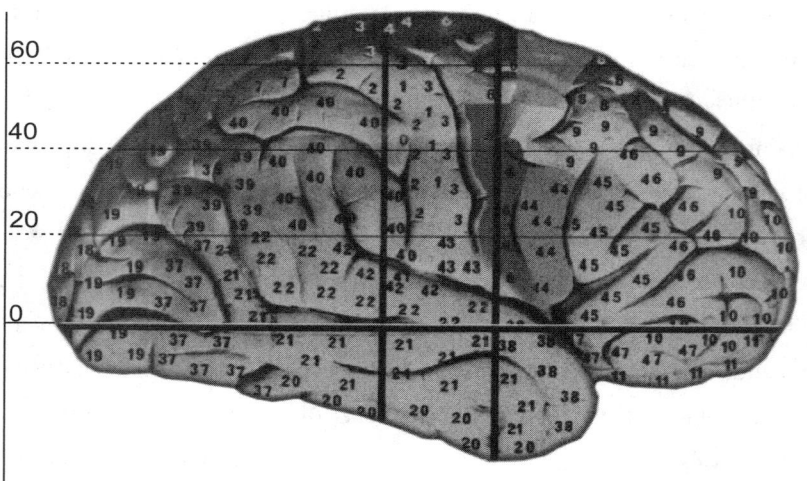

Figure 6.2.
Ventral premotor cortex in monkeys and humans. A. Lateral view of monkey
brain showing the histological and histochemical parcellation of the motor cortex.
Same shadings indicate presumed homologue monkey and human motor areas.
C: central sulcus; ias: inferior arcuate sulsus; L: lateral sulcus; P: principal sulcus;
sas: superior arcuate sulcus. B. Lateral view of the human brain showing the
cytoarchitectonic parcellation of Brodmann and the basal lines (thick lines)
depicted by Talairach and Tornoux. Thin lines indicate z coordinates. Shaded
regions indicate: caudal dorsal premotor cortex (6aα), rostral dorsal premotor
cortex (6aβ), ventral premotor cortex (ventral area 6). Modified from Rizzolatti et
al. (2002).

individuals performing silent speech (Buccino et al., 2004b; Calvert & Campbell, R., 2003; Campbell, R. et al., 2001). Similarly, mirror neurons in area F5 respond to the observation of hand, and mouth ingestive and communicative actions. Broca's area is activated during word listening (Price et al., 1996). Furthermore, an enhancement of motor evoked potential from tongue muscles was demonstrated in subjects submitted to TMS during listening to syllables that required a strong activation of tongue muscles during their production (Fadiga et al., 2002). Enhanced excitability of motor cortex is likely due to the previous activation of Broca's area during speech listening. It was recently demonstrated that mirror neurons activated by both the vision and the sound of an action are present in the monkey area F5 (audio-visual mirror neurons; AVMNs; Kohler et al., 2002). The response of these neurons is specific to the type of action seen and heard. For example, AVMNs respond to peanut breaking when the action is either only observed, or only heard or both heard and observed. AVMNs do not respond to the vision and sound of another action, or to unspecific sounds. These results demonstrate two important properties: a) acoustic input can access action–meaning links by activating action representations in area F5; b) area F5 has the capacity for representing action content independently of the modality used to access this content. Both properties resemble typical features of spoken language.

The proposal that monkey's area F5 and Broca's area are homologue implies the possibility of identifying neuroanatomical features of the ventral premotor cortex in apes that are more similar to the neuroanatomical properties of human Broca's area. In line with this reasoning, MRI studies recently showed a left anatomical asymmetry in the ventral premotor area 44 of apes, similar to that identified in humans (Cantalupo & Hopkins, 2001).

How did Gestures and Sounds Become Associated During Evolution of Communication?

Up to now, we have demonstrated that gestures and vocal calls can co-exist and may have evolved partially independently from each other in non-human primates, with perhaps the exception of apes. However, at a certain stage in human language evolution vocal calls were incorporated into the gestural communicative system. How and when this happened still remains a conundrum.

We speculate that an early step of this process involved the casual production of utterances during the expression of a communicative gesture. Individuals displaying this casual association benefited from this coupling since the sound gave more salience to gesture. This association improved the transfer of information to other group members. Beyond salience, the possibility of using several oro-facial and brachiomanual gestures in association with utterances represents a great advantage in terms of combinatorial power: if gestures and calls are combined in a flexible manner, a rich vocabulary with very few elements can be generated.

A thorough examination of our closest relative the chimpanzee, suggests that the association of utterances with gestures may have started to be expressed in this species. Reports indicate that the communicative brachiomanual repertoire of chimpanzees, compared to that of monkeys, is characterized by new achievements, in terms of richness and complexity (see Parr & Maestripieri, 2003), paralleled by a more complex control of the vocal communicative system (Arcadi, 1996, 2000). Further, it has been observed that these two systems are often used in association (Hopkins & Leavens, 1998; Hostetter et al., 2001; Liebal et al., 2004).

In terms of brain structures involved in the gesture/vocalization association, area F5 of the monkey ventral premotor cortex may have played a crucial role. The above described homology between area F5 and Broca's area leads to the suggestion that, as far as the cortical control is concerned, vocal calls were incorporated into the gestural communicative system and not vice versa. Thus the ventral premotor areas had some evolutionary advantageous features that allowed them to exert a primary role in the control of both gestural and vocal communicative signals. Since "very rarely evolution throws out anything" (de Waal, 2007) or creates something from scratch, the ventral premotor cortex in monkeys was most likely endowed with neurophysiological properties that constituted suitable material for shaping new functions during evolution. One of these neurophysiological properties of area F5 in monkeys is the presence of a large population of neurons controlling both mouth and hand actions. Furthermore, the most lateral sector of area F5 can also control laryngeal muscles, an important aspect for the voluntary production of sounds.

The consequence of the acquisition of a more complex gestural and vocal motor control was that perceptual representations also became more sophisticated. The reason for this increased complexity is that a newly acquired combination of gesture and sound will necessarily produce a new motor representation. In turn, this new representation will begin to be matched with the observed/listened gesture/call by using the mirror neuron matching mechanism. The result of this process will be the understanding of the meaning of the new gesture-sound combination.

Once the first associations between gestures and sounds occurred, a further evolutionary step involved the formation of a richer and more articulated phonatory system which allowed richer combinations between specific gestures and sounds. The anatomical sophistication of the phonatory system and its cortical control rendered this system more efficient than the more primitive vocal-gestural system for the purposes of vocal/speech communication. This stage was probably crucial for the development of a speech-based communicative system (see Rizzolatti & Arbib, 1998).

Conclusions

For evolutionary biologists, anatomical structures devoid of an actual function such as, for example, the pelvis in snakes and leg bones in whales are considered vestiges of previously functional structures in ancestors. Such traces shed light on the evolutionary history of these structures. Similarly, brachiomanual gestures that accompany speech could be considered as vestiges of an antecedent communicative system. However, it is well known that in modern humans spoken language is commonly accompanied by gestures that enrich the communicative message (Goldin-Meadow, 1999; McNeill, 1992). Thus, gestures continue to maintain an important functional value. The intimate relationship between brachiomanual gestures and language has been recently investigated in a series of studies by Gentilucci and his coworkers (Gentilucci, 2003; Gentilucci et al., 2001, 2004). These studies demonstrated that the production of syllables, both in terms of kinematic parameters of mouth movements and of phonetic parameters, can be affected by the simultaneous execution or observation of brachiomanual actions. These findings favor the idea that the control of speech and gestures in humans can partially overlap in the same cortical areas (e.g., Broca's area). A strong evidence for this overlap is provided by brain imaging studies showing an activation of the inferior frontal cortex in deaf people during production of meaningful signs (Petitto et al., 2000).

In conclusion, neurophysiological data support the existence of a hypothetical evolutionary pathway from monkey communication to human language. In our view, cortical control of gestures represents a starting point of the evolutionary process. Vocal calls initially related to emotional behavior, and primarily under subcortical control, subsequently became associated with gestural communication, thus being controlled by the intentional, lateral cortical system (i.e., ventral premotor cortex). This association had the advantage of a rich combinatorial power. We hypothesize that the mirror system, originally evolved as a mechanism for action understanding, became a crucial mechanism for production and perception of communicative gestures. The system continued to maintain its role when gestures became associated with sounds. The anatomo-functional homology of monkey area F5 with human Broca's area confirms the key role mirror neurons played in the evolution of language.

References

Arcadi, A. C. (1996). Phrase structure of wild chimpanzees pant hoots: Patterns of production and interpopulation variability. *American Journal of Primatology, 39*, 159–178.

Arcadi, A. C. (2000). Vocal responsiveness in male wild chimpanzees: Implications for the evolution of language. *Journal of Human Evolution, 39*, 205–223.

Armstrong, A. C., Stokoe, W.C., & Wilcox, S. E. (1995). *Gesture and the nature of language*. Cambridge: Cambridge University Press.

Bonda, E., Petrides, M., Frey, S., & Evans, A. C. (1994). Frontal cortex involvement in organized sequences of hand movements: Evidence from a positron emission tomography study. *Society of Neuroscience Abstracts, 20*, 353.

Buccino, G., Binkofski, F., Fink, G.R., Fadiga, L., Fogassi, L., Gallese, V., Seitz, R. J., Zilles, K., Rizzolatti, G., & Freund, H.J. (2001). Action observation activates premotor and parietal areas in a somatotopic manner: An fMRI study. *European Journal of Neuroscience, 13*, 400–404.

Buccino, G., Vogt, S., Ritzl, A., Fink, G.R., Zilles, K., Freund, H.J., & Rizzolatti, G. (2004a). Neural circuits underlying imitation learning of hand actions: an event-related fMRI study. *Neuron, 42*, 323–334.

Buccino, G., Lui, F., Canessa, N., Patteri, I., Lagravinese, G., Benuzzi, F., Porro, C. A., & Rizzolatti, G. (2004b). Neural circuits involved in the recognition of actions performed by non-conspecifics: An fMRI study. *Journal of Cognitive Neuroscience, 161*, 114–126.

Calvert, G. A., & Campbell, R. (2003). Reading speech from still and moving faces: Neural substrates of visible speech. *Journal of Cognitive Neuroscience, 15*, 57–70.

Campbell, R., MacSweeney, M., Surguladze, S., Calvert, G. A., Mc Guire, P., Suckling, J., Brammer, M.J., & David, A.S. (2001). Cortical substrates for the perception of face actions: An fMRI study of the specificity of activation for seen speech and for meaningless lower-face acts (gurning). *Brain Research Cognitive Brain Research, 12*, 233–243.

Cantalupo, C., & Hopkins, W. D. (2001). Asymmetric Broca's area in great apes. *Nature, 414*, 505.

Cheney, D. L., & Seyfarth, R. M. (1982). How vervet monkeys perceive their grunts. *Animal Behaviour, 30*, 739–751.

Cheney, D. L., & Seyfarth, R. M. (1990). *How monkeys see the world: Inside the mind of another species*. Chicago: Chicago University Press.

Chollet F., DiPiero, V., Wise, R. J., Brooks, D.J., Dolan, R. J., & Frackowiak, R.S. (1991). The functional anatomy of motor recovery after stroke in humans: A study with positron emission tomography. *Annals of Neurology, 29*, 63–71.

Chomsky, N. (1986) *Knowledge of language: Its nature, origin and use*. NewYork: Praeger.

Corballis, M. C. (1992). On the evolution of language and generativity. *Cognition, 44*, 197–226.

Corballis, M. C. (1999). The gestural origins of language. *American Scientist, 87*, 138–145.

Corballis, M. C. (2002). *From hand to mouth: The origins of language.* Princeton N.J.: Princeton University Press.

Corballis, M. C. (2003). From mouth to hand: Gesture, speech, and the evolution of right-handedness. *Behavioral and Brain Sciences, 26*, 199–260.

Darwin, C. (1872). *The expression of emotions in man and animals.* London: John Murray.

De Waal, F. B. M. (1982). *Chimpanzee politics.* New York: Harper & Row.

De Waal, F. B. M. (2007) The Russian doll model of animal (and human) empathy and imitation. In S. Braten (Ed.), *Being moved.* Oslo: Norwegian Academy of Sciences (pp. 49-69).

Fadiga, L., Craighero, L., Buccino, G., & Rizzolatti, G. (2002). Speech listening specifically modulates the excitability of tongue muscles: a TMS study. *European Journal of Neuroscience, 15*, 399–402.

Ferrari, P. F., Gallese, V., Rizzolatti, G., & Fogassi, L. (2003). Mirror neurons responding to the observation of ingestive and communicative mouth actions in the monkey ventral premotor cortex. *European Journal of Neuroscience, 17*, 1703–1714.

Fogassi, L., & Gallese, V. (2002) The neural correlates of action understanding in non-human primates. In M.I. Stamenov & V. Gallese (Eds.), *Mirror neurons and the evolution of brain and language* (pp. 13–35). Amsterdam: John Benjamins.

Fogassi, L., & Ferrari, P. F. (2004). Mirror neurons, gestures and language evolution. *Interaction studies, 5* (3), 343–361.

Fogassi, L., Ferrari, P. F., Gesierich, B., Rozzi, S., Chersi, F., & Rizzolatti, G. (2005). Parietal lobe: From action organization to intention understanding. *Science, 308*, 662–667.

Gallese, V., Fadiga, L., Fogassi, L., & Rizzolatti, G. (1996). Action recognition in the premotor cortex. *Brain, 119*, 593–609.

Gallese V., Fadiga L., Fogassi L. & Rizzolatti G. (2002). Action representation and the inferior pariatel lobule. In W. Prinz & B. Hommel (Eds.), *Common mechanisms in perception and action: Attention and Performance, vol. XIX*, (pp. 334–355). Oxford: Oxford University Press.

Gentilucci, M. (2003). Grasp observation influences speech production. *European Journal of Neuroscience, 17*, 179–184.

Gentilucci, M., Benuzzi, F., Gangitano, M., & Grimaldi, S. (2001). Grasp with hand and mouth. A kinematic study on healthy subjects. *Journal of Neurophysiology, 86*, 1685–1699.

Gentilucci, M., Santunione, P., Roy, A. C., & Stefanini, S. (2004). Execution and observation of bringing a fruit to the mouth affect syllable pronunciation. *European Journal of Neuroscience, 19*, 190–202.

Ghazanfar, A. A., & Hauser, M. D. (1999). The neuroethology of primate vocal communication: Substrates for the evolution of speech. *Trends in Cognitive Sciences*, *3*, 377–384.

Goldin-Meadow, S. (1999). The role of gestures in communication and thinking. *Trends in Cognitive Sciences, 3*, 419–429.

Grafton, S.T., Arbib, M. A., Fadiga, L., & Rizzolatti, G. (1996). Localization of grasp representations in humans by positron emission tomography. 2. Observation compared with imagination. *Experimental Brain Research, 112*, 103–111.

Hast, M.H., Fischer, J. M., Wetzel, A. B., & Thompson, V.E. (1974). Cortical motor representation of the laryngeal muscles in *Macaca mulatta*. *Brain Research, 73*, 229–240.

Hauser, M. D. (1996). *The evolution of communication*. Cambridge: MIT Press.

Hauser, M. D., Chomsky, N., & Fitch, W. T. (2002). The faculty of language: What is it, who has it, and how did it evolve? *Science, 298*, 1569–1579.

Hayes, K., & Hayes, C. (1951). The intellectual development of a home-raised chimpanzee. *Proceedings of the American Philosophical Society, 95*, 105–109.

Hopkins, W. D. & Leavens, D. A. (1998). Hand use and gestural communication in chimpanzees (*Pan troglodytes*). *Journal of Comparative psychology, 112*, 95–99.

Hostetter, A. B., Cantero, M., & Hopkins W. D. (2001). Differential use of vocal and gestural communication in response to the attentional status of a human. *Journal of Comparative Psychology, 115*, 337–343.

Iacoboni, M., Woods, R. P., Brass, M., Bekkering, H. Mazziotta, J. C., & Rizzolatti, G. (1999). Cortical mechanisms of human imitation. *Science, 286*, 2526–2528.

Jürgens, U. (1995). Neuronal control of vocal production in human and non human primates. In E. Zimmerman, J. D. Newman & U. Jürgens (Eds.), *Current topics in primate vocal communication* (pp. 199–206). New York: Plenum Press.

Jürgens, U. (2002). Neural pathways underlying vocal control. *Neuroscience and Biobehavioral Review, 26*, 235–258.

Kimura, D. (1993). *Neuromotor mechanisms in human communication*. Oxford: Oxford University Press.

Kohler, E., Keysers, C., Umiltà, M. A., Fogassi, L., Gallese, V., & Rizzolatti, G. (2002). Hearing sounds, understanding actions: Action representation in mirror neurons. *Science, 297*, 846–8.

Leavens, D. A., Hostetter, A. B., Wesley, M.J., & Hopkins W. D. (2004). Tactical use of unimodal and bimodal communication by chimpanzees, *Pantroglodytes*. *Animal Behaviour, 67*, 467–476.

Libermann, A. M., & Mattingly, I. G. (1985). The motor theory of speech perception revised. *Cognition, 21*, 1–36.

Liebal, K., Call, J., & Tomasello, M. (2004). Use of gesture sequences in chimpanzees. *American Journal of Primatology, 64*, 377–396.

MacLean, P. D. (1993). Introduction: Perspectives on cingulated cortex in the limbic system. In B.A. Vogt & M. Gabriel (Eds.), *Neurobiology of cingulate cortex and limbic thalamus: A comprehensive handbook* (pp. 1–15). Boston: Birkhäuser.

MacNeilage, P. F. (1998). The frame/content theory of evolution of speech production. *Behavioral and Brain Sciences, 21,* 499–546.

Maestripieri, D. (1996). Gestural communication and its cognitive implications in pigtail macaques (Macaca nemestrina). *Behaviour, 133,* 997–1022.

Maestripieri, D. (1997). Gestural communication in macaques: Usage and meaning of nonvocal signals. *Evolution of communication, 1,* 193–222.

McNeill, D. (1992). *Hand and mind.* Chicago: University of Chicago Press.

Paget, R. A. S. (1963). Human speech: Some observations, experiments and conclusions as to the nature, origin, purpose and possible improvement of human speech. London: Routledge and Kegan Paul.

Parr, L. A., & Maestripieri, D. (2003). Nonvocal communication. In D. Maestripieri (Ed.), *Primate psychology* (pp. 324-358). Cambridge, MA: Harvard University Press.

Parsons, L. M., Fox, P. T., Downs, J. H., Glass, T., Hirsch, T. B., Martin, C. C., Jerabek, P. A., & Lancaster, J. L. (1995). Use of implicit motor imagery for visual shape discrimination as revealed by PET. *Nature, 375,* 54–58.

Petrides, M., & Pandya, D. N. (1994). Comparative architectonic analysis of the human and the macaque frontal cortex. In F. Boller & J. Grafman (Eds.), *Handbook of neuropsychology* (pp.17–58). Amsterdam: Elsevier.

Petitto, L. A., Zatorre, R. J., Gauna, K., Nikelski, E.J., Dostie, D., & Evans, A. C. (2000). Speech-like cerebral activity in profoundly deaf people processing signed languages: Implications for the neural basis of human language. *Proceedings of the National Academy of Sciences of the USA, 97,* 13961–13966.

Price, C. J., Wise, R. J., Warburton, E. A., Moore, C. J., Howard, D., Patterson, K., Frackowiak, R.S. & Friston, K. J. (1996). Hearing and saying. The functional neuro-anatomy of auditory word processing. *Brain, 119,* 919–31.

Rizzolatti, G., & Arbib, M. A. (1998). Language within our grasp. *Trends in Neurosciences, 21,* 188–194 (1998).

Rizzolatti, G., Fogassi, L., & Gallese, V. (2000) Cortical mechanisms subserving object grasping and action recognition: A new view on the cortical motor function. In M.S. Gazzaniga (Ed.), *The new cognitive neurosciences* (2nd ed.; pp. 539–552). Cambridge, MA: MIT Press.

Rizzolatti, G., Fogassi, L., & Gallese, V. (2001). Neurophysiological mechanisms underlying the understanding and imitation of action. *Nature Neuroscience Reviews, 2,* 661–670.

Rizzolatti, G., Fadiga, L., Gallese, V., & Fogassi L. (1996). Premotor cortex and the recognition of motor actions. *Cognitive Brain Research, 3,* 131–141.

Rizzolatti, G., Camarda, R., Fogassi, L., Gentilucci, M., Luppino, G., & Matelli, M. (1988). Functional organization of inferior area 6 in the macaque monkey: II. Area F5 and the control of distal movements. *Experimental Brain Research, 71,* 491–507.

Rizzolatti, G., Luppino, G. & Matelli, M. (1998). The organization of the cortical motor system: New concepts. *Electroencephalography and Clinical Neurophysiology, 106*, 283–96.

Rumbaugh, D. M., Beran, M.J., & Savage-Rumbaugh, E.S. (2003). Language. In D. Maestripieri (Ed.), *Primate psychology* (pp. 395–423). Cambridge, MA: Harvard University Press.

Symonian, K., & Jürgens, U. (2003). Efferent subcortical projections of the laryngeal motorcortex in the rhesus monkey. *Brain Research . 974*, 43–59.

Tanner, J. E., & Byrne, R. W. (1996). Representation of action through iconic gesture in a captive lowland gorilla. *Current Anthropology, 37*, 162–173.

Tomasello, M., Call, J., Nagell, K., Olguin, R., & Carpenter, M. (1994). The learning and use of gestural signals by young chimpanzees: A trans-generational study. *Primates, 35*, 137- 154.

Tomasello, M., Call, J., Warren, J., Frost, G.T., Carpenter, M., & Nagell, K. (1997). The ontogeny of chimpanzee gestural signals: A comparison across groups and generations. *Evolution of communication, 1*, 223–259.

Umiltà, M. A., Kohler, E., Gallese, V., Fogassi, L., Fadiga, L., Keysers, C., & Rizzolatti, G. (2001). I know what you are doing. A neurophysiological study. *Neuron, 31*, 155–65.

van Hooff, J. A. R. A. M. (1962). Facial expressions in higher primates. *Symposium of the Zoological Society of London, 8*, 97–125.

van Hooff, J. A. R. A. M. (1967). The facial displays of the catarrhine monkeys and apes. In D. Morris (Ed.), *Primate ethology* (pp. 7–68). London: Weidenfield & Nicolson.

von Bonin, G., & Bailey, P. (1947). *The neocortex of Macaca mulatta*. Urbana, IL: University of Illinois Press.

7

Syllables in Psycholinguistic Theory:
Now You See Them, Now You Don't

Niels O. Schiller

Department of Cognitive Neuroscience, Faculty of Psychology,

Maastricht University

Maastricht, The Netherlands

Are syllables represented in the brain? In the following, I will summarize the views that psycholinguists and neurolinguists take on this question. Presumably, it might be more appropriate to ask "How are syllables represented in the brain?" because few people have disputed the psychological or psycholinguistic reality of the syllable (but see Panconcelli-Calzia, 1934, pp. 119–120). However, syllables have been proven to be notoriously difficult to capture in linguistic terms (for overviews see Bell, A. & Hooper, 1978; Blevins, 1995; Selkirk, 1982), and it has been suggested that "syllables are just epiphenomenal consequences of the necessity of making a succession of auditorily robust modulations in one or more acoustic parameters" (Ohala, 1998, p. 526). Both phoneticians and phonologists (but not psycholinguists) have tried to define the syllable as a universal unit in the language system but "although nearly everybody can identify syllables, almost nobody can define them" (Ladefoged, 1982, p. 220). More than 30 years ago Liberman, I. Y., Shankweiler, Fischer, F. W., and Carter (1974) conducted a study to investigate children's sensitivity to syllables. Results showed that about half of a group of four-year old children were able to correctly determine the number of syllables in spoken words. The same proportion of six-year old children was able to determine the number of phonemes of spoken words correctly (Liberman, I. Y. et al., 1974). This has been interpreted as evidence that syllables are the first sublexical linguistic units that appear in the course of language acquisition and that syllables are accessible earlier than segments or phonemes. Furthermore, speakers can easily manipulate syllables in meta-linguistic laboratory tasks, e.g., syllable reversal (Schiller et al., 1997; Treiman & Danis, 1990), word games (Bagemihl, 1995; Fallows, 1981; Hombert, 1986; Lefkowitz, 1991; Treiman, 1983), or backward talking (Cowan, Braine, & Leavitt, 1985; Hombert; 1973; White, 1955). For instance, in the French secret language *Verlan* the word *verité* becomes *terivé*. Finally, the syllable forms the basis of many linguistic rules such as syllable-initial aspiration in English or syllable-final devoicing in Dutch or German (Kenstowitcz, 1994). Thus, there is plenty of evidence supporting the view that syllables play a role in the speech production process. *Now you see them, ...* However, syllables rarely occur in speech errors (Fromkin, 1971). *... now you don't.* If syllables were independent units, one might expect that syllabic speech errors would regularly occur, just like segmental errors (left hemisphere → *h*eft *l*emisphere). Therefore, it is a legitimate question to ask which role the syllable plays in psycholinguistic models of word production.

Phonological Encoding in Speech Production

Psycholinguistic models of phonological encoding in speech production describe the processes of word form encoding that follow the selection of a word from the mental lexicon (Levelt, 1989; Levelt & Wheeldon, 1994; Lavelt, Roelofs, & Meyer, 1999). Once a word has been selected from the mental lexicon, it has to be encoded in a form that can finally be used to control neuromuscular commands necessary for the execution of articulatory movements (see Guenther, 2003, for a recent overview). When accessing a word's form for phonological encoding, speakers retrieve segmental and metrical information. During segmental encoding, the segments of a word and their order have to be retrieved. For example, for the word *typist* this would be the segments $/t/_1$, $/AI/_2$, $/p/_3$, $/I/_4$, $/s/_5$, $/t/_6$. During metrical retrieval, a metrical frame has to be retrieved, i.e., the number of syllables and the location of the lexical stress. For the example *typist*, the metrical frame would include two syllable slots, the first of which bears lexical stress (e.g., '_ _). Furthermore, the syllable or consonant-vowel (CV) structure of the individual syllables of the word may be retrieved (Dell, G. S., 1988; but see Roelofs & Meyer, 1998). Once the segmental and the metrical information has been retrieved, it is combined during a process called segment-to-frame association. During this process, the previously retrieved segments are combined from word beginning to end with their corresponding metrical frame. The resulting phonological string is syllabified according to universal and language-specific syllabification rules (Roelofs, 1997). A fully prosodified phonological word is generated, which forms the basis for the activation of syllables in a *mental syllabary* (Levelt, W. J. M. & Wheeldon, 1994). Presumably, the units in the syllabary can be conceived of as precompiled articulatory motor programs of syllabic size. These motor programs may be represented in terms of gestural scores, i.e., a phonetic plan that specifies the relevant articulatory gestures and their relative timing (see Goldstein & Fowler, 2003, for a review). The final step includes the execution of these gestures by the articulatory apparatus resulting in overtly produced speech (see Figure 7.1).

One puzzling feature of this process is why segments and metrical frame are retrieved independently from memory when both types of information are reunified slightly later. However, this may only seem puzzling when considering single, isolated word production, but not when the production of words in context is taken into account. For instance, syllabification does not respect lexical boundaries since the domain of syllabification is the phonological word (not the lexical word; Booij, 1995). Let us take the example of the verb *to type*. In its citation form, *type* is a monosyllabic CVC word. Now consider the words *ty.pist* (someone who types; dots indicate syllable boundaries), *ty.ping* (the

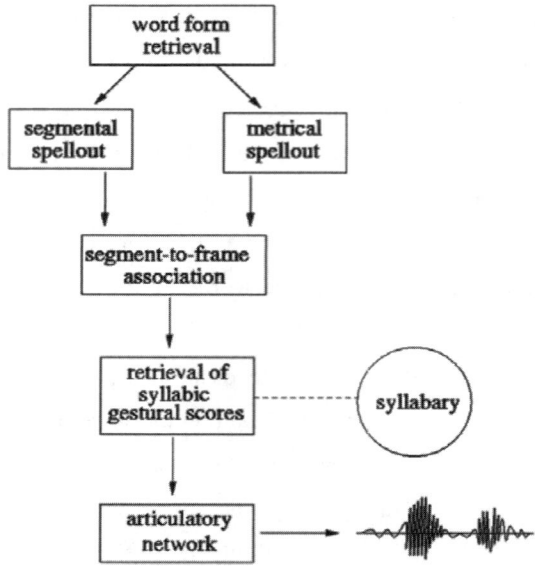

Figure 7.1.
Model of phonological encoding in speech production (slightly adapted from Levelt, W. J. M. & Wheeldon, 1994).

gerund), or the phrase *ty.pe it*. In all of these examples, the coda /p/ of *type* /taɪp/ becomes the onset of a second syllable. In the example *ty.pe it*, it even straddles the lexical boundary between *type* and *it*. Therefore, it is important to bear in mind that segments are not inserted into a lexical word frame, but into a *phonological word* frame. The phonological word, however, is a context-dependent unit. It can solely consist of the lexical word *type* as in *type faster* or unstressed function words like *it* can cliticize to it as in *type it faster*, yielding *ty.pe it* /taɪ.pɪt/. A corollary of context-dependent syllabification in speech production is that it would not make sense to store syllable boundaries with the word forms in the mental lexicon because syllable boundaries will change as a function of the phonological context. The so-called *syllable-position constraint* observed in sound errors (i.e., onsets exchange with onsets, nuclei with nuclei, etc., Shattuck-Hufnagel, 1979) can probably not hold as an argument for stored syllable frames because it may just be a reflection of the general tendency of segments to interact with phonemically similar segments. Therefore, it has been postulated that syllables are not stored with their lexical entries (Levelt, W. J. M. et al., 1999). Rather, syllable boundaries will be generated on-line during the construction of phonological words to yield maximally pronounceable syllables. This architecture lends maximal flexibility to the speech production system in all possible contexts.

However, there are models that assume syllables in the lexicon (Dell, G. S., 1986). In one version of Dell, G. S.'s (1988) theory, structural information about the distribution of consonants and vowels is explicitly represented in terms of so-called CV headers (see also Sevald, Dell, G. S., & Cole, 1995). However, whether or not CV structure information or abstract syllable frames are explicitly represented in the mental lexicon is still a matter of debate (Levelt, W. J. M. & Schiller, 1998; Roelofs & Meyer, 1998).

A mental syllabary

Although Levelt, W. J. M. et al. (1999) do not assume that syllables play a role at an abstract, early planning level in speech production syllables do play an important functional role in their theory. Levelt, W. J. M.'s theory assumes that a so-called *mental syllabary* is involved in speech production (see Figure 7.1). A mental syllabary is a "library of articulatory routines" (Crompton, 1981). The original hypothesis was that pre-compiled motor programs of syllable size could help reducing the computational load during speech production if they form the basic units of articulatory programming (for a critical note see McQueen, Dahan, & Cutler, 2003). From a lexico-statistical point of view this idea is attractive since about 85% of the speech in Dutch (and other Germanic languages such as German and English) can be produced with a relatively small set including less than 5% of all Dutch syllables (Schiller, Meyer, Baayen, & Levelt, 1996; see Figure 7.2). With less than 100 syllables, speakers of Dutch can produce 60% of their speech, and with the 500 most frequently occurring syllables this amounts even to 85% of their speech.

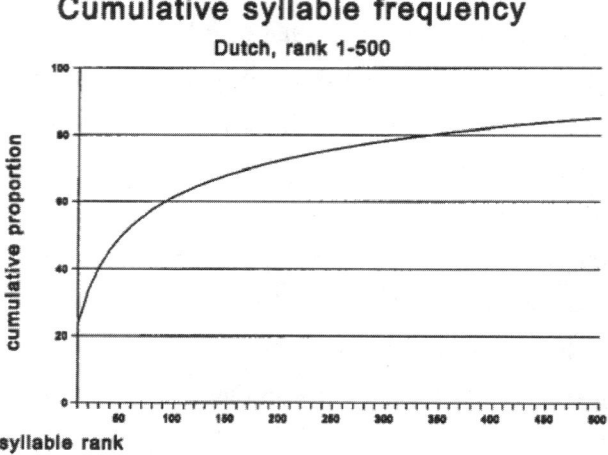

Figure 7.2.
Lexico-statistical distribution of Dutch syllables. Syllable rank is shown from position 1 to 500 on the x-axis; cumulative syllable proportion on the y-axis.

Levelt and Wheeldon (1994) tested the hypothesis of a mental syllabary in an experiment comparing the production latencies of words differing in syllable frequencies. For instance, there were words in the experiment that consisted of high-frequency syllables (e.g., *bo.ter* "butter") and words that were made-up from low-frequency syllables (e.g., *gi.raf* "giraffe") while word frequency was controlled. Results showed that words with high-frequency syllables were named significantly faster than words with low-frequency syllables, independent of word frequency. Levelt and Wheeldon (1994) took this finding as evidence for a separate store from which syllabic units can be recruited during speech production. *Now you see them, ...* Previous evidence, however, indicated that articulation only starts after the whole phonological word has been encoded (Wheeldon & Lahiri, 1997). Thus, the frequency of the first syllable may only have a limited impact because the response to a bisyllabic word can only start after the second syllable has been retrieved. Therefore, Levelt and Wheeldon manipulated the frequency of the second syllable while controlling the frequency of the first and found that the frequency of the second syllable was crucial. However, syllable frequency correlates highly with segment or phoneme frequency. Therefore, Levelt, and Wheeldon's (1994) syllable frequency effect could as well be attributed to segment frequency. When segment frequency was controlled in subsequent experiments, a small set of awkward word stimuli remained and the syllable frequency effect disappeared. ... *now you don't.*

Recently several investigators looked at syllable frequency from different perspectives. Wilshire and Nespoulous (2003) looked at the influence of syllable frequency on phonological errors produced by two French-speaking aphasic patients. The patients were asked to read aloud and repeat 110 polysyllabic word pairs matched for word frequency and syllabic complexity, but differing in word-final syllable frequency. The authors found that performance was not more accurate with words consisting of high-frequency than words consisting of low-frequency syllables. Wilshire and Nespoulous concluded that a "plausible interpretation of the absence of syllable frequency effects [...] is that this variable has no influence on the process of phonological encoding" (Wilshire & Nespoulous, 2003, p. 441). Moreover, they state that their failure to obtain a syllable frequency effect indicates that syllables are not retrieved as representational units nor accessed at the level of phonological encoding.

Similarly, Aichert and Ziegler (2004) investigated the influence of syllable frequency on speech production of ten German patients with apraxia of speech (AOS) using a word repetition task. The materials consisted of 40 bisyllabic words, matched for word frequency and syllabic complexity, but differing in initial syllable frequency. Unlike the previous study, these authors found a tendency towards more segmental errors on words made up of low-frequency syllables. This effect became significant when the most extreme frequency regions were analyzed separately. Aichert and Ziegler (2004) concluded that their findings "indicate that patients with AOS must have access to the syllabary" (Aichert & Ziegler, 2004, p. 153). It seems that patients with an apraxic impairment of speech have access to a mental syllabary, but either the retrieval of the syllabic motor programs or the motor programs themselves are defective.

Recently, Cholin, Levelt & Schiller (2006) conducted a naming study with Dutch speakers using pseudo-words. The reason to employ pseudo-words was that segment frequency could not be controlled when using existing words (see above). All pseudo-words consisted of existing Dutch syllables. In the first experiment, monosyllabic pseudo-words were named in a newly designed symbol-association-naming task. In this task, participants were required to learn to associate a particular pseudo-word either with a left or a right position on the screen. Then a symbol would appear on the screen, and depending on its position (left or right) the corresponding pseudo-word was to be produced. The authors observed a small but significant syllable-frequency effect: pseudo-words consisting of a high-frequency syllables were produced faster than pseudo-words consisting of a low-frequency syllables (Cholin et al., 2006). In a second experiment, the second syllable of bisyllabic pseudo-words was frequency-manipulated, and the naming latencies between pseudo-words including high- or low-frequency second syllables did not differ. Finally, in the third experiment, the first syllable of bisyllabic pseudo-words varied in frequency. A syllable-frequency effect emerged similar to the one in the first experiment. These results strongly support the notion of a mental syllabary to mediate between abstract phonological syllables and phonetic syllables, conceived of as precompiled gestural scores controlling execution of an articulatory motor program. Cholin et al. (2006) concluded that speakers can start articulating a target word when the first syllable is phonetically encoded.

Syllable Priming

The idea of a mental syllabary stimulated even more research. Ferrand, Segui and Grainger (1996) carried out a series of syllable priming experiments and reported a syllable priming effect in French speech production. *Now you see them,* … These authors used the masked priming procedure and found that a visually masked prime ca primed the naming of ca.rotte better than the naming

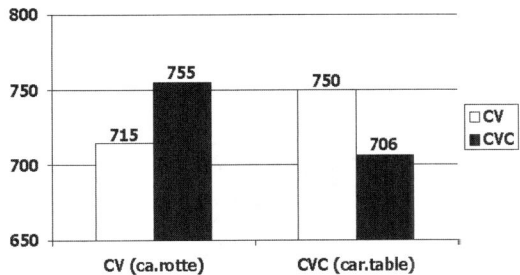

Figure 7.3.
Results of Experiment 4 from Ferrand et al. (1996). Structure of the visual prime (CV or CVC) is shaded. Target picture categories are depicted. On the left are CV words such as *ca.rotte*. On the right are CVC words such as *car.table*). On the y-axis are mean reaction times. Naming latencies are in milliseconds on the x-axis.

of car.table. Similarly, the prime car primed the naming of car.table better than the naming of ca.rotte (see Figure 7.3).

Ferrand et al. (1996) concluded that output phonology must be syllabically structured since the syllable priming effect disappeared in a task that does not make a phonological representation necessary, such as a lexical decision task. This fit nicely with the evidence about syllables as pre-lexical processing units in French speech comprehension (see below). Ferrand et al. (1996) claimed that the mental syllabary model predicts a syllable-priming effect. This account presumed that the prime could pre-activate syllables in the syllabary. Interestingly, Ferrand, Segui, and Humphreys (1997) also report a syllable priming effect for English, although the evidence for syllables as processing units in speech comprehension in English is rather weak (Cutler, Mehler, Norris, & Segui, 1983; Cutler, 1997). Recently, this syllabic effect in English has been replicated in a silent word reading study by Ashby and Rayner (2004) using a parafoveal preview technique although Ferrand et al. (1996, 1997) claimed that the speech-output phonology syllabically structured and did not

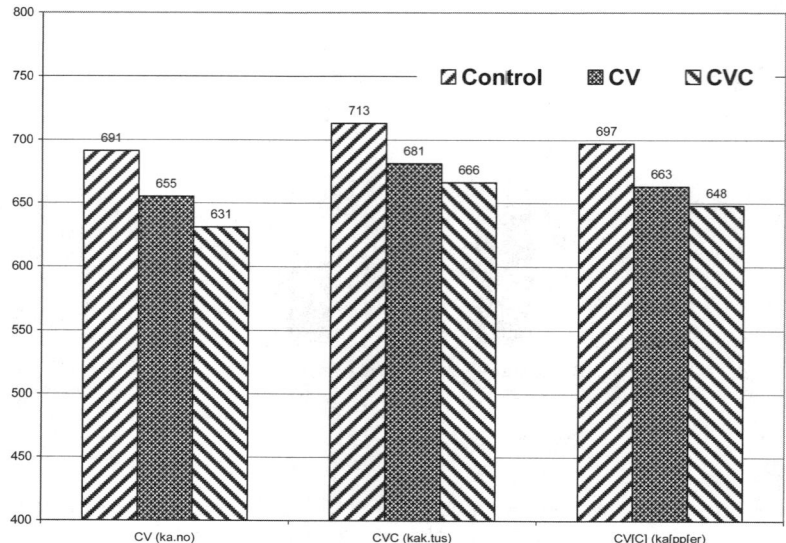

Figure 7.4.
Summary of results of Experiment 1 from Schiller (1998). Structure of the visual prime (CV, CVC, or control, i.e. non-linguistic characters) is color-coded. Target picture categories are depicted (left: CV words such as *ka.no*; middle: CVC words such as *kak.tus*; right: CV[C] words such as *ka[pp]er*; square brackets indicate ambisyllabic consonants) on the x-axis; mean reaction times (naming latencies) in milliseconds on the y-axis.

find a syllabic effect in lexical decision tasks. It should be noted, however, that when using a different technique, i.e., fast priming, no syllabic effect could be demonstrated in reading (Ashby & Rayner, 2004).

However, when Schiller (1998) tried to replicate these syllable priming effects in Dutch speech production, he failed to find syllabic effects. ... *now you don't*. Instead, what he obtained was a clear *segmental overlap effect*, i.e., the more segmental overlap between prime and target picture name, the faster the naming latencies (see also Schiller, 2004). That is, the prime *kan* yielded not only faster responses than *ka* for the picture of a "pulpit" (*kan.sel*) but also for the picture of a "canoe" (*ka.no*) (see Figure 7.4).

Similar results were obtained in the auditory modality, i.e., presenting either /ro/ or /rok/ when Dutch participants were requested to produce either *ro.ken* ("to smoke") or *rook.te* ("smoked"). In fact, in the auditory modality a segmental overlap effect was obtained, i.e., /rok/ was a better prime than /ro/ independent of the target (Baumann, 1995). The failure to find a syllable priming effect in Dutch is in agreement with the statement that syllables are never retrieved during phonological encoding (Levelt, et al., 1999). The syllable priming effect found by Ferrand and colleagues (1996) in French can be accounted for by assuming that segments in the prime are coded with their corresponding syllable structure information. For instance, the prime *pal* pre-activates segments specified for syllable position in the perceptual network, e.g., p_{onset}, $a_{nucleus}$, and l_{coda}. Active phonological segments in the perceptual network can directly affect the corresponding segment nodes in the production lexicon. Therefore, the prime *pal* matches with the target *pal.mier*, but not with *pa.lace* because the /l/ in *pal* is specified for coda and not for onset.

This fits well with the assumption that the syllable is an important pre-lexical processing unit in French. A classical study by Mehler, Dommergues, Frauenfelder, and Segui (1981) showed that when French native speakers are requested to detect a particular target syllable (e.g., *pal*) in an auditorily presented word, they are faster in responding when the target syllable corresponds to the first syllable of the word (e.g., *pal.mier*) than when it does not (e.g., *pa.lace*). Similarly, when the target is a CV syllable (e.g., *pa*), participants are faster in responding to *pa.lace* than *pal.mier* (see Figure 7.5). Mehler and colleagues concluded that the syllable is a pre-lexical processing unit in speech perception. More specifically, syllables may be useful in the segmentation of the incoming speech signal. *Now you see them, ...*

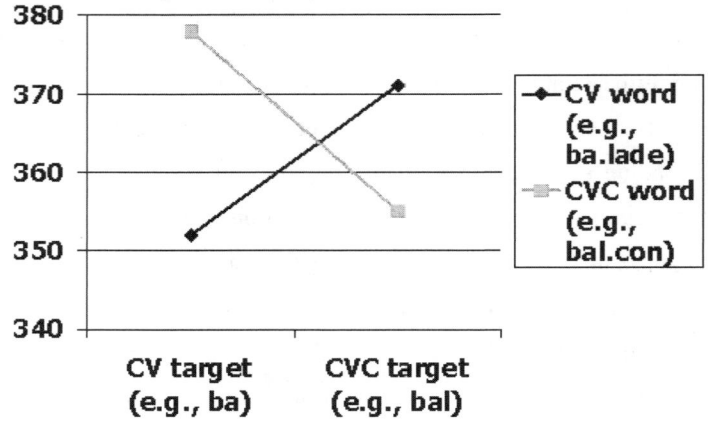

Figure 7.5.
Results of Experiment 1 from Mehler et al. (1981). Structure of the carrier words (CV such as *ba.lade* or CVC such as *bal.con*) is color-coded. Target syllables are depicted (left: CV such as *ba*; right: CVC such as *bal*) on the x-axis; Mean reaction times (monitoring latencies) in milliseconds on the y-axis.

This *syllable match effect* has been replicated in many other Romance languages, but not in Germanic languages (see Cutler, 1997 for a summary). Subsequent research showed that at least the following two factors play a crucial role for obtaining a syllable match effect, i.e., the rhythmic structure of the language and the quality of the pivotal consonant, which follows or precedes the syllable boundary. Germanic languages are stress-timed. That may be the reason that the syllable match effect could not be replicated for these languages. Syllables simply do not play a prominent role for the rhythmic pattern in those languages and therefore they are not used for pre-lexical segmentation; instead, stress is used to segment the incoming speech stream. In contrast, Romance languages have more or less clear syllable boundaries (syllable-timed languages), and therefore syllable match effects can be obtained in those languages. However, it has been shown that the pattern of effects also depends on the nature of the pivotal consonant, which can interact with syllable structure. Content, Meunier, Kearns, and Frauenfelder (2001) assessed the role of the characteristics of the pivotal consonant for the syllable priming effect with pseudo-words. They only found the syllabic effect for liquids (e.g., /l/, /r/, etc.) in a blocked condition, but not for stops (e.g., /t/, /k/, /p/, etc.). Liquids are known to show a higher degree of coarticulation with preceding vowels than stops, and listeners might be able to exploit this when detecting syllables because when they perceive the vowel /a/ in *pal.mier*, they know relatively earlier whether or not a syllable boundary intervenes between the /a/ and the /l/. Therefore, they can detect the syllable *pal* or reject the syllable *pa* relatively quickly. Rietveld and Schiller (submitted) recently obtained similar results for Dutch. The Content et al. (2001) as well as the Rietveld and Schiller (submitted) results argue against a role for the syllable as a pre-lexical segmentation unit and more for a direct phonemic input processing. ... *now you don't.*

The segmental overlap effect is not restricted to Dutch. When Schiller (2000) tried to replicate the Ferrand et al. (1997) results for English with better-controlled material, no syllabic effect was obtained. A segmental overlap effect was found. These English data are interesting. In English there is phonological equivalence between corresponding syllable structures. For example, *pi* /paɪ/ matches phonologically the first syllable in *pi.lot* but not in *pi[l.l]ow* (square brackets indicate ambisyllabicity of the intervocalic consonants), and *pil* /pɪl/ matches phonologically the first syllable in *pi[l.l]ow* but not in *pi.lot*. Nevertheless, the prime *pil* yielded faster responses than *pi* for both *pilot* and *pillow* (see Figure 7.6).

Either the contribution of vowels is less important in segmental priming (Schiller & Costa, submitted) or consonants and vowels have different time courses of activation (Berent & Perfetti, 1995), consonants being faster than vowels and therefore more effective. Further testing revealed no syllable effect in Spanish, but a small segmental overlap effect (Schiller, Costa, & Colomé, 2002), and no syllabic effect in French when a larger set of materials

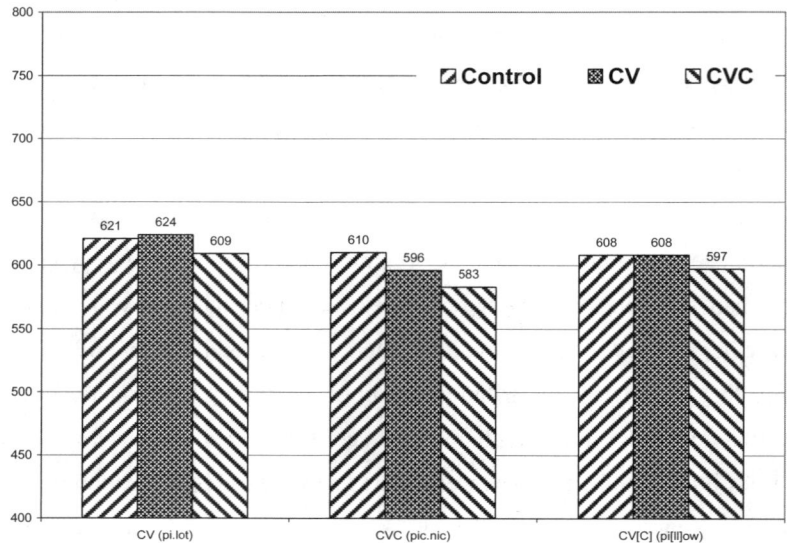

Figure 7.6.
Overview of the results of Experiment 2 from Schiller (2000). The structure of the visual prime (CV, CVC, or control, i.e. non-linguistic characters) is color-coded. Target picture categories are depicted (left: CV words such as *pi.lot*; middle: CVC words such as *pic.nic*; right: CV[C] words such as *pi[ll]ow*; square brackets indicate ambisyllabic consonants on the x-axis the); mean reaction times (naming latencies) in milliseconds on the y-axis.

was tested (Schiller et al., 2002). Taken together, these results support the idea that syllables are not retrieved, but created on-line during phonological encoding.

Although syllables cannot be primed in Dutch, Cholin, Schiller, and Levelt, W. J. M. (2004) found that syllable structure can be prepared in the planning of speech production. These authors hypothesized that masked priming taps a planning level in speech production that is not sensitive to syllabic units. Priming speeds up the spell-out of information from memory, such as segments. However, since syllables are presumably not stored with the word form because syllable boundaries are computed on the fly, syllables cannot be primed. Therefore, Cholin et al. (2004) used a preparation paradigm to investigate whether or not syllables are constructed as part of the phonological word and used to access the mental syllabary. The preparation paradigm was introduced by Meyer (1990, 1991) and further developed by Janssen, Roelofs, and Levelt,

W. J. M. (2002). Participants learned two different categories of item sets, i.e., so-called constant and variable sets. Both sets contained words with initial segmental overlap (e.g., *spui*.en "to drain"; *spui*.de "drained"; *spui*.er "person who drains"; *spui*.end "draining"), but in the variable set, syllable structure varied (e.g., *ro*.ken "to smoke"; *rook*.te "smoked"; *ro*.ker "smoker"; *ro*.kend "smoking"). The past tense form *rookte* is called the *odd-man-out* because its first syllable has the structure CVVC, while all other syllables are CVV. Therefore, in the constant sets, participants can prepare not only the initial segments but also the syllable structure of the first syllable. In the variable sets, in contrary, it was assumed that the odd-man-out would spoil this preparation effect.

Apart from naming the words in a four-item-set, i.e., including four different words (see above), participants named them in a three-item-set which consisted of the same items except for the past tense form. Thus, the three-item-sets were constant for both types of stimuli (e.g., *spui*.en, *spui*.er, *spui*.end vs. *ro*.ken, *ro*.ker, *ro*.kend). Since different item sets cannot be compared directly, the mean naming latencies of all three-item-sets were subtracted from the corresponding four-item-sets and the difference scores were compared. We expected that the four-item-set was relatively more difficult to name in the variable than in the constant condition, even when removing the odd-man-out from the data before conducting the analyses. The reason for this hypothesized outcome is that the syllable structure could be prepared, i.e., the syllabification process can begin to incrementally put the initial segments together and create the first syllable, in the constant but not in the variable sets. In variable sets, the preparation cannot go beyond the retrieval of the initial segments. This is exactly what was found in two experiments (Cholin et al., 2004).

Possibly, the first syllable can be fully prepared for articulation in the constant sets, including the retrieval of the corresponding gestural score from the mental syllabary. In the constant sets all stages prior to articulation, including segmental spell-out, on-line syllabification, and possibly access to the mental syllabary, might contribute to the preparation effect, whereas in variable sets responses can only be prepared up to on-line syllabification. Thus, Cholin et al. (2004) concluded that syllables are probably encoded at the interface between phonological and phonetic encoding.

Metrical Encoding

Syllables may not only be important for segmental encoding, i.e., grouping segments into larger units (*syllable priming* and *mental syllabary*), but also for metrical encoding, i.e., encoding of prosodic features of words such as metrical stress. Probably the most important function of syllables is to bear stress. Metrical stress is a suprasegmental feature that is usually not realized on a single segment but on a number of segments that belong together, i.e., a syllable.

Roelofs and Meyer (1998) investigated how much information about the metrical structure of words is stored in memory. Possible candidates are lexical stress, number of syllables, and syllable structure. In one experiment, for instance, they compared the production latencies for sets of homogeneous bisyllabic words such as *ma.NIER* ("manner"; capital letters indicate stressed syllables), *ma.TRAS* ("mattress"), and *ma.KREEL* ("mackerel") with sets including words with a variable number of syllables such as *ma.JOOR* ("major"), *ma.TE.rie* ("matter"), and *ma.LA.ri.a* ("malaria"). Lexical stress was kept constant (always on the second syllable). Relative to a heterogeneous control condition, there was strong and reliable facilitation for the bisyllabic sets, but not for the sets with a variable number of syllables. This showed that the number of syllables of a word must be known to the phonological encoding system. Hence, this information must be part of the metrical representation of words.

Similarly, the production of sets of homogeneous trisyllabic words with constant stress (e.g., *ma.RI.ne* "navy," *ma.TE.rie* "matter," *ma.LAI.se* "depression," *ma.DON.na* "madonna") and variable stress (e.g., *ma.RI.ne* "navy," *ma.nus.CRIPT* "manuscript," *ma.TE.rie* "matter," *ma.de.LIEF* "daisy") was measured and compared to the corresponding heterogeneous sets. Again, facilitation was obtained for the constant but not for the variable sets. Therefore, one can conclude that the availability of stress information is indispensable for planning of polysyllabic words – at least when stress is in non-default position (see Schiller, Fikkert, & Levelt, W. J. M., 2004 for an alternative). However, CV structure did not yield an effect. When the production latencies for words with a constant CV structure (e.g., *bres* "breach," *bril* "glasses," *brok* "piece," *brug* "bridge"; all CCVC) were compared to words with a variable CV structure (e.g., *brij* "porridge"; CCVV, *brief* "letter"; CCVVC, *bron* "source"; CCVC, *brand* "fire"; CCVCC), relative to the corresponding heterogeneous condition, no difference was found suggesting that the metrical structure speakers retrieve does not contain information about the CV or syllable structure of a word (but see Costa & Sebastián-Gallés, 1998).

To investigate the time course of metrical processing, Schiller, Jansma, Peters, and Levelt, (2005) employed a tacit naming task and asked participants to decide whether the bisyllabic name of a visually presented picture had initial or final stress. Their hypothesis was that if metrical encoding is a parallel process, then there should not be any differences between the decision latencies for initial and final stress. If, however, metrical encoding is a rightward incremental process—just like segmental encoding (Meyer, 1991; Schiller, 2005; van Turennout, Hagoort, & Brown, 1997; Wheeldon & Levelt, 1995)— then decisions to picture names with initial stress should be faster than decision latencies to picture names with final stress. The latter turned out to be the case (Schiller et al., 2005). However, Dutch—like other Germanic languages—has a strong preference for initial stress. More than 90% of the words occurring in Dutch have stress on the first syllable. Therefore, this stress effect might have been due to a default strategy. However, when pictures with trisyllabic names were tested, participants were still faster to decide that a picture name had penultimate stress (e.g., *asPERge* "asparagus") than that it had ultimate stress (e.g., *artiSJOK* "artichoke"; Schiller et al., 2005). This result suggests that metrical encoding proceeds from the beginning to the end of words, just like segmental encoding (see Figure 7.7).

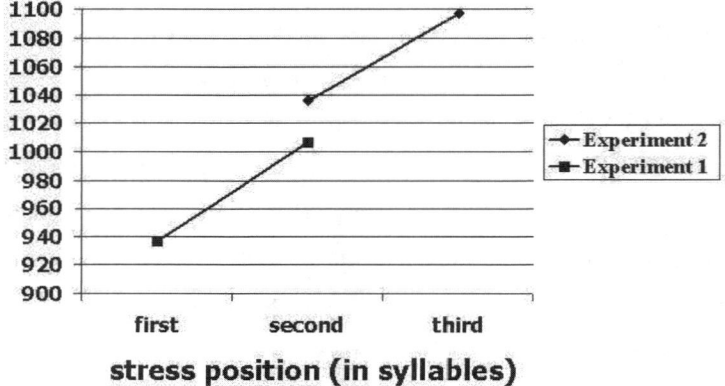

Figure 7.7.
Main results of Experiments 1 and 2 from Schiller et al. (2005). Symbols indicate different experiments. Target picture categories are depicted (left: first syllable stress such as *to.ren*; middle: second syllable stress such as *to.maat* or *as.per.ge*; right: third syllable stress such as *ar.ti.sjok*) on the x-axis; mean reaction times (monitoring latencies) in milliseconds on the y-axis.

Summary and Conclusion

This chapter summarized the role of the syllable in psycholinguistic models of speech production. A detailed model of phonological encoding was described. Evidence in favor of a model where syllables come into play at a relatively late stage in phonological encoding when syllable-sized units are accessed in a mental syllabary was presented. It was argued on the basis of reaction time data that syllables play a role in production planning. Furthermore, the nature of metrical frames was described and it was argued that lexical stress (realized on syllables) is encoded rightward incrementally. It is concluded that syllables fulfill their functional role as stress-bearing units at a late stage in speech production planning, i.e., when the mental syllabary is accessed. However, more research on phonological encoding and the syllabary is necessary to further specify aspects of syllabic representation in the syllabary.

References

Aichert, I., & Ziegler, W. (2004). Syllable frequency and syllable structure in apraxia of speech. *Brain and Language*, *88*, 148–159.

Ashby, J., & Rayner, K. (2004). Representing syllable information during silent reading: Evidence from eye movements. *Language and Cognitive Processes*, *19*, 391–426.

Bagemihl, B. (1995). Language games and related areas. In J. A. Goldsmith (Ed.), *The handbook of phonological theory* (pp. 697–712). Cambridge, MA: Blackwell.

Baumann, M. (1995). *The production of syllables in connected speech*. Ph.D. dissertation, Nijmegen University.

Bell, A. J., & Hooper, J. B. (Eds.) (1978). *Syllables and segments*. Amsterdam: North–Holland.

Blevins, J. (1995). The syllable in phonological theory. In J. A. Goldsmith (Ed.), *The handbook of phonological theory* (pp. 206–244). Cambridge, MA: Blackwell.

Berent, I., & Perfetti, C. A. (1995). A rose is a REEZ: The two-cycles model of phonology assembly in reading English. *Psychological Review*, *102*, 146–184.

Booij, G. (1995). *The phonology of Dutch*. Oxford: Clarendon Press.

Cholin, J., Schiller, N. O., & Levelt, W. J. M. (2004). The preparation of syllables in speech production. *Journal of Memory and Language*, *50*, 47–61.

Cholin, J., Levelt, W. J. M., & Schiller, N. O. (2006). Effects of syllable frequency in speech production. *Cognition*, *99* (2), 205-235.

Content, A., Meunier, C., Kearns, R. K., & Frauenfelder, U. H. (2001). Sequence detection in pseudowords in French: Where is the syllable effect? *Language and Cognitive Processes*, *16*, 609–636.

Costa, A., & Sebastián-Gallés, N. (1998). Abstract phonological structure in language production: Evidence from Spanish. *Journal of Experimental Psychology: Learning, Memory and Cognition*, *24*, 886–903.

Cowan, N., Braine, M. D. S., & Leavitt, L. A. (1985). The phonological and metaphonological representation of speech: Evidence from fluent backward talkers. *Journal of Memory and Language*, *24*, 679–698.

Crompton, A. (1981). Syllables and segments in speech production. *Linguistics*, *19*, 663–716.

Cutler, A. (1997). The syllable's role in the segmentation of stress languages. *Language and Cognitive Processes*, *12*, 839–845.

Cutler, A., Mehler, J., Norris, D., & Segui, J. (1983). A language-specific comprehension strategy. *Nature*, *304*, 159–160.

Dell, G. S. (1986). A spreading-activation theory of retrieval in sentence production. *Psychological Review*, *93*, 283–321.

Dell, G. S. (1988). The retrieval of phonological forms in production: Tests of predictions from a connectionist model. *Journal of Memory and Language*, *27*, 124–142.

Fallows, D. (1981). Experimental evidence for English syllabification and syllable structure. *Journal of Linguistics, 17*, 309–317.

Ferrand, L., Segui, J., & Grainger, J. (1996). Masked priming of word and picture naming: The role of syllabic units. *Journal of Memory and Language, 35*, 708–723.

Ferrand, L., Segui, J., & Humphreys, G. W. (1997). The syllable's role in word naming. *Memory & Cognition, 35*, 458–470.

Fromkin, V. A. (1971). The non-anomalous nature of anomalous utterances. *Language, 47*, 27–52.

Goldstein, L., & Fowler, C. A. (2003). Articulatory phonology: A phonology for public language use. In N. O. Schiller & A. S. Meyer (Eds.), *Phonology and phonetics in language comprehension and production: Differences and similarities* (pp. 159–207). Berlin: Mouton de Gruyter.

Guenther, F. (2003). Neural control of speech movements. In N. O. Schiller & A. S. Meyer (Eds.), *Phonology and phonetics in language comprehension and production: Differences and similarities* (pp. 209–239). Berlin: Mouton de Gruyter.

Hombert, J. M. (1973). Speaking backwards in Bakwiri. *Studies in African Linguistics, 4*, 227–236.

Hombert, J. M. (1986). Word games: Some implications for analysis of tone and other phonological constructs. In J. J. Ohala & J. J. Jaeger (Eds.), *Experimental phonology* (pp. 175–186). Orlando: Academic Press.

Janssen, P. D., Roelofs, A., & Levelt, W. J. M. (2002). Inflectional frames in language production. *Language and Cognitive Processes, 17*, 209–236.

Kenstowicz, M. (1994). *Phonology in generative grammar*. Cambridge, MA: Blackwell.

Ladefoged, P. (1982). *A course in phonetics*. San Diego: Harcourt Brace Jovanovich.

Lefkowitz, N. (1991). Talking backwards, looking forwards. The French language game Verlan. Tübingen: Narr.

Levelt, W. J. M. (1989). *Speaking. From intention to articulation*. Cambridge, MA: MIT Press.

Levelt, W. J. M., Roelofs, A., & Meyer, A. S. (1999). A theory of lexical access in speech production. *Behavioral and Brain Sciences, 22*, 1–75.

Levelt, W. J. M., & Schiller, N. O. (1998). Is the syllable frame stored? [commentary] *Behavioral and Brain Sciences, 21*, 520.

Levelt, W. J. M., & Wheeldon, L. (1994). Do speakers have access to a mental syllabary? *Cognition, 50*, 239–269.

Liberman, I. Y., Shankweiler, D., Fischer, F. W., & Carter, B. (1974). Explicit syllable and phoneme segmentation in the young child. *Journal of Experimental Child Psychology, 18*, 201–212.

McQueen, J. M., Dahan, D., & Cutler, A. (2003). Continuity and gradedness in speech processing. In N. O. Schiller & A. S. Meyer (Eds.), *Phonology and phonetics in language comprehension and production: Differences and similarities* (pp. 39–78). Berlin: Mouton de Gruyter.

Mehler, J., Dommergues, J. Y., Frauenfelder, U., & Segui, J. (1981). The syllable's role in speech segmentation. *Journal of Verbal Learning and Verbal Behavior, 20*, 298–305.

Meyer, A. S. (1990). The time course of phonological encoding in language production: The encoding of successive syllables of a word. *Journal of Memory and Language, 29*, 524–545.

Meyer, A. S. (1991). The time course of phonological encoding in language production: Phonological encoding inside a syllable. *Journal of Memory and Language, 30*, 69–89.

Ohala, J. J. (1998). Content first, frame later [commentary]. *Behavioral and Brain Sciences, 21*, 525–526.

Panconcelli-Calzia, G. (1934). *Die experimentelle Phonetik in ihrer Anwendung auf die Sprachwissenschaft* [Experimental phonetics in its application to linguistics]. Zweite, völlig umgearbeitete und erweiterte Auflage. Berlin: de Gruyter.

Rietveld, T., & Schiller, N. O. (submitted). Phonetic accounts of timed responses in syllable monitoring.

Roelofs, A. (1997). Syllabification in speech production: Evaluation of WEAVER. *Language and Cognitive Processes, 12*, 657–693.

Roelofs, A., & Meyer, A. S. (1998). Metrical structure in planning the production of spoken words. *Journal of Experimental Psychology: Learning, Memory, and Cognition, 24*, 922–939.

Schiller, N. O. (1998). The effect of visually masked syllable primes on the naming latencies of words and pictures. *Journal of Memory and Language, 39*, 484–507.

Schiller, N. O. (2000). Single word production in English: The role of subsyllabic units during phonological encoding. *Journal of Experimental Psychology: Learning, Memory, and Cognition, 26*, 512–528.

Schiller, N. O. (2004). The onset effect in word naming. *Journal of Memory and Language, 50*, 477–490.

Schiller, N. O. (2005). Verbal self-monitoring. In A. Cutler (Ed.), *Twenty-first century psycholinguistics: Four cornerstones.* (pp.245-261). Mahwah, NJ: Lawrence Erlbaum Associates.

Schiller, N. O., & Costa, A. (submitted). The role of the syllable in phonological encoding: Evidence from masked priming?

Schiller, N. O., Costa, A., & Colomé, A. (2002). Phonological encoding of single words: In search of the lost syllable (pp. 35–59). In C. Gussenhoven & N. Warner (Eds.), *Laboratory phonology 7*. Berlin: Mouton de Gruyter.

Schiller, N. O., Fikkert, P., & Levelt, C. C. (2004). Stress priming in picture naming: An SOA study. *Brain and Language, 90*, 231–240.

Schiller, N. O., Jansma, B. M., Peters, J., & Levelt, W. J. M. (2005). Monitoring metrical stress in polysyllabic words. *Language and Cognitive Processes, 21* (1-3),112-140.

Schiller, N. O., Meyer, A. S., Baayen, R. H., & Levelt, W. J. M. (1996). A comparison of lexeme and speech syllables in Dutch. *Journal of Quantitative Linguistics, 3*, 8–28.

Schiller, N. O., Meyer, A. S., & Levelt, W. J. M. (1997). The syllabic structure of spoken words: Evidence from the syllabification of intervocalic consonants. *Language and Speech, 40*, 103–140.

Selkirk, E. O. (1982). The syllable. In H. van der Hulst & N. Smith (Eds.), *The structure of phonological representations. Part II* (pp. 337–383). Dordrecht: Foris.

Sevald, C. A., Dell, G., & Cole, J. S. (1995). Syllable structure in speech production: Are syllables chunks or schemas? *Journal of Memory and Language, 34*, 807–820.

Shattuck-Hufnagel, S. (1979). Speech errors as evidence for a serial ordering mechanism in sentence production. In W. E. Cooper & E. C. T. Walker (Eds.), *Sentence processing* (pp. 295–342). New York: Halsted Press.

Treiman, R. (1983). The structure of spoken syllables: Evidence from novel word games. *Cognition, 15*, 49–74.

Treiman, R., & Danis, C. (1988). Syllabification of intervocalic consonants. *Journal of Memory and Language, 27*, 87–104.

Van Turennout, M., Hagoort, P., & Brown, C. M. (1997). Electrophysiological evidence on the time course of semantic and phonological processes in speech production. *Journal of Experimental Psychology: Learning, Memory, and Cognition, 23*, 787–806.

Wheeldon, L. & Lahiri, A. (1997). Prosodic units in speech production. *Journal of Memory and Language, 37*, 356–381.

Wheeldon, L. & Levelt, W. J. M. (1995). Monitoring the time course of phonological encoding. *Journal of Memory and Language, 34*, 311–334.

Wilshire, C. E., & Nespoulous, J. L. (2003). Syllables as units in speech production: Data from aphasia. *Brain and Language, 84*, 424–447.

White, C. M. N. (1955). Backwards languages in Africa. *Man, 55*, 96.

III: Perception /Action Relationships

8

The Emergent Syllable

John J. Ohala

Department of Linguistics

University of California, Berkeley

Berkeley, California, USA

It is a well-known principle in science that theories must be falsifiable or, as some have put it "unless a theory can be mortally threatened, it cannot live." It is in this spirit that I present the following arguments against the Frame/Content theory about the primacy of jaw oscillations and of the syllable in human speech. I therefore assume the role similar to "the loyal opposition" in the British Parliament. Similarly to other theories, the Frame/Content theory should not be passively accepted without a thorough weighing of alternatives.

The Historical Context of How Evolutionary Theories are Evaluated

A problem for all the sciences of evolution and development—whether phylogenetic or ontogenetic—is how to raise the standard of evidence in support of a theory on origins of an organism or behavior to a level where reasonable people can give it allegiance over competing theories. Darwin's theory of evolution via the natural selection of variants is an example. Experiments seemed not to be possible and quantitative data are difficult to obtain, unlike the case with physics and chemistry. (Today, however, quantification of genes largely overcomes the latter difficulty.) The answer to this issue is strengthening the theory by citing multiple case studies and interlocking point-by-point similarities. A single case study showing a posited pattern is not particularly convincing but 12, 25, 50 such cases showing the same pattern gives increasing credibility to the reality of the pattern. (Boë (this volume) shows how, in ideal cases, the necessary number of similarities can be estimated probabilistically. Darwin's *The origin of species* (1859) as well as his *The expression of the emotions in man and animals* (1872) are such large, fat, volumes because they are, for the most part, filled with case studies. The method of multiple case studies is one of the cornerstones of many sciences where measurements are difficult, e.g., evolution of behaviors, epidemiology, and historical linguistics.

It is instructive to examine the development of this method in historical (comparative) linguistics. Before this scientific breakthrough there were centuries of speculation on family relationships between languages, on the history of particular words, on cognate words in different languages (see, e.g., ten Kate (1723), de Broses (1765), Burnet (Lord Monody) (1773-1792). But there was very little rigor in establishing the similarities between words. Voltaire is reputed to have remarked, sarcastically, that in etymology "[similarity in] consonants count little, and vowels nothing." What the classical grammarians (Gyarmathi, Bopp, Rask, Grimm, among others) did, was to note point-by-point similarities and relationships among large numbers of words.

When comparing the candidate cognate words Latin *pater* and Gothic *fadar*, e.g., they pointed out similarities (e.g., the labiality and voicelessness of the initial consonants) as well as differences (e.g., stop in Latin but fricative in Gothic). The same pattern of similarities and differences appear in many other cognate pairs as exemplified in Table 8.1, where English cognates are given instead of Gothic. From this analysis, these early grammarians were able to extract the generalization that a voiceless stop in Latin corresponds to a homorganic fricative in Gothic (with certain positional exceptions). The number

Table 8.1.
A small sample of cognate words in Latin and English.

Latin	Germanic (English)
pisces	Fish
ped	Foot
tenuis	Thin
tres	Three
centum	Hundred
cornua	Horn
cannabis	Hemp

of regular interlocking similarities exceeded what any reasonable person would say could have originated by chance.

It is very difficult to achieve this level of confidence in any of the variety of interesting and colorful theories proposed on the origin of language and speech especially, I would maintain, on the relevance of concepts like syllabicity.

Chewing as the Seed of Speech

Regarding the origin of speech there have been various proposals that speech precursors are to be found in:

- chewing (Froeschels, 1951; MacNeilage, 1998; Weiss, 1950)
- sound imitation (de Brosses, 1765, and many others)
- iconic gestures of the tongue, lips, etc. made audible (Fonagy, 2001; Paget, 1923)
- physiologically common or necessary sounds (Müller, 1861)
- emotional sounds (cries) that were decoupled from their original stimulus, perhaps for purposes of deception (Müller, 1861)
- and dozens of others

Only one of these places any emphasis on action of the jaw originally associated with chewing.

My point is not to say that the articulations original to chewing were not the precursors to speech but rather to say that there is no way to evaluate this story vis-à-vis the others. All of them have their merits and demerits. As I pointed out elsewhere (Ohala, 1998), there are some points of dissimilarity between chewing and speaking, e.g., in chewing there is a significant lateral movement of the jaw that is missing from speech.

The Importance of Acoustic Modulations in Speech

But my primary misgivings about putting so much emphasis on jaw movements is not to say that they are unimportant but rather that they are subordinate to— or dependent on— an even more important principle of communication using the vocal-auditory channel (or any other channel, for that matter). This principle is that all signals must show syntagmatic contrast, i.e., modulation (Ohala, 1995).

In speech these modulations may be and are in any of several parameters: amplitude, fundamental frequency (F0), spectrum (location of spectral peaks, bandwidths of these peaks, spectral tilt), source characteristics (voicelessness, voicing, creaky voice, breathy voice, etc.), and duration (insofar as certain articulations have an expected or default duration, any deviation from the default constitutes a potential modulation or contrast that can be useful in signaling). Certainly movements of the jaw create modulations in amplitude and spectrum and, in some cases, periodicity, depending on the degree of closure of the jaw. But jaw movement by itself neglects F0 and neglects the fact that other articulatory gestures, especially those of the larynx, velum, the tongue, and the lips (without the help of the jaw) can create such modulations. Would anyone seriously want to argue that laryngeal or source modulations played a secondary role in early hominid vocal communication? For that matter, would anyone serious want to claim that source (laryngeal) modulations play a secondary role in early vocalizations of human infants? Crying, without rhythmic oscillations of any articulator, is the earliest vocalization exhibited by infants. As every parent recognizes, babies early on learn to de-couple crying from actual physical distress and use it to garner special benefits from caregivers. Is this a precursor of vocal symbolization? I make no claims on this point but the idea has as much superficial plausibility as the claim that the gestures found in chewing are the precursors of speech. Some authors have claimed that the first contrastive, i.e., truly linguistic, vocal signals in children involve use of intonation (e.g., Smith, N. V., 1973). When humans developed the cognitive capacity to recognize the signaling possibilities of vocal communication, i.e., when the vocal signals could symbolize and refer to something, is it not plausible that the usefulness of the source modulations would immediately present themselves, especially as these were certainly already familiar to them, being part of the vocal repertory of all known species using vocal-auditory communication (virtually all mammals, birds, some amphibians, some fish)? For the earliest vocal communication then, the syllable seems too advanced.

The Syllable: An Ill-defined Entity

In any case, I believe the notion of the syllable is too ill defined to propose it as a cornerstone of speech.

There have been numerous phonetically discredited definitions or "findings" regarding the nature of the syllable:

- Separate breath pulses that is, pulsatile contractions of the respiratory muscles (Stetson, 1928; but see Ladefoged, 1967; Ohala, 1990).

- Local maxima in vocal tract aperture. This proposal fails to account for the supposed monosyllabicity of words like *spa* or the bi-syllabicity of words in tone languages like [m̀má] or the bi- vs tri-syllabicity of contrasting words like English *lightning* vs. *lightening*.

- Local maxima in sound amplitude. Some of the above words constitute exceptions to this proposal, too.

The notion of "sonority" is often invoked in discussions of syllables: speech sounds are claimed to be arranged at the beginning of syllables in the order of increasing sonority and (perhaps) at the end of syllables in the order of decreasing sonority. The sonority scale (from least to most) is posited to be:

stops – fricatives – nasals – "liquids" – glides – vowels

Thus /ta tra mla smja/ obey this principle; /fta mta lma/ do not. But sonority is an empirically empty concept that can no more be determined for speech sounds than can their temperature (Ohala & Kawasaki-Fukumori, 1997). There is a viable alternative—I return to the idea that what matters is syntagmatic contrast.

Two fundamental changes—vis á vis the supposed sonority hierarchy—are proposed to account for syntagmatic phonological constraints, as outlined in Table 8.2. From this latter view there is nothing anomalous about English *spa*, Mandarin [sz] or [ʂ], words like [spsk] in Nez Perce. It also explains why sequences like the following are avoided in many languages even though they are easily articulated and obey the supposed sonority constraint: [ji wu bw-]. The reason: they make insufficient syntagmatic contrast.

In this new view the syllable is not a basic organizing principle. It is, rather, epiphenomenal; some language-specific organization of a *collection of parametic modulations* (of acoustic variables). Changes in the direction of modulation of one or more (especially more) of these parameters may be taken as "peaks" or "valleys" in the sequence of sounds. There is no plan behind them except, perhaps, for the weight of such patterns in other words in the languages lexicon. In this view the ambiguity in number of syllables in words like English *Brian* vs. *brine, towel* vs. *owl,* is to be expected: some of the modulations in the sound sequences are rather subtle.

I hasten to add, however, that what I've said does not imply that the syllable has no reality. It could be an emergent entity, a grouping that speakers impose on the stream of speech just as, for example, experienced typists impose on frequent letter sequences. If that is true it does not detract from the fundamental organizing principle in vocal-auditory signal systems of syntagmatic contrast which supercedes and may encompass whatever is meant by syllabicity.

Table 8.2.
Comparison of the constraints on sound sequencing. In the case of the proposed constraints under the "RIGHT" heading, the concept of the syllable is unnecessary.

WRONG	RIGHT
Trying to identify a single parameter, sonority, whose empirical correlates are elusive (or non-existent)	Identifying several parameters whose empirical correlates are well known, e.g., the acoustic parameters amplitude, periodicity, spectrum, F0, duration
Claiming that segments arrange themselves according to their inherent value of this parameter	Claiming that segments are arranged according to the relative differences in these parameter. The more these parameters differ between adjacent segments, the better and thus the more commonly they are found in the languages of the world.

Conclusion

My main points are these:

1. The Frame/Content theory that the rhythmic action of the jaw as seen in chewing is the basic frame for articulate speech is interesting but there is no compelling reason to give it any credence.

2. The claim that syllables are somehow the basic unit of speech neglects the difficulty of defining the syllable and neglects the possibility that the more fundamental principle governing speech structure is syntagmatic contrast, including especially source modulations.

References

Bloomfield, L. (1933). *Language.* New York: Holt.
Boë, L. J., Bessiere, P., Ladjili, N., & Audibert, N. (2008). Simple combinatorial considerations challenge Ruhlen's mother tongue theory In B. L. Davis & K.

Zajdo (Eds.), *The syllable in speech production* (pp. 63–93). London: Taylor & Francis.

de Brosses, Ch. (1765). *Traité de la formation méchanique des langues, et de principes physiques de l'étymologie.* 2 vols. Paris: Chez Saillant, Vincent, Desaint.

[Burnet, J. = Lord Monboddo]. (1773–1792). *Origin and progress of language.* (6 vols.) Edinburgh (various printers).

Darwin, C. (1859). *The origin of species.* London: John Murray.

Darwin, C. (1872). *The expression of the emotions in man and animals.* London: John Murray.

Fonagy, I. (2001). *Languages within language: An evolutive approach.* Amsterdam: John Benjamins.

Froeschels, E. (1952). Chewing method as therapy. *AMA Archives of Otolaryngology, 56,* 427–434.

ten Kate, L. (1723). *Aenleidning tot de Kennisse van het verhevene Deel der nederduitsche Sprake.* 2 vols. Amsterdam: Rudolph en Gerard Wetstein.

Ladefoged, P. (1967). *Three areas of experimental phonetics.* Oxford: Oxford University Press.

MacNeilage, P. (1998). The frame/content theory of evolution of speech production. *Behavioral and Brain Sciences, 21,* 499–511.

Müller, M. (1861). Lectures on the science of language, delivered at the Royal Institution of Great Britain in April, May, and June, 1861. London: Longman, Green, Longman, and Roberts.

Ohala, J. J. (1990). Respiratory activity in speech. In W. J. Hardcastle & A. Marchal (Eds.), *Speech production and speech modeling* (pp. 23–53.). Dordrecht: Kluwer.

Ohala, J. J. (1995). Speech perception is hearing sounds, not tongues. *Journal of the Acoustical Society of America, 99,*1718–25.

Ohala, J. J. (1998). Content first, frame later. *Behavioral and Brain Sciences, 21,* 525–527.

Ohala, J. J., & Kawasaki-Fukumori, H. (1997). Alternatives to the sonority hierarchy for explaining segmental sequential constraints. In S. Eliasson & E. H. Jahr (Eds.), *Language and its ecology: Essays in memory of Einar Haugen* (pp. 343–365). Berlin: Mouton de Gruyter.

Paget, R. (1930). *Human speech.* London: Kegan, Paul, Trench, Trubner & Co.

Smith, N. V. (1973). *The acquisition of phonology.* Cambridge: Cambridge University Press.

Stetson, R. H. (1928). *Motor phonetics: A study of speech movements in action.* [Archives néerlandaises de phonétique expérimentale, Tome 3].

Weiss, D. A. (1950). Chewing and the origin of speech. In: H. H. Beebe & D. A. Weiss (Eds.), *The chewing approach in speech and voice therapy* Sasel: Karger.

Young, T. (1819). Remarks on the probabilities of errors in physical observations, and on the density of the earth, considered, especially, with rega–rd to the reduction of experiments on the pendulum. *Philosophical Transactions of the Royal Society of London, 109,* 70–95.

9

Co-occurrence Patterns in the Babbling of Children with a Cochlear Implant *

Karen Schauwers [1,2]

Paul J. Govaerts [1,2]

and

Steven Gillis [1]

[1] *Department of Linguistics*

University of Antwerp

Antwerp-Wilrijk, Belgium

[2] *The Eargroup*

Antwerp-Deurne, Belgium

Prelexical babbling represents an important achievement in children's vocal development. Although the characteristics of babbling (i.e., onset, segmental content) have been studied intensively in the last twenty years or so, it still remains unclear to what extent this prelexical development is autonomous or driven by auditory input and feedback.

---

* The research reported in this paper was supported by a grant from the Science Foundation – Flanders, contract G.0216.05.

Studies of children's motor development seem to imply that the *onset* of babbling is an autonomous event and a motor milestone. Koopmans-van Beinum and van der Stelt (1986) found a particular order in the development of motor functions (including rolling from prone to supine, crawling, pulling up, etc.) in 51 normally developing children. Babbling occupies a specific position in that order. Other studies have argued that the onset of babbling represents a specific step in infants' overall rhythmic development. For instance, Thelen (1981) found a peak period of rhythmic hand-banging around the age of 6–7 months, the age at which babbling normally takes off.

Similarly, the *content* of babbling has been described as autonomous, viz. a direct result of the production of rhythmic mandibular oscillation (Davis & MacNeilage, 1995; MacNeilage & Davis, 1990a, 1990b): the oscillation of the mandible appears to be an independent rhythm generator in babbling. This theory is called the Frame Dominance Theory (henceforth: FDT), in which the term "Frame" applies to the regularity of mandibular oscillation accompanied by phonation resulting in the production of syllable-like output. Elevation of the mandible results in a consonant-like sound, while depression of the mandible results in a vowel-like sound. In this way, babbling (and early speech) is hypothesized to be based on rhythmic close-open movements or cycles of the mandible accompanied by phonation. The dominance of the Frame is considered to result from the virtual absence of an active role of articulators other than the mandible during babbled utterances. Each of the active articulators (i.e., tongue, lips, soft palate) is considered either to remain in resting position during the entire babbling utterance, or to assume a non-resting position at the beginning of the babbling utterance and to retain this position throughout. As a result of this pattern, serial interdependence is considered a hallmark of babbling utterances. This interdependence appears in its most obvious form in the strong trends toward concurrence of consonants (C) and vowels (V). There are two types of interdependency: intracyclical (between adjacent C's and V's) and intercyclical (between two adjacent CV syllables).

Intracyclically, three types of CV co-occurrence constraints are predicted based on FDT: a coronal consonant with a front vowel ("fronted" frames), a dorsal consonant with a back vowel ("backed" frames), and a labial consonant with a central vowel ("pure" frames: production by mandibular oscillation alone, without tongue preconfiguration). MacNeilage and Davis's (e.g., 1990a, 1990b) explanation for these co-occurrence patterns is the presence of a basic biomechanical constraint against tongue movements in the front-back dimension in the transition from the consonant to the vowel. These co-occurrence patterns are also characteristic of children's first words in English (Davis, MacNeilage, & Matyear, 2002) and in other languages studied (see Davis & MacNeilage, 2000 for a review).

Intercyclically, FDT has also implications for patterns of variegated babbling. FDT predicts a significantly higher proportion of changes in the vertical dimension than in the horizontal dimension for consonants as well as for vowels. This patterning is predicted based on the proposed predominance of mandibular over lingual movements in early canonical babbling. These changes in the amplitude of the mandibular cycle result in a stronger trend toward height over front-back dimension changes for vowels (e.g., /dædi/) and in manner over place changes for consonants (e.g., /bawa/).

MacNeilage, Davis, Kinney, and Matyear (1999) also found that the preferred CV co-occurrence patterns in babbling and early words are a recurrent typological pattern. Analyses of intrasyllabic trends in 10 typologically diverse languages revealed that the observed frequencies exceeded the expected frequencies of labial-central CV pairs in 7 languages, coronal-front CV pairs in 7 languages, and dorsal-back CV pairs in 8 languages.

In summary, production based physiological explanations suggest that at the onset of babbling, the serial organization of CV co-occurrences within syllables, and the across syllable variation patterns are not influenced by audition, but are controlled by motor constraints that apply to normally hearing (henceforth: NH) children as well as to hearing-impaired (henceforth: HI) children. The predictions of this theory have been confirmed in NH children supported by an increasing amount of evidence. However, far less evidence is available for HI children. Available evidence on these children with differing access to the auditory speech signal does not unequivocally support a physiologically based theory such as FDT. With regard to the onset of babbling, a pure production system based physiological explanation cannot account for the substantial delay of 15-18 months found in profoundly HI infants (Koopmans-van Beinum, Clement, & van den Dikkenberg-Pot, 2001; Oller & Eilers, 1988). Most HI children produce repetitive vocalizations, but these mainly consist of multiple V syllables without C's (Koopmans-van Beinum et al., 2001). Babbles with multiple CV syllables tend to occur only sporadically (less than 20% according to Oller & Eilers, 1988), and their frequency decreases with age in contrast to a clear increase (i.e., the babbling spurt) seen in NH children. McCaffrey, Davis, MacNeilage, and von Hapsburg (1999) reported the case of an English-learning child who received a cochlear implant (henceforth: CI) at 25 months. A CI is an electronic device that converts the incoming acoustic signal into a coded electrical stimulus that directly stimulates the auditory nerve, bypassing damaged or missing hair cells of the cochlea. The most important difference with conventional hearing aids is the ability of a CI not only to amplify the sound but also to restore the frequency resolution of the cochlea. At 7 and 9 months after implantation, a significant increase of syllabic productions occurred, suggesting that auditory input (by means of a CI) is necessary for the production of syllabic vocalizations. Schauwers, Gillis, Daemers, De Beukelaer and Govaerts (2004) provide evidence for the effect of auditory input and feedback on the onset of babbling: ten profoundly HI infants who received a CI before 20 months of age were followed longitudinally. The results show a linear correlation between the age at implantation and the onset of babbling. All 10 early implanted CI children started babbling within 4 months after the activation of the implant. Thus only the onset of babbling in the 4 youngest subjects occurred at a chronological age comparable to that of NH infants (viz., between 8 and 11 months of age). In addition, all children with a CI demonstrated a clear babbling spurt within 9 months after the activation of the implant.

With regard to babbling *content*, von Hapsburg (2003) performed CV co-occurrence analyses in a group of 6 English-learning children with a mild-to-severe hearing impairment and in a group of 5 English-learning profoundly HI children. The analyses confirmed that when the children produced canonical syllables, the labial-central and coronal-front patterns tended to co-occur at higher rates than other within-category co-occurrence patterns in both groups, similar to NH children. In terms of intercyclical organization, C and V variegation patterns showed higher proportions of V height variegation than front-back variegation, and higher proportions of C manner variegation than place variegation, again in line with predictions of the FDT. These results held for both HI groups.

The aforementioned child who received a CI at 25 months (McCaffrey et al., 1999) also produced significantly higher than expected co-occurrences of labial-central and coronal-front CV's after implantation, which is predicted by FDT. In addition, this CI child also demonstrated the expected preference for consonantal manner variegation, but not the expected height variegation of vowels. Overall, the authors concluded that the babbling utterances after implantation evidenced basic motor propensities, similar to NH children, once the child has had enough listening experience to trigger syllable-like output.

Given the present evidence, it seems that pre-canonical vocalizations may be physiologically driven and probably do not require auditory input, whereas the onset of rhythmic syllable-like vocalizations in canonical babbling requires auditory input. Whether the content of babbling utterances also requires auditory input remains unclear. Therefore, we investigated babbling in 10 profoundly HI children in a Dutch language environment who received a CI between 5 and 20 months of age. The basis of comparison is the babbling of 10 NH children from the same language environment. Several questions will be considered in this report: (1) Do CI and NH children differ from each other in the types of syllabic patterns they prefer to produce? (2) Is the distribution of intra- and intersyllabic babbling patterns in these CI and/or NH children consistent with the predictions put forward by the FDT? and (3) If not, do we see an influence of the environmental language on children's syllabic structure preferences?

Method

Participants

All study participants live in Flanders, the Dutch speaking part of Belgium. The study group consisted of 10 congenitally deaf children of hearing parents without other health problems such as cognitive or motor delays. The children's hearing loss was detected in a neonatal screening program within the first month of life, and a profound hearing impairment (i.e., an unaided pure-tone average or PTA of more than 90 dBHL in the better ear) was confirmed by auditory brain stem response in the first weeks of life. In 7 cases, the cause of deafness was genetic (5 of them were mutations in the connexine-26 gene, which is a commonly found cause of congenital deafness). Nine infants received bilateral hearing aids within 1–4 months after detection of the hearing loss, one child at 8 months after detection. After wearing the hearing aids for several months without any progress (only one child reached a PTA within the speech area with his hearing aids, viz., 47 dBHL), all children received a multichannel Nucleus-24 CI (Cochlear Corp., Sydney, Australia) between 5 and 20 months of age. The PTA with the CI, as measured by pure-tone audiometry at the age of 2 years, increased to 28–53 dBHL, and all children were able to discriminate a set of speech sound contrasts immediately after activation of the implant as assessed by means of the Auditory Speech Sound Evaluation (ASSE, P.J. Govaerts, Antwerp-Deurne, Belgium). All children were raised orally with support of a limited number of signs. Table 9.1 gives an overview of the auditory characteristics of the CI children.

A control group of 10 NH children of hearing parents was selected, and informed consent from the parents to participate in this study was obtained. This group was followed starting at a chronological age of 6–8 months. The recordings were discontinued as soon as the child produced at least 50 word

Table 9.1.
Overview of the auditory characteristics of the CI children.

Subject	PTA unaided (dBHL)	PTA aided (dBHL)	PTA with CI (dBHL) at age 2;0	Age at implantation	Age at activation
RX	117	107	42	0;5.5	0;6.4
AN	120	120	30	0;6.21	0;7.21
MI	120	108	53	0;8.23	0;9.20
YA	103	63	28	0;8.21	0;9.21
EM	115	113	33	0;10 0	0;11.20
RB	117	77	43	1;1.7	1;2.4
AM	120	120	48	1;1.15	1;2.27
KL	93	47	38	1;4.27	1;5.27
JO	113	117	48	1;6.5	1;7.9
TE	112	58	38	1;7.14	1;9.4

types as assessed by the Dutch MacArthur CDI vocabulary list (Zink & Lejaegere, 2002) (range 1;6–1;10). One NH child dropped out at the age of 0;11. No health or developmental problems were present in these NH children.

Data Collection and Transcription

In order to monitor the prelexical period in the CI and NH children, we relied on monthly video recordings taken at their homes. Digital recordings of approximately 60–80 minutes were obtained starting from the first month after activation of the cochlear implant in the case of the CI children, and from the chronological age of 6–8 months in the case of the NH children. Six CI children were also recorded once before implantation. The video sessions consisted of spontaneous unstructured interactions between the child and a parent (and in some cases a sibling).

From each recording a sample of approximately 20 minutes was selected. The sampling procedure was done by the same person for all recordings and aimed at selecting delineated sequences of interactions. Subsequently, these selections were transcribed and annotated according to the CHAT conventions (MacWhinney, 2000). Transcription consisted of an orthographic transcription of the adult's utterances, and an orthographic and phonemic annotation of the lexical items of the child. For the children's prelexical utterances, a dedicated coding system was adopted, which has been described in more detail in Schauwers et al. (2004). Briefly, each vocalization (and more specifically, each "comfort sound") was coded in terms of phonation (uninterrupted or interrupted) and articulation (no articulation, one articulation, or 2+ articulations) according to the model proposed by Koopmans-van Beinum et al. (1986). Each utterance also received a CV-code, i.e., the utterance was broken up into a sequence of consonant- and vowel-like elements. The characteristics of each segment— C or V—were defined in terms of the place and manner of articulation for consonant-like elements, and in terms of the height and the front-back dimension for vowel-like elements. In most cases, the video images provided additional visual information to determine the segmental characteristics.

The Age Period Studied

For each CI and NH participant, data analysis was initiated when the child started canonical babbling, and ended when the child produced at least 10 word types. To determine the age at which the child produced at least 10 different words, we followed the procedure for identifying words proposed by Vihman and McCune (1994). Henceforth, this period is referred to as the *babbling period.*

The onset of babbling in these 10 CI and 10 NH children was reported in Schauwers et al. (2004). The NH children started babbling between 6 and 8 months of age, and the CI children started babbling between 8 and 21 months of age. The CI children produced their first 10 words between the ages of 17 to 26 months. This resulted in a median of 7.5 sessions used for data analysis in the CI group. The NH children reached their 10-word stage between 14 and 20 months of age, resulting in a median of 11.5 sessions for data analysis. One NH child discontinued participation in the study after 6 sessions (from 6 to 11 months of age).

In this paper we will report data of the children's babbling from the onset of babbling up to the 10-word point. For the NH children our database consists of 14,918 babbled syllables (average: 1,492; range: 645–2,643) and 11,921 babbled syllables from CI children (average: 1,192; range: 276–2,354).

Analysis of the Serial Organization of Babbling

Intrasyllabic Co-occurrences

For the analysis of CV co-occurrence patterns, all CV syllables in the corpus of the CI children and the NH children were selected, independently of their position within an utterance. The consonant in each CV syllable was coded in terms of its place of articulation (coronal, labial, dorsal). Vowels were coded as front, central, or back. This approach yielded a 3×3 matrix reflecting the 9 possible co-occurrences of C and V.

In order to assess the predominance of particular CV co-occurrences, we used the same approach as Davis and MacNeilage (1995): the actual prevalence of each CV co-occurrence was compared to its "expected prevalence." The expected prevalence of a CV co-occurrence was calculated from the overall frequencies of the individual consonants and the individual vowels in the corpora (= (row total $\times$ column total) / total of observed CV's). This result represented the prevalence that a specific CV occurs in case of a completely random combination of C's and V's. If the child prefers to use a particular CV sequence rather than other combinations, the observed prevalence of this CV would be higher than the expected prevalence and the ratio of the observed prevalence to the expected prevalence would be higher than 1. This ratio was used to test the FDT proposed by MacNeilage and Davis (1990a, 1990b; Davis & MacNeilage, 1995): three of the nine possible types of CV co-occurrences are predicted to be produced preferentially during babbling, viz. coronal consonants with front vowels (e. g., /ti/), labial consonants with central vowels (e.g., /ma/), and dorsal consonants with back vowels (e.g., /ku/).

Statistical analyses were used to test whether the observed prevalence of each CV-occurrence differed significantly from its expected prevalence. To obtain these results, we converted the binomial parameters (N = total number of

CV-occurrences for one child, p = expected prevalence of a CV-occurrence) into the parameters of a normal distribution with a mean = N*p and a standard deviation = $\sqrt{(N*p*(1-p))}$. This conversion yielded a z-value for each observed CV pattern. The cut-off level for significance was set at 0.05 (-1.96< z < 1.96). Statistical analyses were also used to test whether the observed prevalence of the different CV patterns was different between the NH and CI subjects. To calculate these results, Mann-Whitney U tests were performed with a cut-off level of significance of 0.05.

Inter-syllabic Patterns

The analyses of inter-syllabic patterns were carried out to determine how consonants (place versus manner) and vowels (height versus front-back dimension) varied from one CV syllable to the next. Therefore, all possible pairs of successive CV syllables in the corpora of the CI and NH children were selected. In utterances with more than two syllables, each syllable, except the first and last one, was analyzed twice: once as the first of two syllables and once as the second. If the two syllables were the same, the sequence was characterized as reduplicated. A variegated sequence was defined as a CVCV sequence in which the consonants or the vowels or both were different from each other with regard to place and/or manner of articulation for the C's, and front-back dimensions and/or height for the V's. Voicing differences were not considered.

FDT makes two clear predictions about inter-syllabic variegation patterns: (1) for V's, higher proportions of V height changes are expected than front-back changes; and (2) for C's, more manner variegation is expected than place variegation. A Wilcoxon matched pairs test was carried out to evaluate these predictions within each group (NH and CI). A Mann-Whitney U test was used to investigate whether the observed variegations were different between the NH and the CI group. Cut-off levels of significance were set at 0.05 for all tests.

Table 9.2.
Intrasyllabic CV co-occurrence ratios in the babbling of 10 NH and 10 CI children.

	Front	Central	Back
NH			
Coronal	** 1.2 **	1.0	0.7
Labial	0.7	** 1.0 **	1.4
Dorsal	1.1	1.1	** 0.7 **
CI			
Coronal	** 1.6 **	0.8	0.7
Labial	0.5	** 1.2 **	1.4
Dorsal	0.8	1.3	** 0.9 **

Results

Intrasyllabic Co-occurrences

The co-occurrence matrix of intrasyllabic CV correlations during the babbling period of the NH children and the CI children are given in Table 9.2. The table displays ratios of observed / expected prevalences: the rows represent the articulation places of the C's (coronal, labial or dorsal) and the columns the front-backness of the V's (front, central or back). Black fields mark ratios that are statistically significant from 1 ($p < 0.05$); double asterixes (**) mark ratios that are predicted to be higher than one according to FDT.

For both the NH and the CI group, significantly more Coronal-Front and Labial-Back co-occurrences were observed than expected and significantly less Labial-Front and Coronal-Back co-occurrences were observed than expected. No significant between-group differences were found when comparing the NH and CI children.

Intersyllabic Patterns

Table 9.3 and Figure 9.1 show types of intersyllabic variegations in the NH and the CI children. The NH children show significantly less C variegation than V

Table 9.3.
Types of intersyllabic variegations in the NH and the CI children (median values).

	NH	CI
Vowel	32%	46%
Consonant	24%	21%
Both	41%	28%

variegation (p<0.05) or mixed variegation (p<0.01). Similarly, the CI children show significantly more V variegation than C variegation (p<0.01) or mixed variegation (p<0.05). The CI children show significantly more V variegation than NH children (p<0.05) and significantly less mixed variegation (p<0.01).

Table 9.4 shows the types of intersyllabic C (manner or place) and V (height or front-backness) variegations. In case the intersyllabic variegations consisted of both C and V variegation, half a count was allotted as C variegation and half as V variegation. In both groups (NH and CI) manner variegation is predominant for C's (p<0.05) as predicted by FDT. However, findings about the front-back variegation for V's (p<0.01) contradict the prediction set forth by the

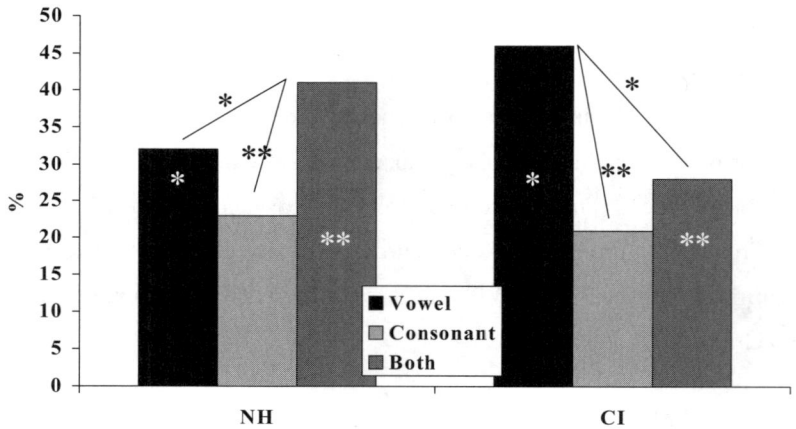

Figure 9.1.
Types of intersyllabic variegations in the NH and the CI children. * and ** mark significant within-group differences at p<0.05 and p<0.01. White * and ** mark significant between-group differences at p<0.05 and p<0.01.

FDT. No statistically significant differences were found between the NH and CI groups. The CI children showed less combined C variegations (place AND manner) than the NH children (25% and 35%, respectively), but this difference was not statistically significant.

Discussion

The present study addressed babbling of early implanted deaf children, with an emphasis on syllabic organization. Deaf children are known to vocalize similarly to hearing children. However, their canonical babbling is retarded or may not occur at all (Oller & Eilers, 1988). In a previous report it was shown that cochlear implantation can initiate the onset of babbling (Schauwers et al., 2004). In this paper, we analyzed NH and CI children's babbles in order to test some of the predictions of the FDT related to serial organization of syllable-like output.

Intrasyllabic Co-occurrences

All children showed a higher than expected intrasyllabic co-occurrence of predicted coronal consonants with front vowels. However, labial consonants also co-occurred with back vowels (Table 9.2). In contrast, the co-occurrence of coronal consonants with back vowels was less than expected, similarly to the co-occurrence of labial consonants and front vowels. Neither of these two co-occurrences is predicted by FDT. No differences were found between the CI group and the NH group in terms of these co-occurrence patterns.

Table 9.4.
Types of intersyllabic consonant and vowel variegations (median values).

	NH	CI
Consonant		
Manner	58%	63%
Place	42%	37%
Vowel		
Front-Back	65%	64%
Height	35%	36%

The findings in the NH group and the CI group are not in line with the FDT. The FDT predicts a high prevalence of coronal-front, labial-central and dorsal-back (the diagonal line in Table 9.2). Only one of these predicted co-occurrences is statistically higher than expected in both groups (viz., coronal-front). The dorsal-back co-occurrence pattern tends to be less prevalent than expected, although again without statistical significance. The ratio is less than 1 in 8 out of 10 NH children and in 7 out of 10 CI children. The other 6 co-occurrence patterns should occur less than expected according to the FDT. This is only the case in 2 of these 6 co-occurrences (viz. the coronal-backs and the labial-fronts). The other co-occurrences have expected prevalence with a ratio of about 1.0. Hence, the strongest unpredicted pattern relative to expectations of FDT is the labial-back co-occurrences (with a ratio of 1.4) in both NH and CI children ($p<0.05$). To a lesser degree, the high prevalence of dorsal-centrals do not favor the FDT either (not statistically significant in either group).

Currently, no working hypothesis exists to explain the observed prevalence of the unpredicted CV co-occurrence patterns. One possible explanation is that these patterns reflect the intrasyllabic co-occurrence patterns of the Dutch language. In order to investigate this possibility, we analyzed the CELEX Dutch lexical database (Baayen, Piepenbrock, & Gulikers, 1995). The phonemic transcriptions of all the word forms from this database (N = 347,150) were investigated, and the word form initial consonant-vowel sequences were categorized and analyzed in the same way as the babbles of our study groups. All 9 possible CV co-occurrences showed ratios that differed from 1 with statistical significance ($p<0.05$), but again not as predicted by the FDT. Two out of 3 co-occurrences that are anticipated to have a high prevalence did so, viz., the coronal-front and the dorsal-back combinations (with ratios of 1.1 for both). However, the labial-central combination had a ratio of 0.9. Similarly, only 4 out of 6 co-occurrences were anticipated to have a low prevalence did so, viz., the coronal-central, coronal-back, labial-front and dorsal-front combinations (with ratios of 0.9, 0.9, 0.9 and 0.7, respectively). The labial-back and dorsal-central combinations had ratios of 1.1 and 1.3, respectively. So whereas the CELEX-data are also not in line with the FDT, they may be able to explain the findings in the babbling of NH children. Indeed, those co-occurrences that have been observed with statistically higher than expected prevalence in the NH children, also occur more often in CELEX. This is the case for the coronal-fronts and the labial-backs. And likewise, those co-occurrences that have been observed with statistically lower than expected prevalence in the NH children also occur less often in CELEX. This is the case for the labial-fronts and the coronal-backs.

Variegation

In both the NH and the CI children, intersyllabic V variegation occurs more often than C variegation. Isolated C variegation is relatively rare in both groups (24% and 21%, respectively; see Table 9.3 and Figure 9.1). However, due to the high number of mixed variegations of V and C, a substantial amount of C variegation was found in the NH children. Overall, 65% of the variegated babbles exhibited C variegation in this population. In contrast, the mixed type of variegation was far less prevalent in the CI children (28%, p<0.01). Thus, although the total frequency of V variegation was similar to that found in NH children, the total frequency of C variegation was less frequent (49%) than in NH children (65%). As mentioned in the results, the types of C and V variegation were not different between the NH and the CI group (more C manner variegation and more V front-back variegation, see Table 9.4). Nevertheless, less combined C variegations were seen in the CI group (25% instead of 35% in the NH group), although not statistically significant.

FDT makes two clear predictions about intersyllabic variegation patterns: (1) for V's higher proportions of V height changes are expected than front-back changes; and (2) for C's more manner variegation is expected than place variegation. Consonant variegation in NH and CI infants' babbling is well in accordance with the FDT predictions: manner variegation (58% and 63%, respectively) is more frequent than place variegation (42% and 37%, respectively). However, V variegation is not in accordance with the predictions of FDT, in either group. Both groups show a preference for front-back variegation (65% and 64%, respectively) instead of height variegation (35% and 36%, respectively).

In order to trace possible influences of the ambient language, we turned to the CELEX lexical database and analyzed consecutive syllables in the Dutch word forms that exhibit both C and V variegation or only C or V variegation (N=406,431). The CVCV sequences were analyzed according to the same categories as the children's babbling data. In Dutch word forms, place variegation (52%) is more frequent than manner variegation (48%). Thus, although the observed C variegation in NH children corroborates the predictions of the FDT, the language that they hear does not. This type of finding supports a production system based argument over a perceptual argument. With respect to V variegation, the word forms from the CELEX database analyzed (N=397,003), revealed a picture that is quite in agreement with the predictions of FDT: height variegation constitutes 59% of all cases and front-back variegation 41%. Yet, NH children appear to prefer otherwise! How can these contradictory findings be reconciled? At present, we can only speculate on the reason. First of all, the data selected from CELEX are types, and hence all frequency data are type frequencies. It may well be the case that instead of type frequencies, token frequencies are required and that type and token frequencies provide different patterns. This topic remains to be investigated. Secondly, CELEX constitutes a database of adult written language. Although it is common practice to consult the CELEX lexical database for frequency data of all sorts, and although frequency differences found in CELEX are often reflected in differences in psycholinguistic experiments, it remains unclear how far findings from this database can be generalized for comparison with spontaneous speech. More specifically, it remains to be investigated whether the syllabic patterns in the spoken language of parents (i.e., infant-directed speech style aka. "motherese") is similar to the distribution of those patterns in the CELEX lexical database.

In conclusion, the babbling content of young implanted deaf children is very similar to that of NH children in Dutch. Intrasyllabic co-occurrence patterns are the same, with a preference for coronal consonants with front vowels and labial consonants with back vowels. Intersyllabic analysis shows similar variegation patterns as such, with more vowel than consonant variegation and mainly manner variegation for consonants and height variegation for vowels. Yet the variegation in CI children seems to be less complex than in NH children. Fewer combinations of consonant AND vowel variegation are observed with less consonant variegation as a result. Whenever there is consonant variegation, it appears to be preferentially simple variegation (manner OR place) rather than complex (manner AND place).

These data suggest the importance of the production system as well as the importance of perceptual learning from the ambient language. They partially support the FDT for intersyllabic patterns but not for intrasyllabic patterns. Observed consonant variegation is in accordance with the FDT. Preferences for CV co-occurrences seem to be more driven by the ambient language than by the FDT, although the ambient language does not seem capable to explain all observed data. Importantly, it remains to be investigated whether analyzing genuine child directed speech would help to understand the origin of these patterns better than utilizing data from adult lexical databases such as CELEX for comparison.

References

Baayen, R. H., Piepenbrock, R., & Gulikers, L. (1995). *The Celex Lexical Database* (Release 2) [CD-ROM]. Philadelphia: Linguistic Data Consortium, University of Pennsylvania.

Davis, B. L., & MacNeilage, P. F. (1995). The articulatory basis of babbling. *Journal of Speech and Hearing Research, 38*, 1199–1211.

Davis, B. L., & MacNeilage, P. F. (2000). An embodiment perspective on the acquisition of speech perception. *Phonetica, 57*, 229–241.

Davis, B. L., MacNeilage, P. F., & Matyear, C. (2002). Acquisition of serial complexity in speech production: A comparison of phonetic and phonological approaches to first word production. *Phonetica, 59*, 75–107.

Koopmans-van Beinum, F. J., Clement, C. J., & van den Dikkenberg-Pot, I. (2001). Babbling and the lack of auditory speech perception: A matter of coordination? *Developmental Science, 4*, 61–70.

Koopmans–van Beinum, F. J., & van der Stelt, J. M. (1986). Early stages in the development of speech movements. In R. Zetterström (Ed.), *Precursors of early speech* (pp. 37–50). New York: Stockton.

MacNeilage, P. F., & Davis, B. (1990a). Acquisition of speech production: Frames, then content. In M. Jeannerod (Ed.), *Attention and performance*, vol. 8 (pp. 453–476). Hillsdale: Erlbaum.

MacNeilage, P. F., & Davis, B. L. (1990b). Acquisition of speech production: The achievement of segmental independence. In A. Marchal (Ed.), *Speech production and speech modeling* (pp. 55–68). Dordrecht: Kluwer Academic Publishers.

MacNeilage, P. F., Davis, B. L., Kinney, A., & Matyear, C. L. (1999). Origin of serial-output complexity in speech. *Psychological Science, 10*, 459–460.

MacWhinney, B. (2000). The CHILDES Project: Tools for analyzing talk: Transcription format and programs (3rd ed.). Mahwah, NJ: Lawrence Erlbaum Associates.

McCaffrey, H. A., Davis, B., MacNeilage, P. F., & von Hapsburg, D. (1999). Multichannel cochlear implantation and the organization of early speech. *The Volta Review, 101*, 5–29.

Oller, D. K., & Eilers, R. E. (1988). The role of audition in infant babbling. *Child Development, 59*, 441–449.

Schauwers, K., Gillis, S., Daemers, K., De Beukelaer, C., & Govaerts, P. (2004). Cochlear implantation between 5 and 20 months of age: The onset of babbling and the audiologic outcome. *Otology & Neurotology, 25*(3), 263–270.

Thelen, E. (1981). Rhythmical behavior in infancy: An ethological perspective. *Developmental Psychology, 17*, 237–257.

Vihman, M. M., & McCune, L. (1994). When is a word a word? *Journal of Child Language, 21*, 517–542.

von Hapsburg, D. (2003). *Auditory constraints on infant speech acquisition: A dynamic systems perspective.* Unpublished doctoral dissertation, University of Texas, Austin.

Zink, I., & Lejaegere, M. (2002). N-CDIs: Lijsten voor Communicatieve Ontwikkeling: Aanpassing en hernormering van de MacArthur CDIs van Fenson et al. Leuven: Acco.

10

The Development of Consonant-Vowel Syllables in Children Following Cochlear Implantation

Jan Allison Moore

Department of Communication Sciences and Disorders

The University of Texas at Austin

Austin, Texas, USA

Multichannel cochlear implantation has been a viable option for providing access to sound for children with bilateral profound sensorineural hearing loss for over twenty years. A cochlear implant (CI) is a surgically implanted prosthesis which bypasses damaged structural or functional abnormalities of the cochlea to provide electrical stimulation of remaining neural elements in the cochlea and auditory nerve. This electrical stimulation leads to a percept of sound. However, hearing through a CI is highly compromised in terms of temporal and frequency resolution, as well as dynamic range of the input signal (Wilson, 1997). Despite these compromises, there is considerable evidence that children can use this signal to develop speech, oral language, and reading skills (Geers, 2003; Spencer, Barker, & Tomblin, 2003; Svirsky, Robbins, Kirk, Pisoni, & Miyamoto, 2000).

A CI system consists of surgically implanted hardware, externally worn hardware, and software to program the device. The surgically implanted device consists of a receiver stimulator, magnet and electrode array. The externally worn hardware includes a microphone, speech processor, and transmitting coil (which also contains a magnet). The magnetic coupling of internal and external hardware allows for the alignment of transmitting and receiving antennas, which makes transcutaneous transmission of the signal possible. The speech processor is programmed with manufacturer-specific software, allowing for adjustment of each patent's individual tolerance for electrical stimulation and preference for sound. Currently, three manufacturers produce cochlear implants approved by the Food and Drug Administration (FDA) for children as young as 12 months of age presenting with bilateral profound sensorineural hearing loss.

Children in the United States have been implanted with CIs since the early 1980s. Since then, most research has concentrated on documenting development of speech perceptual abilities in this population. There has been relatively little focus on identifying speech production patterns in implanted children. Unfortunately, even less emphasis has been given to documenting the emergence of the earliest stages of speech.

The Frame/Content theory (F/C Theory) proposed by MacNeilage and Davis (2000) offers a framework in which to investigate the development of early speech in children following cochlear implantation. The F/C theory attempts to explain the serial organization of speech in typically developing infants. According to the hypothesis, constraints of the child's oral-motor system, rather than the perceptual system, form the primary driving force in patterning of highly predictable syllable shapes. These shapes include the "pure frame" or Labial consonant (e.g., [b, m]) followed by a central vowel (e.g., [a]), the Dorsal consonant (e.g., [k, g]) followed by the back vowel (e.g., [u, o]), and the Coronal consonant (e.g., [t, d, s]) followed by a front vowel (e.g., [e, æ]). These preferred co-occurrence patterns do not appear to be sensitive to the child's ambient language. These typical syllable patterns have been documented in at least 11 different languages through the analyses of both dictionary entries and raw data from adults, young children, and infants (Davis & MacNeilage, 2000; MacNeilage, Davis, Kinney, & Matyear, 2000).

Several researchers have investigated syllable development following cochlear implantation (e.g., McCaffrey, Davis, MacNeilage, & von Hapsburg, 2000; Moore, J. A., Davis, & Tobey, 2004; Prath, 2004; von Hapsburg, 2003). These studies have described in great detail the emergence of speech patterns in a small number of children who have received implants. Detailed analysis of the results allows one to reflect on individual differences. However, the limited data available do not yet provide support for the robust generalization of the F/C theory to this population.

This paper will investigate the development of consonant-vowel (CV) syllable shapes in children with profound deafness who received their implants at different ages. The research questions addressed include the following: 1) Do children with CI follow the expected CV syllable patterns predicted by the F/C theory? 2) Does the age of implantation impact the organization of syllables following CI? 3) How does the examination of group data contribute to the understanding of early speech development in children with CI? 4) How does the serial organization of CV syllables change over time following implantation? 5) What other variables may account for the observed patterns of CV development?

Method

Participants

Fifty-seven children who had received a CI participated in the study. Fifty-five of the children received their implant at The University of Iowa Hospitals and Clinics and are participants in a long-term clinical research program. One child was implanted at The University of Texas Southwest Medical Center in Dallas, Texas and one child was implanted at Brackenridge Hospital in Austin, Texas. The children presented with various etiologies of deafness. All had the onset of deafness by 18 months of age, prior to the development of a full auditory-oral language system. All children presented with bilateral profound hearing loss and minimal or no benefit from appropriately fit amplification prior to implantation.

Table 10.1.
Participant groups and characteristics

Group	Number of Children	Mean age of CI Activation	Range of CI Activation	Data Intervals	Initial Speech Processing Strategy
1	7	19 m; 1 y 7 m	12-27 m	12 m	SPeak, ACE
2	7	33 m; 2 y 9 m	30-37 m	24-48 m	MPeak
3	17	44 m; 3 y 8 m	40-58 m	12-48 m	MPeak
4	16	66 m; 5 y 6 m	61-80 m	12-48 m	MPeak
5	10	132 m; 11y	100-170 m	12-48 m	MPeak, SPeak

None of the children presented with secondary handicapping conditions. Fifty-six of the children had hearing parents. American English was the primary oral language spoken in the home. One child had Spanish as his primary language input. The children were grouped into six categories based on age-of-implantation. The groups and number of participants in each group are shown in Table 10.1 It should be noted that the age-of-implantation ranges are quite diverse across the groups. An attempt was made to stratify the data into more discrete groups. However, insufficient data did not allow for the completion of the statistical analysis. Data for Group 1 was limited to the 12-month post-implant-interval. Data for Group 2 were very limited at the 12 month interval (n=2) but more complete at the other age intervals.

All children in Groups 2-6 used sign supported speech (SSS), a manual code for English (MCE) coupled with spoken English. Sign supported speech was utilized at home as well as in the child's educational environment. Six of the seven children included in Group 1 were exposed to SSS, and used it in varying degrees to develop receptive language skills but none of the children in this group utilized sign as their primary mode of expressive communication. The child from the Spanish-speaking home was not exposed to any sign system at any point during his habilitation. Most of the children attended regular education programs in their home communities with support services which might include a sign language interpreter as well as a speech-language pathologist and teacher of the hearing-impaired. Two of the children attended oral preschool educational programs designed specifically for children with hearing loss.

Device and Speech Processing Strategy

All children were implanted with Cochlear Corporation Nucleus 22 or 24 devices. All children were fit with the most current speech processor and processing strategy available at the time of implantation. The majority of the children were initially fit with the MPeak (Multi-Peak) speech processing strategy (see Table 10.1). This strategy employs 4 to 6 electrodes across the 22 available stimulating electrodes in the cochlea to deliver frequency information of the auditory signal. The strategy operates at a speed of 250 electrical pulses per channel per second, resulting in a maximum of 1500 pulses per second for MPeak. The newer SPeak (Spectral Peak) and ACE (Advanced Combination Encoder) strategies utilize more electrodes for better frequency resolution. The ACE strategy operates at a faster overall rate (14400 pulses per second maximum) for improved temporal resolution of the input signal. For all strategies, the individual patient's electrical dynamic range determines the range of perception for intensity of the signal. All input signals were contained within the dynamic range to avoid auditory discomfort to the patient. The internal components of the Nucleus 22 and 24 devices differ slightly in that the Nucleus 24 device has a slimmer profile, allowing for a less invasive surgical procedure and the addition of two additional ground electrodes. The actual electrode array and number of stimulating electrodes in the two devices was identical. With each advancement in speech processing strategy, overall speech perception scores in adults have increased significantly; however, there is no evidence speech processing strategy or device used has an impact on the emergence of syllable organization explored in the current study (Davis & Morrison, 2004).

Data Collection

Speech data were obtained at yearly intervals for all participants. All sessions were video taped and later transcribed. For children in Groups 2–5, a story re-tell task was utilized to generate a spontaneous, yet structured, speech sample (Tye-Murray, Spencer, & Woodworth, 1995). Data were collected in a laboratory environment. The story-retell task consisted of 6 short stories supported by picture cues. The examiner presented the stories in simultaneous speech and sign (MCE) along with the picture support. Children were asked to retell the story and to use their best speech. Participants who were not capable of forming a narrative were directed to describe the pictures.

The speech samples for children in Group 1 were obtained in spontaneous interaction with their parent or caregiver with both a standard set of toys designed by the author to elicit a variety of vowels and consonants, and toys that were typically used in the family environment. Data were collected in the child's home and in the laboratory. Longitudinal data gathered over 4 years following implantation were analyzed to determine whether there is change in the preferred CV syllable shapes over time.

Data Transcription, Agreement, Reliability, and Analysis

Due to the longitudinal nature of the data set, a number of transcription and reliability protocols were utilized. For children in Groups 2-5, the data were transcribed broadly IPA by two trained Speech-Language Pathologists and percent agreement was calculated (Tye-Murray et al., 1995). Inter-observer agreement averaged 74%. For 37 of the children in Groups 2–5, transcriptions were provided by The University of Iowa Hospitals and Clinics. For 13 of the children in Group 3, the video tapes were also transcribed by the author and trained graduate student clinicians. Thirty percent of each session was transcribed for reliability. Point to point agreement was calculated and exceeded 89% correct for all speech samples for those 13 children. Children in Group 1 have had transcription performed by trained graduate student clinicians. Ten percent of the sample was transcribed for reliability. The Logical International Phonetics Programs or LIPP (Oller & Delgato, 1993) reliability module was utilized to calculate reliability. Inter-observer agreement exceeded 90% for all the children in Group 1. The data were entered into the LIPP program for subsequent analyses of accuracy and syllable shape. Target productions were determined by the child's sign productions along with the overall context of the child's interactions with toys or with their parents.

Data for each group and age interval post implant were analyzed for intrasyllabic CV productions in words for Groups 1-5 and for babbling for Group 1. Babbling was defined as brief, speech-like vocal productions consisting of one or more consonants and vowels not associated with a target production. Laughing, crying, and other non-speech vocalizations were not transcribed. At the word level, intrasyllabic CV patterns in the child's productions were analyzed and compared to their target forms, in an attempt to quantify their accuracy. Syllables including glottals (e.g., /h/) were excluded from the analysis because these speech sounds are not produced in the oral cavity. Syllables were classified according to the F/C theory by place of articulation and observed-to-expected ratios calculated to determine if each pattern occurred significantly above chance. In addition, Chi-square tests of significance were performed for each age interval and group to determine if the observed co-occurrence patterns occurred significantly greater than chance.

Results

Results will be presented in two ways; as a function of hearing age or time post-implantation and over time, considering of the age of activation of the CI.

Table 10.2.
Consonant-vowel co-occurrence patterns observed at the 12-month post-implant interval for word and babbling productions.

Group	N	CV co-occurrence patterns Observed	Syllables Analyzed	Statistically Significant
1	7	**CF, LC,** LB **DB**	1286	Yes
3	14	CC, LF, LB, DC	271	No
4	15	CC, LF, LB, DC	411	Yes
5	9	CC, LF, LB, DC, CB	256	Yes

Post-Implant Interval Across Groups

12-months Post-Implant

CV co-occurrence patterns for this post-implant interval are shown in Tables 10.2 and 10.3. Values exceeding 1.0 indicate CV patterns exceeding chance. Patterns bolded in the shaded boxes are consistent with the F/C theory. Those patterns bolded in unshaded boxes are occurring at greater than chance levels but are not consistent with the frame dominance theory. Chi-square tests of significance exceeded chance for CV productions for Groups 1, 4, and 5 at the 12–month interval. There was insufficient data available for Group 2 to complete statistical analysis. Chi-square tests of significance for the target forms exceeded chance for all groups of children at the 12 month interval.

Data for Group 1 (n=7) was limited to one time interval, 12-months post-implant. A total of 1286 CV syllables were obtained across the 7 children in babbling and word attempts. Predicted CV co-occurrence patterns consistent with the F/C theory were observed (Coronal-Front, Labial-Central, Dorsal-Back) at greater than expected levels. In addition, one other preferred pattern inconsistent with the frame dominance was also observed (Labial-Back syllables). The CV patterns observed occurred significantly greater than chance for the group over all ($\chi 2$ (df = 4) = 16.61, p < .001). A comparison of production forms with target forms in Table10.3 indicates that production and target forms were similar. The youngest group of children (Group 1) showed patterns consistent with the Frame Content theory. Co-occurrence patterns such as Dorsal-Front and Coronal-Back

Table 10.3.
Observed-to-expected ratios for CV co-occurrence patterns at 12 months post implant.

Group	Vowel	Production Consonant Coronal	Labial	Dorsal	Target Consonant Coronal	Labial	Dorsal
1	Front	1.12	0.88	0.88	1.12	0.90	1.19
	Central	0.93	1.11	0.93	0.72	1.24	0.49
N=7	Back	0.89	1.06	1.29	1.49	0.57	1.94
3	Front	0.94	1.05	0.93	0.83	1.22	1.02
	Central	1.17	0.86	1.20	1.32	0.49	1.36
n=14	Back	0.71	1.24	0.66	0.78	1.40	0.53
4	Front	0.84	1.31	0.63	0.90	1.26	0.73
	Central	1.10	0.66	1.55	1.15	0.53	1.69
n=13	Back	1.06	0.99	0.90	0.97	1.16	0.64
5	Front	0.34	1.49	1.07	0.81	1.41	0.48
	Central	1.24	0.79	1.07	1.43	0.28	1.50
N=5	Back	1.00	1.05	0.84	0.83	1.22	1.03

found in the targets were not observed in productions of the youngest children (see Table 10.3). These children produced simpler forms consistent with frame dominance.

Insufficient data was available in Group 2 to complete analysis at the 12-month post-implant interval. For Group 3, several preferred patterns of CV production were observed, but co-occurrences were inconsistent with frame dominance. Statistical analysis of the preferred CV co-occurrence patterns was also non-significant (χ^2 (df = 4) = 8.66, non-significant). The two oldest groups of children (Groups 4 and 5) showed statistically significant CV patterns; however, the patterns observed did not correspond with the F/C predicted patterns. Overall, the speech patterns of two oldest groups of children appeared remarkably similar in their production of CV syllables at 12 months post-implant. Children in Group 4 showed a statistically significant (χ^2 (df = 4) = 24.63, p < .00) preference for the following syllable shapes: Coronal-Central (CC), Coronal Back (CB), Labial-Front (LF), and Dorsal-Back (DB). The oldest group of children in Group 5 had greater than expected productions of Coronal

Table 10.4.
CV co-occurrences observed at the 24 month post-implant interval for word productions. The CV patterns of Coronal-Front (CF), Labial-Central (LC), and Dorsal-Back (DB) are shown in bold.

Group	n	CV co-occurrence patterns Observed	Syllables Analyzed	Statistically Significant
2	6	**CF**, CB, LF, DC	239	Yes
3	16	CC, LF, LB, DC	535	Yes
4	15	CC, LF, LB, DC	568	Yes
5	9	CC, CB, LF, LB, DC	471	No

/Central (CC), Coronal Back (CB), Labial Front (LF), Dorsal Front (DF) and Dorsal Back (DB) syllables. These patterns were statistically different from those occurring by chance (χ^2 (df = 4) = 18.98, significant). Although the children in Groups 3 and 4 did not show a preference for intrasyllabic patterns consistent with frame dominance, the results reflected CV patterns consistent with the target word form patterns shown in Table 10.3.

24 months Post-Implant

Data from children in Groups 2–5 were analyzed at the 24-month post implantation interval. Results at the 24-month interval are shown in Tables 10.4 and 10.5. Values exceeding 1.0 indicate CV patterns exceeding chance. Patterns bolded in the shaded boxes are consistent with F/C predictions. Patterns bolded in unshaded boxes are occurring at greater than chance levels but are not consistent with the frame dominance predictions. For all groups except the oldest group, Group 5, the observed data showed statistically significant intrasyllabic co-occurrence patterns in their syllable production. However, only the youngest implant group, Group 2, showed patterns consistent with F/C theory. Group 2 children showed a significant preference for Coronal-Front syllables (χ^2 (df = 4) = 49.64, significant).

However, they also showed preferred patterns of production for other syllable shapes not predicted by F/C (Coronal-Back, Labial-Front, and Dorsal-Central). For CV syllables produced by the three oldest groups of children (Groups 3–5), a statistically significant preference was shown for intrasyllabic

Table 10.5.
Observed-to-expected ratios for CV co-occurrence patterns at 24 months post implant.

Group	Vowel	Production Consonant			Target Consonant		
		Coronal	Labial	Dorsal	Coronal	Labial	Dorsal
2,	Front	**1.00**	**1.38**	0.21	0.92	**1.21**	0.13
	Central	0.68	0.74	**2.18**	**1.21**	0.61	**2.10**
n=6	Back	**1.33**	0.93	0.50	0.88	**1.15**	0.90
3,	Front	0.94	**1.14**	0.71	0.90	**1.24**	0.60
	Central	**1.09**	0.73	**1.69**	**1.22**	0.49	**1.78**
n=16	Back	0.98	**1.11**	0.66	0.88	**1.27**	0.63
4,	Front	0.82	**1.18**	0.89	0.97	**1.17**	0.44
	Central	**1.22**	0.67	**1.44**	**1.26**	0.46	**1.88**
n=15	Back	0.90	**1.23**	0.57	0.75	**1.42**	0.65
5,	Front	0.84	**1.19**	0.92	0.89	**1.15**	0.97
	Central	**1.09**	0.83	**1.18**	**1.19**	0.65	**1.43**
n=9	Back	**1.02**	**1.07**	0.82	0.90	**1.23**	0.56

co-occurrence patterns not predicted by the F/C Theory. Group 3 showed a preference for Coronal-Central, Labial-Front, Labial-Back, and Dorsal-Central CV syllable productions ($\chi2$ (df = 4) = 25.88, significant) Children in Groups 4 and 5 showed a highly similar preference for the same syllable shapes as Group 3 (CC, LF, LB, and DC). All of these preferences occurred greater than would be expected by chance for children in Group 4 ($\chi2$ (df = 4) = 38.18, significant).

For children in Group 5, statistical significance was not observed ($\chi2$ (df = 4) = 9.16, non-significant). When the word forms produced by the children were compared to the target words, it was concluded that children were able to match the target CV forms consistently at 24 months following implantation.

36 Months Post-Implant

Results for the 36-mont post implant age interval are shown in Tables 10.6 and 10.7. At the 36 month post-implant interval, all children, regardless of age of implant showed a preference for the following intrasyllabic syllable shapes: Coronal-Central, Labial-Front, and Labial-Back. For Group 2, the youngest

Table 10.6.
Consonant-vowel co-occurrences observed at the 36 month post-implant interval for word productions.

Group	n	CV co-occurrence patterns Observed	Syllables Analyzed	Statistically Significant
2	7	CC, LF, LB, DF, DB	291	No
3	14	CC, LF, LB, DF, DC	503	Yes
4	15	CC, LF, LB, DC	822	Yes
5	9	**CF**, CC, LF, LB, DC	391	Yes

children in this comparison, a preference was also observed for Dorsal-Front and Dorsal-Back syllables. Although Dorsal-Back CV syllable shapes are predicted by F/C, the findings did not reach statistical significance (χ^2 (df = 4) = 4.35, non-significant). The Coronal-Central, Labial-Front, Labial-Back, and Dorsal-Central syllable shapes were preferred significantly by the children in Group 3 (χ^2 (df = 4) = 44.76, significant), children in Group 4 (χ^2 (df = 4) = 46.84, significant), and children in Group 5 (χ^2 (df = 4) = 14.15, significant). In addition, the children in Group 3 also showed a preference for the Dorsal-Front syllable shape. Similarly to the other age intervals, target and production CV forms matched consistently across all age groups of children.

.

48 Months Post-Implant

Children at 48 months following implantation showed remarkably similar preference for CV syllable shapes, regardless of the age in which they obtained CI (see Table 10.8). All children showed statistically significant preferences for the following CV syllable productions patterns: Coronal-Central, Labial-Front, Labial-Back, and Dorsal-Central. These patterns are not consistent with the predictions of the F/C theory.

Chi-Square analysis was significant for syllable productions in Group 2. ($\chi2$ (df = 4) = 29.81, significant), Group 3 (χ^2 (df = 4) = 86.35, significant), Group 4 (χ^2 (df = 4) = 33.98, significant) and Group 5 (χ^2 (df = 4) = 19.63, significant). In addition, children in the oldest group, Group 5, also showed a significant preference for the Dorsal-Front and Coronal-Back CV syllable

Table 10.7.
Observed-to-expected ratios for CV co-occurrence patterns at 36 months post implant.

36 m		Production			Target		
Group	Vowel	Consonant			Consonant		
		Coronal	Labial	Dorsal	Coronal	Labial	Dorsal
2,	Front	0.86	1.12	1.00	0.86	1.24	0.76
	Central	1.26	0.83	0.92	1.26	0.46	1.73
n=7	Back	0.94	1.02	1.06	0.92	1.21	0.63
3,	Front	0.71	1.27	1.03	0.79	1.28	0.84
	Central	1.24	0.63	1.44	1.33	0.52	1.45
n=14	Back	0.95	1.25	0.38	0.87	1.22	0.68
4,	Front	0.85	1.32	0.62	1.06	1.04	0.56
	Central	1.18	0.66	1.36	1.28	0.42	1.61
n=15	Back	0.91	1.14	0.89	0.51	1.85	0.58
5,	Front	1.07	1.07	0.65	1.02	1.10	0.41
	Central	1.03	0.82	1.37	1.22	0.43	1.94
n=8	Back	0.85	1.26	0.71	0.75	1.49	0.68

shapes. Once again, these results were inconsistent with the predictions of the F/C theory as shown in Table 10.9.

Age Of Implant Over Time Within Groups

Group 2

Children in Group 2 had their CIs activated at an average age of 33 months. Due to the small number of children in this group (n=6), there was not enough data available at the 12-month post-implant interval to perform statistical analysis. The results of analysis at the 36-month interval indicated non-significant differences. Patterns of CV production over the 24 and 48 month post-activation intervals showed a preference for Labial-Front and Dorsal-Central CV productions. Inconsistency in preference for CV productions over time was observed for all other CV patterns, indicating that preferred patterns observed at the 24-month interval (Coronal-Front, Coronal-Back) were not observed at the 48-month interval.

Table 10.8.
Consonant-vowel co-occurrences observed at the 48-month post-implant interval for word productions.

Group	n	CV co-occurrence patterns Observed	Syllables Analyzed	Statistically Significant
2	6	CC, LF, LB, DC	303	Yes
3	17	CC, LF, LB, DC	831	Yes
4	14	CC, LF, LB, DF, DC	811	Yes
5	9	CC, CB, LF, LB, DF, DC	284	Yes

Groups 3, 4, and 5

CV production patterns produced by the oldest groups of children over time were remarkably similar. The average age of CI activation for the three groups (Groups 3, 4 and 5) was 44 months, 66 months and 132 months, respectively. However, in the oldest group of children (Group 5) the range of age of activation was much greater than in the other two groups. Despite these age differences, preference for specific CV shapes were similar and stable across time. The Coronal-Central, Labial-Front, Labial-Back, and Dorsal-Central CV shapes were most consistently produced over time for all the children following activation of the CI. Although some other CV patterns were also produced, these patterns were not produced consistently. Group 5 had the most diversity in syllable shapes produced. However, the overriding finding was that the patterns were stable from 12 to 48 months post implant and most often did not match the predictions of F/C. Syllable shapes matched their target forms accurately and the targets did not match the expected CV patterns found in American English.

Discussion

It is interesting to consider these divergent results in view of the preponderance of evidence in the typically developing population that hearing children organize their speech following the patterns of CV syllables specified in the F/C theory. There could be a number of factors which lead children with cochlear implants to develop patterns of syllable organization different from those observed in typically developing peers.

Table 10.9.
Observed-to-expected ratios for CV co-occurrence patterns at 48 months post implant.

48 m		Production				Target		
Group	Vowel	Consonant				Consonant		
		Coronal	Labial	Dorsal		Coronal	Labial	Dorsal
2,	Front	0.80	1.29	0.76		1.07	1.04	0.41
	Central	1.27	0.53	1.57		1.14	0.60	2.00
N=6	Back	0.89	1.24	0.62		0.77	1.36	0.65
3,	Front	0.74	1.35	0.69		0.84	1.29	0.67
	Central	1.24	0.57	1.61		1.29	0.48	1.54
n=17	Back	0.97	1.17	0.57		0.82	1.31	0.71
4,	Front	0.85	1.16	1.05		0.90	1.25	0.69
	Central	1.21	0.66	1.16		1.20	0.55	1.48
n=14	Back	0.89	1.24	0.80		0.89	1.23	0.79
5,	Front	0.69	1.31	1.24		0.76	1.41	1.07
	Central	1.13	0.67	1.20		1.17	0.58	1.29
n=5	Back	1.15	1.13	0.46		1.03	1.16	0.45

First, due to the nature of their deafness, these children are not typical. Regardless of the acquisition of audibility provided by the CI, their infancy and, for many children, the majority of their preschool years were spent without usable hearing. The signal provided by the CI is compromised in terms of temporal resolution, frequency resolution, and distinctions within a compressed dynamic range. Following a prolonged period of deafness, audibility alone may not be sufficient to lead to typical CV syllable development. One can see that, in the youngest group, there is a trend to develop more typical syllable shapes. However, these children also produce other syllable shapes not predicted by the F/C theory.

A second issue to be considered is that all of the children in Groups 2 to 5 used a sign system to represent English. The data certainly differ from those gathered from hearing children and from the dictionary counts of syllables previously reported because the children with CI are choosing to use combined voice and sign for some segments of the story and to use sign alone for other words. This strategy leads to a preponderance of preferred spoken words in the sample. For example, the most prevalent word produced in the data across all children was "the" which would be categorized as a Coronal-Central production. Another preferred word was "boy," a Labial-Back production. Interestingly, when one examines the script of the stories told to the children, there is a balance of male and female characters and prevalent use of gender-based pronouns, so the children themselves are using the words "the" and "boy" spontaneously to try to retell the story.

A third issue to consider are the overall language abilities of the children in both speech and sign. These children, even the high performers, exhibit significant delays in oral language development (Svirsky et al., 2000; Yoshinaga-Itano, 2000). In general, language abilities of children with cochlear implants may not match those found in typically developing peers explored by MacNeilage and Davis in their work across language groups. Analysis of the target forms of the words attempted shown in Tables 10.3–10.5 suggest that the children are making accurate attempts of the target forms produced. However, the target forms do not mirror the syllable structure in the language of hearing children who are developing typically. Explicit predictions of the F/C theory suggest that the environmental language is irrelevant for predicting intrasyllabic co-occurrence patterns. In the sample of children with CIs who are implanted after the age of three, language use is likely a very relevant factor in their speech development patterns.

Perhaps the most critical confound in this data set is the story-retell task itself. The task described in this paper was developed to assess speech (Tye-Murray, et al., 1995) and was felt to be advantageous because the stories define the topic of the narrative and makes identification of target words less ambiguous than a free language sample, given the poor speech intelligibility of the children immediately following implantation. Story retell tasks have been used widely as a means to assess the narrative skills of children; however, it is possible that this method would not be appropriate in fine-grained analysis of the nature of the distribution of syllable patterns in speech.

Analysis of the clinician model of the stories bears out this finding. A type-token analysis of the 6 stories indicated a total of 247 words with 99 different words, indicating a type token ratio of .40 indicating a diversity of lexicon used in the samples. Chi-square tests of significance exceeded chance for CV productions of the clinician model; however, the clinician model of CV patterns did not match the patterns expected by frame dominance or the patterns observed in standard American English. However, the CV patterns found in the to produce a preponderance of certain words. The distribution of CV syllable shapes in the clinician model is found in Table 10.10.

Examination of the production and target forms of the three oldest groups of children (Groups 3–5) indicate the children were very accurate in replicating targets. Although the speech samples generated via the story retell task may be adequate to measure global speech production accuracy overtime, it appears this methodology would be inadequate to capture the nature of the distribution of speech sounds or syllable shapes in children. Researchers who investigate narrative language skills in typically developing children and those with language disorders have found that story retell tasks involving pictorial support like the one used in this study lead to language which was manufactured and less natural than narratives elicited with a story generation task (Swanson, Fey, Mills, & Hood, 2005).

Therefore, the task likely biased the sample in some aspects due to these children's poor speech and language skills which led to a preponderance of productions of certain words. However, the same biases have been identified in a free play sample where parents or clinicians encourage multiple productions of key words rather than engaging in conversational exchange with their child. It appears that either methodology can potentially bias the results when working with children with severe language and speech delays, in contrast with children with normal hearing and typical speech and language skills.

Table 10.10.
Observed-to-expected ratios for CV co-occurrence patterns for the clinician model in the story-retell task.

Vowel	Consonant		
	Coronal	Labial	Dorsal
Front	.75	1.27	1.28
Central	1.41	.32	.93
Back	.79	1.52	.72

A fifth issue to consider is the level of sophistication in speech skills prior to implantation. Due to the age at which many of the children received their implant, the structure and quality of the child's speech attempts prior to receiving the implant can not be discounted. Similarly, the maturity of the children's oral-motor mechanism prior to implantation is likely an important factor to consider. Previous works (Higgins, Carney, McCleary, & Rogers, 1996; Moore, 1998) suggest that these children may have preferred patterns of speech production, or the patterns may include non-English types of productions (Chin, 2002). Many patterns identified are deviant and violate the patterns of English phonemes. For many children, audition alone is not sufficient to overcome these patterns. Additionally, it is evident by the preponderance of Labial-Front syllable shapes across all groups that the children with CI still rely heavily on visual properties of speech behavior as these cues provide a model for their own production. Preference for Dorsal-Central and Coronal Central patterns of production might lead us to hypothesize that less visible consonants are followed by neutral vowel productions because the child may limit the use of their oral cavity and produce neutral vowels as a default.

Finally, the children in Groups 2 to 5 utilized a more primitive speech processing strategy than Group 1. It is highly compromised in terms of both frequency and temporal resolution and may contribute to the observed patterns. The MPeak strategy utilized 4 frequency channels at a relatively slow rate as compared to the ACE strategy.

Conclusions

The production of CV syllables as predicted by F/C was observed in the youngest group of children which attests to the primary assumptions of the theory, that the oral motor characteristics of the infant's system given audibility is paramount in the serial organization of early speech. As the age of implantation drops below 12 months of age, we will have the unique opportunity to assess the development of speech in children with CIs at an age which mirrors that of their hearing age-matched peers.

Results from the older groups of children illustrate the critical importance of the task in the assessment of speech production patterns. Although the older children showed intrasyllabic patterns of speech distinctly different from both typically developing children and that of adult speech, their patterns mirrored the clinician model and their own target forms. From the current data set we can not confirm or refute the nature of frame dominance in the serial organization of speech production of older children following cochlear implantation. We can say that many of the children acquire intelligible speech overtime which speaks to the resiliency of these children following years of profound deafness after cochlear implantation.

Acknowledgments

This project was supported by The National Institutes of Health (P50 DC 00242, The University of Iowa Hospitals and Clinics Department of Otolaryngology; R01 HD 277733, The University of Texas at Austin) and the Texas Advanced Research Project. The author expressed gratitude to both The University of Iowa and The University of Texas at Austin for their continued support and cooperation.

References

Davis, B. L., & Morrison, H. M. (2004). *Emergence of inter- and intrasyllabic vocalization patterns in young cochlear implant users.* International Conference on Newborn Hearing Screening, Diagnosis, and Intervention, Cernobbio (Como), Italy: May 27–29, 2004.

Chin, S. B. (2002). Aspects of stop consonant production by pediatric users of cochlear implants. *Language, Speech, and Hearing Services in Schools, 33,* 38–51.

Geers, A. (2003). Predictors of reading skill development in children with early cochlear implantation. *Ear & Hearing, 24* (1S), 59S–68S.

Higgins, M. B., Carney, A. E., McCleary, E., & Rogers, S. (1996). Negative intraoral pressures of deaf children with cochlear implants: Physiology, phonology, and treatment. *Journal of Speech and Hearing Research, 39,* 957–967.

Lee, S.A. (2003). The phonetic basis of early speech acquisition in Korean. Unpublished doctoral dissertation, The University of Texas at Austin. Texas, USA.

MacNeilage, P. F., & Davis, B. L. (2000). On the origin of internal structure of word forms. *Science, 288*, 527–530.

MacNeilage, P. F., Davis, B. L., Kinney, A., & Matyear, C. L. (2000). The motor core of speech: A comparison of serial organization patterns in infants and languages. *Child Development, 71* (1), 153–163.

McCaffrey, H. A., Davis, B. L., MacNeilage, P. F., & von Hapsburg, D. (2000). Multichannel cochlear implantation and the organization of early speech. *The Volta Review, 101* (1), 5–28.

Moore, J. A. (1998). Speech outcomes with cochlear implants: Preliminary results. *Journal of the Academy of Rehabilitative Audiology, 31*, 1–11.

Moore, J. A., Davis, B. L., & Tobey, E. (2004). *Application of Frame-Content Theory to infant speech productions following cochlear implantation.* Poster presented at The International Conference on Newborn Hearing Screening Diagnosis and Intervention, Cernobbio (Como), Italy: May 27–29, 2004.

Oller, D. K., & Delgato, R. E. (1993). *Logical International Phonetics Programs* [Computer software]. Miami, FL: Intelligent Hearing Services.

Prath, S. (2004). *Vocalizations of a 2-year-old Spanish speaking child with a cochlear implant: A case study.* Unpublished master's thesis, The University of Texas at Austin, Austin, Texas, USA.

Tye-Murray, N., Spencer, L., & Woodworth, G.G. (1995). Acquisition of speech by children who have prolonged cochlear implant experience. *Journal of Speech and Hearing Research, 38*, 327–337.

Spencer, L. J., Barker, B.A., & Tomblin, J. B. (2003). Exploring the language and literacy outcomes of pediatric cochlear implant users. *Ear & Hearing, 24* (3), 236–247.

Swanson, L. A., Fey, M.E, Mills, C. E., & Hood, L.S. (2005). Use of narrative-based language intervention with children who have specific language impairment. *American Journal of Speech-Language Pathology, 14*, 131–143.

Svirsky, M., Robbins, A., Kirk, K., Pisoni, D., & Miyamoto, R. (2000). Language development in profoundly deaf children with cochlear implants. *Psychological Science, 11*, 153–158.

von Hapsburg, D. (2003). *The development of speech in children with varying levels of hearing.* Unpublished doctoral dissertation, The University of Texas at Austin, Austin, Texas, USA.

Wilson, B. S. (1997). The future of cochlear implants. *British Journal of Audiology, 31*, 205–225.

Yoshinaga-Itano, C. (2000). *Early identification and intervention: Deaf and hard-of-hearing children of hearing parents.* Paper presentation at the Academy of Rehabilitative Audiology Summer Institute. Snowbird, UT: June 9–11, 2000.

11

Frames and Babbling in Hearing Infants

Florien J. van Beinum

Institute of Phonetics Sciences / ACLC

University of Amsterdam

Amsterdam, The Netherlands

There is a famous story about the ancient Greek forces intending to expand their influence and power. When they arrived at the borders of their territory, they met unknown, unintelligible people who only produced sounds similar to "ba...ba...ba." So the ancient Greeks called them "Barbarians." Herodotus in his "Historiae" (about 450 B.C.; 1926) also mentions that the ancient Egyptians, upon meeting people that did not speak their language, called them "barbarous." In probably the same way, the Russians at their borders met people that, unlike the Mongols, spoke an unintelligible language belonging to the Ural-Altaic language family (Williams, 2001). Hearing their sounds as similar to "ta...ta...ta," they would have named them "Tatars." Obviously, the continual open-close alternation in combination with phonation (actually being "frames" as defined by MacNeilage & Davis, 1990) was perceived as primitive communication of savage, unintelligible persons. The similarity of these vocalization structures with infants' babbling appears evident. These cyclic movements constituting syllabicity by concatenating frames of open-close alternation seem to be one of the most striking characteristics of speech production (MacNeilage, 1998). But is it indeed this concatenation of frames that makes babbling so special within the development of speech since it constitutes the base for syllabicity? Do these "frames" appear at once out of the blue? To answer these questions, we will discuss the hierarchical structure of infants' speech development from birth cry towards babbling and will consider the elements necessary for babbling behavior. Further, we will compare speech development of hearing and deaf infants to better understand the role of audition in the onset of babbling and the use of syllables.

Sensori-Motor Stages in Speech Development

A few decades ago our Amsterdam speech development research group started to study early speech development as a sensori-motor system, based on universal principles of movements of the human speech production instrument: the lungs, the larynx, and the vocal tract (Koopmans-van Beinum & van der Stelt, 1986, 1998). By classifying infants' sound productions in terms of phonation and articulation movements, a hierarchical structure of developmental stages could be demonstrated. It became obvious that speech production in normally hearing children develops in a highly organized way. Due to the universality of the speech production instrument, the sensori-motor classification system was very well suited for describing and comparing the speech development of children who are on their way to becoming users of their mother tongue. But since it was unclear as to what extent early infant vocalization was anatomically and physiologically governed and which aspects represented influences of auditory input and feedback, comparison of the sound productions of very young deaf infants with normally hearing infants was necessary. One question that needed to be examined was why deaf infants do not start babbling in their first year of life (Oller & Eilers, 1988).

When studying the speech communication instrument from the very beginnings, the temporal difference between the perception and the production aspects are quite obvious. Well before birth, the child's auditory system is already able to register various types of sounds (Lecanuet, 1998). In the fifth month of pregnancy, the fetus in the uterus can hear features of sound (e.g., broad-band noise, pure tones, medium and high frequencies, high pressure level). At birth, the infant's auditory system has been functioning intensively for months and has been processing a good deal of information.

For the sound production instrument, the situation at birth is fundamentally different. Apart from sucking and swallowing movements, and from breathing movements, i.e., regular, repetitive movements of the diaphragm that can be seen as prenatal preparatory movements (de Vries, Visser, & Prechtl, 1984), the speech production instrument has not been so active in the uterus. Considering how evolution works, this is hardly a surprise. The actual sources of sound production in infancy are: 1) the lungs and *respiration*, first stimulated during the birth cry; 2) the larynx making *phonation* movements; and 3) the vocal tract making *articulation* movements. Respiration in the neonate is controlled in a rather reflexive way, the other two functions are both secondary: the primary function of the larynx is protecting the lungs, whereas the primary function of the vocal tract at birth is in sucking, chewing, and swallowing.

By basing our description of infant utterances on *phonation* and *articulation* movements, speech development is reduced to its basic characteristics of making movements by means of the speech production instrument. Another advantage of using this approach for the analysis of sound production development is that the early infant sound production system can thus be easily linked up with the generally accepted *"source-filter"* model for adult speech production (Fant, 1960). Within this model, the larynx acts as the basic sound source, whereas subsequently the sound is filtered by the varying shape of the vocal tract and by the movements of the articulation organs.

Human speech is characterized by pitch, loudness, timbre, and duration perceptually, and by periodicity, intensity, spectral components, and physical duration acoustically. Variation, timing, and coordination of the phonation and articulation movements in the speech production mechanism provide segmental as well as supra-segmental speech characteristics, such as vowels, consonants, syllables, intonation patterns, pauses, rate, and rhythm, used in specific languages in diverse ways.

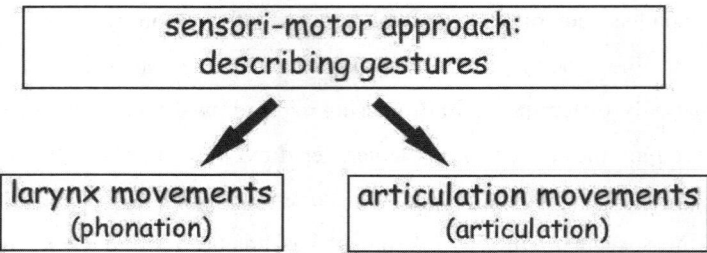

Figure 11.1.

Source-filter model for speech production, applied to the description of infant speech development.

From birth onwards, the infant is equipped with this source-filter system. This system, in principle, is the same source-filter system that adults use during speech production. As a result, our model is pre-eminently suited for the description of infant speech development, as it is for adult speech as well. Thus, this model provides us with the possibility for indicating where in the developmental course the universal, anatomically and physiologically based character of the infant's sound productions become overruled by language-specific features, or where features that reveal the influence of the speech input of the surrounding ambient language can be located.   This model is shown graphically in Figure 11.1.

Building Blocks in Infant Speech Development

Phonation

In order to consider the development of the various building blocks of infant speech separately, we have to start with phonation, which is present from birth. As stated by MacNeilage (1998): *"Infants are born with the ability to phonate, which involves the cooperation between the respiratory and the phonatory*

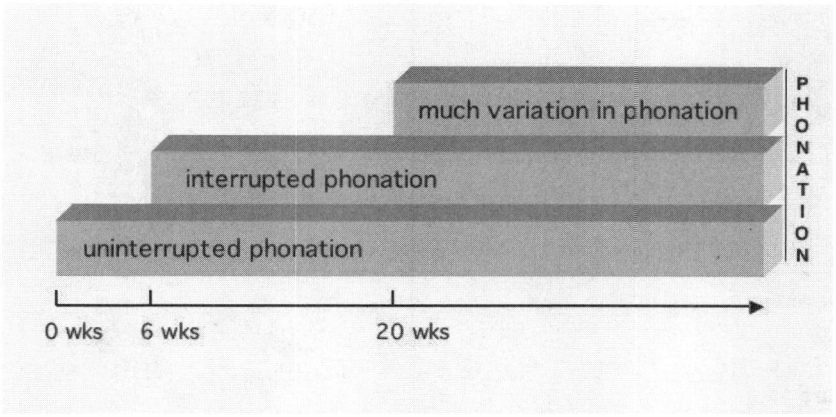

Figure 11.2.
Subsequent steps in the development of the infant phonation system. The listing of ages in weeks along the time span is only meant as a global indication of occurrence.

systems characteristic for all mammals" (p. 504). However, cooperation between these two systems is initially far from perfect and has to be improved by practice during the first weeks. Just after birth, infants' sounds are characterized by simple, uninterrupted phonation. After about six weeks, interrupted phonation within one breath-unit also occurs, resulting in the production of small series of vocalic elements without any articulation movements. From that period onwards, more and more variation in intonation occurs. This new phase in speech development has been called the period of "expansion" (Oller, 1980), "vocal play" (Stark, 1980) or "variegated phonation" (Koopmans-van Beinum & van der Stelt, 1986), all indicating a stage from about four to six month of age in the development of the infant phonation system (see Figure 11.2).

Articulation

Articulation development proceeds in different steps. At about ten weeks of age, the first articulation movements in the vocal tract (the filter) emerge: single closing movements of the pharynx (initially often with much tension), of the jaw

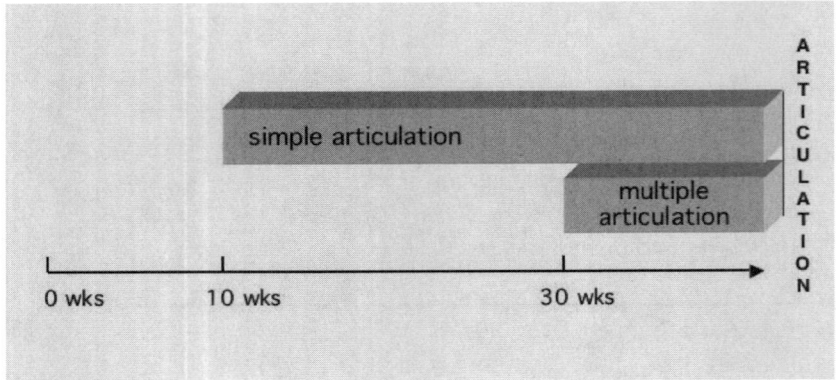

Figure 11.3.
Subsequent steps in the development of the infant articulation system.

and of the lips are noticed, typically in that order. Since most of these simple articulation movements are combined with phonation, pseudo-syllabic forms arise. This stage in speech development is often called "cooing" or "gooing" (Oller, 1980; Stark, 1980). These pseudo-syllabic forms already utilize basic proto-frames as described by MacNeilage (1998). Bloom, K. (1998) also mentions these types of syllabic sounds as early as about three months of age. This period of simple articulation typically occurs before the period of extreme expansion in phonation (see one of the previous sections of this chapter entitled "Phonation"). The most striking development in articulation, however, is at around thirty weeks of age, when cyclic mandibular movements result in the continual open-close alternation called "babbling." These multiple articulation movements constitute the concatenation of syllabic frames, a strong characteristic of adult speech. Consequently, the effect of this new type of infant vocal production on *Combining the Building Blocks of Phonation and Articulation* is obvious: parents believe their infants are saying "papa" and "mama," and they react accordingly. However, this new type of infant vocalization is no more than the next logical step in the development of the infant articulatory system (see Figure 11.3). The listing of ages in weeks along the time span is only meant as a global indication of occurrence. So far we have considered the development of the two sound production sub-systems (phonation and articulation) of the source-filter system separately. It will soon be clear that the coupling of these parts is essential for speech production (see Figure 11.4). Examining changes in *phonation* by following the various steps on the time scale in Figure 11.4, a clear developmental course emerge from simple and uninterrupted phonation via interrupted to complex phonation, with muchvariation in pitch, intensity and duration. Observing changes in *articulation* by following the various steps on the time scale, a clear developmental course becomes apparent as well, going from no articulation, via one simple articulation movement to multiple articulation movements per respiration cycle. However, as it is clear from the model in Figure 11.4, the various developmental steps in phonation do not coincide with the steps in articulation movements. Just as a beginner violin player has to learn to coordinate the movements of his right hand with the substantially different movements of his left hand, so does the infant have to learn to coordinate the movements of the source (phonation) with the movements of the filter (articulation).

In Figure 11.4, arrows indicate the specific coordination milestones, the last one of which includes all general characteristics of later adult speech. Retrospectively seen, the two moments of coordinating phonation with articulation ring in an important stage not only in speech but also in language acquisition, since the new types of utterances already resemble the form (sound structure) of later words (e.g., a (V)CV and a (V)CVCV. . form respectively; V stands for "vowel-like" and C for "consonant-like"). Thus, as soon as phonation and articulation are coupled, the basic frame or syllabic foundation arises in infant vocal behavior.

Development in Motor Coordination

So far, a hierarchical structure in the components of the developing speech production instrument has been shown. However, in order to combine movements of respiration, phonation, and articulation, infants have to coordinate

232 van Beinum

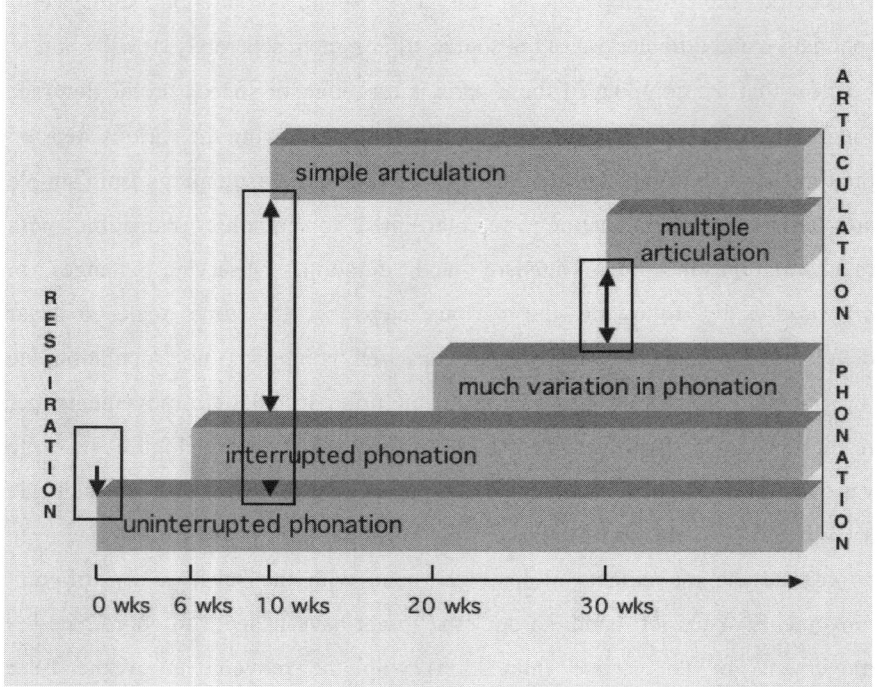

Figure 11.4
Building blocks of the infant sound production system and the three milestones
in the coordination of speech movements. Arrows indicate the specific
moments where respiration, phonation, and articulation have to be coupled.
The listing of ages in weeks along the time sp an is only meant as a global
indication of occurrence.

movements of three separate systems. The scheme in Table 11.1 summarizes the
three coordination milestones. It is assumed that control systems build an
internal model of the speech production system. Thus, internal models or motor
programs are essential for normal movement control and coordination (Kawato
& Gomi, 1992; Thelen, 1981). For that purpose multi-modal control is needed,
at least by auditory and proprioceptive feedback (Thelen, 1991).

Abbs & DePaul (1998) summarized results from several studies stating that
"timing and coordination of speech movement sequences is guided moment-to-
moment by sensory information" (p. 511). Huffman & Henson (1990) mention
that "the interface between auditory and vocalization centers is distributed to all

Table 11.1.
Overview of the coordination milestones in speech development where respiration, phonation, and articulation are coupled.

Coordination milestone	Age	Result
Respiration + phonation	from birth	sound
Respiration + phonation + simple articulation	from ± 10 weeks	basic frame
respiration + phonation + multiple articulation	from ± 30 weeks	concatenation of frames

levels of the brain" (p. 314). These statements together with that of von Hofsten (2002, oral presentation): "…perception and action form loops that allow for online guidance of movements; these loops are also the windows for improving the systems from experience…" brings us to the conclusion that auditory perception must be crucial in the development of speech. One interesting question to be examined is how the lack of auditory perception affects vocalization in deaf infants. Does the lack of auditory perception in deaf children provide an explanation for why they do not start babbling in the first year of life?

Comparing Vocalizations of Deaf and Hearing Infants

In the past, deaf children often remained undiscovered until their second to fourth year of life. Their frequent vocalizations and their activity in multimodal communication disguised the lack of auditory perception. A few years ago, we started a project comparing vocalizations of a group of six deaf (≥ 90 dBHL) and six hearing children, matched for a number of aspects (see Clement, 2004; Koopmans-van Beinum, Clement, & van den Dikkenberg-Pot, 2001a). Monthly audio-recorded vocalizations were examined from 2.5 months onwards from all hearing infants and from some of the deaf, and from 5.5 months of age for all infants.

The deaf infants (five boys and one girl), who were the second or third child in their family, had a genetically based hearing loss of over 90 dB on average in the best ear, established by Auditory Brainstem Response audiometry (ABR) in the first months of life. The loss was confirmed by pure-tone audiometric tests at a later age. All deaf infants participated in early intervention programs and used hearing aids, although not all used them on a regular basis. The parents themselves made the recordings in a face-to-face situation in their homes, in order to create a naturalistic situation during the audio-recordings.

The use of the sensori-motor approach for the classification of early infant vocalizations provides us with a framework to investigate in detail which aspects of these vocalizations actually differ in deaf vs. hearing children. Traditional phonetic transcriptions are not suitable for this analysis since the target words cannot be recognized yet. Further, at this phase in development infant utterances do not yet have the properties that would help identify which specific language is the environmental language. Thus, it is more adequate to use description tools based on universal principles of movements of the human speech production system. In order to make quantitative assessment possible by applying the source-filter based sensori-motor approach, our group developed a system called "AMSTIVOC'" (AMsterdam System for Transcription of Infant VOCalizations; Koopmans-van Beinum, 1999; Koopmans-van Beinum, Clement, & van den Dikkenberg-Pot, 2001b). Within this system, only global characteristics of place and manner of sound production are identified instead of a traditional phonetic-linguistic description.

All non-vegetative comfort utterances of the infants produced during the first 10 minutes of each monthly recording were counted by two trained phoneticians (inter-judge agreement upon vocalizations being non-vegetative comfort utterances: >90%). Next, 50 infant utterances from each recording were selected out of the 10 transcribed minutes evenly divided over that time span, and stored in digital form for further perceptual and acoustic analysis.

Utterances were analyzed for the following characteristics:

- *phonation type*: classifying phonation into one of five possible types, e.g., no phonation (0), simple uninterrupted (1) or interrupted (2) phonation, variegated uninterrupted (3) or variegated interrupted (4) phonation.

- *articulation type*: classifying articulation into one of three possible types, e.g., no articulation movement (0), one articulation movement (1), two or more articulation movements during two- or more-syllabic utterances (2).

- *number of syllables*: the criteria for a syllable or syllable-like element being a minimal rhythmic unit containing a vowel-like phase with or without a preceding or following consonant-like closing phase.

- *structure of the utterance*: indicating co-occurrences of vowel-like (V) and consonant-like (C) elements within each utterance.

- *place of articulation per syllable*: classifying vowel-like elements into one of three possible categories (front, central, or back), and classifying consonant-like elements into one of three possible categories (labial, alveolar, or velar).

Each utterance was coded as belonging to one of five possible types of phonation (inter-judge agreement: 85%) and to one of three possible types of articulation (inter-judge agreement: 91%), based on the classification of movements in infant speech development. The speech analysis program PRAAT (Boersma & Weenink, 1996) was utilized, in order to combine the audible sound form with an oscillographic display. Further, using this program was advantageous for making perceptually based coding decisions easier and more reliable, due to the availability of acoustic analysis techniques such as pitch detection and spectrography.

As our description is based on the movements of the speech production instrument, we can compare deaf and hearing infant speech development, and identify the role of auditory input and feedback. Analyses and results have been published before in more detail (Clement, 2004; Koopmans-van Beinum, Clement, & van den Dikkenberg-Pot, 2001a). Therefore, we summarize the results here as follows.

With respect to the general measures of number of utterances and total duration during the fixed ten minutes time span, it was concluded that:

- deaf infants produce more utterances than hearing infants;
- mothers of deaf infants produce fewer utterances than mothers of hearing infants;
- length of time spent with mother + infant speech together is equal for deaf and hearing infants.

With respect to the specific phonation and articulation analysis for each utterance by means of AMSTIVOC, it was concluded that:

- deaf infants produce more articulations without phonation;
- deaf infants produce more phonations without articulations;
- deaf infants produce fewer variations in their utterances;
- deaf infants do not babble in their first year;
- deaf infants create syllabification by interrupting phonation from 7.5 months onwards;
- utterances of deaf infants differ in number (more) and duration (shorter) from those of hearing infants before the sixth month of life already.

Coordination of Milestones in Deaf Infants

If we consider the components necessary for babbling, i.e., respiration, phonation, articulation, rhythmic motor cyclicity, mimetic capacity, and sensory feedback, we may conclude from our study that deaf children possess the same building blocks of vocalization behavior as their hearing peers. Development in deaf infants proceeds in an order that is similar to hearing children's, with respect to the use of each of the two sound production systems involved in speech (the phonation and the articulation system). This development in the separate systems seems to be physiologically and neurologically governed. In addition, series of repetitive (rhythmic) movements in one of the two sound production systems (phonation only *or* articulation only) are present in the deaf infants at the same time as babbling starts in hearing infants (i.e., repetitive, rhythmic movements in the phonation *and* the articulation system simultaneously), just like the repetitive movements in hammering, chewing, bumping, etc. However, the main differences between deaf and hearing children arise where the two systems need to be coupled. If we consider the three coordination milestones as displayed in Table 11.1, the differences are obvious. Coupling of respiration and phonation is easily achieved since this coordination starts reflexively from birth onwards. Thus, no differences are apparent here. Coupling of respiration, phonation and simple articulation, present from about ten weeks, shows some significant differences between deaf and hearing children. Hearing children produced more vocalizations in which simple phonation was combined with one simple articulation movement, whereas deaf children produced significantly more utterances with one simple articulation movement *without* any phonation (Clement, 2004). Moreover, the variety of articulation movements in deaf children was smaller than in hearing children; contrary to hearing children, the deaf children continued to make movements mainly in the back of the vocal tract, even in their second half year of life, probably because of tactile and kinesthetic influences. This finding is in agreement with results of Wallace, Menn, & Yoshinaga-Itano (2000), who also concluded that consonantal segments in deaf children are almost always glottal.

Another striking difference is significantly longer utterance duration found in the hearing as opposed to deaf children, as soon as phonation is combined with one simple articulation movement at about three months of age (Clement, 2004). This longer duration does not occur in the utterances of deaf children at that age. Results indicate that the initial coupling of phonation and articulation movements, i.e., the second coordination milestone that creates the foundation of the syllabic frame, requires extra production time.

As for the third coordination milestone, i.e., coupling of respiration, phonation and multiple articulation which is present from about thirty weeks and is known as canonical babbling, differences are obvious. Deaf infants do not babble in their first year of life (Oller & Eilers, 1988). Moreover, deaf infants create syllabification by interrupting phonation from about thirty weeks onwards. It seems obvious that, although several components of babbling behavior are present in deaf infants, it is the coupling or coordination of phonation and articulation movements that is insufficient or lacking. Obviously, auditory feedback is necessary for this coordination. Further, this coordination is essential for creating "frames," as described by Davis and MacNeilage for hearing infants (Davis & MacNeilage, 1995). Therefore, babbling is challenging for deaf infants early in development, since problems arise in making the coupling between phonation and simple articulation movements, which is the basis of a frame. The importance of this early basis is strengthened by the results of Yoshinaga-Itano, Sedey, Coulter, and Mehl (1998). The researchers found that children whose hearing losses were identified between birth and the sixth month of age had better receptive and expressive language abilities after intervention than children identified after six months of age.

The capacity to produce a concatenation of syllabic frames resulting in canonical babbling seems to require two abilities. One is a biologically, neurologically governed developmental skill, present in all healthy children to produce repetitive, rhythmic movements. The other is the ability to correctly coordinate the movements of the two elementary sources of sound production: the phonation and the articulation instrument, a skill that requires a well functioning auditory perception system or, at a minimum, some form of auditory feedback.

Conclusions

Speech development has to be considered as two separately developing systems: phonation and articulation. Describing the movements of the speech instrument in the course of the first year of life clearly reveals the different stages in speech production development. Utilizing the sensori-motor approach for the classification of early infant vocalizations allows us to investigate in detail which aspects of the vocalizations of deaf and hearing children differ. Deaf children display the same developmental order as hearing children with respect to the use of each of the two sound production systems involved in speech (the phonatory and the articulatory system). This development of the separate systems is physiologically and neurologically governed. Series of repetitive (rhythmic) movements in one of the two sound production systems (phonation only) are present in the deaf infants at the same time as babbling (i.e., repetitive, rhythmic movements in the phonatory and the articulatory system simultaneously) starts in hearing infants. However, the main differences between deaf and hearing children arise where the two systems have to be coupled. Producing uninterrupted phonation combined with one articulatory movement, and interrupted phonation combined with two or more articulatory movements (i.e. rhythmic, speech like canonical babbling or "frames") is a challenge for deaf infants early in development. Arguably, infants' auditory perception and feedback are a prerequisite for the *coordination of movements* in the two systems together. This becomes the more serious in canonical babbling, since especially in that stage the infrastructure for later speech development is provided. As canonical babbling contains all basic elements of (adult) speech, it is a strong cue to the functioning of the normal speech developmental process. Using the detailed transcription system of AMSTIVOC allows for demonstrating exactly where problems arise in this developmental process. Production of speech is possible due to the two elementary types of movements of sound production: phonation and articulation in combination with respiration, being the foundation for the syllabic frame. A normally functioning auditory perception system or at least some form of auditory feedback seems to be a prerequisite for the ability to correctly coordinate these two elementary types of movements. The foundation for the syllabic frame is already laid before the sixth month of age.

References

Abbs, J. H., & DePaul, R. (1998). Motor cortex fields and speech movements: Simple dual control is implausible. *Behavioral and Brain Sciences, 21*, 511–512.

Bloom, K. (1998). The missing link's missing link: Syllabic vocalizations at 3 months of age. *Behavioral and Brain Sciences, 21*, 514–515.

Boersma, P., & Weenink, D. (1996). Praat, a system for doing phonetics by computer. *Institute of Phonetic Sciences, University of Amsterdam, report 132*. [see also http://www.fon.hum.uva.nl/praat/ for the most recent version].

Clement, C. J. (2004). *Development of vocalizations in deaf and normally hearing infants.* Ph.D.-thesis, University of Amsterdam. Utrecht, The Netherlands: LOT publications, 100.

Davis, B. L., & MacNeilage, P. F. (1995). The articulatory basis of babbling. *Journal of Speech and Hearing Research, 38*, 1199–1211.

Fant, G. (1960). Acoustic theory of speech production. The Hague: Mouton.

Herodotus (about 450 B.C.). *Historiae.* K. Abicht (Ed.), book II, 4th edition (1926), Leipzig: B. G. Teubner.

Huffman, R. F., & Henson, O. W., Jr. (1990). The descending auditory path way and acousticomotor systems: Connections with the inferior colliculus. *Brain Research Brain Research Review, 15*, 295–323.

Kawato, M., & Gomi, H. (1992). The cerebellum and VOR/OKR learning models. *Trends in Neuroscience, 15*, 445–453.

Koopmans-van Beinum, F. J. (1999). AMSTIVOC: Testing and elaborating the AMsterdam System for Transcription of Infant VOCalizations. *Proceedings of the Institute of Phonetic Sciences Amsterdam, 23*, 91–102.

Koopmans–van Beinum, F. J., & van der Stelt, J. M. (1986). Early stages in the development of speech movements. In B. Lindblom & R. Zetterström (Eds.), *Precursors of early speech* (pp. 37–50). Wenner Gren International Symposium Series 44. New York: Stockton Press.

Koopmans-van Beinum, F. J., & van der Stelt, J. M. (1998). Early speech development in children acquiring Dutch: Mastering general basic elements. In S. Gillis & A. de Houwer (Eds.), *The acquisition of Dutch* (pp. 101–162). Amsterdam/Philadelphia: John Benjamins.

Koopmans–van Beinum, F. J., Clement, C. J., & van den Dikkenberg–Pot, I. (2001a). Babbling and the lack of auditory speech perception: A matter of coordination? *Developmental Science, 4*, 61-70.

Koopmans–van Beinum, F. J., Clement, C. J., & van den Dikkenberg-Pot, I. (2001b). AMSTIVOC (AMsterdam System for Transcription of Infant VOCalizations) applied to utterances of deaf and normally hearing infants. In P. Dalsgaard, B. Lindberg & H. Benner (Eds.), *Proceedings of EuroSpeech 2001–Scandinavia*, vol. 2 (pp. 1471–1474). Aalborg University, Denmark: Center for Personkommunikation (CPK).

Lecanuet, J. P. (1998). Foetal responses to auditory and speech stimuli. In A. Slater (Ed.), *Perceptual development: Visual auditory, and speech perception in infancy* (317–355). Hove, East Sussex: Psychology Press.

MacNeilage, P. F. (1998). The frame/content theory of evolution of speech production. *Behavioral and Brain Sciences, 21*, 499–511.

MacNeilage, P. F., & Davis, B. L. (1990). Acquisition of speech production: Frames then content. In M. Jannerod (Ed.), *Attention and performance, XIII Motor representation and control* (pp. 453–476). Hillsdale: Erlbaum.

Oller, D. K. (1980). The emergence of the sounds of speech in infancy. In G. H. Yeni-Komshian, J. Kavanagh & C. A. Ferguson (Eds.), *Child phonology,* vol. I: Production (pp. 93–112). New York: Academic Press.

Oller, D. K., & Eilers, R. E. (1988). The role of audition in infant babbling. *Child Development, 59*, 441–449.

Stark, R. E. (1980). Stages of speech development in the first year of life. In G. H. Yeni-Komshian, J. Kavanagh & C. A. Ferguson (Eds.), *Child phonology.* vol. I: Production (pp. 73–92). New York: Academic Press.

Thelen, E. (1981). Rhythmical behavior in infancy: An ethological perspective. *Developmental Psychology, 17*, 237–257.

Thelen, E. (1991). Motor aspects of emergent speech: A dynamic approach. In N.A. Krasnegor, D. M. Rumbaugh, R. L. Schiefelbusch & M. Studdert-Kennedy (Eds.), *Biological and behavioral determinants of language development* (pp. 339–362). Hillsdale: Erlbaum.

von Hofsten, C. (2002). *The development of manual abilities.* Paper presented at the Euresco Conference: Brain Development and Cognition in Human Infants (Acquafredda Di Maratea, Basilicata, Italy, 7–12 June, 2002, Abstract 27).

Vries, J. I. P. de, Visser, G. H. A., & Prechtl, H.F.R. (1984). Fetal motility in the first half of pregnancy. In H.F.R. Prechtl (Ed.), *Continuity in neural functions from prenatal to postnatal life* (pp. 46–78). Oxford: Blackwell.

Wallace, V., Menn, L., & Yoshinaga-Itano, C. (2000). Is babble the gateway to speech for all children? A longitudinal study of infants who are deaf or hard of hearing. *The Volta Review, 100*, 121–148.

Williams, B. G. (2001). *The Crimean Tatars: The diaspora experience and the forging of a nation.* Leiden: Brill Academic Publishers.

Yoshinaga-Itano, C., Sedey, A., Coulter, D., & Mehl, A. (1998). Language of early- and later-identified children with a hearing loss. *Pediatrics, 102*, 1161–1171.

IV: Acquisition of Speech

12

Teething, Chewing, and the Babbled Syllable

Jeannette M. van der Stelt

Institute of Phonetic Sciences

and

Amsterdam Center for Language and Communication

University of Amsterdam

Amsterdam, The Netherlands

Developmental processes that result in "higher" cognitive functions, like communication, may have their origins in the young infant's physical functioning. Biologically determined sucking and swallowing behavior occurs from about three months onward in a burst-like manner (a sequence of several movements followed by a pause), and these behaviors can be regarded as precursors of turn-taking in a communicative interaction (Kaye, 1977). In this study, we examine teething (also considered a biologically determined process) in relation to infant sound production.

The anatomical and physiological changes in the young infant's oral cavity have traditionally been the domain of medically oriented research. Obviously, in cases of anatomical malformations such as cleft lips and palates, medical attention is the parents' first aid. Speech therapists were among the first to point out effects of oral (feeding) habits on the development of speech production (e.g., Jansonius-Schultheiss, 1985). Thumb sucking, for example, is still a much-debated topic amongst speech therapists, dentists, pediatricians, and psychologists, who are the professionals parents turn to with concerns about their child's speech development. Phoneticians and, to a lesser extent, psycholinguists only became interested in the infant's anatomical and physiological development when the ontogeny of speech production became a focus of scientific interest.

Previous research has established the presence of variability in infant sound production patterns. Results suggest a gradual shaping of early sound qualities into the sounds of the mother tongue by the end of the first year. Serkhane et al. (2002) suggests the presence of two mechanisms in speech development: "exploration of the vocal tract sensori-motor abilities, and the imitation (overt stimulation) of caretakers' language sounds." (p. 45). However, very young infants already possess the ability to imitate. For example, infants have been demonstrated to imitate tongue protrusion at birth (e.g., Meltzoff & Moore, M. H., 1977) and vowel production at 12 weeks (e.g., Kuhl & Meltzoff, 1996). Skoyles (1998) puts forward the hypothesis that "mirror" cells in the brain are specialized in auditory-motor target perception and in linking these perceptions to their execution. During development, these perceptions adapt the articulatory movements to the changes in the vocal apparatus. A major anatomical change is the eruption of incisors, which forces the tongue, the hyoid bone, and the larynx into new positions. This change may potentially facilitate speech motor patterns to better match adult speech.

Previous work (e.g., Koopmans-van Beinum & van der Stelt, 1979; van der Stelt & Koopmans-van Beinum, 1986) described early sound production of babies systematically with regard to phonatory and articulatory movements during one respiration cycle. Knowledge of anatomical and physiological developmental changes in the speech production apparatus is fundamental to this description system. The description was based on the research reports by Bosma (1967, 1977) and Fletcher (1973), characterizing infant oral anatomical and physiological changes over time. Findings about preverbal speech therapy (Boelema-da Costa, 1983; Hendrickx et al., 1976), dentistry in infancy

(Duyzings, 1943), and pediatricians' work (Wasz-Höckert et al., 1968) first including information on acoustics of infant sound production, were also considered when creating the description of infants' early sound production (see the next section).

In this chapter an investigation of the relation between infant sound production and the presence or absence of the first teeth is presented. Results were obtained by means of a parental questionnaire. The results of this inquiry suggest that infants acquire segmental speech movements well before the emergence of babbling. The eruption of the first teeth may be a better marker for the onset of consonant production than the infant's age.

The Infant's Speech Motor Milestones

Infants systematically master the coordination of movements involved in speech production. In a longitudinal study examining speech motor development in two Dutch boys during the first eight months of life, Koopmans-van Beinum & van der Stelt (1979) defined six speech motor milestones during the first year of life. Gradual mastering of muscular coordination of respiration, phonation, and articulation plays a crucial role (see Table 12.1).

The first two milestones have to do with the control over respiration and phonation. The third milestone marks the onset of the uniquely human ability to combine phonation with articulatory movements. The subsequent milestones (4-6) merely show a growing complexity in the motor patterns of speech production.

The first milestone in speech motor development is the ability to produce a sound at the laryngeal level, often as a response to the presence of an interacting adult. The sound has a very short duration since the (relatively small quantity of) outgoing air is forced through the closed glottis into the pharynx.

248 van der Stelt

Table 12.1.
Overview of speech motor milestones during the first year.

Stage	Characteristics	Onset age in weeks
I	Simple, uninterrupted phonation without an articulatory movement within one respiratory cycle.	0 wks
II	Interrupted phonation within one respiratory cycle, without an articulatory movement.	6 wks
III	One single articulatory movement within one respiratory cycle, which can be combined with (I) continuous or (II) interrupted phonation.	10 wks
IV	A decrease in the occurrence of articulatory movements, and an increase in sounds with an uninterrupted phonation, which varies loudness, pitch, and duration.	20 wks
V	Multiple articulatory movements, repetitive or variegated, during one respiratory cycle together with phonatory variation: "babbling."	26 wks
VI	Combinations of all kinds of utterances of the preceding stages, with an onset of referential use of the sounds: phonetically consistent forms and first words.	40 wks

The "syllabic form" in the infant's sound production is already prominently present in the second milestone (from around 6 weeks), which is a sequence of source sounds (e.g., interrupted or aspirated phonation). The ability to interrupt vocal closing activity is needed later for production of voiceless-consonant and vowel repetitions.

The third milestone, often a bi-syllabic sound production (e.g. [aRa], from around 10 weeks), combines phonation and articulation. Only the human primate has been shown to combine these two activities (e.g., Jürgens, 1998). Non-human primates, like chimpanzees, do not segment their vocal sounds into syllables by means of movements of their (feeding) articulators.

The fourth milestone (from around 20 weeks) involves further exploration of potential sounds produced by the voice source only. The infant practices variations in loudness, pitch, and duration. Supra-segmental variability in later-emerging speech can be considered as related to this exploratory activity.

Babbling, which is defined as the production of several articulatory movements during one respiratory cycle with voiced segments, started in the two boys examined at around 26 weeks but, as stated above, a considerable range with regard to the onset of babbling in a group of 51 normal children was identified (van der Stelt & Koopmans-van Beinum, 1986). The babbling infant can produce adult-like multi-syllabic utterances that parents easily recognize as speech-like after only a limited amount of experience (Oller et al., 2001). Oller (1986) has specified "canonical babbling" acoustically: each syllable has a nucleus (vowel-like) and at least one formant transition to the consonantal part. For a babbled utterance to be considered canonical rather than "marginal," additional acoustic criteria with regard to duration, intensity, and pitch must be met. In view of the aim of this chapter, we will not elaborate on these metaphonological and acoustic-phonetic aspects in infant sound productions.

Meaning comes into the infant's sound production when a sound is used consistently in a specific context. From about 39 weeks onwards the child may start to use these "Phonetically Consistent Forms" (PCFs; Dore et al., 1976; Gillis & De Schutter, 1986) that parents may start to recognize when the child uses these PCF consistently in specific situations. First words, usually mono-syllabic, are also reported from about the age of 40 weeks onwards.

The first part of the "Methods" section provides a description of the 6 speech motor milestones, in order to explain to parents the crucial movements in infant sound production which are the *respiration* cycle (breath unit), interrupted or non-interrupted *phonation* and various *articulatory movements* (with regard to place and manner). A total of 23 questions (4 to 5 questions per speech motor milestone) were used in the parent questionnaires to explore developmental patterns of speech sound production.

The Infant's Changing Speech Apparatus

For speech sound production the source-filter model is widely accepted, in its simplest form distinguishing a voiced source (located in the larynx) and a filter (the changing shape of the oral cavity). Sound production, however, is a secondary function of the speech apparatus. The primary function of the larynx is to protect the lungs from liquids and solid materials. The oral cavity has a primary function in feeding. In the course of development, the speech apparatus gradually adapts and subtle coordination of movements involved in speech production is mastered. Auditory perception of speech is thought to be one of the steering mechanisms in the developmental process. Speech-language pathologists have also pointed at the role of proprioception and kinesthetics. Understanding (infant) sound production requires knowledge of the instrument producing the sounds. Bosma (1967, 1977) and Fletcher (1973) have demonstrated the complexity of the anatomical and physiological changes of the infant's speech apparatus. The development of certain motor structures will influence neuro-motor function, and vice versa. This reciprocity is an essential factor in normal development of speech movements (see van der Stelt & Koopmans-van Beinum, 1981).

Respiration and the Larynx

Neonatal respiration is controlled in the respiration center in the brain stem, and inspiratory-expiratory airflow becomes regulated in the course of development. Koopmans-van Beinum & van der Stelt (1986) have used this alternation of inspiration and audible expiration to segment the infant's sound stream. The major part of the infant's utterance durations is determined by duration of the expiration: phonation on the inspiratory part of the respiration cycle does not occur often.

The neonate's larynx is positioned high relative to a short neck. This positioning facilitates protection of the lungs which is three-fold: at the level of the vocal folds, the false vocal folds, and by means of the epiglottis, which can cover the entire larynx entrance during swallowing. In the neonate, the larynx entrance is T-shaped resulting from the relative retardation of the growth of the arytenoids' masses. Initially, infants produce mainly glottal stops and groans in non-cry situations (milestone 1). Gradually, the movements of the arytenoids (and the attached vocal fold muscles) can control glottal closure and tension more efficiently. Thus, the infant can produce sounds with aspiration (an /h/-like quality) and with a changing pitch (milestone 2). The increasing freedom of the larynx to move in cranio-caudal direction permits better control over vocal fold tension, and pitch as well. True phonation is the result of a subtle interplay between respiratory sub-glottal pressure and muscular closing and tension forces in the vocal folds. Around month four, the infant's phonation patterns are quite variegated with regard to pitch, loudness and duration (milestone 4). In the description system proposed by Koopmans-van Beinum & van der Stelt (e.g., 1986), the milestones 1, 2, and 4 represent developmental changes related to the source of speech production.

The Oral Cavity

The newborn mouth is very sensitive for stimuli that are available during feeding. The tongue is relatively large compared to the oral cavity and leaves little masticatory space. The mandible is small in mass and mobile at the temporo-mandibular joint (Bosma, 1977). The muscles attached to the lower jaw move this bone more to the front than they lower the jaw. This positioning is beneficial during breastfeeding (Duyzings, 1943) since the mandible is placed more backwards leaving the nose free for breathing. The flat velum lies on the tongue root and does not touch the back wall of the pharynx as it does in adults (Fletcher, 1973). By slightly flattening the tongue, a vacuum can be created in the oral cavity for milk to flow in. In newborns, sucking and breathing are simultaneous activities interrupted only by swallowing (Bosma, 1967).

Under the constant pressure of the tongue and cheek muscles, the facial skeleton and the oral cavity grows from sutural activities in size and form. Bones only grow at sutures where gristle changes from tough into solid structures, while pressure and muscle activity play an important role in this solidification. Due to an upright position, changes take place especially in the cranial-caudal direction (head-feet direction due to the influence of gravity forces). The mandible has growth sites that permit a harmonious growth parallel with the rest of the facial complex (Fletcher, 1973). Initially, the upper and lower alveolar ridges are lacking: they emerge together with the eruption of the deciduous teeth, thus creating a kind of fence for the tongue, forcing it to a more backward position (Duyzings, 1943). The larynx thus lowers due partially to the effects of a more posterior tongue position, and is permitted more freedom for moving up and down in relation to the trachea or the mandible as well.

Inhibition of oral reflexes is gradually mastered during the first three months of life. Articulatory movements become increasingly voluntarily which explains, for example, the emergence of the uvular trill around 12 weeks of age (see milestone 3). When describing these acquired functional abilities (i.e., practognostic capacities), Hendrickx et al. (1976) argue that, at this point in development, the baby "knows" how to use the apparatus for the production of sound models. Components of existing movements, as for example in the backward "rolling" of the tongue body during swallowing, can be reorganized into new functional movements: creating a constriction between the tongue root and the uvula for the production of the uvular trill. At first, the duration of the utterance is too short for more than one articulatory movement. But the baby masters control over utterance duration and voice control, and then produces sounds that vary enormously with regard to voice qualities. Due to the sensori-motor adaptations in early infancy, carrying out successive mouth movements such as those required for chewing becomes possible from about the 7th month onwards (Boelema-da Costa, 1983). The onset of canonical babbling (at first characterized by repetitive mouth movements) can be explained also by the more adult-like proportions of the facial structures, along with an increased control over the articulators, and the longer duration of the utterances themselves.

The time of eruption of the dental elements is related to birth weight and length, gestational duration, and genetic factors. The developmental state of dentition is often used as an indication for children's age when their chronological age is unknown (for an overview of factors related to the emergence of the deciduous dentition, see Demirjian, 1986, pp. 269-298). According to results reported in a large Dutch survey by Kooi (1982), the deciduous incisors typically emerge in pairs, the first pair being more often the most central one in the mandible (elements 71 & 81, see Figure 12.1). The mean age of eruption for the Dutch population is 32 weeks. Preceding the eruption of incisors, parents often report drooling and diarrhea in the baby, which is possibly caused by temporary tenderness of the mucous. The incisors must "melt" their way out from the mandible bone.

Bosma (1967) considers the teeth as sensors: tiny pressure changes can be perceived precisely, as everyone with a lose tooth knows. In a subtle interplay between tongue and teeth, the eruption process may cause reorganization of articulatory movements into new patterns (Fletcher, 1973). However, when the incisors appear precociously in a newborn baby, the tongue may end up with blisters because the tongue movements for sucking cannot yet be adapted to the limited space in the oral cavity. Infants are also reported to "chew" on objects much more while teething, which may coincide with producing babbling sounds. The mean age for the onset of babbling in a group of 51 normal healthy infants is 31 weeks (the range was from 18 to 48 weeks; van der Stelt & Koopmans-van Beinum, 1986). Thus, the eruption of teeth is likely to be related to the discovery of an articulatory pattern for the audio-motor perception of adult speech (Skoyles, 1998).

Method

The Questionnaire

The hypothesized relation between the eruption of teeth and the quality of infant sound production was studied by means of parent questionnaire. Via an announcement in a popular educational magazine, parents were asked to participate in a research project focused on speech development in children to the age of 24 months. The announcement followed an article on early speech development that disseminated research results of Koopmans-van Beinum and van der Stelt. The reaction to the call for participation was overwhelming. All consenting parents were sent the questionnaire and a return envelope. About 750 questionnaires were returned, often with letters and photographs, and audio recordings. Additionally, parents provided both positive statements (e.g., "I have become more conscious about my baby's behavior.") and negative comments (e.g., "Too many questions that no longer apply to my baby.").

The questionnaire was divided into two parts. The first was concerned with background information about the parents and the baby's history, such as date of birth, weight and length of the baby at birth, and the medical history of mother and baby before and shortly after birth. Several questions focused on siblings and the languages spoken in the home. Parents were asked to indicate the date of the eruption of an element in a scheme of the numbered singular teeth: the upper and lower most central incisors have the numbers 51, 61 and 71, 81 respectively (see Figure 12.1). Participants could also indicate whether they were certain about the eruption date. Children were considered to be without teeth only when parents indicated in the scheme that their child "was too young" or that the question "did not apply to my baby." Age in weeks was calculated by subtracting the date of birth (corrected if pre- or dysmature) from the eruption date.

The second part of the questionnaire focused on the baby's behavioral features that parents observed during the week preceding the completion of the questionnaire. It was expected that this timing would increase reliability of the answers. Behaviors to be observed were grouped together on the questionnaire. Behavioral features included sound production, oral habits, looking and listening, communicative behavior and games, and head, hand and body movements (locomotion).

Speech motor milestones were provided in a "translated" alphabetic form, to be easier for parents than a description based on movements involved. Several questions were formulated for each speech motor milestone to cover various aspects of sound production. Overall, 23 questions were formulated in relation to sound productions. The questions were divided in 5 groups, corresponding to each speech motor milestone proposed (milestones 1 and 2 are grouped together as Laryngeals, see Table 12.1).

Five questions were concerned with production of **laryngeals** (milestones 1 and 2, both without articulations):

1. Does your child produce short pushy sounds while the whole body is moving?

2. Does your baby produce in one-breath unit short sounds by interrupting voice such as a-a-a, u-u-u?

3. Does your baby produce in one-breath unit sounds such as a-uu-u, ah-haa-a, or ahu?

4. Does your baby produce sounds with mouth closed, such as mmmm?

5. Does your baby produce nice soft sounds such as aah, uh, heh?

Four questions focused on sounds produced with only **one articulatory movement** (milestone 3):

6. Does your baby produce in one-breath unit "raspberry sounds" back in the mouth, such as uch, aggr, chru, rrg?

7. Does your baby produce in one-breath unit sounds such as aba, am, hube, upe?

8. Does your baby produce in one-breath unit sounds such as awwa, wu, uwe?

9. Does your baby produce in one-breath unit sounds such as ada, eta, nna, uda?

Five questions were related to the production of **prosodic sounds** (milestone 4):

10. Does your baby produce in one-breath unit sounds that vary in loudness, from loud to soft or vice versa?

11. Does your baby produce high squealing sounds?

12. Does your baby produce loud screaming sounds?

13. Does your baby produce low grumbling sounds?

14. Does your baby produce in one-breath unit sounds that go up-and-down or down-and-up in tone?

Four questions were concerned with **babbling** (milestone 5):

15. Does your baby produce in one-breath unit series of syllables such as apapapapa, umememe, amamama? (not ..am, am, am, or ..ap, ap, ap: the

comma indicates an inspiration pause before the single-syllable sound productions).

16. Does your baby produce in one-breath unit series of syllables such as awawawa, uwewewew? (not ..aw, aw, aw, or ..ew, ew, ew, or ..uwe, uwe, uwe).

17. Does your baby produce in one-breath unit series of syllables such as adadada, tatatatat, nanananan? (not ..eda, eda, eda or ..ta, ta, ta, or   ne, ne, ne).

18. Does your baby produce in one-breath unit series of syllables such as agagaga, kakakak, or nganganga? (not ..ak, ak, ak, or ..ga, ga, ga).

Five questions targeted information about **word and sentence production** (milestone 6):

19. Do you recognize sounds produced by your child that resemble speech, although not really words (timing of turns is resembling talking on the telephone or telling a well-known story from a picture book)?

20. Does your child use one or more words?

21. Does your child imitate words, like a parrot, that you use yourself?

22. Does your child imitate phrases that you use very often, such as "well done" or "that's nice"?

23. Does your child imitate your way of talking, for example with a doll or stuffed animal?

Each question had 6 possible answers:

OYes (unknown onset)	ONot yet
OYes, since this week	ONever has done that
OYes, since (date)	ONo longer since (date)

The current chapter required grouping the three "Yes and "No" answers into just two categories: "Yes" or "No."

The Participants

The 750 questionnaires contained information about 223 children younger than 45 weeks (about 10 months). The upper age limit between the first tooth eruption and the hypothesized change in the quality of sound production was set to 42 weeks. Most children after that age already have the central upper and lower jaw incisors, and are already proceeding to the linguistic stage of first words and sentences. The 223 children included 111 boys (58 with teeth, and 53 without teeth) and 112 girls (58 with teeth, and 54 without teeth). Age of the children was calculated by subtracting the date the parents completed the questionnaire and the baby's (corrected) date of birth.

Data analyses were carried out by means of SPSS 11.5. First of all, the ages of the children at the time of the questionnaire were calculated by subtracting the corrected birth date from the response date. Similar calculations were needed for the ages at which the teeth erupted (parents had indicated those dates in the scheme, see Figure 12.1). Frequency counts resulted in the number of children per gender, per age groups, per dental element, and per (categorized) sound production. In a later stage of this study we have matched children with a

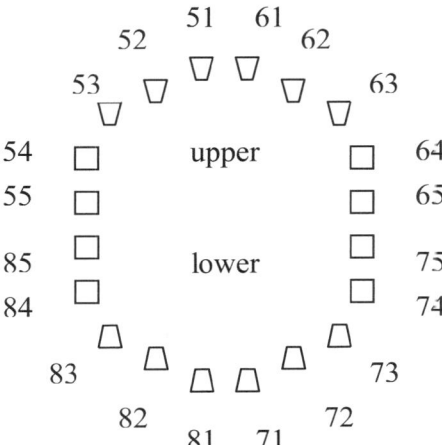

Figure 12.1.
Scheme for the deciduous teeth placed in the upper and lower jaw (mandible).

tooth to a child without a tooth, and no age difference as a criterion. Testing on significant differences is done by means of Pearson's r^2.

Results

Age

The mean age of the 223 children was 27;3 weeks; 26;0 weeks for the boys, and 27;6 weeks for the girls. The children were divided into 10 age groups (see Table 12.2). Up to 14 weeks, there were fewer children since parents are typically too busy attending to their infant during this time. The small group size for the oldest children was due to the cut-off age of about 10 months.

Teeth

Of the 223 children, 116 had one or more teeth (58 boys and 58 girls). The mean age of children with teeth was 34;1 weeks for boys, and 34;5 weeks for girls. This difference is not statistically significant. Thus, gender does not appear to be a differentiating factor with regard to the eruption of the first teeth. The mean age for all children with a first tooth is 26 weeks for boys and 27 weeks for girls, with a wide range from 11;1 weeks to 43;4 weeks. Parents reported that 17

Table 12.2.
Number of boys and girls divided over 10 age groups.

number per group	boys	girls	total
up to 10 weeks	2	3	5
10 – 14 weeks	9	6	15
14 – 18 weeks	12	13	25
18 – 22 weeks	17	10	27
22 – 26 weeks	16	14	30
26 – 30 weeks	13	14	27
30 – 34 weeks	7	17	24
34 – 38 weeks	11	14	25
38 – 42 weeks	17	14	31
42 – 46 weeks	7	7	14
total number	111	112	223

children had one tooth, 57 had two teeth, 9 had three, 13 had four, 6 had five, 9 had six, 1 had seven, and 4 had eight teeth.

There was a clear tendency for the two central incisors (71 and 81) in the mandible to erupt first (see Table 12.3). The mean age between the eruption of the first and second tooth was only 2;1 weeks. In 49 children the tooth numbered '71' was the first tooth, in 41 children tooth number '81'. In 22 children, both 71 and 81 were visible at the same age. Only two children had the upper jaw central incisors (51, 61) as their first teeth. This fact clearly supports the hypothesis that the tongue is pushed more backwards when the child is getting its teeth. As expected, with age the number of children with teeth becomes larger: in the age group 42–46 weeks all children had at least one tooth.

Sound Productions

The validity of results obtained by a parent questionnaire about child behavior might be considered uncertain since the answers cannot be checked. We generated results by stipulating that parents correctly recognize their infant's sound production. Questions related to sound productions are numbered from 1 to 23. Questions focusing on certain behaviors are ordered in a manner reflecting the typical sequence of infant development.

Young infants have been observed to produce laryngeals first. Thus, the first questions on the questionnaire are focused on laryngeals. The production of the first words and sentences is a much later occurring phenomenon. Therefore,

Table 12.3.
Mean age of eruption per element in weeks; days and number of children with a tooth/type:

Gender	51	52	61	62	71	72	81	82
Boys mean age in weeks	33;4	37;2	34;4	36;2	26;5	31;3	27;4	35;6
Number of boys	18	11	21	11	52	3	57	2
Girls mean age in weeks	33;6	31;0	34;3	33;6	27;6	32;6	28;0	33;0
number of girls	12	9	15	10	55	8	52	8
Mean age for all children in weeks	33;5	34;4	34;4	35;1	27;2	32;3	27;6	33;4
number of children	30	20	36	21	107	11	99	10

questions about word and sentence production apply only to children of about nine months and older. As expected, parents of young babies will answer "No" to questions about word and sentence production. Parents of older babies will respond to most questions with a "Yes." Thus, the answers to questions about early sound production will show a higher frequency of "Yes"-answers than questions concerned with babbling and word or sentence production. The decline in the number of "Yes" answers in Figure 12.2 is because older children's parents are likely answer "Yes" to all questions, while the younger children's parents do not. Additionally, Figure 12.2 shows that, within one category of questions, parents recognize certain sounds better than others. Of the "laryngeals" (Questions 1 to 5) sounds 3 and 5 seem to be produced more often than sounds 1, 2 and 4. In the category "simple articulations" (Questions 6-9) sounds 6 and 8 are more frequent than 7 and 9. Clearly, these Dutch children show a preference for certain sound productions in the various categories (or parents recognized these specific sound productions per category better than the other sounds).

Of the **laryngeal sounds**, parents seem to recognize (or remember) sounds asked for via questions number 3 and 5 better than the other sounds in that category. These two laryngeal sounds involve the loose closure of the vocal folds, resulting in sounds with an aspirated segment. These sounds are usually considered by parents to be a rather attractive kind of sound production. Further, the /h/ is a phoneme in Dutch; whereas the glottal stop (the sound focused on in Questions 1 and 2) is not. Question 4 relates to sound production with a closed mouth, which may be either not frequently occurring or not easily recognizable for parents.

Sound Production Questions

Parents often indicate in the category of the **single articulations** that their infant produces back articulations like a uvular /R/ (Question 6), as well as sounds that involve jaw wagging (/w/, questions 8) and mouth closure (/b/, /p/, and /m/ in question 7). The more fronted tongue tip articulations (asked for in question 9)

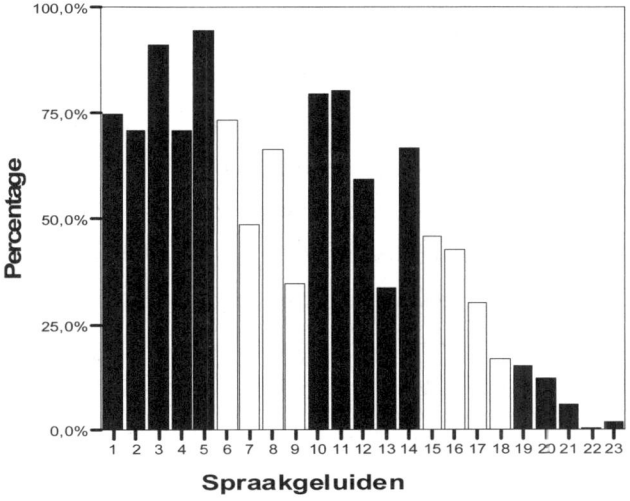

Figure 12.2.
Percentages of "Yes"-answers for questions: 1–5 are laryngeals, 6–9 single articulations, 10–14 prosodic sound productions, 15–18 babbling sounds, and 19–23 words and sentences.In the category of **prosodic sound production,** parents report that growling sounds clearly occur less frequently than other sounds like loudness changes (Question 10), glissandos (Question 14) and screams (Questions 11 and 12). It is reasonable to speculate that parents probably do not attribute growling to their young infant. Another explanation could be found in the children not having a sound model for growling (a dog) in the home.

such as the dentals /t/, /d/, and /n/ occur less frequently. In general, the direction of maturational control progresses from central to peripheral behavior, and from gross motor to more refined movements. We suspect that these maturational effects facilitate the production of mainly back articulations: voluntary tongue root and jaw movements, being closer to the central part of the nervous system, develop earlier than lip and tongue tip control. Possibly, a three month old infant cannot yet control the subtle (as well as swift) tongue tip movements, necessary for the pronunciation of /d/ and /t/.

In the category of **prosodic sound production**, parents report that growling sounds clearly occur less frequently than other sounds like loudness changes (Question 10), glissando's (Question 14) and screams (Question 11 and

12). It is reasonable to speculate that parents probably do not attribute growling to their young infant. Another explanation could be found in the children not having a sound model for growling (a dog) in the home.

The next four questions pertain to **babbling sounds**. The sounds with the bilabial /b/ and /w/ occur somewhat more often than sound productions with dental (tongue tip: /t/, /d/, and /n/) or velar articulations (/k/, /χ/, /γ/, and /g/). The production of the latter sounds increases in frequency only when the child starts to produce variegated variegated babbling.

The age group 42–46 weeks consisted of only 14 children (see Table 12.2) that, in view of the developmental stages, could produce sounds of the sixth milestone (Table 12.1, first words and beyond). As expected, only few children in the older age groups were reported to produce **sentences** and to imitate the parent's manner of speaking and sentences (Figure 12.2, questions 22 and 23). A few parents reported that their children could say **words** (Question 20), and imitate words like "parrot" (Question 21), and intonation patterns (Question 19).

Babbling and Dentition

The effect of age on dentition as well as on speech sound production complicated the comparison of children with and without teeth. Therefore, pairs

Table 12.4.
Number of pairs per age group and number of children with and without teeth.

Age groups		boys	girls	total
14-18 weeks	teeth	1	1	2 pairs
	no teeth	1	1	
18-22 weeks	teeth	3	1	4 pairs
	no teeth	4		
22-26 weeks	teeth	6	1	7 pairs
	no teeth	6	1	
26-30 weeks	teeth	6	3	9 pairs
	no teeth	6	3	
30-34 weeks	teeth	1	5	6 pairs
	no teeth		6	
34-38 weeks	teeth	1	1	2 pairs
	no teeth	1	1	

Table 12.5.
Comparison of sound categories produced by the group and by matched pairs.

	Total group N = 223	Selected pairs N = 60
Laryngeal sounds	80.3 %	86.2 %
Single articulations	55.7 %	59.4 %
Prosodic sounds	64.0 %	67.3 %
Babbling sounds	34.0 %	31.6 %
Words and sentences	7.1 %	4.4 %

of children were selected for comparison. For every child with a tooth a matching child of the same age but without teeth was selected. Overall, 30 pairs of matched infants were analyzed. Matching was possible only in the age groups where some children had teeth and others had not. Table 12.4 displays data from the matched pairs. Matching a boy with a girl (which is permitted since we found no sex differences for teething and sound production) was required twice to form 30 pairs.

The mean age of these 60 children was 25;1 weeks, and ranged from 17;0 to 37;3 weeks. The mean age for the emergence of the first tooth in the 30 children is 22;4 weeks, with a range of 11;0 to 31;4 weeks. This subgroup of 30 pairs of children compares favorably to the total group of 223 children with regard to the sound productions (see Table 12.5). Matching the children for presence or absence of a tooth is restricted to the younger age groups, where both children with and without a tooth occur. Therefore, the children in the pairs tend to produce slightly more "early" sounds (the first three age groups) than the total group.

For each of the 23 questions related to children's sound productions, the number of children with a tooth (30) and without a tooth (30) reported to produce that sound is displayed as in percentages in Figures 12. 3– 12.7 for each group. In the appendix, an overview of the numbers, the percentages, and Pearson's X^2 for each question is shown. Analyzing sound production data from children matched by presence of teeth reveals a tendency for children with teeth to score higher than the children without teeth.

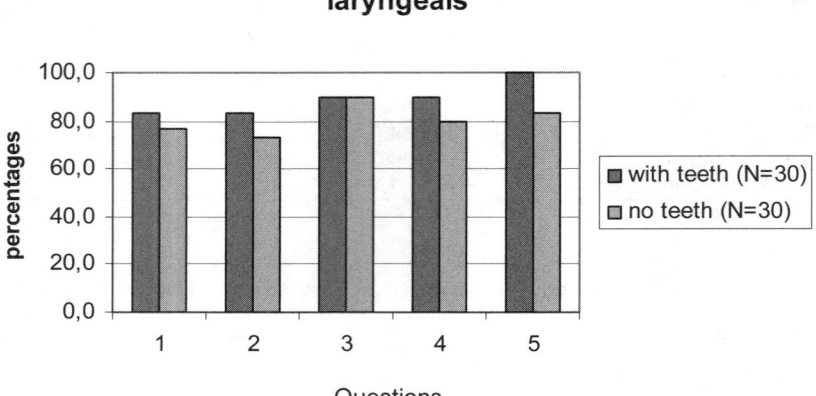

Figure 12.3.
Percentages per group that are reported to produce laryngeal sounds.

Two types of sound production, focused on in questions 21 and 22, are not produced by the paired children. Children with or without teeth score equally high on the laryngeal sound in question 3, the "ahu" sound. Differences are found for the remaining 20 questions. The children with teeth have higher scores in 15 out of the 20 questions Children with teeth scored lower on 5 out of the 20 sounds than the children without teeth (Questions 7, 10, 11, 14, and 18). Three of these lower scores are in the prosodic sounds category where no articulation is involved. Parents of children with teeth report higher frequencies for syllabic sounds and lower frequencies for prosodic sounds than parents of children without teeth. However, the differences in scores of the children with and without teeth are not significantly different.

Discussion

MacNeilage & Davis (2000) propose that "....simple biomechanical properties of the vocal apparatus (e.g., the mandibular cycle and static tongue postures), along with their interaction with the contingencies of movement initiation and the culturally mediated cognitive demands of word formation, have played a key role in both the acquisition and evolution of speech." (p. 530). The "frame first

single articulations

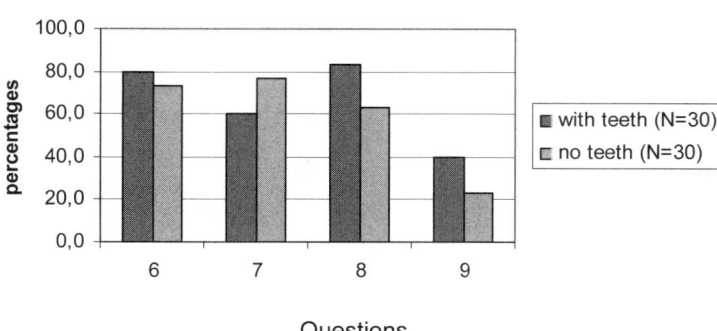

Figure 12.4.
Percentages per group reported to produce sounds with a single articulation.

and then content" theory in the evolution of speech production proposes that babbling is the first universal occurrence of the frame. Our finding, that parents prominently recognize the mere opening and closing of the mouth (/b/ and /w/ productions, questions 15 and 16 in the category of babbling sounds), supports this view. Babbling is thus regarded as the first step towards articulated speech, as proto-words (e.g., MacNeilage & Davis, 2000). Many infant's first words show a remarkable reduplication of syllables. This reduplication process is the major characteristic of canonical babbling, where cycles of mandibular oscillation provide the frame for sound production (MacNeilage, 1998).

Koopmans-van Beinum and van der Stelt (1986) however found that infants from about 10 weeks onward produced sounds with one single articulatory movement per breath unit (Stage III sound productions; see Table 12.1). These sounds were mostly produced with the back of the tongue raised, as in a uvular raspberry, and with the mouth open, resulting in utterances like /aRa/. Sounds produced with one single articulatory movement are most certainly bi-syllabic and involve an articulatory tongue movement. Some mothers reported that their 10-weeks-old infant produced an existing Dutch word "rare," which means "you're a funny one." The parents in this study report this type of sound production most frequently in the category of single articulations (question 6).

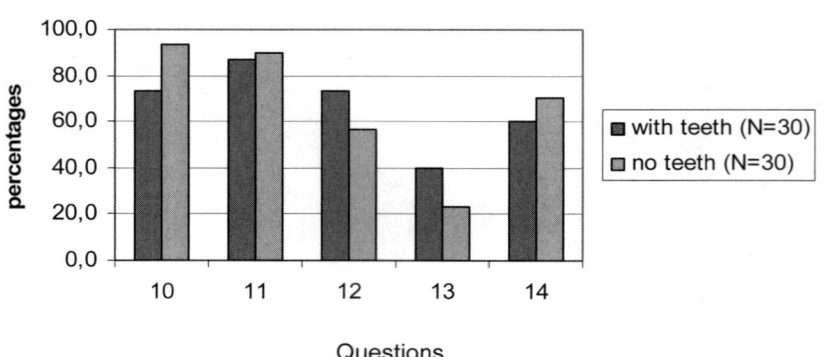

Figure 12.5.
Percentages per group that are reported to produce prosodic sounds.

babbling sounds

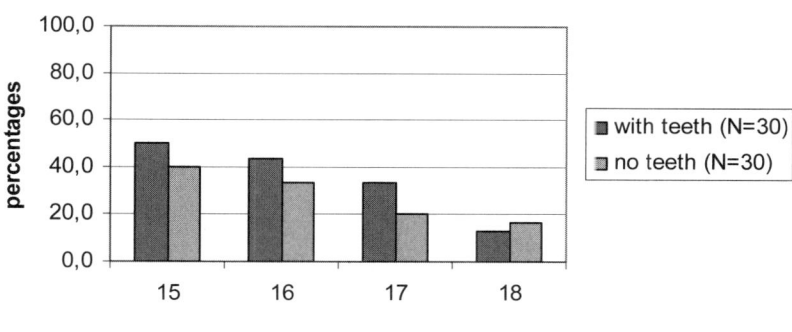

Questions

Figure 12. 6.
Percentages per group that are reported to produce babbling sounds.

Possibly, babbling is not the first occurrence of the frame. The second milestone (see Table 12.1), when the baby can interrupt phonation and restart it in one respiratory cycle, results in a series of vowel-like fragments: /u-u-u/, which is called "vocal babbling" in cleft palate children (occurrence is clearly influenced by the age at which the soft palate is closed surgically, (see Henningsson & Isberg, 1987). In the next stage of sound production, infants start to experiment with content, by making uvular and velar articulations. So, the frame still precedes the content but does the frame predict the content?

words and sentences

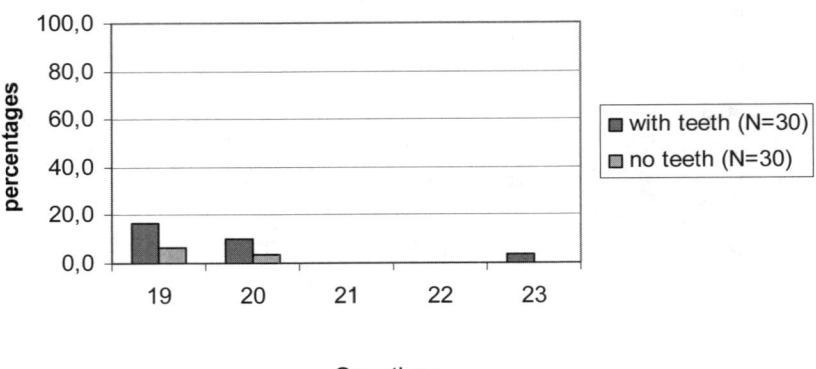

Questions

Figure 12.7.
Percentages per group that are reported to produce words and sentences.

Findings suggest that we must reckon that the eruption of teeth changes speech motor patterns in children, especially when tongue movements are involved. A complicating factor is that tooth eruption and speech movements change in relation to age. Further, the range for the onset of babbling is large (in a group of 51 Dutch infants, the range was 18 to 48 weeks; van der Stelt & Koopmans-van Beinum, 1986). In this group of 223 infants, the first tooth erupted in an age period ranging from 11 to 43 weeks.

In view of the stages (Table 12.1), it is possible that the eruption of a tooth in a three-month-old infant interferes with speech motor patterns in a quite different manner than in a six-month-old. The maturation process in the younger infant permits the child to voluntarily control only the tongue root, while the six-month-old child can already control tongue tip movements. It may be argued that it is the eruption of teeth, not the mere production of frames that predicts the development of content. The more static posture of the tongue in early babbling may only signal a temporary fallback, due to a complete reorganization of the speech motor patterns for the production of multi-syllabic utterances.

Acknowledgments

I owe many grateful thanks to Mrs. Anicka Hillen, since this chapter is based on her master's thesis (Hillen, 2003), which I supervised.

References

Boelema-da Costa, S. P. (1983). Preverbale logopedie (Preverbal Speech Therapy). *Nederlands Tijdschrift voor Geneeskunde, 127* (4), 140–145.

Bosma, J. F. (1967). *Symposium on oral sensation and perception.* Springfield, Illinois, Thomas.

Bosma, J. F. (1977). Structure and function of the infant oral and pharyngeal mechanisms. In J. M. Wilson (Ed.), *Oral-motor function and dysfunction in children: Proceedings of the Workshop at the Division of Physical Therapy* (pp. 33–70). Chapel Hill, NC: University of North Carolina.

Demirjian, A. (1986). Dentition. In F.T. Falkner & J. M. Tanner (Eds.), *Human growth* (pp. 269–298). New York, Plenum.

Dore, J., Franklin, M., Miller, R., & Ramer, A. (1976). Transitional phenomena in early language acquisition. *Journal of Child Language, 3,* 13–28.

Duyzings, J. A. C. (1943). De gevolgen van slechte gewoonten bij zuigelingen en kleuters (The effects of bad oral habits in infants and toddlers). *Tijdschrift voor Tandheelkunde, 50,* 97–404.

Fletcher, S.G. (1973). Maturation of the speech mechanism. *Folia Phoniatrica, 25,* 166–172.

Gillis, S., & De Schutter, G. (1986). Transitional Phenomena Revisited: Insights into the nominal insight. In B.J. Lindblom & R. Zetterström (Eds.), *Precursors of early speech* (pp. 127–142). Basingstoke, Great Britain: Macmillan Press Ltd.

Hendrickx, F. J. P., de Bruecker, J., Lambert, J., Switten, M., & Vrijens-Quintens, R. (1976). Practognosie van de mond. (Oral practognosia). *Logopedie en Akoepedie, 48,* 56–64.

Henningsson, G.E., & Isberg, A. M. (1987). Influence of palatal fistulae on speech and resonance. *Folia Phoniatrica, 39,* 183–192.

Hillen, A. (2003). Relatie tussen het brabbelen en het doorkomen van tandjes (The relation between babbling and the eruption of teeth). *Report 141 of the Institute of Phonetic Sciences of the University of Amsterdam,* The Netherlands.

Jansonius-Schultheiss, K. (1985). Is there a relation between eating and learning to speak? *Proceedings of the Institute of Phonetic Sciences, Amsterdam, 9,* 93–99.

Jürgens, U. (1998). Speech evolved from vocalization, not mastication. *Brain and Behavioral Sciences, 21*, 519–520.

Kaye, K. (1977). Towards the origin of dialogue. In H.R. Schaffer (Ed.), *Studies in mother-infant interaction* (pp. 89–117). London: Academic Press.

Kooi, S. K. (1982). Aspecten van het tijdelijk gebit. (Aspects of the deciduous teeth). Med. Sci. Thesis. Utrecht, The Netherlands: University of Utrecht.

Koopmans-van Beinum, F. J., & van der Stelt, J. M. (1979). Early stages in infant speech development. *Proceedings of the Institute of Phonetic Sciences, Amsterdam, 5*, 30–43.

Koopmans-van Beinum, F. J., & van der Stelt, J. M. (1986). Early stages in the development of speech movements. In B.J. Lindblom & R. Zetterström (Eds.), *Precursors of early speech* (pp. 37–50). Basingstoke, Great Britain: Macmillan Press Ltd.

Kuhl, P. K., & Meltzoff, A. N. (1996). The bimodal perception of speech in infancy, *Science, 218*, 1138–1141.

MacNeilage, P. F. (1998). The frame/content theory of evolution of speech production. *Behavioral and Brain Sciences, 21*, 499–546.

MacNeilage, P. F., & Davis, B. L. (2000). On the origin of internal structure of word forms. *Science, 288*, 527–531.

Meltzoff, A. N., & Moore, M.H. (1977). Imitation of facial and manual gestures by human neonates. *Science, 198*, 75–78.

Oller, D. K., Eilers, R. E., & Basinger, D. (2001). Intuitive identification of infant vocal sounds by parents. *Developmental Science, 4* (1), 49–60.

Oller, D. K. (1986). Metaphonology and infant vocalizations. In B.J. Lindblom & R. Zetterström (Eds.), *Precursors of early speech* (pp. 21–35). Basingstoke, Great Britain: Macmillan Press Ltd.

Serkhane, J., Schwartz, J. L., Boë, L. J., Davis, B., & Matyear, C. (2002). Motor specifications of a baby robot via the analysis of infants' vocalizations. *Proceedings of the International Conference on Spoken Language Processing in Denver*, pp. 45–48.

Skoyles, J. R. (1998). Speech phones are a replication code. *Medical Hypotheses, 50*, 167–173.

van der Stelt, J. M., & Koopmans-van Beinum, F. J. (1981). Note on motor analysis of infant sound. *Proceedings of the Institute of Phonetic Sciences, Amsterdam, 6*, 23–45.

van der Stelt, J. M., & Koopmans-van Beinum, F. J. (1986). The onset of babbling related to gross motor development. In B.J. Lindblom & R. Zetterström (Eds.), *Precursors of early speech* (pp. 163–173). Basingstoke, Great Britain: Macmillan Press Ltd.

Wasz-Höckert, O., Lind, J., Vuorenkoski, V., Partanen, T.J., & Valanné, E. (1968). *The infant cry: A spectrographic and auditory analysis*. London: International Medical Publications, Heinemann.

Appendix

	N=30	with teeth %	N=30	no teeth %	Total number in the pairs=60	%	Pearson's X^2
Laryngeal sounds							
Question 1	25	83.3	23	76.7	48	76.7	0.347
Question 2	25	83.3	22	73.3	47	73.3	0.219
Question 3	27	90.0	27	90.0	54	90.0	1
Question 4	27	90.0	24	80.0	51	80.0	0.278
Question 5	30	100	25	83.3	55	83.3	0.020

	N=30	with teeth %	N=30	no teeth %	Total number in the pairs=60	%	Pearson's X^2
Single articulations							
Question 6	24	80.0	22	73.3	46	76.7	0.542
Question 7	18	60.0	14	76.7	32	53.3	0.301
Question 8	25	83.3	19	63.3	44	73.3	0.044
Question 9	12	40.0	7	23.3	19	31.7	0.113

	N=30	with teeth %	N=30	no teeth %	Total number in the pairs=60	%	Pearson's X^2
Prosodic sounds							
Question 10	25	83.3	23	76.7	48	76.7	0.062
Question 11	25	83.3	22	73.3	47	73.3	0.688
Question 12	27	90.0	27	90.0	54	90.0	0.176
Question 13	27	90.0	24	80.0	51	80.0	0.138
Question 14	30	100	25	83.3	55	83.3	0.520

	N= 30	with teeth	N= 30	no teeth	Total number in the pairs=60		Pearson's
Babbling sounds		%		%		%	X^2
Question 15	15	50.0	12	40.0	27	45.0	0.436
Question 16	13	43.3	10	33.3	23	38.3	0.486
Question 17	10	33.3	6	20.0	16	26.7	0.211
Question 18	14	13.3	5	16.7	9	15.0	0.759

	N= 30	with teeth	N= 30	no teeth	Total number in the pairs=60		Pearson's
Words, sentences		%		%		%	X^2
Question 19	5	16.7	2	6.7	48	11	0
Question 20	3	10.0	1	3.3	47	6.7	0
Question 21	0	0	0	0	54	0	0
Question 22	0	0	0	0	51	0	0
Question 23	1	3.3	1	3.3	55	3.3	0

13

An Acoustical Analysis of Consonant-Vowel Co-occurrences in Babbling: Coronal and Dorsal Contexts

Christine L. Matyear

Department of Communication Sciences and Disorders

The University of Texas at Austin

Austin, Texas, USA

Babbling, often interpreted to mean the senseless gibberish uttered by hysterics or the undifferentiated warbles produced by babies before they learn to speak, means something quite different to speech scientists who study the acquisition of speech in infants. For them babbling is a specific kind of sound: speech-like, but non-linguistic (non-meaningful) strings of consonants and vowels uttered by infants between the ages of seven months and approximately eighteen months. These sounds have very distinctive articulatory, perceptual, and acoustic characteristics: they are made with the same articulators (jaw, lips, tongue, soft palate) as adult speech sounds; they sound very like adult speech sounds; they have the same measurable sound frequency characteristics as adult speech sounds. In some important ways, however, babbling is unique to infants and quite unlike adult speech.

Babbling has been recorded, transcribed, and analyzed by scholars worldwide. These studies have shown that babbling is phonetically very consistent among infants regardless of the ambient language into which they are born. In other words, babbling infants sound more like one another than they do like the adult speakers who surround them. As a result of these findings, the onset of babbling at seven months of age has come to be appreciated as a significant milestone in an infant's progression toward being a speaker and regularities of babbling are seen as useful metrics for assessing development.

A production-based theoretical explanation of babbling has been proposed by MacNeilage and Davis, the Frame/Content (F/C) theory (1990a), which argues that babbling represents a regularization of infant vocalization by rhythmic close/open movements of the mandible (jaw), a step toward the production of the consonant and vowel phonemes (Cs & Vs) of language. During babbling, MacNeilage and Davis have claimed, infants use this mandibular oscillation almost entirely, to the exclusion of independent movements of other speech articulators, to produce the percept of consonants and vowels organized into syllable-like CV sequences.

Some of the most striking consequences of this limited production method are the distinctive CV patterns of babbling, e.g., [ba ba ba] or [dæ dæ dæ]. These patterns are characterized by the co-occurrence of labial consonants (consonants made with the lips) with tongue-central vowels, e.g., [ba], coronal (tongue-front) consonants with tongue-front vowels, e.g., [di], and dorsal (tongue-back) consonants with tongue-back vowels, e.g., [gu]. These dominant co-occurrences in babbling occur, according to MacNeilage and Davis, because the tongue tends to stay relatively stationary while the jaw makes the rhythmic close open alterations that produce the closure for consonantal sounds and the opening for vocalic sounds.

The labial C-central V sequence is the most basic. If the tongue is in a relative static mode resting in the center of the mouth and the jaw is rhythmically closed and opened, the lips will come together and touch one another before the tongue can touch the any part of the palate (the roof of the mouth). The resulting sound, most audible when, as is typical, phonation (voicing) is occurring too, will be syllable-like. It will sound like a CV sequence in which the closed phase is a bilabial stop consonant, e.g., [b], and the open phase is a tongue-central vowel, e.g., [a]. MacNeilage and Davis have called this simplest of CV sequences a "pure frame," a syllable-like utterance in which the jaw does all the work of articulating a CV while the tongue remains passive. These pure-frame syllables may occur as singletons but more often occur in the longer strings of regular, rhythmic, concatenated CVs, e.g., [ba ba ba ba ba], that are most characteristic of babbling.

The other two typical CV co-occurrence patterns, the coronal C-front V, e.g., [di] and the dorsal C-back V, e.g., [gu], differ only slightly from a pure frame. They are made with the tongue either thrust forward or retracted from the central, or neutral, position. Then as the jaw closes and opens rhythmically, either the coronal (front) part of the tongue touches the hard palate (the front part of the roof of the mouth) or the dorsal (back) part of the tongue touches the velum (the back part of the palate, the soft palate). By making such simple articulations, infants can easily produce a range of very adult-like CV syllables in very non-adult-like sequences, e.g., [di di di] or [gu gu gu].

To MacNeilage and Davis, these strong co-occurrence patterns are evidence of motor constraints against the production, during babbling, of individual consonants and vowels in the multitudinous combinations typical of adult speech. They are also evidence of the supremacy of the syllable as the fundamental structural unit of speech. In the process of speech acquisition, they claim, the frame (the syllable) emerges first and only later does the content (the segment). That is, only later does the infant develop the motor control to move the various articulators rapidly and independently of the jaw to produce individual consonants and vowels with unique and contrasting articulatory characteristics. These evident production constraints have been reported in transcription studies of babbling infants from language environments as different as English, Spanish, French, Korean, and Japanese (see Davis & MacNeilage, 2002, for a review).

Questions may arise, however, about some of the reported babbling data. These include questions about the validity of using linguistically-based transcription methods for non-linguistic vocalizations, questions about inter-transcriber agreement, and questions about the utterances that do not follow predicted patterns, that do not seem consistent with the F/C explanation of babbling. The symbols of the International Phonetic Alphabet (IPA) have been developed to permit the phonetic transcription of any speech sound produced in the world's languages, but we might ask whether they are adequate to capture the characteristics of prelinguistic babbling. The degree to which the transcribers in the MacNeilage and Davis study agreed among themselves (personal communication) provides one indication. While agreements about labial sounds [b], were quite solid, more disagreement occurred regarding transcription of coronal [d] and dorsal [g] sounds. In addition, transcribers who did not share the same regional dialect sometimes disagreed about the frontness or backness of vowel sounds. However, there was consistent agreement that velar consonants and back vowels were relatively less frequent in the infant corpus overall that the other two forward pairings—labial-central and coronal-front.

In this chapter we will explore the nature of a set of babbled utterances that seem to contradict the predictions of F/C theory. We will look specifically at a set of babbled sequences that do not seem to be governed by the production constraints described above. These are CVs that were variously transcribed with [d] or [g] and a series of different vowels, some front, some central, some back. We will find that an objective analysis, acoustic measurement of the frequency spectral values of these sounds, provides evidence that these babbles, regardless of how they are transcribed, do in fact manifest the same production constraints that the more frequent, consistently-transcribed, and predicted babbles do. We will find that these utterances are consistent with the predictions of F/C theory. We will offer an explanation of how this might be happening despite the transcription evidence to the contrary.

Background

First, let us review the nature of babbling and what speech scientists have said about it in greater detail. Babbling, as described above, is a characteristic vocal behavior produced by infants, beginning abruptly around seven months of age and continuing though the early stages of language production during the second year. Articulatorily it is defined as rhythmic alternation between a closed and open mouth accompanied by phonation (MacNeilage & Davis, 1993). Perceptually it sounds like strings of alternating consonant and vowel sounds that are speech-like, having a syllabic structure of the form CV, though not evincing any lexical content, that is, not seeming to be used referentially, as words are used in languages. Acoustically, babbling is defined as closed/open cycles of vocal production with at least 10 dB difference in loudness between complete consonantal closure and full vocalic resonance, a CV syllable duration of 100-500 ms, and an absence of extreme (more than two-fold) shifts in fundamental frequency, or pitch (Oller, 1986). Strings of babbled syllables are produced while the vocal folds are vibrating to produce the sound of voicing. To get a 10 dB difference in loudness, the mouth is closing fully to block the emergence of most sound during the consonantal phase and is opening fully to allow sound resonance to emerge during the vocalic phase. The vocal folds are vibrating at a steady rate, so the pitch of the voice does not rise into high squeals or drop into low growls. The jaw is oscillating at a regular rate to give the babbled string a rhythmic quality.

Transcription studies of the babbling phase of infant speech acquisition have consistently reported similar findings with respect to the repertoire of consonantal and vocalic sounds produced and the characteristic organization of these sounds into CV syllables. The most frequent consonants are the labial and coronal (oral) stops [b] and [d], and the labial and coronal nasal (stop)s [m] and [n] (Oller et al., 1976; Vihman et al., 1985; Stoel-Gammon, 1985; Kent & Bauer, 1985; Roug, Landberg & Lundberg, 1989; Oller & Eilers, 1982; Locke, 1983). The first two, [b] and [d] are called stops because air is trapped in the mouth behind closed articulators, and [m] and [n] are called nasals because one of those articulators, the velum or soft palate is lowered to permit air to escape through the nose while the other articulators remain closed.

Vocalic sounds are most often reported to be non-high, non-back. These defining terms refer to the position of the tongue in the oral cavity, from high to mid to low and from front to central to back. Most of the vowel-like sounds in babbling are transcribed like the vowels [ɛ] and, [ae] as in "head" and "had," which are mid- and low–front vowels, and like [ʊ] and [a] as in "hut" and "hot," which are mid- and low-central vowels (Buhr, 1980; Bickley, 1983; Davis & MacNeilage, 1995; de Boysson-Bardies et al., 1989; Holmgren et al., 1986; Kent & Murray, 1982; Kent & Bauer, 1985; Lieberman, 1980; Roug, Landberg, & Lundberg, 1989). As mentioned above, these frequently-occurring consonantal and vocalic sounds also show a strong tendency to co-occur in patterns: labial consonants co-occurring with central vowels, coronal consonants with front vowels, and (though relatively less frequent) dorsal consonants with back vowels (Davis & MacNeilage, 1995).

Again, the theoretical explanation for these co-occurrences (MacNeilage & Davis's Frame/Content theory) is that most of the articulatory variation in babbling results from the close/open mandibular cycle accompanied by sustained phonation (voicing) producing rhythmic alternations of consonantal and vocalic sounds with little independent contribution of the other articulators such as lip, tongue, or velum (soft palate) (MacNeilage & Davis, 1990 a,b). In other words, if the tongue is at rest in neutral position in the center of the oral cavity and the jaw moves up and down (much as it does during sucking and chewing), the upper and lower lips will close to produce a labial consonantal sound, the open mouth will generate central-sounding resonances, and the listener will hear a [bã] [bʌ̃], [mã], or [mʌ̃]. ([˜] is the IPA symbol for a nasalized vowel.) Such CV co-occurrences are considered "pure frames" because the quality of the sounds is a result of basic jaw movement without independent articulatory movements of the tongue or velum. Adding a single additional articulatory movement to the pure frame, a fronting or backing of the tongue or a raising or lowering of the velum, can account for the other typical babbled sequences. If the tongue is in a fronted position, at jaw closure it will most likely make contact with the coronal (front) portion of the roof of the oral cavity, yielding a percept of something more like [dæ] or [næ]. In a similar fashion, a backed tongue will permit a dorsal articulation (a touching of the backmost surface of the oral cavity) and will produce sequences like [go] or [ŋõ]. ([o] is a mid-back vowel, and [ŋ] is a dorsal nasal, pronounced as the "ng" in "sing.") If the velum is raised, blocking the flow of air through the nose, both the consonant and the vowel will tend to be non-nasal like [ba], and if it is lowered the entire CV will tend to be nasal like [mã]. Supporting acoustic evidence includes the finding that, although not always transcribed as such, babbled vowels in nasal consonantal environments tend to be nasalized (Matyear, 1997).

Acoustic analysis of vowel frequencies can also provide evidence about tongue position during CV production. The second highest formant frequency (characteristic resonance or overtone), F2, produced in the oral cavity during the articulation of a vowel is a reliable indicator of tongue position in the horizontal plane (front-central-back). A high value of F2 correlates to a tongue-front vowel, and a low value for F2 correlates to a tongue-back vowel. Evidence from Matyear (1997) shows that vowels in coronal contexts have significantly higher F2 frequency means, that is, are articulatorily more fronted while those same vowels, when they are transcribed as occurring in bilabial contexts have significantly lower means, are articulatorily more central.

For this chapter we will explore the prediction that dorsal closures in babbling are more likely to co-occur with back vowels by acoustically analyzing the F2 values of vowels transcribed in dorsal environments versus the same vowels transcribed in coronal environments. The prediction is that such vowels will have a lower F2 when transcribed in dorsal environments than when transcribed in coronal environments (implying a more backed articulation for vowels in dorsal environments).

CV pairings reported in the highest numbers, labials with central vowels and coronals with front vowels, occur significantly above chance as determined by Chi Square statistical analysis. As a result of their high frequency of occurrence, these particular CV sequences can be interpreted as evidence of articulatory constraints on the developing speech system. That robust finding does not mean, however, that infants cannot produce CV sequences in babbling that do not appear to adhere to these constraints, nor does it mean that infants fail to produce dorsal consonants or high or back vowels. Indeed if they did not produce them, the attempts to compare different vowels in all the consonantal contexts of interest would have been impossible. In fact, the presence of these less frequent babbles forms the focus of this study.

In addition to assessing the acoustic properties of vowels transcribed in dorsal environments compared to the same vowels in coronal environments, some of the issues of reliability in the transcription of babbling are addressed. It might be argued that using the symbols developed for transcribing language is not appropriate for transcribing speech-like, but non-linguistic utterances as there is no evidence that infants are trying to make adult sounds. Languages have distinctive sets of contrastive phonemes, but infants do not show much influence from their ambient languages during babbling. They do not appear to be trying to mimic what they hear. Instead they have repertoires of sounds that are more like those of other infants around the world. This is the reason for using the more superordinate, inclusive phonetic classifications "coronal" and "dorsal" rather than the more English-specific place-of-articulation categories "alveolar" and "velar" to discuss American infant productions.

"Coronal" and "dorsal" refers to either the front half or the back half of the tongue that touches the roof of the mouth during the production of stops, while "alveolar" refers to the specific place just behind the front teeth that the coronal part of the tongue touches during production of the English [d], and "velar" refers the region of the velum, or soft palate, in the back of the mouth, where the dorsum of the tongue touches to make the English [g]. Like English, all languages have coronal and dorsal consonants and each of those sounds will have a very specific place of articulation along the upper surface of the oral cavity, which may or may not be like those of English.

These superordinate categories are used here because there is no reason to believe that the American infant's dorsal articulation is not closer to the hard palate, the center of the roof of the mouth, or closer to the uvula, the fleshy tip at the end of the soft palate, than right at the soft palate as an adult English speaker's would be. Of greater concern, these differences in place of articulation might not be perceived and captured by an English-speaking transcriber whose language has only one dorsal place of articulation. The same potential for transcription bias exists for vowels: the perception of categorical boundaries between front, central, and back vowels is colored by the linguistic experience of the transcriber. Evidence suggests that infants are not producing separate C and V segments at all, in the adult sense, but rather producing a holistic utterance with a dominant articulatory position for the tongue and most of its variation in degree of closure a result of jaw oscillation. There is, thus, little basis to attribute the intentional production of consonant and vowel segments with unique and deliberate places of articulation to the infant.

If babbling is driven by the infant's biological system rather than by the phonology (sound system) of its ambient language and if transcribers are destined by their experience to be biased in favor of the sounds phonemic to their language and training, how valid is phonetic transcription of babbling? Many transcription studies of babbling do not report any measures of inter-transcriber agreement or even of intra-transcriber reliability. When they do, the details of their methodology are vague. The Davis and MacNeilage study (1995) reports the results of inter-transcriber agreement in a straightforward point-to-point analysis of a very large database of babbling. Agreement for consonants was 63–83%; for vowels it was 33–69% (close to chance). The findings upon which F/C Theory is based depend on transcription data. Fortunately, those findings were robust because the unequivocal sounds were so dominant that variability among transcribers did not affect overall conclusions. The study did leave some unanswered questions about the source of the variability though.

This analysis, however, seeks to test the premises of F/C theory without depending entirely upon transcription. One way to assess the nature of the babbled CV is to study the utterance acoustically, measuring the frequency change), termed F2 transition, between the consonantal closure and the vocalic opening. A stable transition for the second formant would imply a lack of tongue movement, regardless of where in the oral cavity the tongue was, and thus the holistic nature of the CV sequence (frame dominance) could be confirmed independently of the transcription.

This chapter therefore presents two hypotheses: (1) the F2 frequency of vowels in coronal contexts should be higher than the F2 frequency of the same vowels in dorsal contexts, indicating that the tongue is more fronted for vowels following tongue-front consonants; and (2) the F2 transition between the closed and opened phases of babbling should remain close to the same frequency, that is, consonant-vowel (CV) transitions should be relatively flat, indicating an absence of tongue movement in the horizontal plane during the entire CV production.

Method

Four infants, two female and two male, were recorded for an hour once a week beginning at age seven months and continuing until they were three-and-a-half years of age. All four were children of monolingual American-English speaking parents. All subjects showed normal results on a hearing screening using sound field techniques. For all four, normal development was established through parent case-history report and the administration of the *Batelle Developmental Screening Inventory*.

Each participant was recorded and transcribed by a single investigator. Recording was performed in the infant's homes, and for this study, data were collected one hour per week for approximately five months, from the onset of babbling to the beginning of first words. Audio-Technica ATW-1031 cordless microphones were affixed to the subject's clothing and transmitted a signal via an Audio-Technica ATW-T31 transmitter to a TEAC ATW-20 digital audio recorder.

Transcription was performed by the recording investigator, and 10% of each session was retranscribed by 1 to 3 trained transcribers. All transcribers were native English speakers. Detailed results of those transcriptions are reported in Davis and MacNeilage, 1995. A convenience sample of 370 CV(C) sequences were selected for acoustic analysis. These tokens were of the form [dV(d)] or [gV(g)], with front vowels, central vowels, or back vowels in second position. Measurements were made of F2 vowel onset ($F2_o$) and F2 vowel steady-state ($F2_v$) frequencies. $F2_o$ was measured at the first glottal pulse after the burst, and $F2_v$ at steady state of the vowel. Analysis of variance was performed on each vowel class with consonantal class as the independent variable and $F2_v$ as the dependent variable. A correlation analysis was made of $F2_o$ as a function of $F2_v$, and a calculation of $F2_v - F2_o$ was performed.

A comparison analysis of two male and one female adult speakers of American-English was completed. One hundred forty four tokens of the same forms as those selected for the infant study were elicited. Data were collected using the same recording apparatus recorded in a laboratory setting. CVC sequences of the desired type were elicited by having the subjects read a prepared list of words containing the appropriate sound sequences and a narrative passage with the same words included. The same data analyses were performed on these tokens.

Results and Discussion

Context Analysis

The effect of consonantal context on vowel F2 frequency was assessed for the 370 infant tokens and 144 adult tokens. The F2 means of six vowels transcribed as [ɪ, ɛ æ, a, ʊ, u] occurring in the context of consonants transcribed as [d ___(d)] were compared with the F2 means of the same vowels occurring in the context [g___(g)]. The number of infant CV tokens were not equally distributed among all CV groups, and the consonants and vowels that composed them did not occur with equal frequency in the infant's output. Some of the

Table 13.1.
Average Infant F2$_v$ by Place of Articulation. *Italic* indicates higher F2 in coronal context. **Bold** indicates a significant difference.

	[d]		[g]	
	n	F2v (Hz)	n	F2v (Hz)
Front V	199	2974	44	**3135**
Central V	76	*2748*	12	2363
Back V	5	*2239*	34	2049

vowels were so infrequent (specifically the back vowels) that the infant vowels were grouped into the superordinate categories of front, central, and back. It was predicted that vowels in coronal contexts would have higher frequency F2 values than the same vowels in dorsal contexts, indicating that the tongue was more fronted. A comparison of the results for infants and adults showed that the predicted effect was only evident in part of the infant data (See Table 13.1).

The infant data showed that for both central and back vowels, F2 means were higher in coronal contexts. For central vowels the difference was significant, but there were not enough tokens transcribed with coronal consonants and back vowels to permit statistical analysis. The F2 means were significantly lower for front vowels transcribed with coronal consonants. This latter finding was unexpected, and difficult to explain.

The results for the adult analysis were closer to expected patterns for adults (See Table 13.2). In 3 of the 6 vocalic classes, [a, ʊ, u], the F2 mean was higher in coronal contexts, and in 3 classes, [ɪ, ɛ, æ], it was lower. In none of the 6 classes was the difference in vowel F2 means significant. These two sets of findings, the infant data and the adult data, imply that adults, in having effectively the same F2 values for each of the vowels regardless of consonantal context, demonstrate independent articulation of vowels and consonants. The tongue is moved to a place of articulation specific to the requirements of the consonant while the jaw makes closure and then to a position in the oral cavity that yields the characteristic resonances of the desired vowel as the jaw opens and then on to the place of articulation for the following consonantal segment.

In contrast, infants, while evidently capable of moving the tongue between open and close movement of the jaw, tend to let the jaw do most of the work and do not move the tongue like adult speakers during the mandibular cycle. The difference in F2 values for the central and back vowels implies that the vocalic sounds that transcribers hear as belonging to the same vowel class in fact are articulated with the tongue more fronted when the tongue is making a tongue front contact with the palate during a coronal consonantal closure and a more tongue-backed articulation during a dorsal closure. In other words, the tongue is not moving independently during the mandibular cycle.

How then can the findings for the front vowels be interpreted? These results indicate that the tongue is more fronted when the vowel occurs in a dorsal context than in a coronal context, a counterintuitive finding. These values imply that independent movement of the tongue is occurring during these CV sequences.

One approach to interpreting the non-predicted findings is to question the accuracy of the transcription of infant babbling sequences. As mentioned above, places of articulation for phonemic lingual stop consonants in English are coronal-alveolar and dorsal-velar. Although palatal allophones (variants) of the velar stop are not uncommon, English transcribers may not be very sensitive to

Table 13.2.
Average Adult F2 by Place of Articulation. *Italic* indicates higher F2 in coronal context. None of the differences were significant.

Vowel	Consonant			
	[d]		[g]	
	n	F_2(Hz)	n	F_2(Hz)
[ɪ]	12	2015	12	2114
[ɛ]	12	1939	12	2958
[æ]	12	1786	12	1833
[ʊ]	12	1350	12	1284
[u]	12	1030	12	1000
[a]	12	1286	12	1247

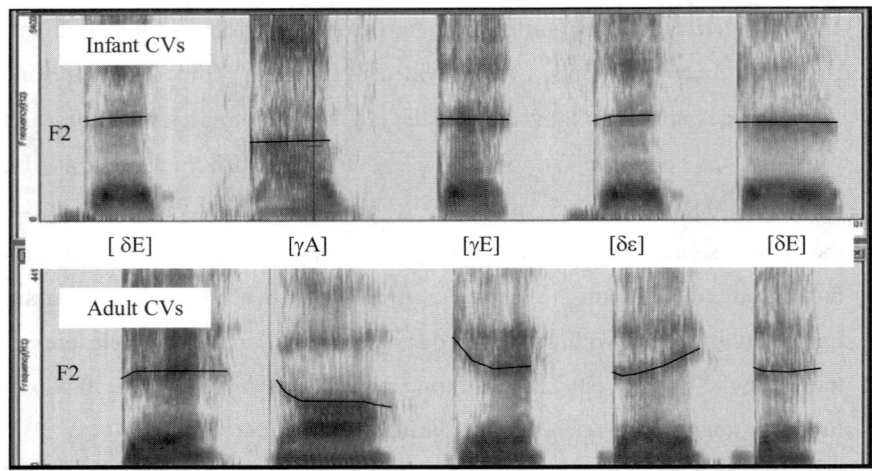

Figure 13.1.
Spectrograms of infant CVs with level F2 transitions and adult CVs with changing transitions.

the acoustic variation between them and may be likely to transcribe them all as velar. Even trained transcribers may not be sensitive to variations in vowel articulation that do not correspond well to their own phonemic repertoire. Thus, relying solely on the transcription of infant babbling for fine-grained distinctions in articulation is unrealistic (Cucchiarini, 1996).

A method to disambiguate the transcriptions of infant utterances that span the boundary between transcriber's phonemic classes is to perform an acoustic analysis. An acoustic analysis that measures the transition of the second formant between consonantal closure and vocalic openness can reveal the presence of and degree of change in tongue front-backness. If a measurement of F2 immediately following the end of a [d] or a [g] and again at the steady-state midpoint of the following vowel shows a significant change in frequency, it maybe inferred that the tongue is moving from its position during stop closure toward a different position during vowel openness. Alternatively, if the transition is relatively flat, it may be inferred that the tongue is not moving to create independent consonants and vowels but rather that the CV alternation is produced primarily by close/open jaw movement. Spectrographic examples of five infant and five adult CV sequences given in Figure 13.1 illustrate the difference.

Another result of such an analysis is the disambiguation of consonantal place of articulation in the transcription of infant utterances. Locus equation studies of adult CV productions (Lindblom, 1998; Sussman, 1998) have shown that the regression lines for F2 onset versus F2 steady-state will have distinctively different slopes for bilabial, coronal, and dorsal productions. If infant utterances are analyzed in a similar fashion, and the slope for coronal CV transitions is significantly different from the slope for dorsal CV transitions, then it can be inferred that infants consistently produce independently articulated consonants and vowels falling into the various C and V categories transcribed. If, however, the slopes are similar, it could be inferred that the co-occurring Cs and Vs are produced with the same lingual articulation and that the transcription is not narrow enough to capture the fine-grained differences in articulation between coronal and dorsal, front and back.

Transition Analyses

The frequencies of vocalic $F2_o$ (vowel) onsets and $F2_v$ vowel (steady-states) were measured for the 370 infant and 144 adult CV sequences. As mentioned above, the infant utterances were spontaneous productions transcribed by trained transcribers whose agreement using a point-to-point agreement rating was between 33–83% (later, a more global agreement analysis produced much higher ratings: 85–98%). The adult utterances were elicited.

The striking finding is that both sets of infant data have practically identical slopes, both effectively 1.000, and little variance as shown in Figure 13.2. These results clearly indicate that for the majority of the utterances measured, the tongue does not move from its position at vowel onset to its position at vowel steady-state. In other words, for most of these utterances the tongue does not move appreciably while the jaw does most of the work in articulating consonant-vowel sequences. For most of these utterances tongue-front consonants do co-occur with tongue-front vowels and tongue-back

Infant CV Co-occurrences: Coronal/Vowel

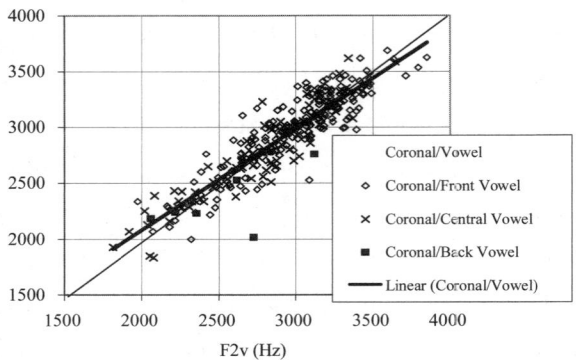

Infant CV Co-occurrences: Dorsal/Vowel

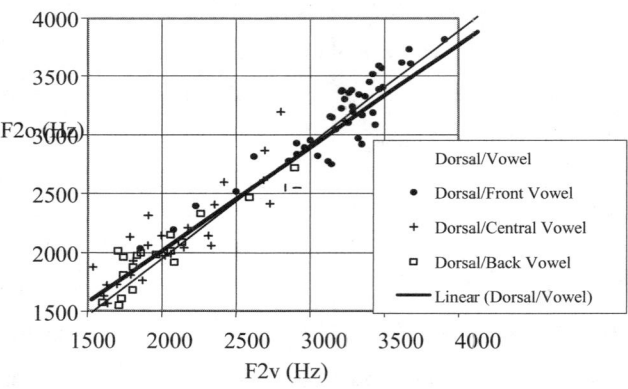

Figure 13.2.
A regression analysis of 280 babbles transcribed as [dV(d)] yielded the following result: R2 = 0.824, SE = 160, y = 0.91x + 262. The analysis of 90 [gV(g)] babbles yielded R2 = 0.941, SE = 160, y = 97x + 234.

consonants co-occur with tongue-back vowels even if the transcription does not always capture the fine details of the articulations.

In contrast, Figure 13.3 shows a regression analysis of 72 adult syllables transcribed as [dV(d)] that yielded the following result: $R^2 = 0.744$, SE = 94, y = 0.4163x + 1136.6. The analysis of 72 [gV(g)] syllables yielded $R^2 = 0.777$, SE = 1160, y = 0.681x + 797.49. These adult results show very different characteristics. The slopes of the two datasets are quite different from one another, neither is close to 1.00, and the data points are not as tightly clustered,

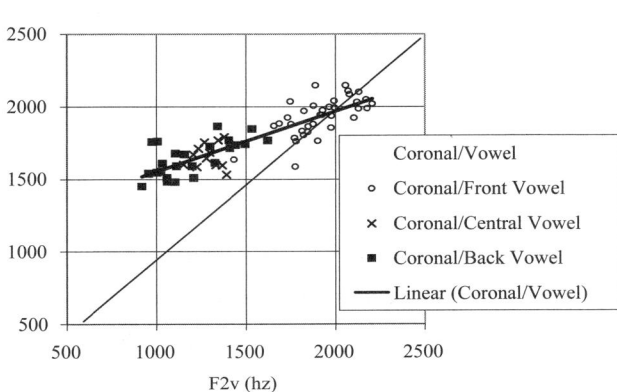

Adult CV Co-ocurrences: Coronal/Vowel

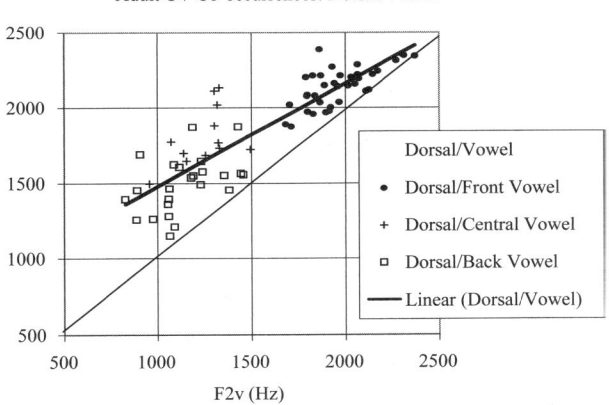

Adult CV Co-occurrences: Dorsal/Vowel

Figure 13.3.
Adult regression analysis.

especially for the [g] tokens. These findings imply a distinctive difference between the articulation of the alveolar consonant and the velar consonant as well as an evident movement of the tongue in the horizontal dimension in order to produce tongue-front consonants with tongue-back vowels and vice versa.

Finally, a simple comparison of the F2 transition ($F2_v - F2_o$) means for infant vowels and adult vowels shows that infant $F2_v$ values differed from $F2_o$ values by an average of 2 Hz (a non-significant amount), while adult F2 values varied by an average of 281 Hz (a significant amount). It is hard to escape the conclusion that adults evince more independent articulatory control of the tongue and jaw during CV production than infants do.

Overview

Overall, the results of these acoustic analyses leave us with a clearer picture of the infant's developing sound production system. Evidently driven by the same basic motor functions used for such ingestive acts as licking, sucking, and chewing, infants at about seven months begin to produce speech-like sounds by rhythmically closing and opening the jaws while producing voicing. This powerful dominance of the mandibular cycle permits infants to produce a repertoire of three classes of consonants and three of vowels with a minimum of other articulatory movements and no evident intentionality. Note though, that the nine possible combinations of labial, coronal, and dorsal consonants with front, central, and back vowels do not occur with equal frequency. Three combinations are significantly more common than others: the labial-C/central-V, coronal-C/front-V, and dorsal-C/back-V sequences.

Still, we need to explain the presence in transcription studies of the other six non-preferred co-occurrences. They could be random variances; they could be intentional excursions away from motorically governed, holistic productions toward cognitively governed, linguistic segmental productions; they could be mis-transcriptions. The evidence presented above shows the presence of some small amounts of variance probably caused by occasional random tongue movements during the mandibular cycle. Beyond that, the absence of any reason to suspect intentionality leaves only the likelihood of transcription error to explain the exceptions.

The regression data with their distribution of F2 values along a regression line with a slope of approximately 1.000 show very convincingly that the tongue it tends to stay during vocalic opening wherever it is positioned during consonantal closure. It may be the case that listeners have transcribed some tokens too broadly or inaccurately, either because of perceptual ambiguity in the sound or because of the inadequacies of their transcription conventions coupled with their inescapable transcription bias. Regardless, the evidence implies that these infants were producing utterances with little if any independent movement of the tongue. Though these findings may offer a gentle indictment of the accuracy of some babbling transcription, they also provide both a very strong confirmation of the conclusions previously based entirely on the more robust of those transcriptions, and an explanation of the apparent discrepancies.

References

Bickley, C. (1983). Acoustic evidence for phonological development of vowels in young children. Paper presented at the Tenth International Congress of Phonetic Sciences, Utrecht, Holland.

Boysson-Bardies, B. de, Halle, P., Sagart, P. L., & Durand, C. (1989). A cross-linguistic investigation of vowel formants in babbling. *Journal of Child Language, 16,* 1–17.

Buhr, R. D. (1980). The emergence of vowels in an infant. *Journal of Speech and Hearing Research, 23*(1), 73–94.

Cucchiarini C. (1996). Assessing transcription agreement: Methodological aspects. *Clinical Linguistics and Phonetics, 10*(2), 131–155.

Davis, B. L., & MacNeilage, P. F. (1995). The articulatory bases of babbling. *Journal of Speech and Hearing Research, 38,* 1199–1211.

Holmgren, K., Lindblom, B., Aurelius, G., Jalling, B., & Zetterström, R. (1986). On the phonetics of infant vocalization. In B. Lindblom & R. Zetterstrom (Eds.), *Precursors of early speech* (pp. 51–63). New York: Stockton Press.

Kent, R. D. & Bauer, H. R. (1985). Vocalizations of one-year-olds. *Journal of Child Language,* 12, 491–526.

Kent, R. D., & Murray, A. D. (1982). Acoustic features of infant vocalic utterances at 3, 6, and 9 months. *Journal of the Acoustical Society of America, 72,* 353–365.

Lieberman, P. (1980). On the development of vowel production in young children. In G. Yeni-Komshian, J. F. Kavanaugh, & C. A. Ferguson (Eds.), *Child phonology, Vol. I: Production* (pp. 113–142). New York: Academic Press.

Lindblom, B. (1998). An articulatory perspective on the locus equation. *Behavioral and Brain Sciences, 21,* 274–275.

Locke, J. (1983). *Phonological acquisition and change.* New York: Academic Press.

MacNeilage, P. F., & Davis, B. L. (1990a). Acquisition of speech production: Frames then content. In M. Jeannerod (Ed.), *Attention and performance XIII: Motor representation and control* (pp. 453–475). Hilldale, NJ: Lawrence Erlbaum.

MacNeilage, P. F., & Davis, B. L. (1990b). Acquisition of Speech Production: The Achievement of Segmental Independence. In W. J. Hardcastle & A. Marchal (Eds.), *Speech production and speech modeling* (pp. 55–68). Kluwer: Dordrecht, Holland.

MacNeilage P. F., & Davis, B. L. (1993). Motor explanations of babbling and early speech patterns. In B. Boysson-Bardies, S. de Schoen, P. Jusczyk, P. MacNeilage & J. Morton (Eds.), *Developmental neurocognition: Speech and face processing in the first year of life* (pp. 341–352). Dordrecht: Kluwer Academic Publishers.

Matyear, C. L. (1997). *, acoustical study of vowels in babbling*. Unpublished Doctoral Dissertation, The University of Texas at Austin, Department of Linguistics.

Matyear, C. L., MacNeilage, P. F. & Davis, B. L. (1998). Nasalization of vowels in nasal environments in babbling. *Phonetica, 55*, 1–17.

Oller, D. K. (1986). Metaphonology and infant vocalizations. In B. Lindblom & R. Zetterstrom (Eds.) *Precursors of early speech* (pp. 21–35). Basingstoke, Hampshire: MacMillan Press.

Oller, D. K. & Eilers, R. E. (1982). Similarity of babbling in Spanish- and English-learning babies. *Journal of Infant Language, 9*, 565–577.

Roug, L., Landberg, I., & Lundberg, L. J. (1989). Phonetic development in early infancy: A study of four Swedish children during the first eighteen months of life. *Journal of Child Language, 16*, 19–40.

Stoel-Gammon, C. (1985). Phonetic Inventories, 15-24 Months: A longitudinal study, *Journal of Speech and Hearing Research, 28*, 505–512.

Sussman, H. M., Fruchter, D., Hilbert, J., & Sirosh, J. (1998). Linear correlates in the speech signal: The orderly output constraint. *Behavioral and Brain Sciences, 21*, 241–299.

Vihman, M., Macken, M., Miller, R., Simmons, H., & Miller, J. (1985). From babbling to speech: A reassessment of the continuity issue. *Language, 60*, 397–445.

14

Syllables, Segments, and Sequences: Phonological Patterns in the Words of Young Children Acquiring American English

Carol Stoel-Gammon

and

Beate Peter

Department of Speech and Hearing Sciences

University of Washington

Seattle, Washington, USA

The syllable plays a key role in MacNeilage's Frame/Content theory of the development of speech in children and in his concept of the evolution of language in humans. MacNeilage proposes that the basic consonant-vowel syllable type developed from the closing (for consonant production) and opening (for vowels) mandibular movements associated with chewing and sucking. These movements constitute the "frame" of a syllable and the particular consonants and vowels within the frame form the "content," hence the term "Frame/Content theory" of the evolution of speech (MacNeilage, 1998; MacNeilage & Davis, 2000; 2001). According to MacNeilage (1998), the content that occurs within the syllable frame is influenced by movements of the jaw with no independent movements of the tongue, resulting in the likelihood of more frequent occurrences of particular consonant-vowel (CV) sequences.

Specifically, it is argued that (1) consonants produced with a constriction in the front of the mouth are more likely to precede front vowels (e.g., /di/); (2) consonants produced with the lips (i.e., with no tongue involvement) will be strongly associated with central vowels (e.g., /ba/); and (3) consonants produced with a constriction in the back of the mouth will be associated with back vowels (e.g., /ku/).

MacNeilage and colleagues have examined consonant-vowel sequence patterns in both babbling and speech with a large dataset for babble and a somewhat smaller set for early speech (Davis & MacNeilage, 1995; Davis, MacNeilage, & Matyear, 2002; Gildersleeve-Neumann, Davis, & MacNeilage, 2000; MacNeilage, Davis, & Matyear, 1997) in English. The findings they present for both babble and speech show strong support for the predicted CV patterns, namely that labial consonants precede central vowels; coronal consonants precede front vowels; and dorsal consonants precede back vowels. In a review of the early words of children acquiring English, Stoel-Gammon (1983) cited a number of studies that reported a coronal consonant-front vowel pattern.

This chapter focuses on phonological patterns of words produced by young children acquiring American English, with particular attention to CV sequential patterns and characteristics of onset consonants in words. The analyses examine these patterns from a different perspective than that of MacNeilage and colleagues. In their studies of children's word productions, speech samples are collected in the homes; word productions are phonetically transcribed and analyzed in terms of co-occurrence patterns. The analyses are based on word tokens, thus including multiple productions of the same word. In contrast, the analyses presented here are based on word types, where each word represents only one data entry regardless of how many times it was produced. This "dictionary" approach is similar to one taken by MacNeilage and colleagues in their analyses of adult languages (e.g., MacNeilage, Davis, Kinney, & Matyear, 2000). The second difference between our studies and those of the MacNeilage group is that our analyses are based on the target form (i.e., the correct production) rather than transcription of the child's pronunciation of the word. This approach allows us to examine phonological patterns of early word productions from a variety of perspectives and compare the findings with those of MacNeilage, Davis and colleagues.

Overview

We present three studies, based on different data sets and having different purposes. The first study examines phonological properties of words targeted by young children acquiring American English and is based on analyses of words from the MacArthur Communicative Developmental Inventory (CDI; Fenson, Dale, Reznick, Thal, Bates, Hartung, Pethick, & Reilly, 1993; Stoel-Gammon, 1998b). The CDI words were analyzed to determine the following characteristics: (1) general syllable shape patterns; (2) manner and place of articulation of onset consonants in the words; (3) front-back features of the stressed vowels in the words; and (4) sequential patterns of onset consonants and stressed vowels. We looked at the entire set of words in the CDI and then divided the words into two groups based on age of acquisition, to see if the phonological patterns differed by age.

In the second study, we present a re-analysis of data from an article by Tyler and Langsdale (1996), who analyzed the phonology of words produced by children aged 18–24 months with particular attention to CV sequences. In this re-analysis, we compare findings for word types and word tokens.

The third study focuses on characteristics of onset consonants in English with particular attention to the frequency of words beginning with /b/. Within this study, three data sets are analyzed: (1) words produced by children in adult-child dialogues; (2) words spoken to children in the same adult-child dialogues (i.e., child directed speech); and (3) words in the adult lexicon based on dictionary counts.

Study 1:

Phonological Characteristics of the Words from the MacArthur Communicative Developmental Inventories

Stoel-Gammon (1995; 1998) examined general phonological characteristics of children's early vocabulary by analyzing words from the MacArthur Communicative Development Inventories (CDI), a checklist of commonly used words and phrases that yields a parent report of the child's productive vocabulary (Fenson et al., 1993). In a previous analysis, Dale and Fenson (1993; 1996) examined responses to the CDI and assigned an age of acquisition to each word on the list, defined as the age at which the word appeared in the vocabularies of at least half the children in a particular age group. Using this metric, the age of acquisition for the words *daddy* (the first word to meet the criterion), *sleepy*, and *tomorrow* were ages 11.5 months, 25.35 months, and 29.25 months, respectively. The present analysis of the CDI is based on all words that met the criterion for age of acquisition by 30 months, a total of 598 words.

Characteristics of Syllable Shapes in CDI Words

The analysis of the children's vocabulary from the CDI in terms of syllable shape revealed the following patterns: of the 598 words in the data set, 356 (60%) are monosyllables and 218 (36%) are disyllables; 32 words (5%) are formed of three syllables, and only 7 (1%) have more than three syllables. The most common word shapes in terms of CV structure, in descending order of frequency, are CVC (30%), CVCV (9%), CCVC (8%), CVCC (7%), and CV (6%). Stress placement is extremely uniform across the sample. Of the 242 words with more than one syllable, 218 (90%) have stress on the first syllable. If monosyllabic words are classified as having stress on the first syllable, 96% of the words have stress on the first syllable.

Characteristics of Initial Consonants in CDI Words

In word-initial position, stop consonants constitute the most frequent manner class in the 598-word data set, accounting for 43% of segments. Fricatives and affricates represent the next most frequent manner class (29%), followed by liquids (6%), nasals (7%), and glides (5%). Vowels occur in word-initial position in approximately 9% of all words. In word-final position, stops occur most frequently (30% of words), followed by vowels (29%), fricatives and affricates (17%), nasals (13%), and liquids (11%).

In terms of place of articulation of word-initial consonants, labial consonants (/p, b, f, v, m, w/) account for 33% of the CDI words; coronal consonants (/t, d, θ, ð, s, z, ʃ, tʃ, dʒ, n, r, l, j/) occur in 40% of words; dorsal consonants and glottal /h/ account for 18% of words. In word-final position, labial consonants are relatively infrequent, occurring in only 9% of words, while coronals represent the most frequent consonant class, occurring in 51% of target words. Velar consonants and vowels occur in final position in 12% and 28% of target words respectively. The proportional occurrences of labial consonants and vowels exhibit striking asymmetries by position. Labials appear frequently in onset position and rarely in coda position, while the reverse pattern holds for vowels.

Characteristics of Vowels in CDI Words

To obtain a general picture of vowels in words on the CDI, we categorized all stressed vowels in terms of the front-back dimension. MacNeilage and colleagues have suggested that the lack of support for their hypotheses regarding consonant-vowel sequences may be due to differences in vowel classification (MacNeilage, Davis, Kinney, & Matyear, 2000). In an effort to adopt the classifications used by the MacNeilage group when coding the front-back dimension for vowels, we classified all low non-front vowels (categorized as back vowels by some researchers) as central, as they are in the analyses of MacNeilage and colleagues. We used Longman's *Dictionary of American English* (1997) for the classification of vowels; for those words in which a vowel had two possible pronunciations, e.g., watch (/wɑt∫/ vs. /wɔt∫/), we categorized the vowel as being central. Our analysis of the stressed vowels in the 598-word sample from the CDI revealed that front vowels (/i, ɪ, e, ɛ, æ/) occur in nearly half the words (n=288), accounting for 48% of this data set. Central vowels (/ʌ, a, ɝ/) and back vowels (/u, ʊ, o, ɔ/) occur in roughly equal proportions, accounting for 21% and 18% of the sample, respectively. Diphthongs (/aɪ, aʊ, ɔɪ/) occur in 13% of the words.

CV Sequences in CDI Words

As noted previously, the present study examines CV sequential patterns in early meaningful speech by analyzing word types reported by parents on the CDI. Our corpus for the CV sequential analysis consisted of CDI words that begin with a sequence of singleton consonant followed by a stressed vowel (n=415). We followed MacNeilage's protocol in analyzing these sequences by calculating observed and expected occurrences of sequences and then determining the ratio of observed-to-expected occurrences. A ratio greater than 1.00 would indicate that a particular CV sequence occurs more frequently than expected. Additionally, we computed chi square statistics to search for evidence that the place classes for consonants and vowels are not mutually independent, where significant p values do not necessarily support any particular hypothesis, but rather describe unusual deviances from random distributions.

The results of our first analysis are presented in Table 14.1, based on place of articulation of word-initial consonants (singleton consonants only) and front-back classification of the following stressed vowels in the set of 415 words. The left portion of Table 14.1 shows the observed occurrences of each consonant and vowel class, and the right portion shows the ratios of

Table 14.1.
Observed frequencies of CV co-occurrences and ratios of observed/expected
co-occurrences of CDI words. L = Labial, C = Coronal, D = Dorsal, G = Glottal.
Cells for which the F/C theory predicts ratios > 1.00 are in bold italics.

	Observed				Observed/Expected Ratio			
	Consonants				Consonants			
Vowels	C	L	D	G	C	L	D	G
Front	82	72	19	19	*1.00*	1.00	0.91	1.08
Central	36	40	13	7	0.88	*1.12*	1.25	0.80
Back	39	25	11	6	1.13	0.83	*1.25*	0.81
Diphthong	20	18	2	6	1.02	1.05	0.40	1.42

$$\chi^2 = 7.27, df = 9, p = 0.61$$

observed-to-expected frequencies for these data, where a ratio substantially above 1.00 indicates an interaction between consonant and vowel place of articulation. Cells for which the Frame/Content theory predicts ratios greater than 1.00 are indicated in bold italics.

Table 14.1 shows that occurrence patterns of some CV sequences in target words are similar to those reported by MacNeilage and Davis. Specifically, the ratios of two of the predicted sequences exceed 1.00: the labial consonant-central vowel ratio is 1.12 and the dorsal consonant-back vowel ratio is 1.25. However, two other CV patterns also exceed 1.00, including coronal consonant-back vowel (1.13) and dorsal consonant-central vowel (1.25). A Chi-square test of independence revealed that the distribution of observed-to-expected frequencies was not statistically significant at the conventional alpha of 0.05, compared to those expected under random conditions ($\chi^2 = 7.27$, df = 9, $p = 0.61$); in other words, we could not find sufficient evidence to reject the null hypothesis, according to which vowel place and consonant place are independent of each other. We analyzed the data a second time without the category of glottal place of articulation, as MacNeilage and Davis do not include this category in their analyses. The results of the second analysis show trends similar to the first, in that the ratio of observed-to-expected dorsal consonants

Table 14.2.
Observed frequencies of CV co-occurrences and ratios of observed/expected co-occurrences of CDI words by age of acquisiticn. L = Labial, C = Coronal, D = Dorsal, G = Glottal. Age 1: words acquired by 22.80 months; Age 2: words acquired between 22.82 and 30.00 months. Cells for which the F/C theory predicts ratios > 1.00 are in bold italics.

		Observed				Observed/Expected Ratio			
		Consonants				Consonants			
	Vowels	C	L	D	G	C	L	D	G
AGE 1	Front	33	35	13	12	*0.94*	0.93	1.11	1.41
	Central	16	27	8	2	0.80	*1.26*	1.20	0.41
	Back	17	14	4	2	1.22	0.93	*0.86*	0.59
	Diphthong	12	8	1	3	1.33	0.82	0.33	1.36

$$\chi^2 = 10.34,\ df = 9,\ p = 0.33$$

AGE 2	Front	49	37	6	7	*1.04*	1.09	0.66	0.77
	Central	20	13	5	5	0.98	*0.89*	1.28	1.27
	Back	22	11	7	4	1.05	0.73	*1.74*	1.00
	Diphthong	8	10	1	3	0.76	1.33	0.50	1.49

$$\chi^2 = 8.40,\ df = 9,\ p = 0.50$$

followed by back vowels was 1.23 while the ratios for labial consonants followed by central vowel and for coronal consonant followed by front vowel were 1.09 and 1.01, respectively. As in the first analysis, the Chi square test of independence did not reach statistical significance at the conventional alpha of 0.05 ($\chi^2 = 5.62$, df = 6, $p = 0.47$).

Table 14.3.
Observed frequencies of CV co-occurrences and ratios of observed/expected co-occurrences of CDI words, without glottals and diphthcngs. L = Labial, C = Coronal,   D = Dorsal. Cells for which the F/C theory predicts ratios > 1.00 are in bold italics.

	Observed			Observed/Expected Ratio		
	Consonants			Consonants		
Vowels	C	L	D	C	L	D
Front	82	72	19	*1.14*	1.15	0.96
Central	36	40	13	0.97	*1.24*	1.28
Back	39	25	11	1.25	0.91	*1.29*

$\chi^2 = 8.19$, df = 4, $p = 0.08$

Age-Related Patterns

It is possible that the CV sequence patterns predicted by the Frame/Content Theory are present in a child's early lexicon and then disappear as vocabulary size increases. To examine this possibility, we divided the words from the CDI into two groups of nearly equal size: the first 207 words (these words are acquired, on average, by 22.80 months) and the next 208 words (acquired between 22.82 and 30.00 months). We then analyzed the two data sets to determine occurrences of CV sequences. The only discernible developmental patterns in the two data sets consist of a labial consonant-central vowel association at Age 1 where the ratio of observed-to-expected frequencies was 1.26, and a dorsal consonant-back vowel association at Age 2 with a ratio of observed-to-expected frequencies of 1.74. However, once again, the occurrences of CV sequences did not reach statistical significance. Table 14.2 summarizes these findings. Taken together, the analyses of forms attempted presented in Tables 14.1 and 14.2 do not yield findings that conform to the CV patterns predicted by the Frame/Content theory for the lexical targets actually produced by young children.

Our final analysis of the CDI data set is more restricted, excluding words with glottal onsets (i.e., /h/) and words in which the stressed vowel is a

Table 14.4.
Observed frequencies of CV co-occurrences without glottals and diphthongs and ratios of observed/expected co-occurrences of CDI words, by age of acquisition. L = Labial, C = Coronal, D = Dorsal. Age 1 includes words acquired by 22.80 months; Age 2 includes words acquired between 22.82 and 30.00 months. Cells for which the F/C theory predicts ratios > 1.00 are in bold.

		Observed			Observed/Expected Ratio		
		Consonants			Consonants		
	Vowels	C	L	D	C	L	D
AGE 1	Front	33	35	13	*1.03*	0.95	1.07
	Central	16	27	8	0.79	*1.16*	1.05
	Back	17	14	4	1.23	0.88	*0.76*
		$\chi^2 = 2.93$, df = 4, $p = 0.57$					
AGE 2	Front	49	37	6	*0.91*	0.96	0.58
	Central	20	13	5	0.90	*0.82*	1.18
	Back	22	11	7	0.94	0.66	*1.57*
		$\chi^2 = 6.54$, df = 4, $p = 0.16$					

diphthong, as these categories do not appear in MacNeilage's analyses; this reduced data set consists of 337 words. Table 14.3 shows the findings for the entire set of these words and Table 14.4 presents an analysis by age. It can be seen that, with this more restricted set of data, predictions of the Frame/Content thoery are more strongly supported, although none of the p values reach the 0.05 level of significance.

CDI Analyses: Discussion

Tables 14.1-14.4 present a series of analyses of consonant-vowel interactions based on words reported on the CDI. The analyses focused on the occurrence of CV sequences in these words with particular attention to the sequences predicted by the Frame/Content theory for the actual productions of young children: coronal consonant-front vowel sequences; labial consonant-central vowel sequences; and dorsal consonant-back vowel sequences. Although some of observed-to-expected ratios exceeded 1.00, there was no particular CV sequence that occurred consistently in all the analyses; moreover, several sequences not predicted by the theory occurred at higher than expected frequencies in word targets reported, e.g., coronal consonant-back vowel. Chi square tests of independence failed to reach statistical significance at the conventional alpha of 0.05, with p values ranging from 0.08 (the only value less than 0.1) to 0.61.

Other studies have also examined the predictions of the Frame/Content theory with mixed results; some investigations showed support for the theory, others did not. In a discussion of research that failed to find the predicted CV sequences (e.g., Oller & Steffens, 1994; Tyler & Langsdale, 1996; Vihman, 1992), MacNeilage and colleagues state that the lack of support may be due to differences in vowel classification (MacNeilage, Davis, Kinney, & Matyear, 2000) or to methodological differences in data analysis. As noted above, our analyses adhered to MacNeilage and Davis's approach in terms of vowel classification; furthermore, we used the same methods for calculating observed-to-expected ratios. One important difference between our data and those of MacNeilage is the size of the data set. Given a larger number of word types, or an analysis of children's actual productions of CDI targets, it is possible that our findings would support the predicted co-occurrence patterns more consistently. Another difference is the one noted at the outset: our analyses are based exclusively on word types for word targets, while MacNeilage's are based on phonetic transcription of actual tokens produced by children. The study described below examines the differences using a single set of data and analyzing word productions separately by types versus tokens.

Study 2:
Types versus Tokens in Tyler and Langsdale (1996)

The goal of this study was to determine if there were marked differences between CV co-occurrence patterns in analyses of word types and word tokens. The data are from a study by Tyler and Langsdale (1996) examining consonant-vowel interactions in phonetic transcriptions of spontaneous word productions

Table 14.5.
Ratios of observed/expected CV co-occurrences from Tyler and Langsdale (1996) excluding cluster onsets. Analysis of types on the left, of tokens on the right. L = Labial, C = Coronal, D = Dorsal. Cells for which the F/C theory predicts ratios > 1.00 are in bold italics.

		Types			Tokens		
		Consonants			Consonants		
Age	Vowels	C	L	D	C	L	D
18 Mo	Front	*0.67*	0.94	1.68	*0.96*	0.98	1.22
	Central	1.06	*1.00*	0.91	0.83	*1.06*	1.17
	Back	1.27	1.07	*0.38*	1.27	0.93	*0.54*
		$\chi^2 = 3.27; p = 0.51$			$\chi^2 = 4.09; p = 0.39$		
21 Mo	Front	*0.86*	1.14	0.84	*1.03*	1.07	0.69
	Central	0.96	*1.02*	1.02	0.71	*1.07*	1.24
	Back	1.37	0.67	*1.33*	1.41	0.78	*1.06*
		$\chi^2 = 3.71; p = 0.45$			$\chi^2 = 11.44; p = 0.02$		
24 Mo	Front	*0.97*	0.91	1.21	*0.86*	1.19	0.60
	Central	0.85	*1.14*	0.87	0.93	*0.96*	1.25
	Back	1.25	0.95	*0.85*	1.28	0.81	*1.12*
		$\chi^2 = 2.65; p = 0.62$			$\chi^2 = 12.85; p = 0.01$		

of 15 children, five each at the ages of 18, 21 and 24 months. The authors report that their findings did not support MacNeilage's predictions; however, the analyses presented in the article did not include ratios of observed-to-expected occurrences of CV sequences, thus making it difficult to directly compare them to MacNeilage's work. In the re-analysis below, we calculated observed-to-expected ratios and Chi square statistics using Tyler and Langsdale's data. To conform to MacNeilage's methods, we eliminated words with cluster onsets and reclassified the vowel /a/ as central (Tyler and Langsdale classified /a/ as a back vowel). As in our analyses of words from the CDI, this study is based on the phonological form of the target word. Table 14.5 shows the observed-to-expected ratios of CV sequences for each age. The left side of Table 14.5 represents word types produced at each age and the right side of the table shows the analysis of word tokens from the same data set. The number of types analyzed for the three age groups (18, 21, and 24 months) consisted of 57, 110, and 146 words, respectively. In those same age groups, the word token counts were 199, 295, and 371, respectively.

Although there are clear differences between the statistical results for types and tokens, the CV co-occurrence patterns differ from those predicted by the Frame/Content theory. Of the 18 predicted CV pattern occurrences across child ages and linguistic forms (types and tokens) only eight had ratios that exceeded 1.00; moreover, several of the predicted ratios were well below 1.00. Interestingly, the coronal consonant-back vowel sequence, which is not predicted by the Frame/Content theory, consistently occurred at higher than expected frequencies in both types and tokens and in all age groups. This pattern was also observed in the CDI analysis of productions of younger children presented in Study 1. In the Tyler and Langsdale data, the ratio of dorsal consonant-back vowel sequences at 18 months was substantially below 1.00 while the same sequence at 21 and 24 months exhibited much higher ratios, particularly in the analysis of tokens; the dorsal consonant-back vowel sequence was also observed at higher observed-to-expected ratios in the older age group in the CDI data. This change may indicate a developmental trend, but more data are needed to confirm this hypothesis. It should also be noted that the distribution of consonant and vowel place classes for tokens at 21 and 24 months showed a statistically significant structure, but only the dorsal consonant-back vowel sequence at 24 months occurred in proportions predicted by the Frame/Content theory. The other two predicted sequences occurred less frequently than predicted, while the high numbers of coronal consonant-back vowel sequences observed in this data set contradict the hypothesis. Even with the small sample size, coronal consonant-back vowel sequences showed a statistically significant pattern

Regarding the statistical effects of comparing sequential patterns in word types with those in word tokens, the following observations are offered: First, in the data from Tyler and Langsdale (1996), we found much lower chi square p values in the tokens than in the types, presumably the result of multiple productions of individual words. To cite an example, in the published data set

(Tyler & Langsdale, 1996, pp. 173–174), 8 of the 18 word tokens exhibiting the dorsal consonant-back vowel sequence at 24 months count were productions of *go(es)*, supporting both a high observed-to-expected ratio for a sequence predicted by MacNeilage and a highly significant value in the Chi square test. Also contributing to a significant *p* value, but not supporting MacNeilage's predictions, is the high number of occurrences of the coronal consonant-back vowel sequence; in this case, 12 of the 37 tokens were instances of the word *no,* and 6 tokens were the word *two*. Second, the *p* values for the token analyses decreased sharply with increasing age, while those for types remained extremely high. These divergent findings can, in part, be attributed to differences in sample size, with number of tokens increasing across ages from 199 to 295 and 371 for 18 months, 21 months, and 24 months, respectively, while the numbers of types, though increasing with age, were much smaller: 57 different words at 18 months, 110 at 21 months, and 146 at 24 months.

Studies 1 and 2:
Summary and Discussion

In sum, the analyses presented above examined CV co-occurrence patterns in target words from two sets of data: (1) the MacArthur Communicative Developmental Inventories (a word list) and (2) a study of spontaneous speech in children 18, 21 and 24 months that analyzed type and token counts of the target words separately (Tyler & Langsdale, 1996). The CDI data were examined in a number of ways, first with all consonants and vowels, then with a more restricted set of segments (e.g., excluding glottals; excluding diphthongs). Co-occurrence patterns were also examined longitudinally in both sets of data.

In light of MacNeilage and colleagues' investigations of children's actual production patterns showing strong evidence of particular CV sequential patterns: coronal consonants preceding front vowels; labial consonants preceding central vowels; and dorsal consonants preceding back vowels, we wished to investigate the sequential patterns in the target words of young children acquiring English to determine if they conformed to the predictions of the Frame Content theory. Our findings showed that although some patterns were found in some of our analyses and at some ages, none of the patterns occurred consistently within or across the data sets. Tables 14.1–14.5 show the ratios for the CV sequences of interest, where 12 ratios are presented for each CV sequence. Ratios exceeding 1.0 were as follows: 4 (of 12) for coronal consonant-front vowel sequences; 8 for labial consonant-central vowel sequences; and 7 for dorsal consonant-back vowel sequences. The most consistent CV pattern in our data was coronal consonant-back vowel for which the observed-to-expected ratio exceeded 1.0 in 11 of the 12 possible cases.

There were no clear developmental patterns in either the CDI data or the data from Tyler and Langsdale (1996), apart from the observation that the dorsal consonant-back vowel sequence was observed more prominently in the older age groups than in the younger ones in both studies. The CDI study, which analyzed types only, showed a high observed-to-expected ratio (1.57) for this sequence in the older age group, although the chi square test of independence did not reach statistical significance ($p=0.16$). In the data from Tyler and Langsdale (1996), the dorsal consonant-back vowel sequence was associated with a slightly elevated observed-to-expected ratio (1.12) in the token analysis at 24 months, and the chi square test of independence yielded strong evidence to assume that the place classes for consonants and vowels are not mutually independent ($p=0.01$).

The differences between the patterns we observed and the patterns documented by MacNeilage and colleagues can be attributed to a number of factors. First, our study is based on analyses of word types; thus, multiple productions of words such as *mommy, daddy* or *no* will not alter our findings. If these words were produced accurately in terms of place of articulation, multiple productions of *mommy* (labial initial consonant followed by a central vowel) and *daddy* (coronal initial consonant followed by a front vowel) would provide support for the predicted CV sequences, while the word *no* (coronal initial consonant followed by a back vowel) would not.

A "dictionary" based analysis of word types is not influenced by this kind of frequency effect. The Tyler and Langsdale (1996) data illustrate the statistical consequences of analyzing tokens as opposed to types, both in terms of data structures (i.e., multiple counts of the same word, which results in a weighted analysis) and sheer corpus size. Table 14.5 shows that the chi square tests of independence yielded substantially lower p values for tokens than for types. In studies of CV patterning in adult languages, MacNeilage and colleagues (Davis et al., 2002; MacNeilage, Davis, Kinney, & Matyear, 2000) based their analyses on word types, as we have done. An analysis of 2,348 words of English with initial stops or nasals (MacNeilage et al., 2000) revealed that the observed-to-expected ratios for CV sequences exceeded 1.0 for coronal stops and nasals followed by front vowels and for dorsal stops followed by back vowels; the labial consonant-central vowel ratio was 1.0. Statistical tests of significance were not provided. These findings suggest that the CV sequential patterns predicted by the Frame/Content theory are present in the adult lexicon for English. Our analyses, in contrast, indicate that they are not present in the lexicon of young children acquiring English.

The second difference between the present studies and those of MacNeilage is that our analyses are based on the target form rather than a transcription of the child's actual production. This factor would influence the outcomes if the pronunciation errors children make create CV sequences predicted by the Frame/Content theory. In terms of early speech errors, Stoel-Gammon (1983) noted a number of studies of individual children who substituted [d] for target /b/ in words in which /b/ occurred before a front vowel (e.g., the word *baby* was produced as [didi]), resulting in the predicted coronal consonant-front vowel sequence rather than a labial consonant-front vowel sequence. However, this error pattern is not frequent across children and, when present, tends to occur for only a brief period, usually disappearing by 16-18 months. Young children rarely make mistakes in place of articulation of labial and coronal consonants, with the exception of instances of consonant assimilation and labial substitutions for the interdental fricative /θ/ (Grunwell, 1985; Hare, 1983). Examination of Stoel-Gammon's data on the first words of 55 children (2002) showed that only two of the 117 words with initial labials in the target form were produced with an error in place of articulation of the labial consonant; the 90 words with initial coronal consonants were very similar: only two words exhibited an error of place of articulation of the target coronal. The only way to determine if there are systematic differences in place of articulation of consonants and/or vowels in target form of children's words and the actual production of these words is to analyze a common set of data using both approaches.

Study 3:
Syllable Shapes and Segmental Features
in Adult and Child Targets

In their studies of babble and early speech, MacNeilage and colleagues investigated not only CV patterns but also characteristics of consonant place within and across syllable sequences (e.g., MacNeilage & Davis, 1996; MacNeilage, Davis, & Matyear, 1997; Davis, MacNeilage, & Matyear, 2002). In comparing consonantal patterns in babble and speech, MacNeilage, Davis, & Matyear (1997) noted an increased use of labial consonants in initial position that coincided with appearance of first words. They argued that this represented a "regression" to an easier articulatory movement, under the assumption that CV syllables with labial consonants are primarily a consequence of jaw movement with no change in tongue position. When children begin to produce words, they are faced with an added cognitive load associated with word productions and thus there is a need to minimize articulatory movement complexity at this stage of development.

We have also examined word-initial consonants in child speech and noted a preference for labial consonants (Peter, 2001; Peter & Stoel-Gammon, 2001; Stoel-Gammon, 1998; Stoel-Gammon & Peter, 2002). Of particular interest to us was the finding that the preference did not extend to all labial consonants, but was especially strong for words with /b/. In a previous analysis of words from the MacArthur Communicative Developmental Inventories (CDI), Stoel-Gammon (1998) reported that, among English-speaking children in the US, words beginning with /b/ accounted for 22 of the first 100 words acquired, based on Dale & Fenson's age-of-acquisition data (1993; 1996). Of the 598 words from the CDI acquired by 30 months of age, 10.7% began with /b/. By comparison, the proportional use of initial /p/ was 4% in the first 100 words and 8.7% in the larger data set.

One might propose that the adoption of /b/ words into a child's early vocabulary was due primarily to semantic and/or pragmatic factors and that possibility cannot be ruled out at this point. However, if we look at the /b/ words from the CDI, no obvious pragmatic or semantic features emerge. The first 22 words, listed in order of acquisition on the CDI, are as follows: *bye, ball, baby, book, bottle, balloon, bird, banana, bath, bubbles, boat, bear, belly button, bug, bunny, bite, bicycle, blanket, bed, bee, block, button.* We have attributed the pattern to lexical selection (Peter & Stoel-Gammon, 2001; Stoel-Gammon, 1988), a phenomenon whereby children select words for their productive vocabulary based, in part, on phonological features of the word. In most cases, children choose words with sounds and syllable structures that are within their productive phonetic repertoire.

Lexical selection was noted by Ferguson and Farwell (1975) in their seminal paper on the phonology of first words; they reported that, in the early stages of lexical acquisition, children showed a preference for words with certain sounds or particular syllabic shapes and avoidance of other sounds and/or syllabic shapes. For example, one of the children in Ferguson and Farwell's study had an unusually high number of words with fricatives in her early vocabulary (and she was able to produce fricatives); Stoel-Gammon and Cooper (1984) noted a child who exhibited a preference for words with medial or final /k/ (see also Vihman, 1981). Lexical selection in young children was assessed, and confirmed, experimentally by Schwartz, & Leonard (1982) using nonsense words. More recent investigations have shown that this phenomenon extends beyond the period of the first words (Fletcher, Chan, Wong, Stokes, Tardif, & Leung, 2004; Stoel-Gammon, 1998).

Other factors that may influence the high occurrence of /b/-initial words in a child's vocabulary include the frequency of occurrence of such words in the adult lexicon and/or in adult speech addressed to children. The analyses below examine these factors by analyzing phonological characteristics of word-initial consonants in three datasets: (1) children's speech when interacting with adults; (2) adult speech to children; and (3) the adult lexicon in English, based on dictionary counts. As in the studies presented previously, all analyses are based on word types.

Data Sets

The lexicon of young children was constructed from the spontaneous speech of 16 children, age 11 through 31 months. It consisted of 714 word entries. Samples were taken from 16 caregiver-child dialogues published in the CHILDES database (MacWhinney, 1995). These same samples provided the data for a lexicon of child-directed speech, consisting of 1,053 different words. *Webster's Pocket Dictionary* (1997) served as the source for determining word-initial phoneme distribution of types in adult speech, as reported in Stoel-Gammon (1998). The present corpora include singleton onsets as well as clusters; words with cluster onsets were infrequent the CHILDES dialogues.

Word-Initial Consonants in the Data Sets

Our analysis of consonant onsets of words is based on type counts, excluding vowel-initial words; for child-to-adult speech, that reduced lexicon consists of 625 words and for adult-to-child speech, it contains 941 words. To investigate the nature of word-initial consonants from the three sampled populations, we profiled these consonants in two ways: (1) grouped into the articulatory place

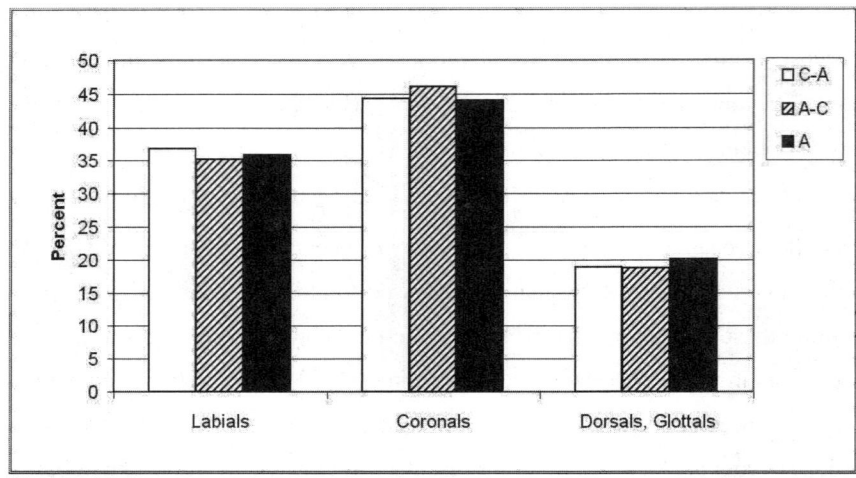

Figure 14.1.
Percentages of initial consonants, by place of articulation, of word types in three data sets: C-A: child-to-adult speech (from CHILDES dialogues); A-C: adult-to-child speech (from CHILDES dialogues); A: adult lexicon (from a dictionary).

classes of labials, coronals, and dorsals/glottals, and (2) as individual phonemes. The profiles by articulatory place classes were strikingly similar across the three data sets. Word-initial labial consonants accounted for approximately 36% of the types, coronal consonants accounted for approximately 45% of types, and dorsal and glottal consonants (/k, g, h/) for approximately 19%. These proportions are very similar to the analyses of the CDI presented in the previous section. Figure 14.1 shows the distributions.

Figure 14.1 confirms that labial consonants are frequent in both input to children and children's output.. proportional occurrences of labial-initial words in both child-to-adult and adult-to-child speech, as shown in Figure 14.2 Analysis of the occurrence of word-initial labial and coronal consonants as a function of the children's ages (with the three youngest participants excluded because of their limited vocabulary) reveals that there is a slight increase in

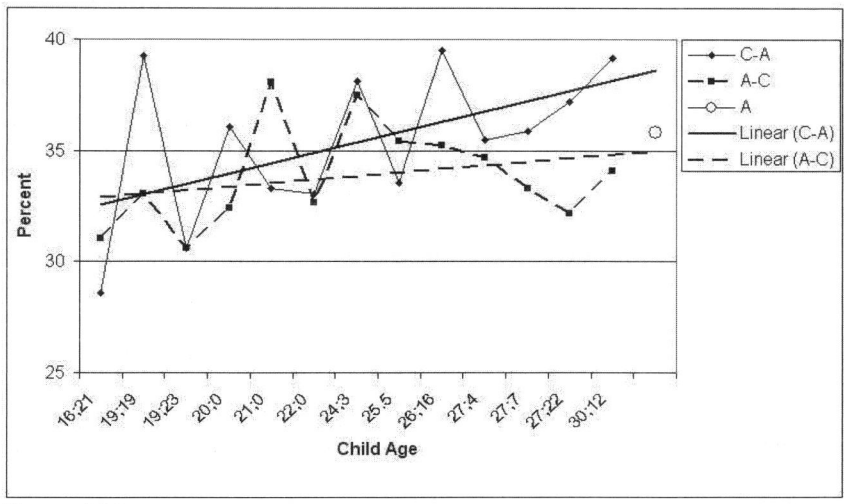

Figure 14.2.
Percentages of word types with labial-initial consonants in three data sets: C-A: child-to-adult speech (from CHILDES dialogues); A-C: adult-to-child speech (from CHILDES dialogues); A: adult lexicon (from a dictionary).

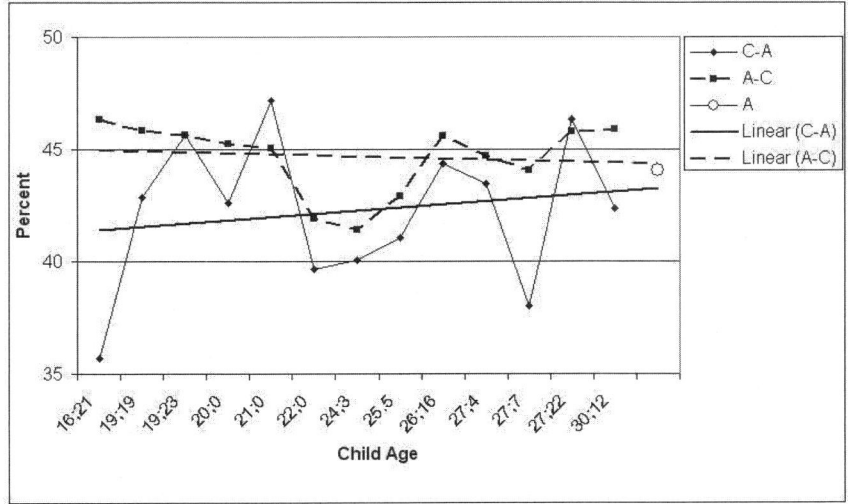

Figure 14.3.
Percentages of word types with coronal-initial consonants in three data sets: C-A: child-to-adult speech (from CHILDES dialogues); A-C: adult-to-child speech (from CHILDES dialogues); A: adult lexicon (from a dictionary).

the proportions of coronal-initial words, shown in Figure 14.3, change only minimally. Overall, Figures 14.1–14.3 reveal strong similarities in proportional occurrence of labial and coronal consonants in the three data sets, both in terms of cumulative lexicons and across age of participants; in contrast, analysis of onsets by individual phoneme distribution reveals substantial differences across the data sets. Figure 14.4 presents comparisons of the data sets by word-initial consonant; within each place class, the consonants are ordered by frequency of occurrence in the child-to-adult data set.

As shown in Figure 14.4, the most frequent word-initial phoneme in the child-to-adult data set is /b/, accounting for 12.2% of all word types. The occurrence of /b/ words in the children's speech is somewhat higher than in adult speech to children (9.9%) and substantially higher than /b/words in the adult lexicon (6.4%). In contrast, /p/-initial words are more prevalent in the adult lexicon (11 %) than in the child-to-adult data sets (7.7%). The preference for /b/ words but not /p/ words suggests that children are selecting words based on a single phoneme rather than the class of labial stops. The differences between proportional occurrence of /b/ and /p/ cannot be explained by a general preference for voiced consonants as previous analyses have shown that, after /b/, the most frequent initial consonant phonemes /k,t,s,p/ are voiceless (Stoel-Gammon, 1998).

Although the phoneme-based analysis in Figure 14.4 shows that /b/ was the most frequent word-initial consonant in the child-to-adult data set, the proportion of /b/ words is considerably lower than the Stoel-Gammon's analysis (1998) of early-acquired words (n=100) from the CDI which revealed that 22% of words began with /b/ while only 4% began with /p/. If the CDI phoneme-based analysis excludes words with vowel onsets (comparable to the analyses in Figure 14.4), the proportion of /b/ words increases to 25%. The CDI analyses include words acquired as early as 11 months, a period when children produce a

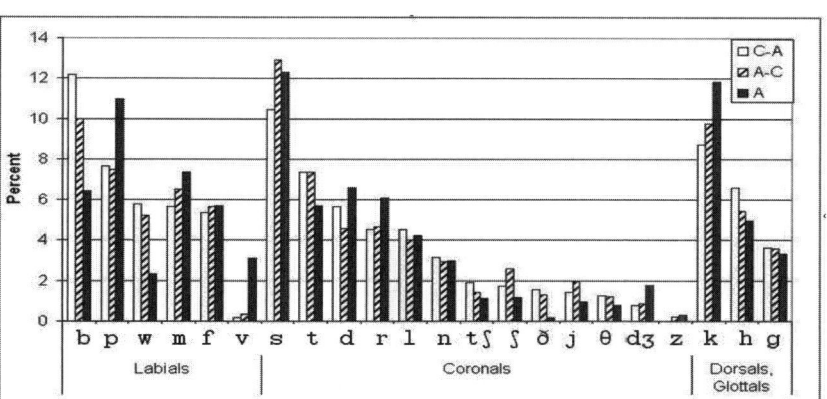

Figure 14.4.
Percentages of word-initial consonants in three data sets: C-A: child-to-adult speech (from CHILDES dialogues); A-C: adult-to-child speech (from CHILDES dialogues); A: adult lexicon (from a dictionary). Within each place class, the consonants are ordered by frequency of occurrence in the child-to-adult data set.

very high proportion of /b/ words; in contrast, our analyses of the CHILDES data set includes productions from children 16-30 months. The differences in proportional occurrence of /b/ words between the CDI and CHILDES data sets results from the fact that the cumulative averages from the CHILDES database are weighted towards the older participants, who contributed more words and a greater variety of word-initial consonants to the lexicon.

We also examined developmental changes in occurrence of /b/ words in the children's speech to adults and adult speech to children by constructing trajectories for the prevalence of /b/-initial words across the ages of the children in the sampled dyads. Excluded were the youngest three children because their limited vocabulary did not allow for the construction of a meaningful word-initial phoneme distribution. Figure 14.5 shows the trajectory for occurrence of /b/ words in 13 samples from children aged 16;21 (months; days) to 30;12. If the speech samples from the youngest three children had been included, we assume that the proportion of /b/ words at the youngest ages would be even higher, based on data from the CDI. Included in Figure 14.5 are the percentages

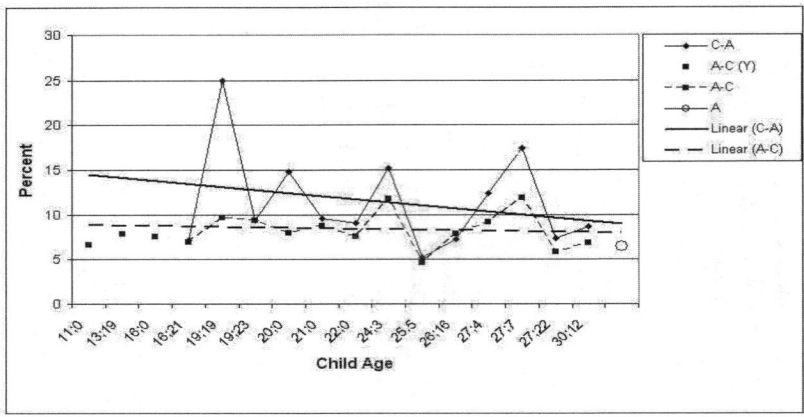

Figure 14.5.
Percentages of /b/-initial words in child-to-adult and adult-to-child speech from CHILDES dialogues. C-A: child-to-adult speech; A-C (Y): adult-to-child speech in the youngest three dyads; A-C: adult-to-child speech in 13 samples; A: adult lexicon. Child ages are on the horizontal axis. The y axis is autoscaled.

of /b/ words from the adults in the earliest three dyads. In the case of /b/ words spoken by the children, a decreasing trend towards the adult norm is evident.

This decrease is consistent with the process of lexical selection as described by Ferguson and Farwell (1975). Additionally, we observed (1) a matching decrease in /b/-initial words in the adult-to-child speech as a function of the child's ages, and (2) percentages of /b/ words in adult-to-child speech similar to the adult norms in the dyads involving the youngest three children, who produced few word types in the adult-child interactions. To gain a better perspective of the developmental patterns for /b/ words, we also examined occurrences of /s/ in the CHILDES dialogues. As shown in Figure 14.4, /s/-initial word types account for a high proportion of the data in all three data sets. Figure 14.6 shows that these words increase proportionally with child age for child-to-adult speech. The linear C-A trajectory in Figure 14.6, like the trajectory of /b/ words, is consistent with the idea of lexical selection, in this case illustrating the flipside of the construct, as very young children are presumed to avoid words with phonological characteristics that are beyond their

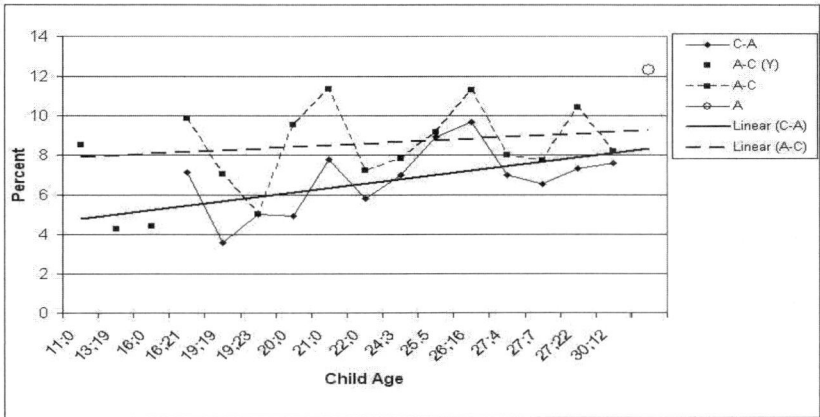

Figure 14.6.
Percentages of /s/-initial words in child-to-adult and adult-to-child speech from CHILDES dialogues. C-A: child-to-adult speech; A-C (Y): adult-to-child speech in the youngest three dyads; A-C: adult-to-child speech in 13 samples; A: adult lexicon. Child ages are on the horizontal axis. The y axis is autoscaled for range from 0.

productive capabilities. As was the case with /b/ words, the adult-to-child percentages show a matching trend in the dyads involving the 13 older children, however the dyads involving the three youngest children did not exhibit a consistently adult-like distribution of /s/ words, unlike in the pattern for /b/ words.

In order to investigate these trends more fully, a greater number of participants and a greater age range across the child participants would be necessary. It would be especially intriguing to study the phonological profiles in adult speech directed at pre-verbal children, compared with data such as those presented here. It is possible that caregivers show phonological profiles of word-initial consonants similar to those in adult-directed speech during this period and begin to adjust their patterns to those of their children as first words emerge and increase in number. Our observations of the distribution of /b-/ words in the speech of adult caregivers of preverbal children support this hypothesis.

Study 3:
Summary and Discussion

Study 3 examined the use of initial consonants in word types, using dialogues from the CHILDES database (child-to-adult speech and adult-to-child speech) and the adult lexicon; in some cases these analyses are aligned with data from the CDI, providing a comparison with the characteristics of targets attempted in the early child lexicon. With reference to place of articulation, the findings show that all data sets exhibit a high proportion of labial and coronal consonants, with labials accounting for approximately 36% of all initial consonants and coronals for approximately 45%. Clear differences across data sets emerge when word types are examined by individual phoneme rather than place class. Our analyses show that the phoneme /b/ has a special status in the lexicon of young children acquiring English; in the data sets included in the present study, this single phoneme accounted for 9% to 25% of initial consonants in word types, thus supporting the notion of a lexical selection pattern for such words.

The child data cited in Study 3 reveals a systematic decline in proportional use of /b/ word types between onset of first words (around 11 months) and productions at 30 months. The observed decline does not mean that fewer /b/ words are produced; rather, the proportional decline stems from increased use of other initial consonants in the children's productions. In sum, our analyses of proportional use of word types beginning with /b/ reveal the following patterns: (1) CDI words, 11-20 months: 25% of consonant-initial words begin with /b/;   (2) CDI words 11-30 months: 10.7% of consonant-initial words begin with /b/; (3) linear analysis of child-to-adult speech from 16.21 months to 30.12 months: /b/ word types average 12.2% with a declining trend.

It is worth noting that, regardless of age or of data set, /b/ is consistently the most frequent initial phoneme in children's word types. The extensive use of /b/ words supports the notion of lexical selection, i.e., that children's choice of words to include their vocabulary is based, at least in part, on phonological characteristics of the target words. Whereas /b/ is the most frequent word-initial phoneme for types in child speech, /b/ word types were second in frequency in adult-to-child speech, with /s/ types being most frequent. In the adult dictionary, by contrast, /b/ words occupy Rank 6 while /s/ words rank highest. This finding suggests that the high proportion of /b/ words in child speech is not merely a reflection of use in adult speech, but a true preference for words beginning with /b/. Our understanding of the role of lexical selection in early child speech would benefit from further investigation focusing on adult-to-child speech in the prelinguistic period and on use of labial consonants, with attention to /b/, in languages other than English.

If we consider the notion of lexical selection in interpreting the findings from the first two studies presented above, it would appear that the target forms of children's early words include a variety of CV sequence patterns with no preference for particular CV sequences. As far as we are aware, all research to date has indicated that lexical selection is based on phonological characteristics of overall word shape (presence/absence of clusters; open/closed syllables) and/or on presence of particular consonantal phonemes or phoneme classes. Possible influences of vowels or of particular CV sequences on the construction of a vocabulary should be investigated.

Summary

We have presented three studies of the phonological characteristics of early words produced by children acquiring American English. In Studies 1 and 2 we analyzed target forms of reported words to determine if the CV co-occurrence patterns were similar to those predicted by the Frame/Content theory. Based on analyses of babble, early word productions and adult languages, the Frame/Content theory predicts observed-to-expected ratios greater than 1.0 for particular CV sequences: coronal consonant-front vowel sequences; labial consonant-central vowel sequences; and dorsal consonant-back vowel sequences in actual child predictions. Our analyses of reported word targets did not support these predictions, neither in terms of predicted observed/expected ratio nor in terms of statistical hypothesis testing (see Tables 14.1–14.5). The most frequently and consistently seen sequence in these two studies was coronal consonant-back vowel, a sequence that is not predicted by the Frame/Content theory.

We have noted several possible explanations for the fact that our results do not support those of the MacNeilage group. Our methodology differed in that we used word types, not tokens; we used targets, not transcriptions of actual productions; and, in addition to calculating observed/expected ratios, we performed statistical hypothesis testing via chi square analysis.

Study 3 examined initial consonants in children's productions when interacting with an adult and in two sets of adult data, speech directed to children and in the adult lexicon, based on a dictionary analysis. All three analyses in Study 3 are based on word types. Our findings show that the majority of words in the three data sets begin with labial or coronal consonants; across the data sets, approximately 36% of words begin with a labial consonant and approximately 45% begin with a coronal consonant. When these consonant classes were examined in terms of individual phonemes, substantial differences emerged on two levels, namely between the individual phonemes within a given place class and between the data sets. For instance, compared to the two sets of adult speech data, the child data showed a strong preference for word types beginning with /b/ while /p/ was less prominent. For these two phonemes, the child-directed adult speech showed frequencies that fell between the adult data from the dictionary and those produced by young children. When viewed as a function of the child ages, /b/ words showed a declining trend in both the child speech and child-directed adult speech, while /s/ words showed the opposite pattern. From this we conclude that (1) the individual phonemes within place classes show phonological profiles that are far from homogeneous; (2) the word onset profiles in the child productions were not caused by the adult input, but, rather, driven by the child; (3) the onset profiles in the child productions were consistent with the construct of lexical selection, where the majority of the selected words have onsets that are typically mastered at an early age; and (4) adults interacting with young children make adjustments in their onset profiles that approximate those of the children.

Several questions remain. For instance, it is not yet known to what extent languages other than English show the patterns and developmental trends presented here. It would also be enlightening to observe onset distributions in adult speech directed at preverbal children, compared to adult speech directed at children across several years past the onset of first words. Such a study would further investigate our hypothesis that caregivers adjust their onset profiles to those of their young children once the children begin to talk. In terms of methodology, it would be helpful to systematically examine the statistical effects of analyzing tokens vs. types, and to conduct reliability testing of perceptual vowel classification. Finally, within the general context of the Frame/Content theory, it would be interesting to investigate word codas and their association with the preceding vowel to see if any patterns consistent with oral motor considerations emerge.

References

Dale, P. S., & Fenson, L. (1993, July). *LEX: A Lexical Development Norms Database* [Computer program]. Seattle, WA: University of Washington, Department of Psychology.

Dale, P. S., & Fenson, L. (1996). Lexical development norms for young children. *Behavior Research Methods, Instruments, & Computers, 28,* 125–127.

Davis, B. L., & MacNeilage, P. F. (1995). The articulatory basis of babbling. *Journal of Speech and Hearing Research, 38,* 1199–1211.

Davis, B. L., MacNeilage, P. F., & Matyear, C. (2002). Acquisition of serial complexity in speech production: A comparison of phonetic and phonological approaches to first word production. *Phonetica,* 59, 75–107.

Fenson, L., Dale, P., Reznick, J.S., Thal, D., Bates, E., Hartung, J., Pethick, S., & Reilly, J. (1993). *MacArthur Communicative Development Inventories (CDI).* San Diego, CA: Singular Publishing Group.

Ferguson, C. A., & Farwell, C. (1975). Words and sounds in early language acquisition: Initial consonants in the first fifty words. *Language, 51,* 419–439.

Fletcher, P., Chan, C., Wong, P., Stokes, S., Tardif, T., & Leung, S. (2004). The interface between phonetic and lexical abilities in early Cantonese language development. *Clinical Linguistics and Phonetics, 18,* 535–545.

Gildersleeve-Neumann, C. E., Davis, B. L., & MacNeilage, P. F. (2000). Contingencies governing production of fricatives, affricates and liquids in babbling. *Applied Psycholinguistics, 21,* 341–63.

Grunwell, P. (1985). *Phonological assessment of child speech.* Windsor, England: NFER-Nelson.

Hare, G. (1983). Development at 2 years. In J.V. Irwin & S. P. Wong (Eds.), *Phonological development in children* (pp. 55–69). Carbondale, IL: Southern Illinois University Press.

Longman's Dictionary of American English, 2nd ed. (1997). White Plains, NY: Pearson Education.

MacNeilage, P. F. (1998). The frame/content theory of evolution of speech production. *Behavioral and Brain Sciences, 21,* 499–546.

MacNeilage, P. F., & Davis, B. L. (1996). From babbling to first words: Phonetic patterns. *Proceedings of the first ESCA tutorial and research workshop on speech production modeling.* Autrans, France, 155–157.

MacNeilage, P. F., & Davis, B. L. (2000). Origin of the internal structure of words. *Science, 288,* 527–531.

MacNeilage, P. F., & Davis, B. L. (2001). Motor mechanisms in speech ontogeny: Phylogenetic and neurobiological and linguistic implications. *Current Opinion in Neurobiology, 11,* 696–700.

MacNeilage, P., Davis, B., Kinney, A., & Matyear, C. (2000). The motor core of speech: A comparison of serial organization patterns in infants and languages. *Child Development, 71,* 153–163.

MacNeilage, P., Davis, B., & Matyear, C. (1997). Babbling and first words: Phonetic similarities and differences. *Speech Communication, 22,* 269–77.

MacWhinney, B. (1995*). The CHILDES project: Tools for analyzing talk* (2nd ed.). Mahwah, NJ: Lawrence Erlbaum Associates.

Oller, D. K., & Steffens, M. L. (1994). Syllables and segments in infant vocalizations and young child speech. In M. Yavaš (Ed.), *First and second language phonology* (pp. 45–61). San Diego, CA: Singular Press.

Peter, B. (2001, November). *Lexical selection: Phonologic patterns in the word choices of toddlers.* Paper presented at the American Speech-Language-Hearing Association Convention, New Orleans, LA.

Peter, B., & Stoel-Gammon, C. (2001, April). *Input and output: Comparing phonologic patterns in child-directed speech vs. child speech.* Paper presented at the 2001 Child Phonology Conference, Boston, MA.

Stoel-Gammon, C. (1983) Constraints on consonant-vowel sequences in early words. *Journal of Child Language, 10,* 455–57.

Stoel-Gammon, C. (1995, April). *What children say: A phonological analysis of the target words acquired by young American children.* Paper presented at the Child Language Seminar, Bristol University, England.

Stoel-Gammon, C. (1998). Sounds and words in early language acquisition: The relationship between lexical and phonological development. In R. Paul (Ed.), *Exploring the speech language connection* (pp. 25–52). Baltimore: Paul H. Brookes Publishing Co.

Stoel-Gammon, C. (2002). Intervocalic consonants in the speech of typically developing children: Emergence and early use. *Clinical Linguistics and Phonetics, 16,* 155–168.

Stoel-Gammon, C. & Cooper, J., (1984). Patterns of early lexical and phonological development. *Journal of Child Language, 11,* 247–271.

Stoel-Gammon, C., & Peter, B. (2002, July). *Phonological development and lexical selection: The case of /b/.* Paper presented at the IX International Congress for the Study of Child Language and the Symposium on Research in Child Language Disorders. Madison, WI.

Tyler, A., & Langsdale, T. (1996). Consonant-vowel interactions in early phonological development. *First Language, 16,* 159–191.

Vihman, M. M. (1981). Phonology and development of the lexicon. *Journal of Child Language, 8,* 239–265.

Vihman, M. M. (1992). Early syllables and the construction of phonology. In C. A. Ferguson, L. Menn & C. Stoel-Gammon (Eds.), *Phonological development: Models, research, implications* (pp. 393–422). Timonium, MD: York Press.

Webster's Pocket Dictionary (1997). Springfield, MA: Merriam-Webster.

V: Modeling and Movement

15

The Target Hypothesis, Dynamic Specification and Segmental Independence

Björn Lindblom

Stockholm University

Stockholm, Sweden

and

The University of Texas at Austin

Austin, Texas, USA

One of Peter MacNeilage's early contributions is a seminal paper entitled "Motor control of serial ordering in speech" (MacNeilage 1970). It offers a critical review of work on speech production seen in the broader context of non-speech motor mechanisms. The topics highlighted include the physiological nature of speech units. In particular, the article considers the status of "*spatial targets*" and the possibility that the goals specified by control commands are articulatory in nature.

It also discusses the classical concept of *motor equivalence* (Hebb 1949; Lashley 1930)—the ability of the motor system to come up with alternative solutions to reaching a given goal if the default movement path is unexpectedly unavailable, as in "compensatory articulations," MacNeilage concludes that "*...the essence of the speech production process is ... an elegantly controlled variability of response to the demand for a relatively constant end*" (1970, pg.184). In other words, like movements in general (Bernstein, N. 1967; von Hofsten, 1993), motoric speech events are defined in terms of the downstream consequences of the muscular activity rather than in terms of that activity itself. This conclusion has since been strongly reinforced by a great deal of experimental evidence on speech (Guenther, 1995; Lindblom, 1990; Löfqvist, 1997; Perkell, 1997).

In this chapter I would like to create a link to MacNeilage (1970) by returning to the idea of "target" and to the mechanisms underlying motor equivalence. In particular, I will address the ability of motor mechanisms to adaptively produce consistent and unique trajectories between targets under changing conditions and despite external disturbances. I will show that those two topics, targets and the generation of movement paths, can be combined in a revealing way with a third more recent theme of MacNeilage's research (MacNeilage & Davis, 1990), *viz.,* the problem of how children achieve *segmental independence*, i.e., go from early holistic vocalizations to the adult end-state of segmentally organized speech. Ultimately, this theme concerns the question where phonetic structure comes from in development and evolution.

From Targets to Phonetic Gestures

To pursue these themes we first need to take a selective walk through the recent history of phonetics. It will take us from the timeless, static targets of the 60s to the dynamically specified gestures of more current approaches.

The practice of describing speech sounds in terms of static articulatory attributes can be traced back to the earliest stages of phonetic history (Jespersen, 1926). In the literature on acoustic phonetics the term "target" became popular about 40 years ago when Stevens and House (1963) reported formant frequency measurements for American English vowels embedded in a variety of consonantal contexts. The formant patterns of the vowels exhibited significant changes systematically related to the place and manner of the consonantal environments. This work implied that the formant displacements associated with a given phoneme did not necessarily arise from distinct context-specific vowel variants but reflected a unique articulatory goal and a sluggish response of the speech production system. Others were stimulated by these findings to examine how formants varied with context and vowel duration as in "vowel reduction"' (Lindblom, 1963), and the extent to which formant patterns at consonant onsets and offsets were coarticulated with the preceding and following vowels in VCV sequences (Öhman, 1966, 1967). The quantitative analyses of these studies converged in showing that individual consonants and vowels were associated with single "targets" and that their variable acoustic correlates were due to an interaction between context and articulatory system dynamics. The evidence accordingly suggested a strong isomorphism between phonetic categories and articulatory processes and the possibility of identifying speech units with timeless, static "targets."

This interpretation is not unproblematic. One problem concerns its perceptual implications. It is reasonable to assume that what a talker controls in production is what the listener wants in perception. If so, it would seem that the target theory implies that speech perception is basically a matter of recovering static targets. Experimental data indicate that visual and auditory systems are more sensitive to changing stimulus patterns than to purely static ones (Kandel & Schwarz, 1981). A paradox emerges: If perception likes change, why assume that speech control is based on static targets? An instructive example is provided by the "moving-edge" detectors found in frogs (Lettvin et al., 1959): *"The frog .... is not concerned with the detail of stationary parts of the environment of the world around him. He will starve to death surrounded by food if it is not moving."*

Strange (1989 a & b) drew attention to this problem. She showed that subjects were able to identify vowels with high accuracy although the center portions of CVC stimuli had been removed. She concluded that vowel perception is possible also in "silent-center" syllables although they lack information on the alleged target retaining only short portions from the initial and final transitions. Abandoning the target concept, she proposed that vowels be "... *conceived of as characteristic gestures having intrinsic timing parameters (Fowler, 1980). These dynamic articulatory events give rise to an acoustic pattern in which the changing spectrotemporal configuration provides sufficient information for the unambiguous identification of the intended vowels.*"

Several theoretical frameworks make the assumption that the "phonetic gesture" represents the basic unit of speech (Browman & Goldstein 1990; Fowler 1994; Liberman & Mattingly, 1989). These approaches share the assumption that what we perceive is the articulatory activity of the vocal tract and that the fundamental units of that process are the *dynamically specified* phonetic gestures. Gesture is often used informally in phonetics to describe a movement observed in an experimental record. However, gesturalists use the term in the technical sense of a primitive of phonetic theory and intend it as a replacement of traditional entities like vowel and consonant (Studdert-Kennedy, 2005).

Munhall and Löfqvist (1992) reported fiberoptic observations of laryngeal opening and closing movements. Their subjects pronounced *Kiss Ted* at varying tempos stressing either the first or the second syllable. At slow rates two gestures were identified, one for [-s-], another for [-t-]. At fast tempos these gestures merged into a single movement. Munhall & Löfqvist modeled the range of observed patterns by adding the curve shapes for slow movements at various degrees of temporal overlap. The simulated curves matched the observed shapes well, suggesting that the resultant movement was made up of two unaltered gestural components blended into a single composite motion. A reduction of the gestural amplitudes further improved the match at fast rates. This study illustrates gestures as building blocks and gestural *phasing* and *amplitude modulation* as postulated in articulatory phonology.

The work of Studdert-Kennedy deserves special attention as we address the origins of segmental independence. It presents an extension of the gesturalist perspective to the development and evolution of speech. It departs from traditional approaches, in part because it places the study of spoken language in the broader framework of evolutionary biology, in part because of its application of a gesturalist program.

Studdert-Kennedy (2005) argues that, as candidates for the basic units of speech, consonants and vowels have to be rejected for three reasons: (1) They are *"purely linguistic,"* not substantive entities; (2) They are *"compound units"* made up of 'features' which are also descriptive, purely linguistic lacking substance. Moreover, features are static and hence incapable of capturing the complex ever changing flow of rapid, parallel articulatory movements of fluent speech. (3) Since discrete units *"... corresponding to consonants and vowels are not to be found in the acoustic signal* phoneticians tend to assume that they *"exist only in the minds of speakers and hearers."* Such a *"...retreat into cognition will not do."*

In contrast, the phonetic gesture offers several advantages. "First, as a unit of phonetic action the gesture can be directly observed by a variety of techniques … Second, because the gesture is not intrinsically linguistic, we can trace a continuous path from infant prelinguistic mouthings and vocalizations through babbling and early speech to the mature phonological system … Third, the gesture takes a step toward the desired evolutionary account of the origins of consonants and vowels, and their descriptive features, by viewing them as recurrent, complex, cohesive patterns of gesture and sound" and "…as dynamic units of phonetic action, temporally coordinated gestural structures, rather than as static "beads on a string."

As a key aspect of an evolutionary account of language, Studdert-Kennedy invokes the *Particulate Principle* of self-diversifying systems (Abler, 1989) which governs all natural systems that *"make infinite use of finite means."* The merit of this principle is that it *"brings language within the natural sciences by generalizing its combinatorial, hierarchical structure across other domains,"* and that it *"invites a view of language as a hierarchy of increasing scope and complexity, growing, by stages, from basic symbol use and combinatorial phonetics, .. to the elaborate structures and mechanisms of recursive syntax."*

Back to Targets and How to Reach Them

Articulatory phonologists (e.g., Goldstein, 2003) refer to the task-dynamic framework of Saltzman and colleagues (Saltzman & Kelso, 1987; Saltzman & Munhall, 1989) for a mathematical definition of gesture. The "... *dynamical specification for each gesture includes a spatial goal, which is the equilibrium position for the (point attractor) dynamics.*" (Studdert-Kennedy & Goldstein, 2007). For a given task, movement is modeled as a second-order, time-invariant system for which the equation of motion can be written as

$$m\frac{d^2x(t)}{dt^2} + b\frac{dx(t)}{dt} + k(x(t) - x_0) = 0 \qquad (1)$$

The constants *m*, *b* and *k* represent mass, friction and stiffness respectively, *x(t)* is displacement and x_0 is the position at which the system will come to rest (Saltzman & Kelso, 1987, pg. 86). In phonetic terms, *x(t)* is the articulatory trajectory and x_0 is its spatial target. Strictly speaking this definition of gesture does not get rid of the notion of target.

An appealing aspect of the task-dynamic model is its ability to model motor equivalence. Consider such a task: the case of producing a labial closure normally and in the presence of a perturbation. Lindblom et al. (1987) investigated the durational structure of Swedish mono-, bi- and trisyllabic words produced under normal and bite block conditions. The test words were samples of *reiterant* speech: e.g., ['bab:ab] was produced according to the stress pattern of *Baghdad*. In a similar way, ['bab:abab] corresponded to *Arafat* etc. Bite blocks created jaw openings ranging between 20 and 25 mm which necessitated compensatory action in the articulation of [b] segments. The main results were that all subjects were able to produce adequate compensatory lip closures for [b] in all positions. Bite block segment durations matched those of the normal test words within ±15 ms. Movement records indicated that the *compensations were characterized by more extensive and larger lip displacements.*

"Labial closure" has two meanings: 1) the closing of the lips (dynamic); 2) the state of closed lips (static). What remained invariant across the experimental conditions? The answer is: reaching the equilibrium position of closed lips, not the kinematic paths of the lips which were markedly different in N and BB items. Hence, if the gesture is an *observable*, it is context-dependent and would therefore be problematic as a basic unit of speech. This kinematic non-invariance means that the mechanical constants of Eq. (1) have to be recalibrated for each context. This could be done by adjusting the stiffness term which, for a given task, correlates with the peak derivative of the displacement curve (Ostry et al., 1983). Such retuning is target-dependent.

The BB experiment highlights the fact that the goal of closed lips is primary. The method of reaching it is secondary since it depends not only on the goal but also on the lips' current position and the situation. As the lips move toward closure, a number of acoustic consequences occur: The formant transitions from V to [b], stop gap, buildup of oral pressure, release of overpressure and [bV]-transitions. Bearing in mind that these events arise largely from the non-linear articulation-to-acoustics mapping, we realize that the minimal specification of the goal for [b]: lip closure, is responsible for considerable acoustic changes. Accordingly, a static command is compatible with a dynamically rich output—in other words, with a signal relevant to perception. This observation represents a small, but relevant step towards resolving the static-dynamic paradox.

To recapitulate: As gesture is examined more closely, we find that the differences between the gestural and target-based accounts become less pronounced. A possible reason why gesturalists avoid the term "target" may be the fact that their thinking is rooted in ecological psychology. Gibson, the founder of this school, recommended restraint in postulating internal representations (Shepard, 1984). Hence "retreating into cognition" should be avoided. This advice readily applies to the term "target" which implies an *intended* mental goal and therefore becomes problematic. However, ultimately intentionality needs to be addressed and, as Shepard points out, Gibson never got to the end of his own ecological story.

Evidence from Work on Non-Speech Movements

The preceding interpretations are compatible with the analysis of many tasks in the non-speech literature. A recent review (Todorov, 2004) presents a comprehensive evaluation of current theories of motor function. The proposals compared include the Equilibrium Point Hypothesis (Feldman & Levin, 1995), dynamical systems (Kelso, 1995) and optimal control (OC) accounts. The latter derive movement by optimization which means that first the task is specified; then movement details are filled in by a strategy optimizing the performance. OC models are sometimes referred to as "*minimum X*" models, X standing for a "cost" defined in terms of e.g., jerk, torque change, energy, time or variance. The larger part of the review is devoted to the OC accounts since, it is argued, competing frameworks (e.g., the EPH) require pre-specification—that is, "a detailed input description of how the desired goal should be accomplished." In contrast, OC models only need a specification of the goal as input. Movement details are then supplied using a best performance control strategy. According to Todorov, optimal feedback control models currently offer the best unified explanations for a wide range of observations on a variety of experimental tasks including kinematic regularities, motor synergies, motor redundancy (equivalence) and speed-accuracy trade-off phenomena.

From this work, we conclude that a pervasive trend is to model motor performance postulating high-level goals (targets, "via points"), on the one hand, and mechanisms most suitable for attaining those goals, on the other. This dissociation lends support to viewing target control in speech production as primary. It also recommends caution in attributing "dynamic specification" to the input level of speech production since the kinematics of articulatory movement owes a great deal of its smoothness and temporal characteristics to the low-pass filtering of mechanical, neuromuscular and sensorimotor mechanisms.

Developmental Implications

The preceding remarks can be restated from a developmental perspective. We hypothesize that the end-state of phonetic learning involves the mastering of two processes: targets and a method for reaching them. Targets are learned from the ambient input. Their fine tuning presupposes trial-and-error experiences relying heavily on imitation—the child's ability to map sensory speech patterns onto the corresponding motor effector commands (Locke, 1993; Meltzoff & Moore, 1997; Rizzolatti et al., 1996). We will here assume that finding the optimal movement paths between targets is the work a general-purpose mechanism (henceforth the GPM) that speaking shares with other goal-directed motor activities. Its role in speech is similar to what it does in e.g., reaching and grasping, in the sense of applying to sequences of possible, but arbitrary spatial goals (via points). GPM (optimal smoothing) is assumed to develop in parallel with the targeting.

Can this ability to adaptively produce movement between arbitrary targets be algorithmically defined? One positive answer is provided by DIVA, a computational model of speech acquisition (Guenther, 1995). This model derives the direction and velocity of an articulator from its current location to an arbitrary target. Accordingly, it exemplifies the GPM mechanism proposed here.

EMFO, a Quantitative Model of Phonetic Learning

Next we take our discussion one step further by incorporating these general purpose mechanisms into a highly simplified, but fully formalized algorithm of phonetic learning, EMFO (*emergent phonetic organization*).

EMFO makes two points. First, it hypothesizes that language-independent articulatory constraints play a significant role in children's attempts to replicate the phonetic patterns of their native languages. Second, assuming that the end-state of phonetic learning is the mastery of the target-guided GPM, EMFO demonstrates that such a mechanism strongly biases learning towards the re-use of targets, i.e., "segmental independence."

EMFO "listens," "speaks," "imitates," "remembers," and "learns." It does those things only in a loose way and admittedly without providing much detail. In this sense it is highly incomplete. However, with respect to the components most essential to the argument, it offers a rigorous, numerical treatment: Possible articulations are specified in terms of Principal Components, a dynamic, biomechanically motivated measure of "Articulatory cost" is introduced and the interaction of "ambient exposure," "imitation," and "learning" is governed by a set of "Learning equations."

Possible Articulations

To define the notion of "possible articulation'" we used articulatory measurements from X-ray tracings. The source of these observations is the Stockholm University X-ray films made in collaboration with colleagues at Danderyd's Sjukhus (Branderud et al., 1998). The present project used a subset of about 500 images from a single male speaker of Swedish. Tracings of all acoustically relevant contours were made using the Osiris software. The tongue contours were quantified by resampling them at 25 equidistant "fleshpoints" (x/y-coordinates). A Principal Components analysis was then performed on these tables (Lindblom, 2003). The output of this method is a formula that describes all observed contours and allows one to interpolate between them.

$$s(i,x,v) = w_i(i,v)PC_1(x) + w_2(i,v)PC_2(x) + \cdots (2)$$

where PCn(x) refers to a principal component, wn(i,v) contains the weights for the ith articulatory profile, x is fleshpoint number and v selects horizontal or vertical fleshpoint coordinates, a small number of PC:s is sufficient to produce highly accurate specifications. The formula expresses the idea that any observed contour is a linear, weighted combination of a set "cardinal" tongue shapes (=PC:s).

This body of data was searched for strongly constricted configurations with a place of articulation ranging from maximally posterior (pharyngeal) to maximally anterior (dental). The final set came from vowels ([i], [u], [a]) and stop consonants (g(i),g(u),[d] and []).Figure 15.1 (left panel) shows the dorsal constrictions. The shapes obtained from tracings are drawn in bold (pharyngeal, uvular, velar, and palatal). The thin contours were derived by interpolating between the PC representations of the bold cases. Average profiles for [d] and [d̪] were also included. A total of nine constrictions were selected. Figure 15.1 (right panel) illustrates the derivation of open configurations from one of the constrictions (pharyngeal in bold) and a contour obtained by averaging the PC specifications of the total inventory of tracings (dashed line). The latter shape is *neutral* in that it lacks a pronounced constriction. The three thin contours are PC-based interpolations between the constricted and the neutral shapes. This procedure was followed for all the nine constricted configurations yielding 27 open articulations.

Given these procedures we defined "possible articulation" as a smooth movement made within a fixed time frame (approximating the duration of a syllable) from a constricted to a more open articulation. The patterns are thus

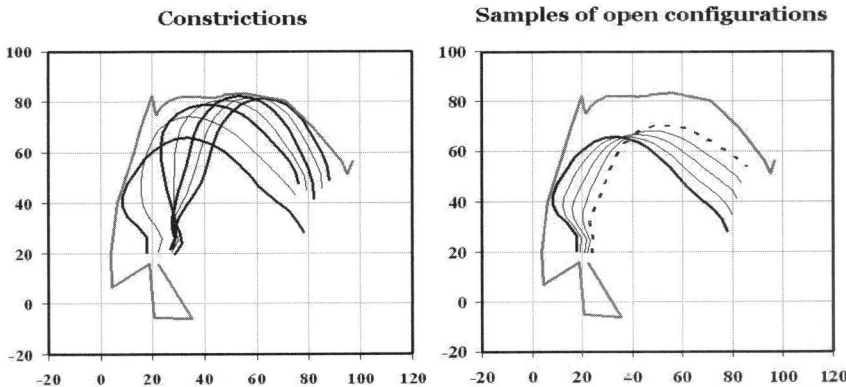

Figure 15.1.
The left panel shows dorsal constrictions. The right panel illustrates the derivation of open configurations from one of the constrictions (pharyngeal in bold) and a contour obtained by averaging the PC specifications of the total inventory of tracings (dashed line). This procedure was followed for all the nine constricted configurations, yielding 27 open articulations.

speech-like and similar to CV syllables. However, there is no explicit pre-specification of segmental structure since the way in which EMFO ends up representing these forms depends on the constraints under which it operates.

Articulatory Cost

"Articulatory ease"' has long played a role in phonetics as an explanatory principle. The difficulty of quantifying it in a non-ad hoc way has made it controversial. However, biology teaches us that the activation of a single muscle, or a single nerve fiber, is necessarily associated with a physiological energy cost (McArdle et al., 1996). There is a sizeable experimental literature indicating that locomotor movements are shaped so as to minimize such costs (Anderson & Pandy 2001; Hoyt & Taylor, 1981). For speech these costs are small (Moon & Lindblom, 2003). The question arises whether the brain ignores them, or favors the use of similar criteria in shaping big and small movements. The present position is that there is sufficient evidence on both speech (Lindblom, 1983; Nelson et al., 1984) and non-speech (Todorov, 2004) indicating that it is unlikely that energetics can be ignored with impunity in studying speech movements.

The present attempt to quantify "articulatory cost" is based on measuring *how far and fast* a given articulator moves from its rest position. Suppose we wanted to investigate the energy cost of forcing a spring-mass system to move sinusoidally with a certain amplitude and frequency. Knowing the mass, the damping and the stiffness of the system, we would use the equation of motion to derive the time-varying force required for this task. From there the energy expended could then be computed. Such an exercise is biomechanical and neglects certain physiological energy costs (Biewener, 1990). Nevertheless, biomechanical considerations allow us to infer that, everything else being equal, increasing the amplitude (its deviation from rest) of a fixed-duration movement will cost more energy (Nelson et al., 1984).

Figure 15.2 compares the rest position with one of the constrictions. The two contours are each specified by 25 points. Straight lines have been drawn to

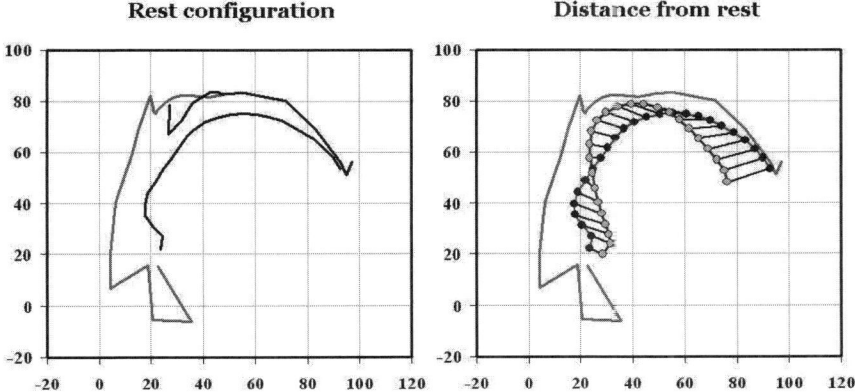

Figure 15.2.
Rest configuration and constriction configuration.

connect identically numbered points. In EMFO the "articulatory cost" of moving the tongue between rest and a specific target, in a fixed time interval, is proportional to the articulatory distance between the two articulations. The distance between two arbitrary contours a(x) and b(x) is defined as the root mean square distance:

$$\text{dist}\,(a,b) = \sqrt{(\sum_{1}^{25}[a(x)-b(x)]^2)/25} \qquad (3)$$

The left panel displays the rest position of the present subject recorded during quiet breathing. The jaw is in a high position producing passive closed lips. Breathing occurs through the nose, as indicated by the lowered velum. Presumably to facilitate this activity, the tongue is fronted so as not to cause any pharyngeal obstruction to the expired air.The right panel of EMFO utterances involve a motion from rest to a closed state and from there to an open vocal tract. We can generalize Eq (3) to a sequence of two events. The cost incurred by a second event should depend on how far the first and the second articulations are from each other in articulatory space. This reasoning leads- to the following formula (shown in Figure 15.3) for the articulatory cost of an EMFO trajectory from $a(x)$ to $b(x)$:

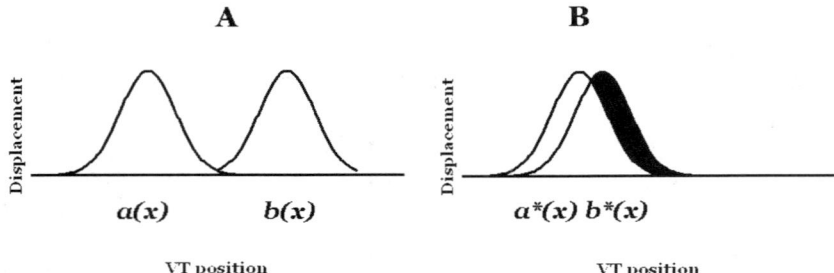

Figure 15.3
Articulatory cost of an EMFO trajectory.

$$\text{A-cost}(a,b) = \text{dist}[rest(x) - a(x)] + \text{dist}[a(x) - b(x)] \quad (4)$$

This figure is a stylization of how the formula works. The horizontal line represents the resting state of the vocal tract. In A, muscular forces modify this line giving rise to a certain initial pattern of deviation from rest (left peak). A short time later another perturbation occurs somewhat more remote from the first (right peak). In B, similar activities occur but the places of articulation of the two peaks are very similar.

Eq (4) tells us that A is more costly than B since the distance between *a(x)* and *b(x)* is greater than that between *a*(x)* to *b*(x)*. This result provides a preliminary but principled basis for saying that processes of assimilation are simplifications.

When Eq (4) is applied to the items of the EMFO phonetic space, several noteworthy observations can be made. Figure 15.4 shows articulatory costs for EMFO utterances plotted against the place of articulation of their open configurations. The data points connected by line segments form six groups, each associated with a specific constriction location. Dental constrictions show the lowest, pharyngeals the highest values. There is considerable context-dependence as indicated by the rising and falling patterns of these groups. Circles have been added to indicate the minimum value for each place. In other words, EMFO prefers onsets combined with endpoints whose places of articulation are identical or close to each other— a finding reminiscent of results

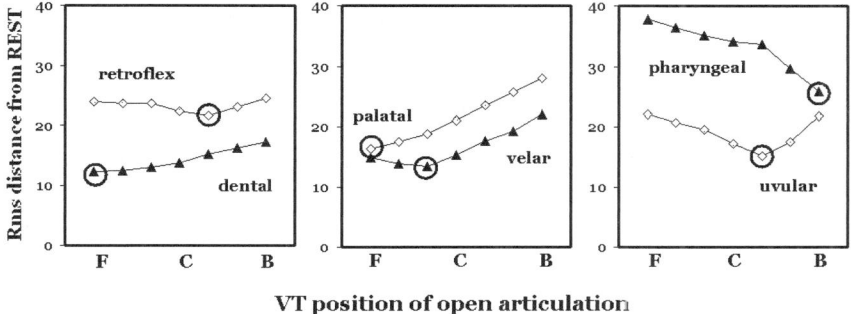

VT position of open articulation

Figure 15.4.
"Articulatory costs" (i.e., RMS distance) plotted against the place of articulation of the open configuration. F, C and B refer to front, central and back articulations. Left diagram compares dental with retroflex onsets; Middle figure: palatal with velar constrictions; Right panel: uvular with pharyngeal items. Circles mark the minimum values for the individual constriction.

reported by Davis and MacNeilage (1995) for babbling. These authors examined a large number of babbles with respect to their (pseudo)-segmental content. Consonant-like segments were classified as alveolar, labial and velar. Vowel-like elements were sorted as front, back and central. There was a strong tendency for consonant-vowel sequences to show an assimilatory pattern dental consonants co-occurring with front vowels, velars with back vowels and labials with central vowels.

Labial closure was not included among the EMFO patterns. This articulation resembles the rest position with respect to closed lips and the unspecified tongue position. The articulatory costs of movements from a labial closure would thus come mainly from the opening movement and could be expected to be comparable, or smaller than, those for dental onsets. If this assumption is correct, articulatory cost could be invoked to explain the preference for the labial, coronal (dental/alveolar) and dorsal (palatal/velar) points of articulation in the world's languages (Maddieson, 1984) and the *co-occurrence* patterns observed in early speech (Davis & MacNeilage, 1995; MacNeilage & Davis, 1993).

Learning Equations

The next step in developing EMFO is to give the articulatory cost table a role in a simulated learning task. We stipulate that, at the end of this task, EMFO develops either of two motor representations:

1. Each pattern is learned as a whole.
2. Each pattern is learned by finding the minimum input needed to produce that pattern. It is assumed that, by optimization, this process invokes the GPM and automatically chooses no more than two targets (the onset and endpoint of movement path).

We will refer to the first option as *Gestalt coding*. It is dynamically specified in that the detailed shape of the trajectory is pre-specified. The second alternative which derives from a "least action" or "minimum redundancy" condition we call *target-based coding.*

Recall that the input patterns to EMFO were profiles. This typical shape suggests that speech motor control does not attempt to change the default response of the strongly damped effector system described as smooth speech-like movements implying s-shaped articulatory trajectories with near Gaussian velocity and that no more than two targets should be needed to specify most speech transitions. Had a movement more complex than the s-shape been selected a larger number of targets or via points would have been needed. The fact that speech transitions do not elaborate on the basic s-shape may also have a perceptual motivation. It seems to go hand in hand with the finding that the perceptual differences between linear, exponential or logarithmic transitions are very subtle (Carré, personal communication).For each item of the ambient input, EMFO simulates learning by recalibrating its articulatory preference score, a number derived from its articulatory cost (Figure 15.5 and more below). In response to an ambient pattern EMFO tries to imitate it. As this process is repeated, sensory references are built and the initial motor representation is strengthened. In the model this activity takes the form of an input-based incrementation of the preference score. EMFO tracks the amount of practice

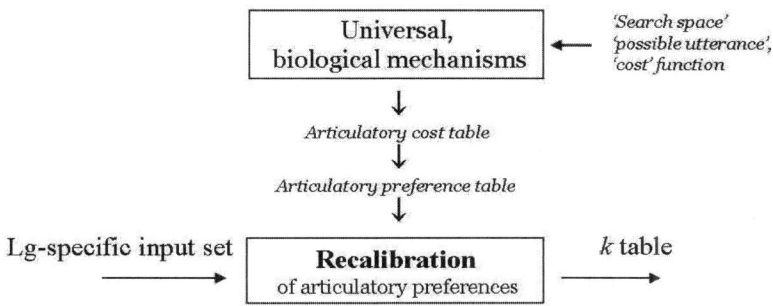

Figure 15.5.
Block diagram illustrating the organization of EMFO.

needed for each item. It stops the process when the item's preference score is equal to one. Accordingly, EMFO copies what it is exposed to but some patterns are easier than others and are therefore acquired faster. Thus copying interacts in a significant way with the articulatory costs of the items to be learned.

Articulatory preference scores were obtained from the articulatory costs by normalizing them (Eq. 5). This move turns the scores into probabilities. If EMFO were to select and produce utterances by pure chance, it would generate a distribution in which *co-occurrence patterns* would be strongly favored: e.g., dental onsets would be followed by front open vocal tracts and back onsets would be combined with back open articulations.

$$p_{ij} = \frac{A_{ij}}{\sum_{i=1}^{9}\sum_{j=1}^{27} A_{ij}} \qquad (5)$$

where A_{ij} is the articulatory cost associated with the item with constriction i and open articulation j, and p_{ij} is its preference score, a number between 0 and 1.

The progress of learning is represented by *learning equations*. Gestalt coding is described in the following recursively applied expression:

$$p_{ij}(\text{new}) = p_{ij}(\text{old}) + k_{ij} * \varepsilon) \qquad (6)$$

where $p_{ij(\text{new})}$ and $p_{ij(\text{old})}$ are the preference scores after and before applying Eq. (6) respectively, ε is a small arbitrary increment and k_{ij} keeps track of the current amount of "practice." "Practice" is interpreted as the number of times that an item has been both heard and imitated at the same time. The item in question is considered acquired when $p_{ij(\text{new})}$ is equal to one. In this mode of learning, the amount of practice needed for any given item is given by:

$$k_{ij} = (1 - p_{ij}) / \varepsilon \qquad (7)$$

where p_{ij} is the original preference score as defined in Eq. (5).

Target-based coding is described as follows. Again the expression is applied recursively:

$$(p_{ij}(\text{new}) = p_{ij}(\text{old}) + k_{ij} * \varepsilon * (1 + r) \qquad (8)$$

where r is a *re-use factor* defined as:

$$r = w(i) + z(j) \qquad (9)$$

Here $w(i)$ and $z(j)$ reflect the degree of activation along the *ith* and *jth* dimensions respectively. In this mode of learning, the amount of practice needed for any given item is given by:

$$k_{ij} = (1 - p_{ij}) / \varepsilon * (1 + r) \qquad (10)$$

Comparing Gestalt and target-based coding— that is, comparing Eqs. (7) and (10)— we see that the effect of the re-use factor is to return a smaller value of k_{ij} for target-based coding. In other words, an item is learned faster if its targets are used also by other items. Figure 15.6 shows the articulatory preference table as a matrix with constrictions in rows and open vocal tracts in the columns. Two hypothetical input sets are shown. In A the items differ maximally with respect to both onsets and endpoints. In B onsets and endpoints are recombined into a three-by-three system. The cells with the cross symbol have identical positions.

For simplicity, we assume that the elements occur with equal frequency and in sufficiently close succession to be regarded as "synchronous" on a low-resolution time scale. Recall that the "ease" with which A and B are learned is

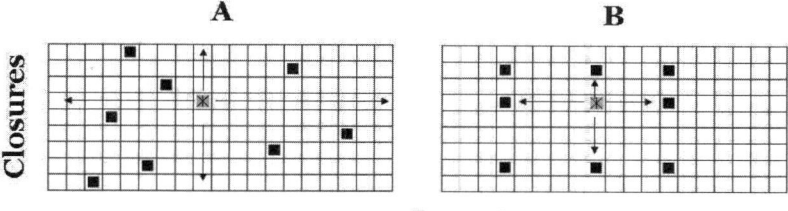

Open articulations

Figure 15.6.
Comparing degrees of re-use. The diagrams refer to two hypothetical input sets, consisting of nine items. Columns quantize the continuum of open VT states. Rows ten represent the closure dimension. The location of the cross symbols is identical in the two matrices. In A the nine items differ completely both with respect to onsets and endpoints. B shows a 3-by-3 arrangement which implies that both the onset and the endpoint of the cross item are used twice by other cells. The point made in the text is that case B would be learned much faster than A if it is the "targets" rather than the entire movement paths that are learned.

measured in terms of k (Eq. 7). We also note that the acquisition of A or B produces a table listing the k values of the input forms (Figure 15.5).

The "time" it takes it master A is equal to the time it takes to learn its most difficult articulation. Each item has to be acquired as one coherent, unanalyzed pattern. Accordingly, with respect to the cross symbol item, the Gestalt model makes no difference between A and B. It learns that item with a fixed delay determined by its preference score, and unaffected by the configuration of the system.

For B the object of learning is not the Gestalt but only the minimum information needed to produce it, that is, its targets. The recalibration applies only to targets. The acquisition of the GPM is not item specific. It is target-independent. Since B re-uses the targets of the cross item in other items, the scores of those items also get updated when the cross item is presented. In Eq. (8) this updating is made by the re-use factor.

In A the re-use factor of the cross item is zero. Practicing that item does not facilitate learning any other items. By contrast, the cross item of B has a re-use factor of 2 for both the onset and the endpoint dimensions. Consequently, r

= (2+2) = 4 which imposes a significant modification on the preference score. As already remarked, this means that re-use speeds up the learning process.

Discussion

Targets and the Frame/Content Theory

Infant vocalizations show a developmental pattern that is similar for children from different language backgrounds. The following milestones were observed in a comparison of Dutch, English, and Swedish children's vocal productions (Roug et al., 1989). Reflexive vocalizations; cooing; vocal play, reduplicated and variegated babbling. Reduplicated babbling is characterized by the rhythmic alternation between open and closed jaw producing utterances such as [bababa]. Variegated (nonreduplicated) babbles are utterances involving a change in place of consonant articulation and/or of vowel quality, e.g., [badi]. The last two stages occur during the second half of the first year with the proportion of variegated utterances increasing markedly.

The Frame/Content theory (MacNeilage, 1998) interprets canonical babbles, the "pure frames," as produced by the up and down movement of the mandible. As the child becomes capable of recruiting additional articulators this frame is modified: first in a crude way so as to fix the tuning of the oscillation for the entire utterance–e.g., "fronted frames" such as [dɛdɛ], later with a finer temporal control of the spatial modulation so as to produce variegated utterances in which vowel and consonant elements are varied. According to the theory, it is from these patterns that adult syllables emerge. Conceivably, it is at this non–reduplicated stage that we begin to see the first signs of "segmental independence" (MacNeilage & Davis, 1990).

These observations can be readily fitted into the framework of target learning and inter-target movement control. They imply that that the child's ability to reset a sequence of target specifications and make target-directed movements improves as both temporal and spatial control becomes more finely differentiated.

Phonetic Re-use Experimentally Observed in Development

Schwartz. and Leonard (1982) report a lexical learning experiment in which they presented 16 invented lexical concepts, each represented by nonsense words, to 12 children with vocabularies of no more than five words. Half of these items had phonetic characteristics previously seen in the children's production. Half of them were phonetically novel. The authors conclude that the children imitated, and spontaneously used, words earlier and in greater numbers when the items were phonetically compatible with existing patterns, thus providing some preliminary evidence of developmental re-use.

EMFO adds detail to the design of this type of study. To test the learning algorithm empirically it would be necessary to control, not only for the current state of the child's phonology, but for perceptual experience and the organization of the ambient sound system.

On Articulatory Ease

If predictions are to be made about the role of articulatory constraints, sophisticated, independently motivated measures of articulatory cost must be devised. Ladefoged points out that articulatory ease must necessarily be given a language-dependent definition (Ladefoged, 1990) because speakers of different languages rate the difficulty of a given segment depending on whether it forms part of their system or not. Menn (1983, pg. 21) favors a similar extended view suggesting that ease of articulation should include production routines already acquired as a factor affecting the learnability of a new sound: *"... physiological causes are only one factor in determining 'ease of articulation for the individual child. The other factor, and I propose that it is the major factor, is the state of the child's knowledge at a given time ... [1] is "easier" than [j] only because this child happens to have found out how to make an [1] first."* EMFO addresses this problem at the recalibration stage where the universal articulatory cost scores interact with the language-specific sensory and motor activations.

Patterns of Phonetic Re-use in Phonetic Inventories

In the past, several attempts have been made to explain the patterning of vowel and consonants in phonetic inventories. The idea that sound systems are the way they are because language use puts a premium on perceptual distinctiveness is a traditional one in phonetics. Diehl et al. (2003) proposed that the auditory representation of vowels be based on both temporal and spectral information. Motivated by evidence from auditory physiology this representation was found to produce a vowel space in which contrasts along the open-close dimension were more strongly favored than front-back distinctions. This result significantly improved the distinctiveness-based predictions of vowel systems.

However, distinctiveness alone is unlikely to satisfactorily account for the typological facts. Maddieson (1984, pg. 16) asked: if perceptual contrast shapes vowel systems why is /i ẽ a̤ o̤ ʉ/ not favored over the presumably less distinctive, but more common /i e a o ʉ/? The example suggests that articulatory factors are at work. Lindblom and Maddieson (1988) sorted the segments of the UPSID database into three classes of articulatory complexity: Basic, Elaborated and Complex. They found that inventory size was a good predictor of the relative proportions of B, E and C segments (Size Principle) offering support for the view that articulatory constraints play a causal role in shaping phonetic inventories.

Nevertheless, even if distinctiveness and articulatory factors were combined it is not likely that such a move would be sufficient either, because the typological data clearly indicate that the predictions need a mechanism of re-use. The following remarks by Ohala (1979) drive home that point (with a formulation currently referred to as the MUAF Principle): *"Rather than maximum differentiation of the entities in the consonant space, we seem to find something approximating the principle which would be characterized as "maximum utilization of the available distinctive features." This has the result that many of the consonants are in fact, perceptually quite close— differing by a minimum, not a maximum number of distinctive features.*" EMFO identifies a possible behavioral basis for this principle.

Summary

In this chapter we explore the following claim: What children develop in the early stages of learning their mother tongue is a mastery of phonetic targets (defined via points) on the one hand and an ability (not specific to speech) to make movements between arbitrary points in a functionally defined anatomical work space (finding optimal movement paths) on the other.

To give this hypothesis a more rigorous formulation we present a numerical algorithm of phonetic learning, EMFO. The model introduces a biomechanically motivated measure of articulatory cost that fairly closely matches the preferred vowel-consonant place co-occurrences reported for children's early productions. Second, EMFO is used to explore two hypotheses about the nature of speech units, specifically the developmental end-state of their motor representations: (1) Maximal pre-specification of movement dynamics (Gestalt coding) and (2) minimal pre-specification (target-guided smoothing). The latter strategy promotes the learning of phonemically coded input sets, whereas Gestalt coding offers no advantage for such sets. Despite its simplicity EMFO throws new light on the question of *how segmental independence can arise behaviorally, rather than from explicit genetic pre-specification.*

References

Abler W. (1989). On the Particulate Principle of self-diversifying systems, *Journal of Social and Biological Structures, 12*,1–13.

Anderson F. C. & Pandy M. G. (2001). Dynamic optimization of human walking, *J Biomech Eng., 123*, 381–390.

Bernstein N. (1967). The coordination and regulation of movements, Pergamon: London.

Biewener A. A. (1990). Bio-mechanics of mammalian terrestrial locomotion, *Science, 250*, 1097–1103.

Branderud P., Lundberg H. J., Lander J., Djamshidpey H., Wäneland I., Krull D. & Lindblom B. (1998). X-ray analyses of speech: methodological aspects, in *FONETIK 1998*, KTH: Stockholm.

Browman C. P. & Goldstein L. (1990). Gestural specification using dynamically-defined articulatory structures, *J Phonetics, 18*, 299–320.

Davis B. L. & MacNeilage P. F. (1995). The articulatory basis of babbling, *J Speech Hearing Research, 38*, 1199–1211.

Diehl, Lindblom B. & Creeger C. P. (2003). Increasing realism of auditory representations yields further insights into vowel phonetics, *Proceedings of the 15th International Congress of the Phonetics Sciences*, CDROM ISBN 1-876346-48-5 © 2003 UAB.

Feldman A. G. & Levin M. F. (1995). The origin and use of positional frames of reference in motor control, *Behav Brain Sci., 18*, 723–744.

Fowler C. A. (1990). Coarticulation and theories of extrinsic timing, *J of Phonetics, 8*, 113–133.

Fowler C. A. (1994). Speech perception: Direct realist theory, 4199–4203 in Asher R. E. (Ed.): *Encyclopedia of Language and Linguistics*, Pergamon: New York.

Goldstein L. (2003). Emergence of discrete gestures, 85–88 in *Proceedings of the 15th ICPhS*, CDROM ISBN 1-876346-48-5 © 2003 UAB.

Guenther F. H. (1995). Speech sound acquisition, coarticulation, and rate effects in a neural network model of speech production, *Psychological Review, 102*, 594–621.

Hebb D. O. (1949). *The organization of behavior*, New York: Wiley.

Hoyt D. F. & Taylor C. R. (1981). Gait and the energetics of locomotion in horses, *Nature, 292*, 239.

Jespersen O. (1926). *Lehrbuch der Phonetik*, Teubner: Leipzig.

Kandel E. R. & Schwarz J. H. (1981). *Principles of neural science*, Edward Arnold: London.

Kelso J. A. S. (1995). *The self-organization of brain and behavior*, MIT Press: Cambridge, MA.

Ladefoged P. (1990). Some reflections on the IPA, *J of Phonetics, 18*, 335–346.

Lashley K. S. (1930). Basic neural mechanisms in behavior, *Psychological Review, 37*, 1–24.

Lettvin J. T., Maturana, H. R., McCulloch W. S., Pitts W. H. (1959). What the frog's eyes tells the frog's brain, *Proc. of the IRE, 4 (11), 1940–1951*.

Liberman A. M. and Mattingly I. (1989). A specialization for speech perception, *Science, 243*, 489–494.

Lindblom B. (1963). Spectrographic study of vowel reduction, *J Acoust Soc Am, 35*, 1773–1781.

Lindblom B. (1990). Explaining phonetic variation: A sketch of the H&H theory, 403–439 in Hardcastle W J & Marchal A (Eds.). *Speech Production and Speech Modeling*, Dordrecht: Kluwer.

Lindblom B. (2003). A numerical model of coarticulation based on a Principal Components analysis of tongue shapes, *Proceedings of the 15th*

International Congress of the Phonetics Sciences, CDROM ISBN 1-876346-48-5 © 2003 UAB.

Lindblom B., Lubker J., Gay T., Lyberg B., Branderud P. (1987). The concept of target and speech timing, 161–181 in Channon R & Shockey L (Eds.): *In honor of Ilse Lehiste,* Dordrecht: Foris.

Lindblom B. & Maddieson I. (1988). Phonetic universals in consonant systems, 62–78 in Hyman L. M. & Li C. N. (Eds.): *Language, Speech and Mind,* London & NewYork: Routledge.

Locke J. L. (1993). *The child's path to spoken language,* Harvard University Press: Cambridge, MA.

Löfqvist A. (1997). Theories and models of speech production, 404–426 in Hardcastle W. J. & Laver J. (Eds.): *The Handbook of Phonetic Sciences,* Blackwell: Oxford.

McArdle W. D., Katch F. I. & Katch V. L. (1996). *Exercise physiology,* Baltimore: Williams & Wilkins.

MacNeilage P. F. (1970). Motor control of serial ordering in speech, *Psychological Review, 77,* 182–196.

MacNeilage P. F. & Davis B. L. (1990). Acquisition of speech production: The achievement of segmental independence, 55–68 in Hardcastle W. J. & Marchal A. (Eds.): *Speech Production and Speech Modeling,* Dordrecht: Kluwer.

MacNeilage P. F. & Davis B. L. (1993). Motor explanations of babbling and early speech patterns, 341–352 in Boysson-Bardies B., de Schonen S., Jusczyk P., MacNeilage P. F. & Morton J. (Eds.): *Developmental neurocognition: Speech and face processing in the first year of life,* Kluwer: Dordrecht.

MacNeilage P. F. (1998).The frame/content theory of evolution of speech production, *Behavioral and Brain Sciences 21,* 499–546.

Maddieson I. (1984). *Patterns of sound,* CUP: Cambridge.

Meltzoff A. N. & Moore M. K. (1997). Explaining facial imitation: a theoretical model, *Early development and parenting, 6,* 179–192.

Menn L. (1983). Development of articulatory, phonetic and phonological capabilities, in Butterworth B (Ed.): *Language Production II,* Academic Press: London.

Moon S. J. & Lindblom B. (2003). Two experiments on oxygen consumption during speech production: vocal effort and speaking tempo, in *Proceedings of the 15th International Congress of the Phonetics Sciences,* CDROM ISBN 1-876346-48-5 © 2003 UAB.

Munhall K. G., Vatikiotis-Bateson E. & Kawato M. (2000). Coarticulation and physical models of speech production, in Broe M. B. & Pierrehumbert J. (Eds.): *Papers in Laboratory Phonology V,* CUP: Cambridge.

Nelson W. L., Perkell J. S. & Westbury J. R. (1984). Mandible movements during increasingly rapid articulations of single syllables: Preliminary observations, *J Acoust Soc Am 75(3),* 135–147.

Ohala J. J. (1979). Chairman's introduction to the Symposium on Phonetic Universals in Phonological Systems and their Explanation, 184–185 in

Proceedings of the Ninth International Congress of Phonetic Sciences, Institute of Phonetics, University of Copenhagen.

Öhman S. (1966). Coarticulation in VCV utterances: Spectrographic measurements, *J Acoust Soc Am, 39(1)*,151–168.

Öhman S. (1967). Numerical model of coarticulation, *J Acoust Soc Am, 41*, 310–320.

Ostry D. J., Keller E. & Parush A. (1983). Similarities in the control of the speech articulators and the limbs Kinematics of tongue dorsum movement in speech, *J Exp Psy, 9(4), 622–636.*

Perkell J. S. (1997). Articulatory processes, 333–370 in Hardcastle W. J. & Laver J. (Eds.): *The Handbook of Phonetic Sciences*, Blackwell: Oxford.

Rizzolatti G., Fadiga L., Gallese V. & Fogassi L. (1996). Roug L., Landberg I. & Lundberg L. J. (1989). Phonetic development in early infancy: A study of four Swedish children during the first eighteen months of life, *J Child Language, 9,* 319–336.

Saltzman E. & Kelso J. A. S. (1987). A dynamical approach to gestural patterning in speech production, *Psychological Review, 94(1)*, 84–106.

Saltzman E. & Munhall K. G. (1989). A dynamical approach to gestural patterning in speech production, *Ecological Psychology, 1*, 333–382.

Schwartz R. G. & Leonard L. B. (1982). Do children pick and choose? An examination of phonological selection and avoidance in early lexical acquisition, *J Child Language, 9,* 319–336.

Shepard R. N. (1984). Ecological constraints on internal representation: Resonant kinematics pf perceiving, imagining, thinking and dreaming, *Psychological Review, 91(4)*, 417–447.

Stevens K. N. & House A. S. (1963). Perturbation of vowel articulations by consonantal context. An acoustical study, *Journal of Speech and Hearing Research, 6*, 111–128

Stevens K. N. (2003). Acoustic and perceptual evidence for universal phonological features, *Proceedings of the 15th International Congress of the Phonetics Sciences,* CDROM ISBN 1-876346-48-5 © 2003 UAB.

Strange W. (1989a). Dynamic specification of coarticulated vowels spoken in sentence context. *J Acoust Soc Am, 85(5),* 2135–2153.

Strange W. (1989b). Evolving theories of vowel perception. *J Acoust Soc Am, 85(5), 2081–2087.*

Studdert-Kennedy M. & Goldstein L. (2007). Launching language: the gestural origin of discrete infinity, In Christiansen, A. & Kirby S. (Eds.): *Language Evolution: The States of the Art*, Oxford: Oxford University Press, 55-69.

Studdert-Kennedy M. (2005). How did language go discrete?, 47–68 in Tallerman M. (Ed.): *Language origins: Perspectives and evolution*, Oxford: Oxford University Press.

Todorov E. (2004). Optimality principles in sensorimotor control, *Nature Neuroscience, 7*, 907–915.

Vatikiotis-Bateson E., Hirayama M., Wada Y., Gracco V. & Kawato M. (1993). Generating articulator motion from muscle activity using artificial neural networks, *Annual Bulletin Research Institute of Logopedics and Phoniatrics (RILP), 27*, 67–77.

Von Hofsten C. (1993). Prospective control: A basic aspect of action development, *Human Development, 36,* 253–270.

16

Jaw Cycles and Linguistic Syllables
in Adult English

Melissa A. Redford [1]

and

Paul van Donkelaar [2]

[1] Department of Linguistics

The University of Oregon

Eugene, Oregon, USA

[2] Department of Human Physiology

The University of Oregon

Eugene, Oregon, USA

In this chapter, we examine whether ideas from Professor MacNeilage's Frame/Content theory of the evolution of speech production (MacNeilage, 1998) apply to linguistic syllables in adult speech. The relevant ideas are that jaw movement is independent of segmental articulation, and that the jaw is recruited to help solve the serial order problem for speech. Specifically, MacNeilage argues that in ontogeny and phylogeny, speech-like behavior— the production of consonant-vowel strings—first emerges when phonation is married to the cyclic open-close movement of the jaw. The result of this marriage is the proto-syllable: a structured segment grouping, which becomes elaborated with time as motor control of the tongue, lips, and velum becomes more sophisticated.

Together with Professor Davis and other colleagues, MacNeilage has amassed substantial evidence to support the hypothesis of a Frame/Content mode of speech production in development (e.g., Davis & MacNeilage, 1995; MacNeilage, Davis & Matyear, 1997; MacNeilage & Davis, 2000).

The specific questions addressed in this chapter are as follows. Does the jaw cycle continue to define syllables in adult speech, as suggested by the cross-language distribution of certain hallmark patterns of a Frame/Content mode of production (MacNeilage, Davis, Matyear, Kinney, 2000)? Second, is jaw movement subordinate to segment articulation, as suggested by more traditional articulatory phonetic accounts of jaw movement in speech (e.g., Gracco, 1994; Perkell, 1969; Stone & Vatikiotis-Bateson, 1995)?

The initial data we present suggest that jaw movement is influenced, but not tied to segmental articulation. However, the data also suggest that any functional correspondence between the jaw cycle and the syllable is weak at best. Whereas a weak correspondence between the cycle and the syllable may be sufficient to condition sound change in the directions predicted by an extended Frame/Content theory (e.g., MacNeilage et al., 2000), it is insufficient to explain syllable production in the adult. Instead, it may be that syllabic motor routines are so highly practiced that their execution can be achieved in the same integrated and holistic sense described for individual segments (e.g., Fowler & Saltzman, 1993) and without consistent reference to the frame upon which they were originally organized.

The Hypothesis

Redford (2000) hypothesized that the Frame/Content mode of production might be extended to adult speech to provide an explanation for several phonological and phonetic patterns associated with linguistic syllables. The argument departed from two observations and an assumption. The observations were (1) that segments within a syllable are organized so that they increase and decrease in sonority according to the Sonority Sequencing Principle (SSP; Clements, 1990; Hooper, 1972; Selkirk, 1982;); and (2) that sonority correlates with jaw openness, such that more sonorous segments are articulated with more jaw opening than less sonorous segments (Lindblom, 1983). The assumption was that sonority sequencing reflects segment sequencing according to the jaw cycle (as in Lindblom, 1983; Butt, 1992). Redford reasoned that if the SSP is central to a definition of a syllable, as is generally assumed (see, e.g., Kenstowitcz, 1994), and the jaw cycle explains the SSP, then the jaw cycle could provide an articulatory basis for the syllable.

If the jaw cycle provides an articulatory basis for the syllable, then it should explain other syllable-related phonological and phonetic patterns beside the SSP. Redford (2000) argued that it could. To take a phonological example, Redford argued that the cross-language preference for syllable-onsets over syllable-offsets (Bell & Hooper, 1978) might emerge from the oft-noted asymmetry between jaw opening and closing (Gracco, 1994; Hanson, 1973; Kuehn & Moll, 1976; Kay, 1985) In particular, the faster closing movement of the jaw might disfavor consonantal articulation because of the speed-accuracy trade-off (Fitts, 1954), assuming that faster jaw closing is a property of the cycle and is independent of linguistic targets.

The hypothesis that the jaw cycle provides a frame for segmental articulation in adult speech as it does in child speech is attractive because of its power to explain a wide variety of syllable-related sound patterns. The hypothesis is at odds, however, with the view derived from the study of adult segmental articulation. The dominant view in adult articulatory phonetics is that jaw movement follows from segmental articulation (e.g., Perkell, 1969; Gracco, 1994; Stone & Vatikiotis-Bateson, 1995). The jaw is raised during the consonant and lowered during the vowel. If the jaw follows segmental articulation, then jaw height maxima and minima represent consonant and vowel targets respectively, and the alternation between the two (i.e., the cycle) is a mere epiphenomenon of consonant-vowel sequencing in language.

Evidence for this segment-first view of jaw movement comes from the fact that the jaw maxima and minima can be predicted by the location and degree of vocal tract constriction that defines segmental articulation. For instance, consonants that are made with greater and more anterior constrictions of the vocal tract are associated with more jaw raising than those that are made with lesser or more posterior constrictions (Keating, Lindblom, Lubker, Kreiman, 1992). However, the maximal vocal tract constrictions achieved by the tongue are not always temporally aligned with maximal jaw closure (Stone & Vatikiotis-Bateson, 1995). This is surprising if the jaw is part of the coordinative structure that defines segmental articulation (Fowler & Saltzman, 1993), and leaves open the possibility that jaw movement is independently specified.

In summary, it is possible to identify two competing views of jaw movement in speech. One view follows from the Frame/Content Theory and suggests that segmental articulation is timed to correspond to the jaw cycle in such a way that syllables can be defined by cycles. The other view follows from articulatory phonetics and suggests that segmental articulation constrains jaw movement, such that cycles emerge from segment sequencing restrictions within syllables. The experiments described below were aimed at corroborating one or the other of these views by examining the relationship between jaw cycles and English syllables in adult speech.

The Production of CVC, CCVC, CVCC Syllables

The goal of this experiment was to determine the relationship between the jaw cycle and segment groupings that we would intuitively characterize as syllables in adult English.

Methods

One male and two female native English-speaking adults participated in the experiment. All three spoke a West-coast dialect of American English. The participants produced CVC, CCVC, and CVCC syllables in the frame sentence "Say ____ eight times." The different syllables all shared the same vowel, /ɑ/, and one of three consonants, /ɹ, l, t/, that occurred in either the onset or offset position and either as a singleton onset or as the internal member of a cluster.

For example, the stimuli for the /ɹ/ series were /ɹɑt/ *rot*, /tɑɹ/ *tar*, /tɹɑt/ *trot*, /tɑɹt/ *tart*. As in this example, labial segments were avoided for all stimuli, so as not to interfere with the measurement of jaw kinematics. Participants produced each of the stimuli 5 times in individually randomized orders for a total of 60 tokens per speaker (20 per series × 3 series).

Procedure

Speakers were seated in a darkened room and read the stimuli off a computer monitor. Stimulus presentation was controlled by software that automatically randomized the stimuli, presented each for several seconds, and then advanced to the next after a short interval. Jaw movement and speech acoustics were recorded simultaneously by two separate computers during the subjects' responses. Jaw movement was recorded on one computer using a Watsmart system consisting of infrared light emitting diodes (LEDs) and two infrared-sensitive cameras. Two LEDs were used. The one that measured jaw movement was attached to a neoprene chin-guard that was taped below the chin to the speaker's mandible. The other marker was attached to the bridge of the nose to provide a reference point for the jaw movement. Speech acoustics were captured by a high quality microphone and recorded directly onto the second computer. The stimulus presentation computer simultaneously triggered the jaw movement and the speech acoustic recording computers at the beginning of each trial. The following acoustic and movement measures were then made on the recordings.

Acoustic Duration

Segment onsets and offsets were identified using standard phonetic procedures (e.g., Klatt, 1976): the acoustic waveform was displayed as a spectrograph and an oscillograph. Following an obstruent consonant or vowel closure, the boundaries of liquid consonants were identified at the beginning of periodicity and the corresponding rise in signal amplitude. Following a vowel, the boundaries were identified at an abrupt decrease in energy and frequency changes in the waveform. The boundaries between liquid consonants and the vowel nucleus of the syllable were determined by a change in the waveform, a decrease in overall energy, and a low F3 for /ɹ/ and an antiformant between F1 and F2 for /l/. The boundaries of stop consonants were identified at the offset/onset of adjacent vowels or liquids as indicated by an abrupt decrease or increase in the energy of the periodic waveform. If a stop was released in final position, stop duration was measured from the offset of periodicity on the initial border to the offset of aspiration on the final border. Otherwise the final border was measured as the onset of the following vowel in *eight*. This practice allowed for measurement consistency, but it probably overestimated the actual articulation time of a final stop. The stimuli also included the alveolar fricative /s/ (e.g., /stɑk/ *stock*). The boundaries of this segment were identified at the onset to the offset of noisy energy.

Movement Measures

Next, the temporal onsets of the segments were aligned with the jaw movement waveform and the cycle maxima (peaks) and minima (troughs) were identified for the target syllable (see Figure 16.1). The duration, displacement and velocity of jaw movement were calculated for the demicycle, that is, the portion of the cycle corresponding to either the movement from cycle peak to trough or the movement from cycle trough to peak. Several additional measures were also made to describe the relationship between the jaw cycle and the articulation of the target segments in the syllable. Specifically, jaw height at segment onset was calculated for the shared consonants, /ɹ, l, t/, and vowel, /ɑ/. The time of segment onset from the relevant cycle peaks (for the consonants) and troughs (for the vowel) was also calculated. Figure 16.1 depicts these latter measurement types.

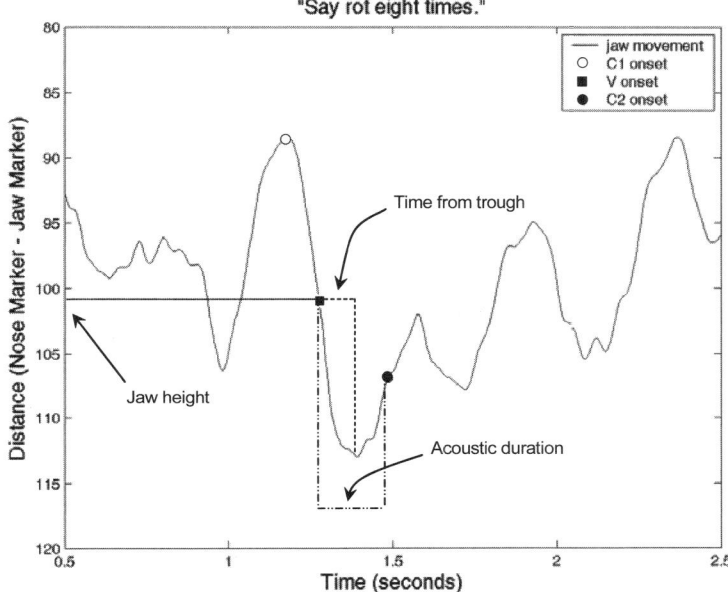

Figure 16.1.
The movement waveform is shown for the target syllable *rot* in the frame "Say ___ eight times." The temporal onsets of the acoustic segments are plotted on the waveform. The figure also shows how measures relating segmental articulation to the jaw cycle were calculated. The example measures are for the /ɑ/ in *rot*.

Predictions

The hypothesis that segmental articulation follows jaw movement predicts that the segments of a syllable will be timed to correspond to the opening and closing movement of the cycle. Syllable onsets will be articulated during the opening phase of a cycle, and syllable offsets will be articulated during the closing phase. Internal members of a cluster will be articulated further from the peak of the cycle and closer to its trough.

The hypothesis that jaw movement follows from segmental articulation predicts that the target jaw position should be reached at approximately the same time during the articulation of a segment regardless of syllable position. So, for example, in the V___V frame of the present experiment, the proportion of a consonant articulated during opening or closing should not be affected by syllable position.

Results

Overall, the results suggest a correspondence between the jaw cycle and syllable structure, but jaw movement is also clearly influenced by segmental articulation. We present the results on demicycle characteristics for different syllable positions, followed by the results relating segments-by-position to location within the cycle.

Demicycle Characteristics

Demicycle characteristics were analyzed as the first step in the evaluation of the relationship between the cycle and the syllable. Demicycle duration, displacement, and peak velocity covary and so were entered as dependent variables in a 3-way multivariate analysis of variance (MANOVA) with Speaker, Syllable (C<u>C</u>V, <u>C</u>V, V<u>C</u>, V<u>C</u>C), and Consonant (r, l, t) as fixed factors. The test showed that the variables jointly varied systematically with Syllable and Consonant [Pillai's Trace, $F = 8.144$, $p < .01$] and with Speaker and Syllable [Pillai's Trace, $F = 4.693$, $p < .01$]. The presence of Speaker differences in particular obscured the expected asymmetry in opening and closing peak velocity, as indicated by the lack of an effect of syllable position in a follow-up univariate analysis on peak velocity. However, other follow-up analyses showed an asymmetry in displacement—opening displacement was greater than closing displacement [$F(1, 135) = 158.276$], and a corresponding asymmetry in duration [$F(1, 135) = 14.654$, $p < .01$].

Neither speaker differences nor differences between consonant types obscured the effect of syllable structure on the variables. Follow-up univariate analyses adjusted for multiple comparisons indicated that demicycles associated with the articulation of complex onsets and offsets were greater in duration, displacement, and velocity than those associated with the articulation of simple onsets and offsets [duration, $F(1, 135) = 77.993$, $p < .01$; displacement, $F(1, 135) = 23.805$, $p < .01$; peak velocity, $F(1, 135) = 7.541$, $p < .01$]. This latter result is most likely due to the sequential articulation of consonants rather than to syllable shape per se.

In sum, duration and displacement were greater during jaw opening than during jaw closing, and during the articulation of complex onsets/offsets than during the articulation of simple onsets/offsets.

Segment Height and the Cycle

The relationship between segment articulation and the jaw cycle was evaluated more directly by analyzing jaw height at the onset of segment articulation. Jaw height (measured as the difference between the nose and jaw markers) at segment onset was evaluated as a function of Speaker, Syllable, and Consonant. Consonant height at segment onset was significantly affected by Syllable [$F(3, 135) = 10.076$, $p < .01$] and Consonant [$F(2, 135) = 8.506$, $p < .01$], but not by the interaction of these factors or by interactions with Speaker. Both singleton consonants and those in a cluster were initiated at a more open point on the cycle in syllable-offset position than in syllable-onset position. The alveolar stop was initiated at a more open point on the cycle than either alveolar liquid. In contrast, vowel height at onset interacted with Syllable and Consonant [$F(6, 135) = 2.575$, $p < .05$], but the fact that neither factor alone significantly affected height indicated significant variability across the different Syllable and Consonant combinations.

Given the lack of an effect of Syllable on vowel height at onset, the Syllable effect on consonant height is more easily understood as resulting from the asymmetry of the opening and closing demicycles than in terms of segment duration characteristics.

Segment Duration and the Cycle

The final analysis was aimed at directly testing the relationship between segments and the cycle. The hypothesis that segment groups are sequenced according to the jaw cycle predicted that consonants in onset position would be articulated during the opening phase of the cycle and those in offset position would be articulated during the closing phase. The alternative prediction was that syllable position would be irrelevant, and that target jaw positions would be reached at the same time during the articulation of the consonant. With respect to vowels, only the hypothesis that jaw movement follows segmental articulation makes the specific prediction that the target jaw position for vowels should be reached at the same time during vowel articulation regardless of syllable shape.

To evaluate the predictions, we calculated the proportion of consonant articulation within the cycle. For onset position (CVC or CCVC) this meant subtracting the duration of articulation prior to the first peak of the cycle from the total duration of the consonant, and then dividing the adjusted duration by the total duration. A similar procedure was applied to offset position (CVC or CVCC), but the adjusted duration was that which occurred prior to the second peak in the cycle. So, the measure indicated the proportion of consonantal articulation during jaw opening for onset position and during jaw closing for offset position.

Figure 16.2 shows the proportion of consonantal duration articulated within the cycle for consonants in the different syllable positions and onset/offset types. This significant effect of Syllable interacted with Speaker [$F_{(6, 135)} = 6.889$, $p < .01$] and Consonant [$F_{(6, 135)} = 3.890$, $p < .01$], but the general pattern captured by the simple effect [$F_{(3, 135)} = 25.021$, $p < .01$] was evident in spite of the systematic variation. In particular, and as shown in Figure 16.2, a larger proportion of consonantal articulation occurred during the opening phase for consonants in onset position and during the closing phase for consonants in offset position than vice versa.

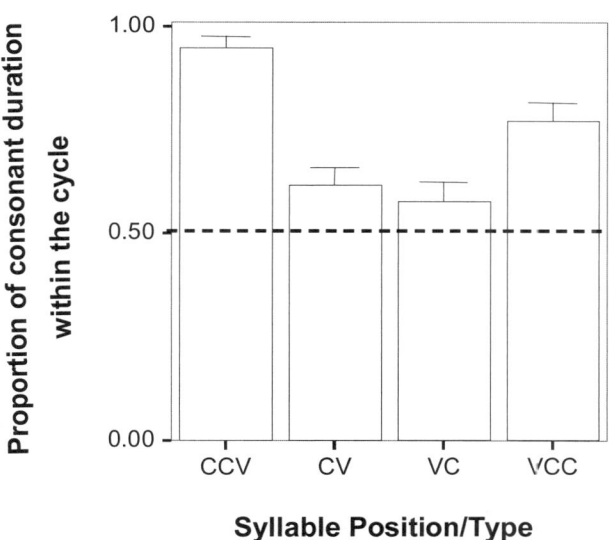

Figure 16.2.
The proportion of consonantal articulation within the cycle is shown as a function of the target segment's location: CCV, CV, VC, VCC. The duration of articulation following or preceding a peak (consonantal target) was divided by the total duration of articulation to obtain the proportions shown in the figure. If the jaw had peaked midway through the articulation of the consonant, then the proportions would all be at .50, or even with the dotted line.

Figure 16.2 also suggests directionality in the relationship between jaw movement and segmental articulation. If cycle peaks represent the consonantal target for the jaw, then we can see that this target was achieved at different points during the articulation of the consonants in different syllable positions. For instance, the target was attained roughly 40% through articulation of simple onsets (CVC), and closer to 60% through articulation for simple offsets (CVC).

The difference in target attainment as a function of syllable shape is more striking for vowels, if the cycle minimum is taken as the articulatory target for the vowel. Figure 16.3 shows that proportion of vowel duration prior to the trough varies for the different syllable types.

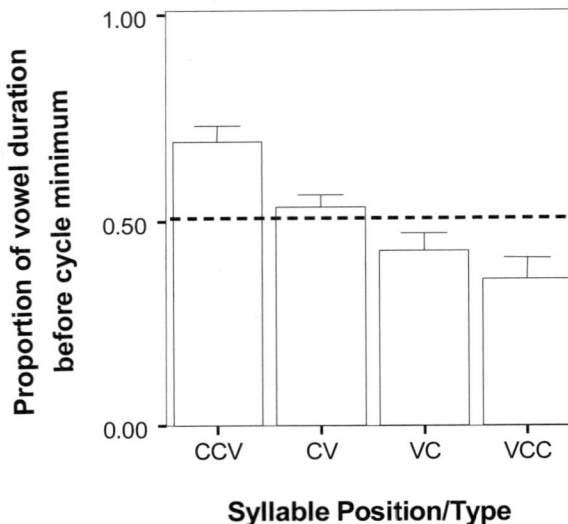

Syllable Position/Type

Figure 16.3.
The proportion of vowel articulation prior to the cycle trough (vocalic target) is shown as a function of the target segment's location: CC̱V, C̱V, VC̱, VC̱C. If the jaw had troughed midway through the articulation of the vowel, then the proportions would all be at .50, or even with the dotted line.

As shown in Figure 16.3, the vowel target is attained roughly 70% through the vowel in CCVC syllables and roughly 40% though in CVCC syllables. Univariate analyses with Speaker, Syllable, and Consonant as fixed factors confirms systematic differences by syllable position and type [$F(3, 135)$ = 15.414, $p < .01$], even though the differences interact to a certain degree with speaker and consonant type as well [$F(12, 135) = 2.670$, $p < .01$]. This result is not predicted by the view that jaw movement merely follows from segmental articulation. It is more consistent with the finding of greater jaw displacement in initial position than in final position, attributes that follow from the jaw cycle.

Discussion

Experiment 1 examined jaw movement as a function of syllable position and type. The relationship between segmental articulation and jaw movement was then explored. Overall results point to the importance of syllable structure in sequential articulation of segments. It is not clear from this experiment whether jaw movement defines the syllable or is defined by it. For example, the direction of the opening and closing asymmetry was not predicted, but is arguably better understood as a suprasegmental rather than a segmental effect. In the present context, the smaller displacement during jaw closing relative to jaw opening could signify that final consonants were undershot, consistent with other accounts of syllable position-dependent differences in segmental articulation (Redford & Diehl, 1999; Sussman, Bessell, Dalston, Majors, 1997). On this view, the observed differences between opening and closing could have been determined by linguistic factors, for instance, by the need for greater perceptual distinctiveness in onset position.

On the other hand, it is possible that the asymmetry result argues for the priority of sequential coarticulatory constraints on jaw movement, which would de facto argue against the idea of any meaningful relationship between the cycle and the syllable. For example, the relevant VCV and VCCV sequences were meant to be identical, but the vowel offset in the initial part of the frame, *say*, is more closed than the onset of the vowel in the latter part of the frame, *eight*, due to the diphthongization of the mid-front tense vowel in American English. So the latter part of the syllable-final diphthong in *say* could have boosted the initial peak of the cycle associated with the target syllable, thereby increasing displacement from peak to trough during opening relative to closing.

To determine whether observed relationships between the cycle and the syllable reflects more than segment-to-segment coarticulatory constraints, we conducted an additional experiment. Sound sequences were held constant and syllable boundaries were varied by inserting a word boundary either before or between two identical consonants.

Boundary Manipulations on VCCV Sequences

The goal of this experiment was to assess whether the relationship observed between the jaw cycle and syllable structure in Experiment 1 represented a meaningful relationship or a fortuitous consequence of coarticulatory constraints on the sequential articulation of segments.

Methods

Speakers, procedures, and measurements were identical to Experiment 1. The stimuli were different. The target stimuli were adjacent words that created an intervocalic two-consonant sequence. Syllable structure was manipulated via boundary location while segmental content was held constant: *high trot* vs. *might rot, my slot* vs. *nice lot, my snot* vs. *nice knot, my stock* vs. *nice talk, hi Scott* vs. *nice cot*. The stimuli were repeated 5 times, and produced in randomized order in the frame sentence "Say___eight times." Speakers used the same intonational contour for the V.CCV and VC.CV segmentations.

Results

Overall, results indicate a complex relationship between suprasegmental structure, segmental articulation, and jaw movement. Jaw movement differed as a function of boundary location, but it appeared that the direction of influence was from suprasegmental structure to jaw movement and not vice versa. The suggestion that suprasegmental factors influence jaw movement and not segmental factors is based on the results, which suggest that jaw movement is somewhat independent of segmental articulation. In particular, there appears to be only a loose temporal connection between the attainment of maximal jaw closure and consonantal articulation. The evidence suggests, though, that consonantal articulation may be timed to correspond to aspects of the cycle. In particular, the onset of consonantal articulation may be timed to correspond to particular jaw heights. Below, boundary-dependent differences in the relative acoustic durations of C1 and C2 are noted first, then the results on demicycle characteristics are presented, followed by the results on the relationship between segmental articulation and jaw movement.

Acoustic Duration

The literature on phonetic juncture indicates that segmental duration is affected by position relative to a boundary (see, e.g., Klatt, 1976... for a classic description of the correlations between linguistic structure and patterns of segment duration). Such boundary-dependent changes in acoustic duration were also noted in the present experiment. The relative acoustic duration of C1 and C2 in the VCCV sequences was analyzed in a 3-way ANOVA with Speaker, Boundary (VC.CV, V.CCV), and Sequence (-tr-, -sl-, -sn-, -st-, -sk-) as factors. Results showed that the measure of relative consonantal duration, namely, a C1-C2 duration ratio, was significantly affected by boundary location across all speakers and all sequence types [$F(1, 120) = 310.36$, $p < .01$]. A pre-consonantal (V.CCV) boundary was associated with larger ratios; long C1s and short C2s. A transconsonantal (VC.CV) boundary was associated with smaller ratios; C1s and C2s of similar durations.

Although the relative duration of C1 and C2 varied with boundary location, the total consonantal duration (C1+C2) did not. Instead, the total consonantal duration varied differently for different combinations of Boundary and Sequence [$F(4, 120) = 12.759$, $p < .01$]. Unlike consonantal duration, the relative acoustic duration of V1 and V2 were not systematically affected by boundary location or any other variable. That is, there were no significant effects of Speaker, Boundary, or Sequence on a V1:V2 ratio.

Demicycle Characteristics

As a first step towards evaluating the relationship between suprasegmental patterns and the jaw cycle, demicycle characteristics were evaluated according to the fixed factors of Speaker, Boundary, and Sequence.

A MANOVA with closing duration, displacement, and peak velocity as dependent variables showed that these variables varied jointly with all three factors [Pillai's trace, $F = 2.771$, $p < .01$]. The effect of Boundary alone on the variables was also significant [Pillai's trace, $F = 10.849$, $p < .01$]. A MANOVA on opening duration, displacement, and peak velocity showed systematic variation by Sequence [Pillai's trace, F = 11.816, p < .01], but no other factors or combination of factors affected the dependent variables associated with jaw opening. Follow-up univariate analyses on the closing variables showed that only closing duration varied systematically with Boundary [$F(1, 120) = 30.751$, p < .01]. Closing duration was longer when the boundary occurred before the consonant sequence (e.g., *high trot*) than when it occurred between the consonants (e.g., *might rot*).

Longer closing durations leading into the articulation of a complex onset (e.g., *high trot*) were not due to differences in peak or trough height. The simple effect of Boundary was absent in 3-way univariate analyses of these two variables. Sequence did, however, systematically affect peak height [$F(4, 120) = 150.646$, p <.01]. Post hoc tests showed that the distance between the nose and jaw marker was smallest (i.e., greatest closure) for peaks associated with stimuli that had intervocalic -*tr*- sequences (p < .01). There were no other significant differences in peak height between other sequence types.

Overall, these results suggest that jaw movement is affected by suprasegmental structure, but not in the way that would be expected. If the syllable and the cycle were functionally related, then the articulation of V.CCV sequences would have resulted in greater duration/displacement during jaw opening, not jaw closing.

Segment Height and the Cycle

Analyses showed that neither vowel nor consonant height varied systematically with boundary location. Jaw height varied systematically, though differently, for V1 and C1 with different combinations of Speaker, Boundary, and Sequence [V1: $F(8, 120) = 2.404$, p < .05; C1: $F(8, 120) = 4.228$, p < .01]. Different Speaker and Boundary combinations affected C2 and V2 height differently as well [C2: $F(2, 120) = 4.471$, p < .05; V2: $F(2, 120) = 4.014$, p <.05]. Although there were no systematic effects of Boundary on jaw height, Sequence was found to systematically effect the height of C2 [$F(4, 120) = 22.751$, p < .01].

Post hoc tests showed that /ɹ/ was systematically initiated with a higher (more closed) jaw position than any of the other consonants (p < .01). Height at initiation did not differ between the other consonants /l, n, t, k/. Overall, these results suggest that jaw height at the onset of articulation is correlated with segmental variables, but not with suprasegmental variables.

Segment Duration and the Cycle

As in Experiment 1, the relationship between syllable structure and the jaw cycle was tested by analyzing the proportion of C1 and C2 articulated during jaw closing and jaw opening respectively. This analysis indicated some significant differences as a function of the fixed factors that were not in the anticipated direction. A relationship between syllable and cycle would predict that the proportion of C1 articulated duration the closing portion of the cycle would be less for a V.CCV than for a VC.CV segmentation, and that the proportion of C2 articulated during the opening cycle would be greater for a V.CCV than a VC.CV segmentation. Results are inconsistent with this prediction, and are in the opposite direction for C2.

The proportion of C1 articulated during the closing portion of the cycle differed with different combinations of Boundary location and Sequence type [$F(4, 119) = 3.334$, $p < .05$]. Variability was such that there was no simple effect for Boundary (see Figure 16.4). The proportion of C2 articulated during the opening portion of the subsequent cycle also differed with different combinations of Boundary location and Sequence type [$F(4, 119) = 2.511$, $p < .05$], but the simple effect of Boundary was also significant [$F(1, 119) = 17.626$, $p < .01$]. Nonetheless, variability in the timing of C2 with respect to the offset/onset peak was also high (see Figure 16.4).

Figure 16.4 shows histograms for proportion of C1 in cycle 1 and proportion of C2 in cycle 2. C1 is most often articulated almost entirely during the closing phase of cycle 1, and similarly for C2. In other words, neither singleton onset nor complex onsets are usually coarticulated with the following

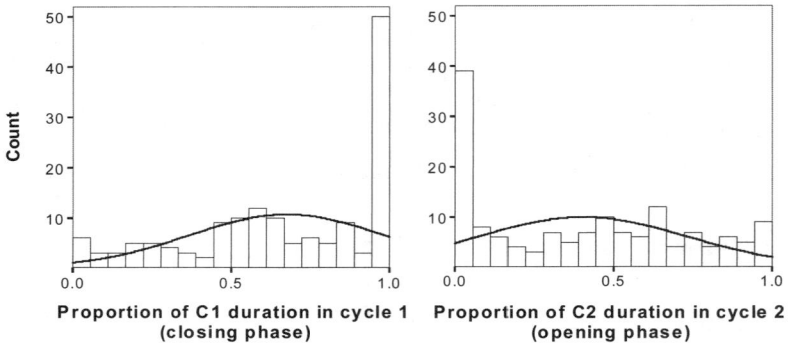

Figure 16.4.
Histograms show the variability associated with the articulation of consonants relative to the peak. In the majority of cases, C1 and C2 are articulated during the closing phase of cycle 1.

vowel—the vowel to which they belong according to linguistic segmentations of the sequences.

The result that both consonants are usually articulated during the closing phase of cycle 1 rather than during the opening phase of cycle 2, particularly during production of V.CCV stimuli, was unexpected. In order to evaluate whether this surprising result was due to differences in the displacement of the closing and opening phases in cycle 1 and cycle 2 respectively, we compared the phases on this variable. Two-tailed t-tests showed that closing displacement in cycle 1 was greater than opening displacement in cycle 2 [$t(149) = 11.925$, $p < .01$]. A corresponding asymmetry in duration was also found, but this asymmetry presumably interacted with Boundary, as described in the section on demicycle characteristics.

It is likely that the difference in opening and closing displacement followed from the asymmetry of the vowels in the sequences. V1 was the diphthong /ɑi/, V2 was the monophthong /ɑ/. The vowel asymmetry translated into an asymmetry in the degree of opening attained in the two cycles. Maximal opening for cycle 1 was greater than that attained in cycle 2, as indicated in a two-tailed t-test [t(149) = 11.925, p < .01].

A possible interpretation of results is that the consonants were preferentially articulated during the closing phase of cycle 1 rather than the opening phase of cycle 2 as cycle 1 had more "room" relative to cycle 2. The finding that a greater proportion of C2 was articulated during jaw closing in V.CCV relative to VC.CV stimuli might have been due to the longer closing durations of the cycle associated with the initial portion of the V.CCV stimuli.

Discussion

The results from Experiment 2 suggest that the jaw cycle reflects aspects of suprasegmental structure, but there is little to suggest a constant or functional relationship between the cycle and linguistic syllable of adult English. The closing phase that followed V1 was longer for stimuli associated with V.CCV type stimuli than for those associated with VC.CV types. This lengthening was unexpected. The expectation had been that jaw opening for V2 would be lengthened to accommodate the articulation of a complex onset. It is difficult to attribute the effect to segmental duration, since total consonantal duration was not different for V.CCV and VC.CV stimuli. However, if the slowing was due to segmental duration, then it would have to be due to differences in relative duration. C1 was longer and C2 was shorter in V.CCV stimuli than in VC.CV stimuli.

Although Experiment 2 provides little evidence for a functional relationship between the syllable and cycle in adult language, it also provides little evidence for the view that jaw movement is defined by segment-to-segment articulatory constraints. Consonant timing varies greatly with respect to maximal jaw closing, and this variation is not systematically related to any of the factors explored in the present Experiment. Because of variation in when the jaw peaks vis-à-vis consonant articulation, it is hard to imagine that jaw closure represents a well-defined consonantal target, as the segment-first view would seem to predict. Instead, consonants and vowels appear to be timed to coincide with spatial location on the cycle. Segments were initiated at similar jaw heights regardless of suprasegmental structure or other characteristics of the cycle.

General Discussion

In spite of the relationship between sonority and jaw height (e.g., Lindblom, 1983), results from present study indicate that the relationship between the syllable and the jaw cycle may be fortuitous rather than functional. Segments usually appear to be initiated at the same spatial location in a jaw cycle, but the cycle appears not to impose a strict temporal constraint on segmental articulation. A consonant that is initiated at a particular height can be initiated either during the upward or downward trajectory of the cycle, depending on where there is enough room to articulated it. Our phenomenological sense of segment groupings therefore cannot be defined or clarified in terms of the cycle, at least for adult English. Overall, present evidence disfavors the hypothesis argued for in Redford (2000), which pushes the Frame/Content mode of speech production into adult language to define the online production of syllables.

The alternative hypothesis that jaw movement follows segmental articulation, is not supported by the evidence either. There is a strong sense in which jaw movement appears to be independently specified, as suggested by the neurophysiological data reviewed in MacNeilage (1998). First, the maximal opening and closing movements do not seem to reflect segmental targets, as shown above. Second, a single jaw cycle can span one to many segments. So, the question remains, why does the jaw move during speech? And, does this movement reflect anything other than the vestiges of babbling or inaccurate target attainment and inertia on the part of a slow and massive articulator? Given (1) the role of the jaw during the development of speech production (viz. Davis & MacNeilage, 1990); (2) some correspondences between the cycle and adult syllables; and (3) the potential of jaw movement to help explain a variety of syllable-related patterns in language (see section 2 above), we continue to expect that the cycle organizes segments in adult speech at some level and/or under certain conditions. We will test this expectation in future research by moving away from the over-practiced utterances focused in the present study to measure jaw movement during sequence learning tasks, with novel sound combinations.

References

Bell, A., & Hooper, J. B. (1978). Issues and evidence in syllabic phonology. In A. Bell & J. B. Hooper (Eds.), *Syllables and segments* (pp. 3–22). Amsterdam: North Holland.

Butt, M. (1992). Sonority and the explanation of syllable structure. *Linguistische Berichte, 137*, 45–67.

Clements, G. N. (1990). The role of the sonority cycle in core syllabification. In J. Kingston & M. Beckman (Eds.), *Between the grammar and the physics of speech* (pp. 283–333). New York: Cambridge University Press.

Davis, B. L., & MacNeilage, P. F. (1995). The articulatory basis of babbling. *Journal of Speech and Hearing Research, 38*, 1199–1211.

Fitts, P. A. (1954). The information capacity of the human motor system in controlling the amplitude of movement. *Journal of Experimental Psychology, 47*, 381–391.

Fowler, C. A., & Saltzman, E. (1993). Coordination and coarticulation in speech production. *Language and Speech, 36*, 171–195.

Gracco, V. J. (1994). Some organizational characteristics of speech movement control. *Journal of Speech and Hearing Research, 37*, 4–27.

Haggard, M. (1973). Correlations between successive segment durations: Values in clusters. *Journal of Phonetics, 1*, 111–116.

Hooper, J. B. (1972). The syllable in phonological theory. *Language, 48*, 525–540.

Keating, P., Lindblom, B., Lubker, J., & Kreiman, J. (1994). Variability in jaw height for segments in English and Swedish VCVs. *Journal of Phonetics, 22*, 407–422.

Kelso, J. A. S., Vatikiotis-Bateson, E., & Kay, B. (1985). A qualitative dynamic analysis of reiterant speech production: Phase portraits, kinematics, and dynamic modeling. *Journal of the Acoustical Society of America, 77*, 266–280.

Kenstowicz, M. (1994). *Phonology in generative grammar*. Cambridge, MA: Blackwell.

Klatt, D. (1976). Linguistic uses of segmental duration in English: Acoustic and perceptual evidence. *Journal of the Acoustical Society of America, 59*, 1208–1221.

Kuehn, D.P., & Moll, K.L. (1976). A cineradiographic study of VC and CV articulatory velocities. *Journal of Phonetics, 4*, 303–320.

Lindblom, B. (1983). Economy of speech gestures. In P. MacNeilage (Ed.), *The production of speech* (pp. 217–246). New York: Springer.

MacNeilage, P. F. (1998). The frame/content theory of evolution of speech production. *Behavioral and Brain Sciences, 21*, 499–546.

MacNeilage, P. F., & Davis, B. L. (2000). On the origin of internal structure of word forms. *Science, 288*, 527–531.

MacNeilage, P. F., Davis, B. L., & Matyear, C. L. (1997). Babbling and first words: Phonetic similarities and differences. *Speech Communication, 22*, 269–277.

MacNeilage, P. F., Davis, B. L., Matyear, C. L., & Kinney, A. (2000). The motor core of speech. *Child Development, 71*, 153–163.

Perkell, J. (1969). *Physiology of speech production: Results and implications of a quantitative cineradiographic study*. Cambridge, MA: MIT Press.

Redford, M. A. (2000). An articulatory basis for the syllable. Doctoral dissertation, University of Texas at Austin, 2000. *Dissertation Abstracts International, 61*, 1127.

Redford, M. A., & Diehl, R. (1999). The relative perceptual distinctiveness of initial and final consonants in CVC syllables. *Journal of the Acoustical Society of America, 106*, 1555–1565.

Selkirk, E. (1982). The syllable. In H. van der Hulst & N. Smith (Eds.), *The structure of phonological representation* (pp. 337–383). Dordrecht: Foris.

Stone, M., & Vatikiotis-Bateson, E. (1995). Trade-offs in tongue, jaw, and palate contributions to speech production. *Journal of Phonetics, 23*, 81–100.

Sussman, H. M., Bessell, N., Dalston, E., & Majors, T. (1997). An investigation of stop place articulation as a function of syllable position. *Journal of the Acoustical Society of America, 101*, 2826–2838.

Sussman, H. M., MacNeilage, P. F., & Hanson, R. J. (1973). Labial and mandibular dynamics during the production of bilabial consonants: Preliminary observations. *Journal Speech and Hearing Research, 16*, 385–396.

VI: Alternative Perspectives on the Syllable

17

The Syllable in Sign Language: Considering the Other Natural Language Modality

Wendy Sandler

Department of English Language and Literature

The University of Haifa

Haifa, Israel

The research program developed by Peter MacNeilage seeks to derive aspects of phonological organization from fundamental physical properties of the speech system, and from there to arrive at reasonable hypotheses about the evolution of speech. Speech is the dominant medium for the transmission of natural human language, and characterizing its organization is clearly very important for our understanding of language as a whole. Speech is not the only medium available to humans, however, and a comprehensive theory of the nature and evolution of language has much to gain by investigating the form of language in the other natural language modality: sign language, the focus of this chapter.

Like spoken languages, sign languages have syllables, the unit that will form the basis for comparison here. As a prosodic unit of organization within the word, sign language syllables bear certain significant similarities to those of spoken language. Such similarities help to shed light on universal properties of linguistic organization, regardless of modality. Yet the form and organization of syllables in the two modalities are quite different, and I will argue that these differences are equally illuminating. The similarities show that spoken and signed languages reflect the same cognitive system in a nontrivial sense. But the differences confirm that certain key aspects of phonological structure must indeed be derived from the physical transmission system, resulting in phonological systems that are in some ways distinct.

The bulk of the chapter is dedicated to a discussion of the syllable in signed languages, pointing out ways in which the unit resembles its spoken language counterpart and also describing how it differs. After a brief introduction to sign language phonology (in Sections 2 and 3), motivation is presented for use of the term, "syllable" in a physical modality that is very different from the oral-aural modality of spoken language. While the notion of 'sentence' or 'word' may be easy to conceive of in a manual-visual language, 'syllable' takes more convincing, which is what Section 4 attempts. The sign language syllable is distinguished from other units such as the word and morpheme, and phonological evidence is presented for the reality of the syllable as a phonological and prosodic element. Differences between the syllable in spoken and signed language are highlighted in Section 4.3. One important difference is the presence of an oscillating mandible as a syllable frame in spoken language (MacNeilage, 1998), and the absence of a comparable frame in sign language. Another is the availability of greater articulatory range to the primary articulator in sign language—the hand(s)—than to what might be considered the spoken language counterpart, the tongue. I will suggest in Section 5 that phonetic differences underlie phonological differences, providing support for MacNeilage and Davis (2000) position that (some of) the phonological form of language is determined by the physical system.

The evolutionary context that motivates this volume requires us to ponder the implications of the descriptions and analyses to be presented. Section 6 provides some remarks on this issue that grow out of the discussion that precedes it. The fact that there are differences in syllable (and other phonological) organization in the two language modalities does not imply that the oral and manual modalities are mutually exclusive. They have too much in common to sustain that view. Nor does it require us to assume that the medium of transmission is essentially extraneous to the structure and organization of language. The latter view is refuted by the fact that some phonological structure clearly derives from the physical properties of the system and is therefore different in each modality. Instead, we need a theory that explains both commonalities and differences in phonological organization, differences that were chiseled out of the raw material in each modality. And the theory needs a plausible scenario for how this language capacity could have evolved.

Such a theory must not only explain our species' unique endowment for a complex linguistic system; it must also explain our extraordinary capacity to use two different systems. I suggest bimodalism as a starting point for developing a comprehensive theory of the kind described. Specifically, natural languages in the two modalities evolved from complementary aspects of the **same** system, and bimodalism is still apparent in each kind of language if you know where to look.

Two Kinds of Natural Language

Sign languages are natural languages arising spontaneously wherever a group of deaf people has an opportunity to gather and meet regularly (Klima & Bellugi, 1979; Sandler et al., 2004; Senghas et al., 2004). Sign languages are not contrived communication systems, nor is there a single, universal sign language. Instead, there are hundreds of natural sign languages in deaf communities worldwide (Woll et al., 2001). Sign languages are acquired by children in the same stages and time frame as spoken languages (Meier, 1991). Both deaf and hearing children acquire sign language natively if sign language is the primary language in the home. Signed and spoken languages share many significant linguistic properties at all levels of structure (Sandler & Lillo-Martin, 2002, 2006). Certain key areas of the brain are active in the control of spoken and sign language (Emmorey, 2002). And sign languages subserve the same full range of communicative functions as spoken languages, including artistic forms such as poetry (Klima & Bellugi, 1979; Sandler & Lillo-Martin, 2002, 2006; Sutton-Spence & Woll, 1999). A large body of literature on the topic demonstrates that sign languages are full and complex languages with rich expressive capabilities. It is safe to conclude, then, that speech and language are not synonymous. Instead, speech is one primary medium for language, and sign is another.

Sign Languages Have Phonology

The first strictly linguistic investigation of sign language was that of William Stokoe (1960), working on American Sign Language (ASL). That work was seminal because it established a characteristic of sign languages that makes them clearly comparable to spoken languages, a characteristic that is perhaps least expected a priori. That property is duality of patterning (Hockett, 1960). This means that languages have both a meaningless level of structure—in spoken languages, a finite list of sounds which combine in various constrained ways to make words—and a meaningful level of structure—words and sentences. Duality is a fundamental property of language, responsible for its capacity to generate an enormous lexicon of meaningful words from a very small number of meaningless building blocks. Despite their iconic and gestural origins, Stokoe showed that there is also a meaningless level of structure in a sign language, and inaugurated the field of linguistic research on sign language. He showed that signs are not holistic gestures, as they may appear to be at first glance, but rather that they are made up of a small and finite set of meaningless components. Subsequent research showed that there are constraints on the ways in which these components combine to create the words of sign languages (e.g., Battison, 1978; Mandel, 1981), and that the form of a word may change in predictable ways in different morphophonological contexts (e.g., Liddell and Johnson, R., 1986; Sandler, 1987). Together, these discoveries demonstrate that sign languages have phonology. With a meaningless phonological level, sign languages have the building blocks of a potentially large lexicon.

On the basis of minimal pairs formed by substituting a single feature of handshape, location, or movement in a sign, Stokoe proposed these categories as the three basic formational parameters of signs. Stokoe proposed that each handshape, location and movement of the ASL inventory should be compared with a spoken language phoneme. However, he believed that the inter-organization of these elements within a sign is different from the spoken word, that the elements occur simultaneously, not sequentially like consonants and vowels in spoken words. Other researchers have found evidence of some sequential structure within a sign, although it is more limited than is typical in spoken words (Liddell, 1984; Sandler, 1989). My own work adopts nonlinear theories of phonology and morphology (e.g., Goldsmith, 1976; McCarthy, 1981) to create a model of sign language structure that reveals both simultaneous and sequential properties (Sandler, 1986; 1989; Sandler & Lillo-Martin, 2006). The analysis of the syllable presented in Section 4 assumes this model.

Simultaneous and Sequential Structure in the Sign

In a typical sign, the hand, in a particular configuration, begins in one location and ends in another. For example, JUST-THEN, from Israeli Sign Language (ISL), is illustrated in Figure 17.1. The hand configuration (HC) is

The hand begins at a location (L) a proximal distance above the nondominant hand, and moves (M) to a location in contact with that place of articulation. A partial representation of JUST-THEN is shown in Figure 17.2.

Figure 17.1.
JUST-THEN (ISL)

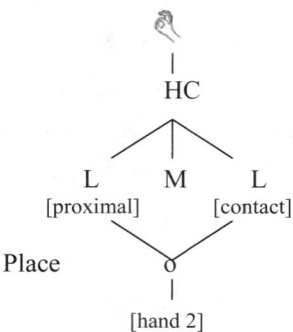

Figure 17.2.
Partial representation of JUST-THEN

    The model used for the representation is the Hand Tier model (Sandler, 1986, 1989), motivated by the interaction of sequential and simultaneous elements in sign language phonology and reveals both in its representation. In JUST-THEN both the Hand Configuration and the place of articulation are simultaneous, in the sense that they are invariant across the sign. But the two locations, [proximal] and [contact] are articulated sequentially. While sequential structure is an important and salient characteristic of spoken language, it is less obvious in most signs. Nevertheless, there is compelling evidence that sequentiality is indeed present in the phonological structure of signs.

    First, there are some minimal pairs distinguished only by one feature in a sequential position within the sign. Like *chap* and *chat* in English, the signs CHRISTIAN and COMMITTEE are distinguished by the final segment only, as pictured in Figure 17.3 and illustrated schematically in Figure 17.4.

    While these minimal pairs, distinguished by sequentially occurring features, are admittedly rare, more evidence for sequentiality is found in the morphophonology of sign languages that have been studied. For example, verb agreement is marked on the first and last locations of a sign. The hand begins at

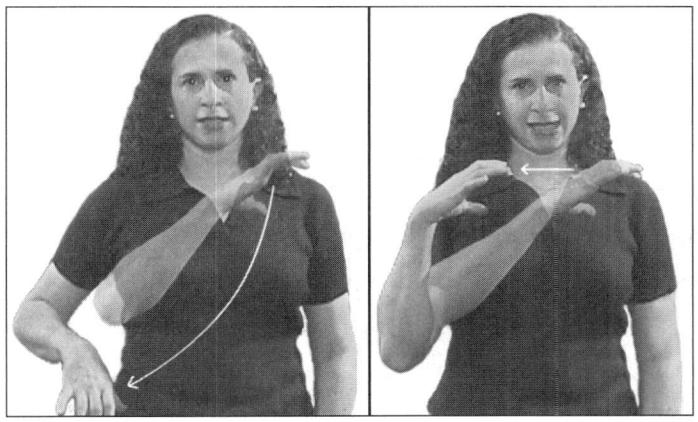

a. CHRISTIAN   b. COMMITTEE

Figure 17.3.
Minimal pair in ASL distinguished by sequentially occurring features.

a location designated as the spatial locus for one referent, typically the subject, and ends at a locus designated as the locus for another referent, typically the object (Liddell, 1984; Padden, 1988). Two pictures of the ISL verb SHOW appear in Figure 17.5. In the first, SHOW agrees with first person subject and second person object, and in the second, with second person subject and first person object. To sign I-SHOW-HER, the sign would begin at the first person

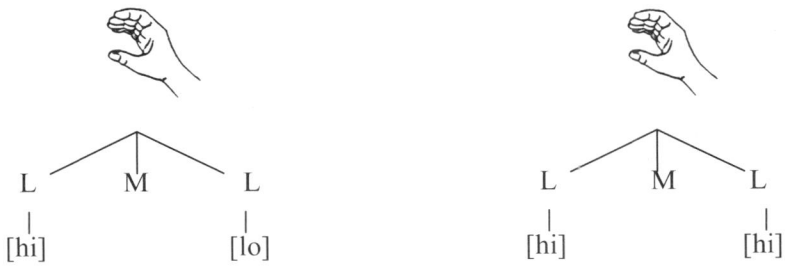

Figure 17.4.
Schematic representation showing features distinguishing CHRISTIAN and COMMITTEE in the final segment of each word.

locus like I-SHOW-YOU, but end at a different locus, the one established for the relevant third person referent. In order to make such distinctions, signers must attend to sequential structure. This sequentiality is reflected in Figure 17.6.

The signs in 17.5 each involve three morphemes: the verb itself and two agreement markers. Examples such as these demonstrate that there is some sequential structure in sign language phonology. Still, the basic form of these signs is the same as that of the monomorphemic sign JUST-THEN, shown in 17.1 and 17.2 above, despite their morphological complexity. All have the canonical structure, LML. In the next section, this structure is shown to be monosyllabic.

The Syllable in Sign Language

Much of the following material summarizes a more detailed treatment in Sandler and Lillo-Martin (2006). In order to demonstrate convincingly that it is useful to adopt the term "syllable" in the description of visually perceived languages, we must show that the unit labeled bears significant similarity to the syllables of spoken languages. This section will demonstrate that syllables of sign language are the anchor to which lower meaningless elements are bound, that they are required to explain morpho-phonological processes, and that they are prosodic in nature. In all these ways, they are like spoken language syllables. I will also

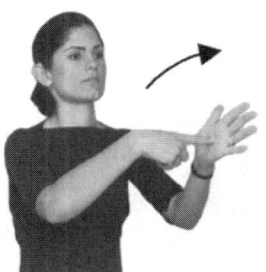

a. I-SHOW-YOU   b.YOU-SHOW-ME

Figure 17.5.
Verb agreement

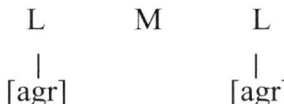

Figure 17.6.
Agreement is marked on the first and last locations.

describe the differences that also exist between syllables in the two modalities.

The sign language syllable is defined as a single movement, be it path movement of the hand(s) from one location to another, internal movement (such as opening or closing of the hand), or both simultaneously (Brentari, 1998). An example of a sign with path movement only is ISL JUST-THEN, pictured in Figure 17.1.

To argue that sign languages have syllables, it is first necessary to distinguish the syllable from other kinds of structure, such as the morpheme or word. The two sign languages, ASL and ISL, each have many words that are both monomorphemic and monosyllabic, like JUST-THEN shown in Figure 17.1. Monomorphemic but disyllabic words like ISL REVENGE, shown in Figure 17.7 can also be found.

In the verb agreement example in Figure 17.6, a word may consist of several morphemes but still be monosyllabic. And finally, bimorphemic words, like many compounds or words with sequential affixes like ISL SEE-SHARP

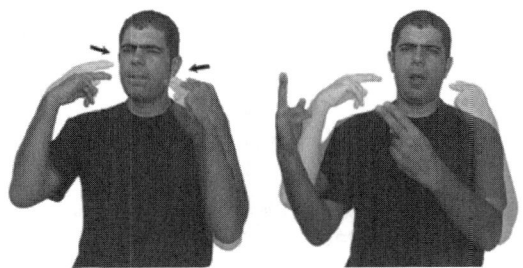

Figure 17.7.
Monomorphemic disyllabic sign: ISL REVENGE

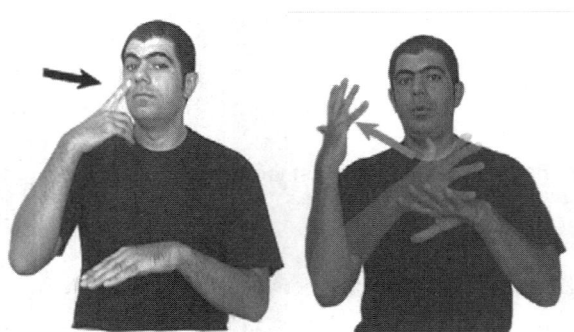

Figure 17.8.
Bimorphemic disyllabic sign: ISL SEE-SHARP ("to discern by seeing").

("discern by seeing") shown in Figure 17.8, may also be disyllabic.

    The different relationships between syllables and meaningful units that are found in sign languages are summarized in Table 17.1. By far the most common kinds of words across sign languages are the first and third shown in bold in Table 17.1, i.e., words that are monosyllabic regardless of morphological structure. Forms that are considered to have more than one syllable for the purposes of Table 17.1 are only those that have two different syllables; reduplicated forms are not included. The relation between syllable and word

Table 17.1.
The word, the morpheme, and the syllable are distinguished by their co-occurrence patterns. All the possibilities shown are attested, but those in bold are most common.

ω | μ | σ	ω | μ /\\ σ σ	ω | /\\ μ μ \\/ σ	ω /\\ μ μ | | σ σ
monomorphemic monosyllabic	monomorphemic disyllabic	**bimorphemic monosyllabic**	bimorphemic disyllabic

reveals a clear modality effect in most spoken languages, especially those with morphological complexity.

In sign language, despite the non-isomorphism between word and syllable, there is an overwhelming tendency for words to be monosyllabic (Coulter, 1982). I refer to this as the monosyllable conspiracy (Sandler, 1999a).

We can see this conspiracy at work where morphologically complex words that either diachronically or underlyingly have more than one syllable reduce to the canonical monosyllable. Lexicalized compounds in sign languages provide an example. In all languages, compounds may become lexicalized where the juxtaposition of the two words is entered as a single word in the lexicon. One indication that a compound has become lexicalized is a meaning that cannot be predicted from the words from which it was originally formed. For example, a *blackboard* does not necessarily have to be black. Another is phonological change, such as fusion. The Hebrew word for soccer is the lexicalized compound *kaduregel* from words meaning "ball" (*kadur*) and "foot" (*regel)*. In the compound, we do not get a geminate (lengthened) [r] sound from the adjacent [r]s in the two words (**kadurregel*); instead, one [r] is deleted.

Returning to the monosyllable conspiracy in sign language, we see an example in one of the lexicalized ASL compounds for the concept FAINT, formed from MIND+DROP, pictured in Figure 17.9. An example of a sign with handshape change and path movement together is DROP, shown in Figure 17.9. MIND and DROP each consists of one syllable in isolation, but in the compound FAINT, the form is not disyllabic as simple concatenation of the two words would predict. Instead, it reduces to a single syllable, represented in 17.10. The autosegmental relation between the hand configurations and the locations under compound reduction, shown in Figures 17.9 and 17.10 is one of the phenomena that motivated the Hand Tier Model (Sandler, 1987, 1989).

Many lexicalized compounds in ASL and ISL reduce to one syllable, and some affixed forms do as well (Sandler, 1999a). We witness a conspiracy toward monosyllabicity in this phenomenon when it is taken together with the overwhelming preponderance of monosyllabic simple words in sign language

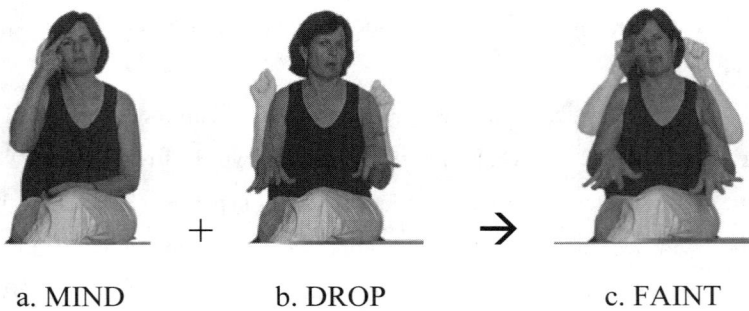

a. MIND   b. DROP   c. FAINT

Figure 17.9.
Hand configuration assimilation in an ASL compound.

lexicons, as well as the tendency for productive morphological processes such as verb agreement to produce monosyllabic words as well. Sign languages seem to prefer monosyllabic words. But in order to justify the existence of the syllable as a phonological and prosodic unit, additional evidence is needed.

Evidence for the Syllable

The first piece of evidence for the syllable as a prosodic unit, then, is the mere fact that signs with one movement (or two simultaneously) are the optimal form in sign languages. As the syllable is not isomorphic with the word (see Table 17.1), the fact that this particular prosodic structure predominates gives us a reason to refer to it in describing the structure of the sign. Several other pieces of evidence for the syllable in American Sign Language have been proposed. Brentari and Poizner (1994) provide evidence that the syllable is a unit of

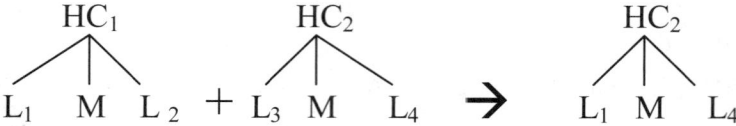

Figure 17.10.
Two syllables reduce to one, producing the canonical, monosyllabic form of a sign (Sandler, 1989, 1999a).

phonological organization by showing that timing of handshape change is different within a syllable than during transitional movements between syllables. The handshape change in a sign like DROP shown in Figure 17.9 is coordinated with, and evenly distributed over, the beginning and ending of the syllable, demarcated by the two locations. However, the handshape change that obligatorily occurs phonetically during the transitional movement between signs is not so coordinated with the last location of one sign and the first location of the next, neither in timing nor in relative distribution of finger movement.

Another reason to believe in syllables is stress assignment in disyllabic signs. Most newly formed compounds and some lexicalized compounds retain the two syllables that are underlyingly present in the two member signs. In such ASL compounds, the second syllable is stressed (Klima & Bellugi, 1979). In contrast, ASL nouns derived through reduplication have stress on the first syllable (Supalla & Newport, 1978).

It is not only stress assignment rules that make reference to the syllable. When ASL verbs are reduplicated under aspectual inflection, the reduplication rule copies only the final syllable (Sandler, 1989). Specifically, if a compound is monosyllabic like FAINT, the whole compound will reduplicate under a temporal aspect inflection such as Habitual (to derive "faint habitually"). But if the compounds have not reduced to a monosyllable and remain disyllabic, like the ASL compound BLOW-TOP (literally, HEAD+EXPLODE-OFF, meaning "explode with anger," only the final syllable undergoes reduplication in the Habitual form. It is clear that these phenomena, (see Table 17.2) are singling out

Table 17.2.
Evidence for the syllable in American Sign Language

1. The optimal form of the sign is a monosyllable (Coulter 1982, Sandler, 1989, 1999a)
2. Handshape change is organized by the syllable unit (Brentari and Poizner, 1994)
3. The final syllable of compounds receives stress (Klima and Bellugi, 1979)
4. The first syllable of reduplicated nominals receives stress (Supalla and Newport, 1978)
5. The final syllable of verbs is reduplicated for temporal aspect inflection (Sandler, 1989)

a prosodic unit, the syllable, not a morphological or lexical unit. It is specifically the rhythmic aspect of the syllable unit at work in each of these constraints and processes, and rhythmicity is prosodic by definition.

Similarities between Spoken and Signed Syllables

Three central characteristics of sign language syllables make them comparable to syllables in spoken language. First, syllables organize lower units of phonological structure. In spoken language, syllables are organized around the nucleus, typically a vowel, and the surrounding consonants usually rise in sonority before the nucleus and fall in sonority after it. Different languages have different constraints on the number of consonants that can occur in the onset and the coda, and on the relative distance in degree of sonority that must exist between adjacent consonants. English clusters that begin with a stop can maximally be followed by one other consonant, which must be a liquid or glide (e. g., *proud, plus,* and *puce,* not **pnack* or **pfack*). In addition, phonological rules may refer to syllables or syllable positions. For example, one of the environments for stop aspiration in English is the onset of stressed syllables.

Now we return to sign language. As we have seen, the timing of handshape change is controlled by the syllable. Although the shape of the hand usually changes in the transitional movement between signs, that change, which is not within a syllable, is uneven in shape and in timing, which leads to the conclusion that the syllable organizes the timing of the units it contains. Using a different model of sign phonology from the on assumed here, Brentari (1998) argues further that all phonological elements that are dynamic have the syllable as their domain.

Second, in neither modality is the syllable unit isomorphic with morphosyntactic structure. It is not the word or the morpheme that is reduplicated in verbal aspect inflection, but the syllable. Similarly, it is the syllable and not the morpheme that receives stress in nominals derived through reduplication.

Finally, syllables in both language modalities are prosodic units. We can see this by their participation in rules and processes that are themselves prosodic in nature, such as reduplication (McCarthy & Prince, 1986) and stress assignment. In fact, it is the prosodic property of "one-movementness" that defines the optimal phonological word in sign language (Sandler, 1999a), and not properties of any nonprosodic unit such as morphemes or lexemes. These observations identify a universal of human language, regardless of modality: a prosodic level of structure that is relevant for linguistic organization and rules, but that cannot be subsumed as part of the morphosyntactic system. Prosodic constituents at higher levels have also been shown to exist in sign languages: the phonological word, the phonological phrase, and the intonational phrase in ISL.

Differences

Considering the fundamental lack of similarity in modality of transmission, it is quite striking that the phonological organization of spoken and signed languages should share a prosodic unit at the sublexical level of structure—the syllable. But there are differences as well. Differences in the physical properties of the manual-visual system have reflexes in the organization of the syllable and its role in the phonology.

Because of its many degrees of freedom in the articulation of signs, the primary articulator of sign language, the hand, is sometimes compared with the tongue in spoken language. Many signs involve both hands, but I do not deal with this articulatory option here because it does not bear on the present discussion But unlike the tongue and other articulators of spoken language, the hand is not framed by the inherent rhythmic properties of another articulator that might be compared with the jaw. So, where the spoken syllable is framed by the oscillation of the mandible (MacNeilage, 1998), no parallel to jaw oscillation can be found in sign language (Meier, 2002). In addition, the hand surpasses even the tongue in its articulatory range (Sandler, 1989). First, different combinations of fingers can be selected, for example:

Second, most of these groups can be configured in one of four different positions. Demonstrated here only with the all-five fingers group, positions are respectively open, closed. bent or curved:

Third, the hand can be positioned in any of several different orientations; two examples are:

Finally, the hand can touch or approximate any of a large number of places of articulation on the body. I consider only places of articulation in relation to the body that can be considered system internal and ignore those places of articulation in space. Whether these spatial places are truly linguistic entities is a matter of current controversy (see Sandler and Lillo-Martin, 2006, for discussion). The ASL signs SICK and TOUCH in Figure 17.11 illustrate just two such places. The Hand Tier model (Sandler, 1989; Sandler & Lillo-Martin, 2006) proposes four major body areas—the head (e.g., Figures 17.8—left side, (17.10—left side), the trunk (e.g., Figure 17.3)—the nondominant hand (e.g., Figures 17.1, (17.10—right side) and the nondominant arm—and nine more

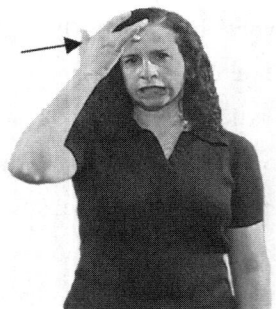

a. SICK   **b. TOUCH**

Figure 17.11.
Two different places of articulation (ASL)

specific "settings" (such as [hi]—[contralateral], etc.) at each of those major areas. Figures 17.9 above and 17.11 below illustrate two out of the nine possible different settings on the head, ipsilateral in the sign DROP illustrated in Figure 17.9, and central in the sign SICK, illustrated in Figure 17.11.

So even a global comparison between the hand and the tongue is very rough indeed, as the hand has many more degrees of freedom, and it is not grounded within a constricting and oscillating articulator like the jaw.

The phonetics and phonology of the sign language syllable are different from those of its oral counterpart in other ways as well. Unlike spoken syllables in many languages, sign language syllables cannot have clusters of two different locations which might be compared to consonant clusters. Due to the nature of the system, there must be a movement between any two different locations. Similarly, any path movement must by definition traverse the space between two locations, so that it would also be difficult to argue for movement clusters (diphthong-like entities) within a single syllable. Another characteristic of the spoken syllable absent in the sign syllable is an asymmetry between the onset and the rhyme, both in terms of constraints on the constituents (the rhyme is more limited in type and number of segments) and in terms of the role each plays in the phonology (stress assignment cares about the weight of rhymes but not of onsets). Unlike spoken syllables, the syllables of sign language exhibit no onset-rhyme asymmetries; the first and last L do not differ from one another in their articulatory properties or in the role each plays in the system.

In spoken languages, syllables are relevant for the distribution of intonational tunes. Typically, the tunes are aligned with stressed syllables, either within a focused constituent or at a prosodic constituent boundary. While it has been demonstrated that sign languages have intonational systems, conveyed by facial expression, the unit with which intonational tunes are aligned is a larger prosodic constituent, such as the whole phonological or intonational phrase, and not a single syllable within it, stressed or otherwise (Nespor & Sandler, 1999; Sandler, 1999b). Such "tunes" in sign language have been given the label, *superarticulatory arrays* (Sandler, 1999b).

The role of sonority or acoustic resonance in determining the internal organization of the syllable is another important characteristic of the spoken syllable that has no clear analogy in sign language. Spoken syllable onsets rise in relative sonority toward the peak, the syllable nucleus (typically the vowel), and their codas fall in sonority from there, yielding syllables like *plans*, and not like **lpasn*. While several researchers have proposed that sign languages have sonority in the form of relative visual salience (e.g., Brentari, 1990, 1998; Perlmutter, 1992; Sandler, 1993), and even that this relative salience has an effect on the internal structure of the syllable, it is unlikely that useful comparisons can be made regarding a relationship between sonority and syllable organization in the two language systems (see Sandler & Lillo-Martin 2006 for an explanation). The difficulty in finding a parallel stems from a fundamental difference in the architecture of the two transmission systems. In spoken language, the source of energy is the lungs. Relative sonority of the acoustic signal is determined by properties of the vocal tract filter. Sign language has no such distinction between signal source and filter: the signal is perceived directly.

Adding these differences to the other differences in sequential structure outlined above, such as the impossibility of complex onsets, nuclei, or codas, leads to the conclusion that there is no direct analogue to syllable nuclei and margins (vowels and consonants), and that relative sonority is not likely to play a role in sign language syllable organization that is analogous to its role in spoken language. This position, which contrasts in some ways with my own earlier work (Sandler, 1989, 1993), is expanded in Sandler and Lillo-Martin (2006).

Constructing a Lexicon: Less Feature Variegation within the Sign Syllable, but More Phonetic Features in the System

Previously, evidence was presented for sequential structure in sign. However, the segmental structure of sign language is different from spoken language in the following way: most of the features in a monosyllabic sign always characterize all of its segments. It is this broadness in scope of most features that gives the sign its simultaneous feel. The sign JUST-THEN, pictured in Figure 17.1 and represented schematically in Figure 17.2 illustrates this characteristic.

In the three segments of *fit* [fIt], there is a good deal of variegation in the features and feature values from segment to segment. In addition, few of the features and feature values of any one segment are predictable from the features in the other segments. For example, the rhyme, [It], could easily occur with a different onset, such as [+voiced, +sonorant, +nasal], as in *knit* [nIt]. Or, the onset and nucleus of *fit* could occur with a different coda, such as a voiced lateral sonorant, to produce *fill* [fIl]. The vowel could easily have different features as well, e.g., [+low, -back], to produce *fat* [fæt]. That is, for any feature and feature value in one segment, the features and their values in the other segments are largely unpredictable. And none of the features and values are the same throughout the three segments. While a feature like [voice] or [high] may have the same value throughout a syllable (as in *deal* or *king*, resp.) typically most of the other features will be different. The overall impression is of a sequence of three different segments.

In contrast, in the typical sign, JUST-THEN, almost all the features and their values are the same in the three segments. In all three segments, the index finger is selected and closed (touching the thumb). The palm is oriented downward. The place of articulation is the nondominant hand (h2). Only the features [proximal] in the first segment and [contact] in the last segment differ. While in the English word fit, there are no features that characterize more than two adjacent segments, in the ISL sign JUST-THEN, almost all feature specifications characterize all three segments. This is not an accident associated with this particular sign. Typically there is variation in only one feature in the segments within a sign language syllable. Because so much is the same throughout the sign language syllable, the overall impression is one of simultaneity rather than sequentiality. Some researchers have argued that constraints on production, perception, and short-term memory conspire to create simultaneity of linguistic structure in sign language (e.g., Bellugi & Fischer, S., 1972; Emmorey, 2002).

Signs typically have only one syllable and share most of the same features within that syllable. In principle, this characteristic might limit the potential a sign language has for creating a large number of phonologically distinct and developing a large enough lexicon for adequate communication. Another modality difference may resolve this potential limitation; the number of phonological features available to each system. Comparing phonological models that propose a universal set of features for each modality, sign languages have many more phonological features than spoken languages. Halle (1992) proposes that spoken languages use 18 phonological features to make all the distinctions of their phonological inventories, while Sandler and Lillo-Martin (2006) propose that sign languages require 30, a set almost twice as large as spoken language. Other models of sign language phonology propose larger numbers of features. Other sign language phonologists have motivated different feature inventories, but none of them smaller than 30. Brentari's (1998) carefully detailed model based on American Sign Language proposes 46 features, and van der Kooij's (2002) model of Sign Language of the Netherlands, which strives to minimize redundancy, proposes 39.

An interpretation of these facts is inspired by work by Nettle (1995) comparing ten languages on the basis of two variables, the size of the segment inventory and the length of the word. He found a significant correlation between the two: the smaller the segment inventory, the greater the mean word length. The languages at the two extremes were Nahuatl and !Xu. Nahuatl has an inventory of 23 distinct segments and a mean word length of 8.69 segments, while !Xu has 119 segments and a mean word length of 4.02. Presumably, all 147 segments in !Xu can be distinguished using Halle's 18 distinctive features.

The explanation is simple, and lends itself neatly to the issue at hand. The correlation found by Nettle is compensatory. All natural languages are faced with the same cognitive requirement to furnish a very large lexicon. This can be achieved either by providing a large enough pool of distinctive segments to choose from, or by providing long enough words to enable different combinations of segments in a string. We may extend this line of reasoning to the somewhat different but comparable issue of syllable internal variegation and feature inventory in signed and spoken languages. Spoken languages have a relatively small number of features but many options for variegation, in this case, for different feature combinations across a syllable (even a syllable with a small number of segments, like *fit*). Sign languages, on the other hand, have a large number of features but very limited variegation across a syllable. According to this reasoning, the limited variegation within a sign syllable is compensated for by the large number of features available for constructing syllables.

The Relation Between the Physical System and Phonology

Many qualitative and quantitative differences in the nature and organization of the syllable in the two natural language modalities have been demonstrated. Differences are attributed to the nature of the physical system of transmission. In spoken language, the syllable frame is provided by jaw oscillation, and content is provided by different configurations of the tongue and lips within the confines of the frame. In sign language, there is no frame to constrain the range or rhythm of the syllable, and the hand articulator has many more degrees of freedom for configuration, movement, and articulation. This added freedom results in a larger number of phonological features in sign than spoken language phonology, a capacity counterbalanced by a limited amount of variegation within a syllable.

These differences between sign and the spoken language syllables provides support for MacNeilage and Davis's research program seeking to derive phonological properties from the physical system of transmission (MacNeilage & Davis, 2000). The differences also suggest that such a program will ultimately be more explanatory than one that assumes that a great deal of phonology is arbitrarily furnished by Universal Grammar. In light of the sign language system, it seems non-explanatory to take for granted that a feature like [coronal] or a constraint like NO CODA is universally generated for all human language. How then to explain a feature like [head] or a constraint like ONE

FINGER GROUP in sign language? This is an allusion to Mandel's (1981) Selected Finger Constraint, which states that only one group of fingers may be selected in a morpheme. The effect of this constraint is also evident within the syllable. Are we endowed with two UG's? This is not likely.

But the similarities between the syllables of signed and spoken languages are significant as well. First, in each modality the syllable organizes lower phonological elements. Second, the syllable is distinguishable from the morpheme and the word, and nonisomorphic with those structures in both modalities. And third, the syllable is in essence a prosodic unit, a unit that is part of the rhythmic system and not part of the lexical system. It is perhaps especially interesting that there is a strong rhythmic effect in sign language in the form of the monosyllable "conspiracy" despite the fact that there is no oscillating mandible to provide a rhythmic frame.

There are many other phonological similarities in the two systems beyond those found in the syllable (Sandler & Lillo-Martin, 2006). For example, both systems have sequential structure (Liddell, 1984; Sandler, 1986), autosegmental structure (Sandler, 1986, 1989), hierarchical organization of phonological features (Corina and Sagey, 1989; Sandler, 1987, 1993a), discrete assimilation rules (Sandler, 1993b), a distinction between lexical (structure-preserving) and postlexical (non-structure-preserving) phonological processes (Padden & Perlmutter, 1987; Sandler, 1993b, 1999a), and a hierarchy of prosodic constituents (Nespor & Sandler, 1999; Wilbur, 1999x). These similarities show that essentially the same cognitive system underlies language in both modalities, and it is necessary for a comprehensive theory of language to account for these similarities as well as differences. These and other similarities also mean that some properties of phonology are **not** directly derivable from the physical system; we must look to higher levels of organization to account for them, as I have argued elsewhere (Sandler, 2006). A theory of the evolution of language must also take this array of discoveries into account.

Bimodal Language and its Origin

The existence of natural language in the manual/visual modality shows that speech does not equal language. Sign language shares key properties with spoken language, including the existence of a phonological level of organization. This phonology is forged from the physical transmission system in tandem with higher level organizing mechanisms. The discovery that humans can "do" language in two different modalities may lead to a variety of conceptions of the nature of the human language capacity. One might assume, for example, that oral and manual language are just different instantiations of the same thing, and that the difference is essentially trivial. However, we have seen that this is not the case. Instead, phonological differences are far-reaching and require theoretical motivation and explanation. An opposing conclusion is that the two modalities are actually so different that they instantiate language in ways that are mutually exclusive. That is, humans have the capacity for two distinct language systems. But this view is also inadequate, as it overlooks two essential properties of these language systems. First, the similarities are also far from trivial. Second, the modalities are not mutually exclusive. Instead, both manual and oral channels are exploited by deaf and hearing alike, in the service of language, an observation that I will expand below. These properties lead to a third theory. The third theory, which can only be painted in broad strokes here, holds that language is essentially bimodal. We evolved to use **both** the hands and the mouth as the vessels of language. Each modality brings a different aspect of a **unified** capacity present in all human linguistic communication (Sandler, 2003).

In his contribution to this volume, Peter MacNeilage proposes that "A theory of the evolution of speech must *begin* with a conception of what it is like now, even though it cannot end there." Extending the notion of "speech" to consider "language transmission" more generally, we see much evidence for bimodalism. First, is the fact that humans are capable of both spoken and sign language. The second piece of evidence comes from manual gestures that universally accompany and supplement speech, the importance of which has attracted a good deal of attention in recent years (McNeill, 1992, 2002). Hearing children gesture with their hands before they speak. As they begin to acquire spoken words, they first use either a spoken word or a gesture but not together (Goldin-Meadow, 2003). This complementary distribution of speech and gesture in small children suggests that the two perform the same function for them. Only after they begin to develop an explicitly linguistic system does gesture become an auxiliary communicative mode. When it does, this supplementary mode becomes important: hearing people across all cultures augment their spoken language with iconic (and other) manual gestures (McNeill, 1992). A rapidly growing body of research shows that these gestures often add information relevant to the verbal signal, but not present in it. They are part of the message.

Furthermore, bimodalism is bimodal: Deaf people also augment their language with gesture. For them, the primary linguistic signal is made mainly by the hands, and the gestures are made with the mouth. Just as speakers use hand gestures to describe visual properties of referents, signers express visual, tactile, and even auditory impressions with mouth gestures that co-occur with the signed linguistic description (Sandler, 2003). In fact, the mouth is very active during signing, performing a variety of linguistic (non-gestural) functions as well (Boyes-Braem & Sutton-Spence, 2001).

Added to this view of the way things are now is research that hints at an evolutionary precursor to bimodal language, specifically, research on mirror neurons in monkeys (see Fogassi, this volume). Mirror neurons are located in a brain region proposed to be homologous with Broca's area in humans. These neurons discharge when the monkey performs certain actions, and also when the monkey observes the experimenter performing the same action. Rizzolatti, Fogassi, and colleagues (Gallese, Fadiga, Fogassi, & Rizzolatti, 1996) hypothesize that this phenomenon underlies imitation as a learning mechanism used by humans in the translation of perceived phonetic gestures into motor commands in speech. Particularly intriguing in this regard is the discovery that some mirror neurons discharge when either the hand or the mouth moves, but only when the movements have the same goal, i.e., in response to the same "behavioral meaning" (Gentilucci and Rizzolatti, 1990) Extrapolation tempts the following speculation: there is a neural substrate in primates that links meaning and its physical expression, regardless of whether that expression is oral or manual.

It may well be that the form of the earliest human language was fully bimodal, recruiting both oral and manual expression equally. Oral transmission emerged as primary for hearing individuals at some point in our evolutionary history, but manual expression survives as an option for both the deaf and the hearing, and robust vestiges of a bimodal system remain in both primarily oral and primarily manual modalities, e.g., in the form of co-language gesture.

Conclusion

Comparing the syllable unit of sign language to spoken language reveals differences and similarities in phonological organization across the two modalities. The differences demonstrate clearly that part of phonological organization is linked directly to the physical mode of transmission. This argues for an approach that attempts to derive some of phonology from physical properties of the system and against an approach stipulating a universal pool of formational elements that are generated arbitrarily. The similarities in syllables (and in other aspects of phonology described elsewhere) suggest that some characteristics of phonological organization arise from higher levels of patterning common to both modalities—in the case of syllables, the systemic distinction and interaction between the individual articulatory events involved in producing a meaningful element and its more global prosodic traits. Both kinds of organization result in predictable properties in the phonology of language in each modality. It is an extraordinary fact about humans that we have a natural command of two kinds of phonology, each grounded in a dramatically different physical modality, the oral/aural modality and the manual/visual modality.

In the spirit of the research program to which this volume is dedicated, we must use our conception of the present in order to probe the past. To do this, we focus on four observations that fall out from the discussion presented here.

(1) Phonological similarities between modalities are fully universal across all languages; (2) phonological differences between modalities are fully general across languages in each modality; (3) humans have a natural ability to use both modalities; and (4) language in each physical modality is supplemented by meaningful co-linguistic gesture transmitted in the other. Add to this the intriguing possibility that mirror neurons in other primates that respond equally to hand and mouth actions are precursors to some aspects of language. Taken together, these observations suggest that speech and sign are part of a single bimodal language system well grounded in earlier stages of evolution.

Acknowledgments

I am grateful to Peter MacNeilage for useful discussion and comments on this paper.

References

Bellugi, U. and Fischer, S. (1972). A comparison of signed and spoken language. *Cognition, 1,* 173–200.

Brentari, D., & Poizner, H. (1994). A phonological analysis of a Deaf Parkinsonian signer. *Language and Cognitive Processes, 9(1).* 69–99.

Boyes-Braem, P., and Sutton-Spence, R.l (Eds.). (2001). *The Hands are the Head of the Mouth: The Mouth as Articulator in Sign Languages. International Studies on Sign Language and Communication of the Deaf, 39,* Hamburg: Signum Verlag.

Corina, D. and Sagey, E. (1989). Are phonological hierarchies universal? Evidence from American Sign Language. *Proceedings from Escol, 6,* Columbus, Ohio: Ohio University Press, 73–83.

Coulter, G. (1982). On the nature of ASL as a monosyllabic language. Paper presented at the annual meeting of the Linguistic Society of America. San Diego, CA.

Current Issues in ASL Phonology, Phonetics and Phonology, (2004). Volume 3. 103–129. New York: Academic Press.

Emmorey, K. (2002). Language, *Cognition, and the Brain: Insights from Sign Language Research.* Mahwah, NJ: Lawrence Erlbaum Associates.

Fogassi, Leonardo and Ferrari, Pier Francesco. (2008). Mirror neurons and the evolution of communication and language. In Davis, B. L. & Zajdo, K. (Eds.) *The Syllable in Speech Production,* London: Taylor & Francis.

Gallese V., Fadiga L., Fogassi, L., Rizzolatti G. (1996). Action recognition in the premotor cortex. *Brain, 119 (2):*593–609.

Gentilucci, M. and Rizzolatti G. (1990). Cortical motor control of arm and hand movements. In Goodale, MA (ed.), *Vision and Action: The Control of Grasping.* Norwood NJ: Ablex. 147–62.

Goldin-Meadow, S. (2003). *Hearing Gesture: How our Hands Help us Think.* Cambridge, MA: Belknap Press of Harvard University Press.

Goldsmith, J. (1976). *Autosegmental Phonology.* Doctoral Dissertation. MIT, Cambridge, Mass. [Published 1979. New York: Garland Press]

Halle, M. (1992). Phonological features. *International Encyclopedia of Linguistics, vol 3.* W. Bright (Ed.), Oxford: Oxford University Press. 207–212.

Hockett, C. F. (1960). The origin of speech. *Scientific American*, 203, 88–111.

Klima, E. & Bellugi, U. (1979). *The Signs of Language.* Cambridge, MA: Harvard University Press.

Liddel, S. (1984). THINK and BELIEVE: Sequentiality in American Sign Language. *Language, 60*, 372–392.

Liddell, S. and Johnson, R. (1989). American Sign Language: The phonological base. *Sign Language Studies, 64*, 197–277.

MacNeilage, P. F. & Davis, B. L. (2000). On the origin of internal structure of words. *Science, 288.* 527–531.

MacNeilage, P.F. and Davis, B. L. (2001). Motor mechanisms in speech ontogeny: phylogenetic, neurobiological and linguistic implications. *Current Opinion in Neurobiology, 11,* 696–700.

MacNeilage, P. F. (1998). The frame/content theory of evolution of speech production. *Behavioral and Brain Sciences, 21.* 499–546.

MacNeilage, P. F. (2008). The frame/content theory. In Davis, B. L. & Zajdo, K. (Eds.) *The Syllable in Speech Production*, London: Taylor & Francis.

Mandel, M. (1981). *Phonotactics and Morphophonology in American Sign Language,* Unpublished Doctoral Dissertation, University of California, Berkeley.

McCarthy, J. (1981). A prosodic theory of nonconcatenative morphlogy, *Linguistic Inquiry, 12*, 373–418.

McCarthy, J. and Prince, A. (1986). *Prosodic Morphology.* Unpublished Ms. University of Massachusetts, Amherst, and Rutgers University, New Brunswick, NJ.

McNeill, D. (1992). *Hand and Mind: What Gesture Reveals about Thought.* Chicago: University of Chicago Press.

McNeill, D. (2004). *Language and Gesture.* Cambridge, UK: Cambridge University Press.

Meier, R. (1991). Language acquisition by deaf children. *American Scientist, Vol. 79.* 60–70.

Meier, R. (2002). Why different, why the same? Explaining effects and non-effects of modality upon linguistic structure in sign and speech. In Meier, R. P. Cormier, K., & Quinto-Pozos, D. (Eds.), *Modality and Structure in*

Signed and Spoken Languages, Cambridge: Cambridge University Press 199–223.

Nespor, M. & Sandler, W. 1999. Prosody in Israeli Sign Language. *Language and Speech, 42,* 143–176.

Nettle, D. (1995). Segmental inventory size, word length, and communicative efficiency. *Linguistics, 33.* 359–367.

Newport, E. & Meier, R. (1985). The acquisition of American Sign Language. In D. Slobin (Ed.), *The Cross-Linguistic Study of Language Acquisition, Vol. 1.* 881–938. Hillsdale, NJ: Lawrence Erlbaum Associates.

Padden, C. and Perlmutter, D. (1987). American Sign Language and the architecture of phonological theory. *Natural Langaueg and Linguistic Theory, 5,* 335–375.

Padden, C. (1988). *Interaction of Morphology and Syntax in American Sign Language.* New York: Garland Publishers. [1983: Doctoral dissertation, University of California, San Diego]

Sandler, W. & Lillo-Martin, D. (2002). Natural sign languages. In Aronoff, M. & Rees-Miller, J. (Eds.), *The Handbook of Linguistics.* Oxford: Blackwell. 533–562.

Sandler, W. & Lillo-Martin, D. (2006). *Sign Language and Linguistic Universals,* Cambridge, UK: Cambridge University Press.

Sandler, W. Meir, I., Padden, C., and Aronoff, M. (2005). The emergence of grammar in a new sign language. *Proceedings of the National Academy of Sciences, 102 (7),* 2661–2665.

Sandler, W. (1986). The Spreading Hand Autosegment of American Sign Language, *Sign Language Studies, 50,* 1–28.

Sandler, W. (1987). Assimilation and Feature Hierarchy in ASL, A. Bosch, B. Need, and E. Schiller, (Eds.)., *Chicago Linguistics Society Parasession on Autosegmental Phonology,* 266–278.

Sandler, W. (1989). Phonological Representation of the Sign. Dordrecht: Foris.

Sandler, W. (1993a). Sign language and modularity. *Lingua, 89(4),* 315–351.

Sandler, W. (1993b). Linearization of Phonological Tiers in ASL, in G. Coulter, (Ed.), *Current Issues in ASL Phonology, Phonetics and Phonology Volume 3,* San Diego: Academic Press. 103-129.

Sandler, W. (1999a). Cliticization and Prosodic Words in a Sign Language, in T. Hall and U. Kleinhenz, (Eds.), *Studies on the Phonological Word.* Amsterdam: Benjamins. (*Current Studies in Linguistic Theory*). 223–255.

Sandler, W. (1999b). The Medium and the Message: Prosodic Interpretation of Linguistic Content in Sign Language. *Sign Language and Linguistics, 2(2),* 187–216.

Sandler, W. (2003). On the Complementarity of Signed and Spoken Languages. In Y. Levy and J. Schaeffer (Eds.), *Language Across Populations: Towards a Definition of SLI.* Mahwah, N.J.: Lawrence Erlbaum, 383–409.

Sandler, W. (2004). Phonology, phonetics and the nondominant hand. In L. Goldstein, D. Whalen, and C. Best (es.) *LabPhon 8.* Berlin, New York: De Gruyter.

Senghas, A., Kita, S., & Ozyurek, A. (2004). Children creating core properties of language: Evidence from an emerging sign language in Nicaragua. *Science, Vol 305.* 1779–1782.

Stokoe, W. (1978). [1960]. *Sign Language Structure.* Silver Spring, MD: Linstok Press.

Supalla, T. and Newport, E. (1978) How many seats in a chair? The derivation of nouns and verbs in American Sign Language in P. Siple, (Ed.). 91–133.

Sutton–Spence, R. & Woll, B. (1999). *The linguistics of British Sign Language: An introduction.* Cambridge, England: Cambridge University Press.

van der Kooij, E. (2002). *Phonological Categories in Sign Language of the Netherlands.* Unpublished Doctoral Dissertation. University of Leiden. Utrecht: Holland Institute of Lingustics.

Wilbur, R.B. (1999). Stress in ASL: Empirical evidence and linguistic issues. *Language and Speech, 42,* 229–251.

Woll, B., Sutton-Spence, R., & Elton, F. (2001). Multilingualism: The global approach to sign language. In Lucas, C. (Ed.) *The Sociolinguistics of Sign Languages.* Cambridge, England: Cambridge University Press. 8–32.

18

When the Babble Syllable Feeds the Foot in a Point

Christian Abry

Virginie Ducey

Anne Vilain

and

Claire Lalevée

Institut de la Communication Parlée

Université Stendhal

Institut National Polytechnique de Grenoble

Grenoble, France

Peter MacNeilage and Barbara Davis have promoted a longstanding companion program for grounding developmentally—then phylogenetically—speech motor control within the Frame/Content Theory (FCT, MacNeilage, 1998). Like many other researchers who discussed and supported FCT with data from their own field and ambient language, we are deeply indebted to this impetus for French baby studies and potential for links with primatology (Abry & Schwartz, J. L., 2004, Abry et al., 2004).

The first gift we offered some years ago to Peter, was a comment to the *Behavioral and Brain Sciences* FCT debate (Abry et al., 1998), drawing his attention to data published quite simultaneously by a few aphasiologists. They listed productions of "brothers" of Broca's first patient "Tan", named for his remnant utterance "tan, tan." We coined it later, as a tribute, frame aphasia, in a more detailed account (Abry et al., 2002). Frame aphasia reappeared recently under the broader heading of phoneme encoding and monitoring, especially with a mental syllabary concern, in a neuropsychological "Syllables in the brain" issue (Code, 2005a). To avoid any future ambiguity concerning this "frame" of frame aphasia, it must be clear that it denotes (like jargon aphasia means the production of jargon) the generation of frames produced by neural "degeneration," together with the degeneration of segmental content. Hence content aphasia will mean conventionally the (rare) impairment of the frame, saving the production of content (see the dissociation table in Code, 2005a, pg. 132).

Since these frame aphasics suffered from "la grande aphasie de Broca" (Global Aphasia), their so-called Non Meaningful Recurring Utterances or Non Lexical Speech Automatisms ("Titi," "dodo," "tsetsetse…, etc.) were not supported by the counterproposal made in the BBS debate by some opponents, who argued against the medial Supplementary Motor Area as a locus of frame control, proposing that the Left Inferior Frontal Gyrus region could work for both frame and content. MacNeilage termed our support an "insuperable problem" undermining their lumped lateral locus view.

Finally a dissociation of frame aphasia from content aphasia was rendered possible by contrasting "Tantan's brothers" versus a left posterior SMA hemorrhage case tested by Ziegler et al. (1997; both ultimately tabulated in Code, 2005a, pg. 132). Our nascent/remnant (roughly: baba=tantan) proposal is reactivated now by Code (2005b) under his formulation "First in/Last out?", which gives frame aphasia a place in the evolution of language issue.

There is, however, a difference between remnant frame aphasia and nascent canonical babbling, which lies in CV co-occurrences (MacNeilage & Davis, 1999, 2001). Since this BBS debate, SMA and pre-SMA studies (e.g., Kennerly et al., 2004) have supported the "premotor frame," not in the sense of a rhythmic pattern generator (not to speak of the lack of inhibition of basal ganglia circuit output, due to an immature or deficient frontal-striatal system), but as a self-pacer for generating voluntary action, via anterior cingulate cortex, probably like rhythmic play, solitary babbling, including jaw wagging, etc. (1).

Our second gift was to invite Peter and Babs to the "Vocalize to Localize" international seminar we organized in Grenoble—with an evolutionary "from meerkats to humans" deixis bias in speech and gesture—in January 2003. And finally we pushed them into the pit to debate, in the resulting special double issue (Abry et al., 2004), with Arbib (2005), who challenged, and changed on this occasion his rather hand-biased view of language, making the proposal of "interweaving protosign and protospeech," "Let's struggle…" answered Peter with his relaxing accent (MacNeilage & Davis, 2005).

Before offering our present gift, let us remember that Gift is "poison" in German, as ambiguous as Greek dosis and French poison coming from Latin potione. To be frank we do not hope that any of these proposals will leave Peter peaceful amidst scientific controversies: they are raised by his endeavor in asking such a fundamental question as "From what primate capacity does speech originate?" More, he will go on making his case even worse by perseverating towards more specific questions, giving his own grounded motor control answers. His answers concern no less than the origin of basic speech units, which have remained until now the property of linguist's intuitive axiomatics: syllables, segments, and finally the word.

Our Present Gift: Testing the *Babbling/Pointing* Ratio

Today we will present data that seem to support our way of coping with the inescapable relationship between *phonology* and *semantics*. Our final aim is to link the rhythmic control of the babble syllable (at 7 months), with the semiotic control of *deixis* in discrete pointing (at 9 months), to integrate babbling into a *Point-Foot* template. This is ultimately the template of the first word (at 12 months). The proposal that the babble syllable would feed the word is not new: *frame dominance* for Babs and Peter (Davis et al., 2002), *vocal motor scheme* for Marilyn Vihman (McCune & Vihman, 2001), are proposals supported by data in favor of articulatory filtering in first words.

But links between the semantic unit and its expression would still remain a miracle, if we used templatic word phonology as another name for saying that the lemmatic word has a rather stable morphonological manifestation. To our present knowledge, there is still no proposal of a control for this unit comparable with the syllable cycle control, embodied in an articulator neural system. We will say the arm instead of the jaw, a new frame in search of its neural correlates. Thus we view our proposal as a needed extension of the *Frame/Content theory*, with the *Speech Frame* [SpF] being finally embedded into the *Sign Frame* [SiF], i.e., *a Framework for two Frames*. Like the embodiment of the abstract phonological syllable, the abstract unit best fitted for interfacing the control of the SpF-syllable with the control of the word-SiF, is also a well known metric unit. The *foot* is prosodically controlled, stressed, intonated, focused, etc. It is already available in (Homeric) poetics, and till now in post-SPE phonologies. This unit is particularly appropriate to take into account the typical one-two syllables in first words. The foot is also able to integrate in adults 1-3 syllables (e.g., in English *muse, music, musical, musically*). Thus we propose that the semiotic-deictic pointing gesture —a semantic grabber for so-called lexical fast mapping, and a syntactic precursor for that-connectives— be the main control unit shaping the foot, hence a *Point-Foot*.

This Babble *syllable/Point-Foot* proposal will become testable by analyzing the ratio between distributions of durations of the babbling cycles and strokes of pointing gestures in babies. If the first word can contain two syllables this ratio must be a *harmonic ratio* 2:1. We will have to make a quantification of the (preferred) behavioral speech and gesture regimes or modes. The first meaning for *mode* is a biocybernetic frequency or resonance. There has been one pioneer experiment in establishing the preferred frequency of the mandibular system (since Sorokin et al., 1980). And coupling of the arm and the mandibular systems, after many purely rhythmic speech-tapping tasks (say a musical activity for the brain!), is still in its exploration phase. What will become clear from the present results is that mean duration decreases with age, for pointing, and for jaw cycle as well: both are faster in adults. Hence this is not due to the mass-size factor (growth) in computing the eigen frequencies of the jaw and the brachial system. It is more likely to neural maturation, e.g. to myelination, but not only (cf. synaptogenesis and the maturation of neurotransmitter systems). The second meaning of *mode* is a statistical dominance in behavioral biometrics, the highest number of occurrences: that's the one we will deal with here.

We will evaluate the implications of a three-step proposal. First, (1a) if the rhythm of canonical babbling has a 3Hz mode, (1b) then a two-syllable first word—if it is chunked from the canonical babbling flow (before a language-specific tuned metric of trochaic... iambic intra-word reorganization)— will tend to have a duration of about 600-700ms. Secondly, (2a) if this first word is controlled by a *foot* template, (2b) then the same tendency towards isochrony must be observed in the duration of a monosyllabic first word. Third, (3a) if the first-word-foot is templated by the pointing gesture, (3b) then the pointing duration of, say, a stroke will take about the same 600-700ms.

We will use statistical tendencies as a first test-approach: namely the peak of occurrences, i.e., the mode in the distribution of babbling cycle duration (or frequency) values, and the mode for pointing stroke durations. The ratio of the two modes should tend to be 2:1. We will also analyze longitudinally one baby who is in the general pointing profile, but displays a marked reduction in stroke duration around the beginning of first words. This relationship could be problematic for a pointing/syllable ratio.

The Pointing Stroke Mode

Our measurements were performed on a video corpus of 6 French children, filmed at home every two weeks between 6 and 18 months; a total of about 57 hours (recorded by Stefanie Brosda in 1999-2000). Since children started canonical babbling earlier or later than 7 months, some were videoed more than others (from 18 to 23 sessions), their follow up stopping around 17 months. The corpus was available for investigation of spontaneous pointing, since there was no eliciting procedure. As expected, domestic baby ethology is as difficult as

414 Abry, Ducey, Vilain, and Lalevée

non-human primatology in the wild! Two hundred and seventy six pointing *and* vocalizing events were measurable, approximately the same as 207 conflict screams collected from 37 chimpanzees during a 5 months field survey (Slocombe & Zuberbühler, 2005).

The presence of a pointing gesture was observed from 7;20 to 17;18. First occurrences were observed in children, from 7 months to 10 months. The more general start occurred at around 9 months, a classical date for the so-called "imperative pointing" emergence. The 276 events located were measured from the first visually detectable onset of motion, in an image by image inspection (i.e. each 40ms); the same for the end of Movement Time (5). Figure 18.1 displays a raw cumulative distribution, obtained with MT or duration of the strokes plotted

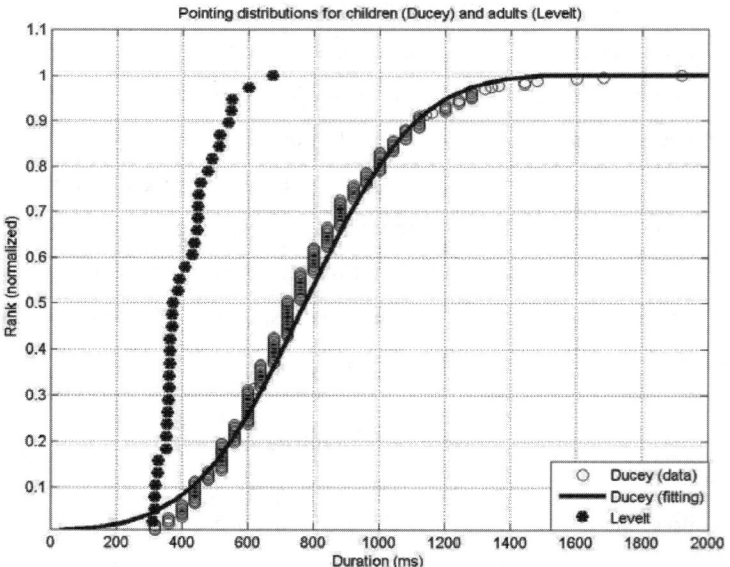

Figure 18.1.
Cumulative frequency curve (rank-duration) for the 276 pointing strokes (circles) of 6 French children in between 6 and 18 months (measured by Ducey, this contribution), fitted by a Gaussian approximation. Levelt *et al.* (1985) mean durations of adults pointing with the right hand (while uttering Dutch deictics), available for 38 conditions (stars), are plotted for comparison (both curves normalized in rank).

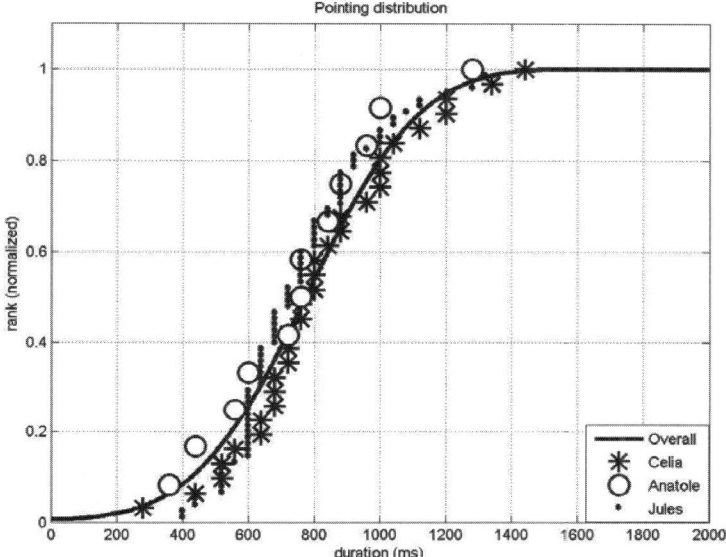

Figure 18.2.
Normalized distributions of pointing strokes for Célia, Anatole and Jules. Their data are rather close to the overall distribution curve obtained from the 6 children (cf. Figure 18.1).

in x and the rank of these duration values in y (here normalized for further comparisons, see below). Figure 18.2 displays normalized distributions of pointing strokes for Celia, Anatole, and Jules and Figure 18.3 details results for Lise, Nicolas, and Tom.

Values run from 280ms to 1920ms (a very slow early pointing stroke, see Fig 18.4). Mean was 776ms with ±267ms as one standard deviation; the gaussian approximation is fitted on the raw data. We plotted a comparison with adults using means of the 38 *right* hand experiments in Levelt et al. (1985), for which MT was available (obtained via SELSPOT tracking, MT=TE for Right Hand only, MT=TA-T1, MT=Execution time). Depending on the number of choice in deictics (*this/that "lamp,"* in Dutch *dit/dat "lampje"*), direction and distance of LED-targets (left/right field; near/far), MT mean values ranged from 313ms (one deictic, for the near-right direction among two LEDs, instantaneous "on-line" response) to 675ms (two deictics, for far left direction among four LEDs, and "offline" response, i.e., after the lamp lighted on, waiting for the experimenter's question "which light?" before starting). As a whole, spontaneous child points are slower than adults, evidencing a maturational factor. Normalized rank presentations of each child (since the number of observations collected for each was different) *vs.* the overall fitted curve, show that three children (Figure 18.2) were closer to the overall mean (A: 763ms±255; J: 768ms±222; and C: 826ms±261), while the others (Figure 18.3) were either faster (T 680ms±239) or slower (N: 926ms±291; and L: 927ms±313). From 9 to 17 months (omitting two occurrences at 7-8 months), there is a clear decreasing trend in means and distributions, from a decrease towards 800ms from 10 to 14 months over 1s to about 600ms at 15-17 months (Figure 18.4). Again, maturation corresponds to faster gestures.

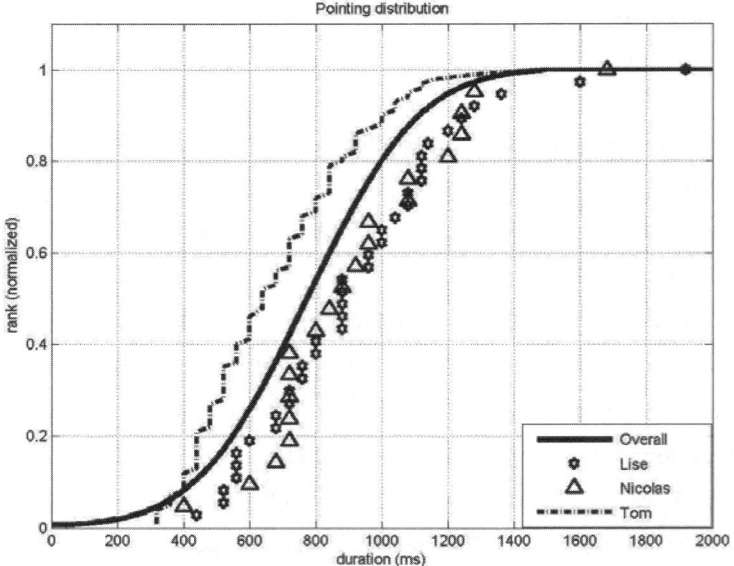

Figure 18.3.
Normalized distributions of pointing strokes for Lise, Nicolas and Tom. Their data are rather faster (Tom) or slower (Lise and Nicolas) than the overall trend obtained from the 6 children (cf. Figure 18.1).

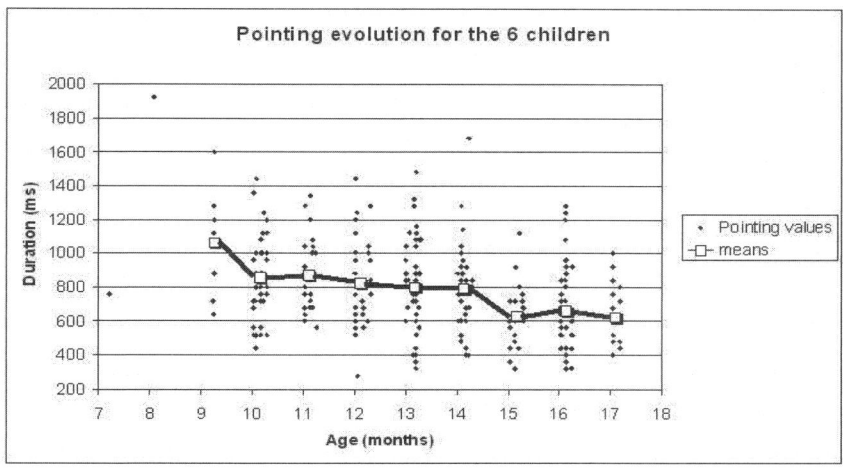

Figure 18.4.
Evolution of pointing stroke durations (diamonds) for all 6 French children in between 6 and 18 months (data are plotted with a decimal x-scale, <month,days>, in order to get a visual grouping by months). Apart the first isolated points (no one 6 months and two 7-8 months), pointing starts at 9 months, and goes on decreasing in overall mean durations —after a period of about 800ms between 10-14 months— towards 600 ms at 15 months.

The syllable cycle mode and the resulting
Babbling/Pointing ratio

There is a huge variation among the many measurements of syllable duration made by different researchers, due obviously to too many factors (see for the clear influence of linguistic patterns of American English, French and Welsh, Vihman et al., 2004). We will take Thelen's proposal (1981) as an anchor point for canonical babbling: canonical babbling settles into the same periodicity as other rhythmic activities. To our knowledge, the first movement recording of rhythmic activity of babies, about this stage (6), was performed on their hands, with the OPTOTRAK system to test Petitto's amodal language rhythm hypothesis (Petitto et al., 2001). Pettito reported that rhythm of signing (hearing) babies had very early (as soon as the 6 months canonical babbling stage for speech exposed children) a low frequency (1Hz) component that was not met in the manual activity of speech exposed babies (Petitto et al., 2001; details in Petitto et al., 2004, for the 3+3 babies recorded at 6, 10, 12 months). This claim remains controversial, being not replicated in any other survey (as discussed in Petitto et al., 2004). Moreover this low frequency appears very soon (6 months). It could be interpreted as repetitive pointing, a very frequent gesture in sign language, especially in child databases. Signing babies could be rather precocious in first signs (e.g., Bonvillian et al., 1985). For the purpose of anchoring our predictions, we will assume the non-controversial distribution of hand rhythmic activities displayed by both signing and non signing babies. This distribution peaks at 3Hz for the 3 non sign-exposed, and the 2.5Hz mode for the 3 sign-exposed is not significantly different. Consequently, by adding to Thelen's general rhythmic stage (i) a precise claim of maturational isofrequency control for the hand and the mouth, we can then predict that, (ii) with this proviso of canonical babbling jaw (mandibular) rhythmic activity being not different from arm-hand rhythmic activity (7), both will run about 3Hz, and finally, that (iii) in order to include 2 jaw cycles, a discrete pointing gesture will afford a stroke of about 1.5 Hz.

But what is the support for the proposal, that babbling cycle runs about 3Hz, like these 6 babies' hands? We used the source/filter approach of Koopmans-van Beinum and van der Stelt (1993) in AMSTIVOC for labeling our corpus. They note that "Initially [up to 4-5 months], large differences exist between the mean values of syllable-sized units duration, but as soon as the stage of canonical babbling is reached at about 6-7 months, the mean durations are more or less equal for the four Dutch children, with a mean value of 424 ms, or an articulation rate of 2.36 syllables/second. However, the relative slowness of the production system at this age may be illustrated by the fact that this value is still about twice as long as the mean syllable duration given by De Boysson-Bardies et al. (1981), for a French child at the age of one and a half. Den Os (1990) studying temporal properties in the speech of one Dutch child between one and three years of age, reports a mean articulation rate of about 3 syllables/second. Koopman-van Beinum (1992) obtained articulation rate values of 6.44 syllables/second for read aloud speech and 6.7‾ syllables/second for conversational speech for a Dutch professional adult speaker." (Koopmans-van Beinum and van der Stelt , 1993: 76). Taken together these results show clearly a maturational trend towards faster babbling/syllable cycles. We can add to these meager canonical babbling rate measurements, data from Bickley et al. (1986) on one child. They tested DFT (Fourier transform) *vs.* AC (autocorrelation function) from the envelope, i.e., intensity curve, of the babbling signal. Both delivered a scattering of frequencies around 3Hz (their Figure 18.3). They showed that evidence of rhythm could be gained 2 months earlier (at about 6 months) than transcription diagnosis of canonical babbling (8 months). As concerns our own data, repetitive measurements of syllable trains (CVCVCV…; including disyllabic CVCV's or S1S2, see below), displayed in syllable cycle durations a large variation scattering around 370ms, i.e., 2.7Hz.

Coming back to the mean stroke of 776ms, this confirms a 2:1 ratio, i.e., the predicted harmonic ratio of *two syllables to one point*. This result demonstrates that the two systems can function in harmony. In order to get the capacities of the two systems, the global approach we used first was neutral with respect to supposed word semantics. We considered no intra-event pointing-syllable relationship. A more detailed approach is needed to show that the realization of this global capacity is as individualized and longitudinal as possible.

A Closer Look at C's Metric: Pointing, Syllables, and Words

We have seen that C was a child behaving in the mean profile of the group for pointing (see Figure 18.2). But contrary to the other children she did not exhibit a monotonously decreasing duration. She presented a rather sudden change between 11 (900ms) and 13 months (940ms), namely at 12 months (540ms), when the appearance of her first words was corroborated (by at least one of the 6

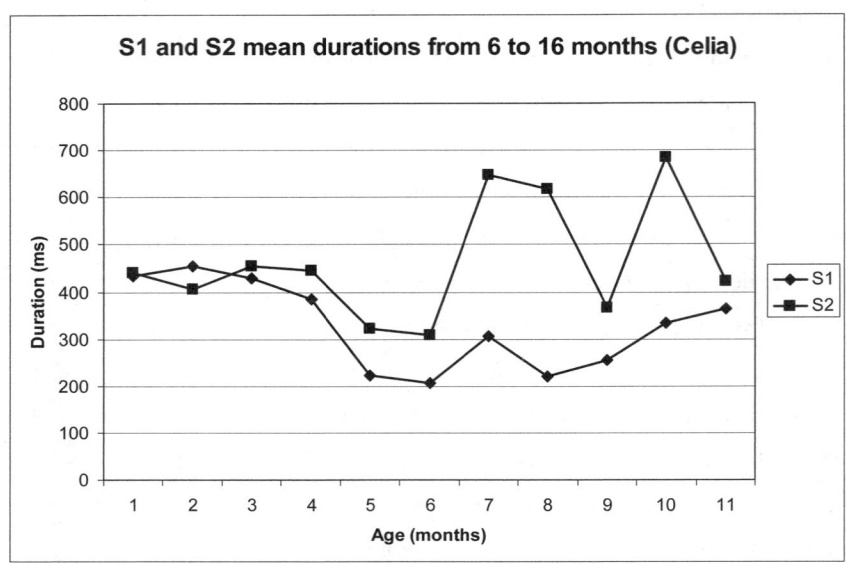

Figure 18.5.
Evolution of the cycle durations of first (S1: diamonds) and second (S2: squares) syllables in Célia's performances from 6 to 16 months. Notice the increase in S2 about the emergence of her first words at 12 months.

criteria in Vihman & McCune, 1994). In Figure 18.5, the first (S1), and second (S2) syllables, starting both in isochrony from above 400ms (2.5Hz) at 6-8 months, fell towards 200ms (S1) and 300ms (S2) at 10-11 months. Just before appearance of first words at 12 months, the second syllable jumps clearly to a duration above 600ms and oscillates between 400ms and 600-700ms for the remaining 13-16 months (which ends at 2.5Hz again). This profile is somehow smoothed when the ratio S2/S1 within each measured item is plotted (Figure 18.6), evidencing clearly the jump at 12-13 months, where the second syllable becomes 2.5 times longer than the first, followed by a decrease of this ratio in the 14-16 months.

This behavior is also illustrated by another French baby (Konopczynski, 1998, pg. 186, her Figure 18.2). This child displayed the same changes in the pattern of syllables. First and second syllables started with isochrony at 8 months (about 4Hz) and increased in duration around first words, the second

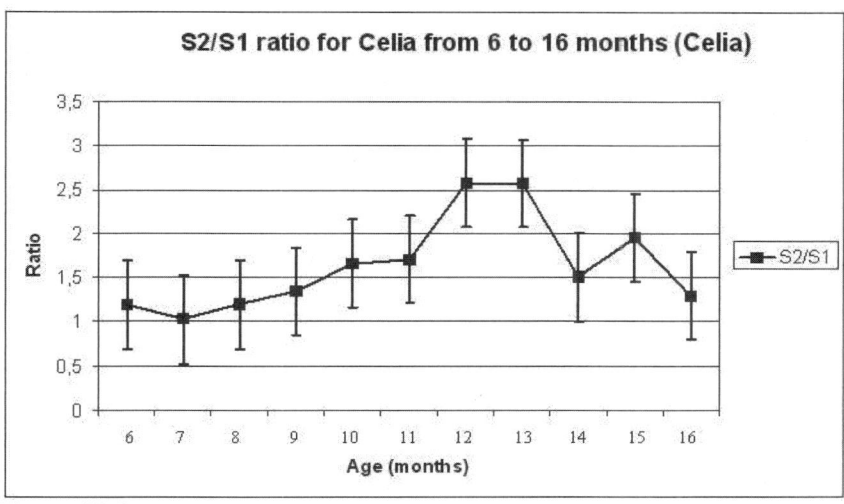

Figure 18.6.
Evolution of the S2/S1 (second over first syllable) ratio for Célia. This ratio evidences the metric change at the same first word period, one-year-old (cf. Figure 18.5).

syllable reaching a maximum at 12 months, followed by a decrease at 15 months. They oscillated in parallel, keeping their values apart, their overall mean duration at about 300ms (3.3Hz) at 2 yrs. Taken together these observations could be a cue that the French iambic pattern is acquired (in babbling) about the first words.

So what about first words and pointing in our data? A simple addition would show, at least for C (see Figure 18.5), that a 12 months CVCV sequence with S1+S2 above 900ms could not be contained within her 540 ms mean foot… But this is not the story. C's CVCV words corresponding to these pointing gestures were between 450-650ms (with a mean of 527ms). Consequently she has no foot-frame/syllable-content problem, her maximum 12 months word point being 680ms. Thereafter she will produce longer exemplars of pointing. Thus when babbling syllables decrease, then increase with the emergence of the first words —evidencing this acquisition of a S1S2 hyper-French pattern (where S2/S1=2.5, a trend which is maintained in Cs 12-13 months words)—these words are not made up simply by chunking out of the babbling flow the first and the second syllables. Thus, there is here an autonomous production of words parallel to this re-patterning in babbling. This result does not mean that such metric (prosodic) changes are independent.

More Questions Left than Answers?

Our 2:1 harmonic ratio links flexibly the two frame claims that, as well as the jaw is the lip and tongue carrier in the babble syllable cyclicity, the arm-hand is the carrier of the index finger in the slow exploratory tipping and in faster pointing discrete gestures. This doesn't mean that the syllable *is* the jaw, nor the foot it feeds with one-two cycles *is* the arm. It indicates that these articulator constraints are harnessed by their neural control structures. Obviously the setting or device that allows a baby's brain to become able to turn the brain of his mother towards its region of interest, only by eye, then by point and voice (older children do sometimes turn forcefully with their hands the head of the inattentive mother!) remains a mysterious black box which is just beginning to open. Dub it Speech Sign Sharing Intention Mechanism (S3IM), as we can play, by elaborating from SAM (Shared Attention Mechanism) of Baron-Cohen (1995), beyond Tomasello et al. (in press) SIM proposal: this would be just referring to inflated/deflated intentional assumptions on mind-reading, unless the deictic devices are more constrained (more by Leslie et al., 1998; than Pylyshyn, 2000).

Meanwhile, we will continue to argue that these two Speech and Sign Frames are the two first frontlines, before going beyond babbling and pointing: they are the roots of phonology and semantics. Both are needed in order to acquire later the specific syllabic structure and the lexicon and grammar of the ambient language. To invoke "early pattern-finding skills" for perceptual and motoric templates—since babies are as good "pattern-extractors" as sound discriminators, and categorizers, (see Tomasello, 2003:28-31)—remains too unconstrained even to account for these only two basic questions: (1) Why syllables? And (2) why one-two syllables in the first words?

Saying that children are imitating motherese leaves totally unanswered the evolutionary issue, i.e., affords no constraints for a coherent evo-devo approach, an endeavor favored by Peter, and other precursors, for deriving language from non-language. "Pattern finding" will account for language pattern-learning in the lexicon, in phonology, and in morpho-syntax. But before fishing words with constructions by ear (and eye), before wording out even a simple lumped "What's that?"—uttered in your baby's style—you need a fishing rod, say voice grunts and (eye, arm) points (McCune et al., 2003). We will argue that this fishing rod is a tool for both the word phonological template and for morpho-syntax, giving ground to demonstratives (Diessel, 1999), giving rise to relativizers and complementizers (from English that-that-that, to Classical Nahuatl in-in-in, etc.: what we can call "that-grammars"), to noun determinants (German "das Haus"/Swedish "huset," French "l'homme"/ Rumanian "omul," etc.), to verb person marking (Latin "ille venit," French "il vient," etc.), and finally giving shape to morphology by grammaticalized cliticization. There is no in-principle reason for not using these processes in development (as promoted, for example, by Vihman, 1999).

Deixis with nascent signs and words is conceivably *enactivated* in the neuron and nerve circuits of the jaw and the arm. Babies need both in order to succeed optimally in capturing jointly semantics and phonetics available in their interactive world. Thus they will step into their own words by stabilizing their *syllables* within a *foot*.

Acknowledgments

To Stefanie Brosda for the legacy of her corpus; to Romain Trollat for measuring C's babbling; to Coriandre Vilain for his help in graphics and statistics; and to Alain Arnal and Christophe Savariaux for management of the video files. Special thanks to Barbara Davis who did far more than polish the rubbish of our English. Research for this contribution has been supported by a European project within Origin of Man, Language, and Languages ("COG-

Speech") and the ACI on Complex Systems in Social Sciences of the French Cognitique Programme" ("Pati Papa?").

References

Abry, C., Boë, L. J., Laboissière, R. & Schwartz, J. L. (1998). A new puzzle for the evolution of speech? *Behavioral and Brain Science, 21*, 512–513.

Abry, C. & Schwartz, J. L. (2004). Language origins: A puzzle with many pieces. In Schwartz, J. L.(Ed.) *Dossier Origine du langage, Primatologie, 6*, 353–366.

Abry, C., Stefanuto, M., Vilain, A. & Laboissière, R. (2002). What can the utterance "tan, tan" of Broca's patient Leborgne tell us about the hypothesis of an emergent "babble syllable" downloaded by SMA? In J. Durand & B. Laks (Eds.) *Phonetics, Phonology and Cognition,* (pp. 226–243). Oxford: Oxford University Press.

Abry, C., Vilain, A. & Schwartz, J. L. (2004). "Vocalize to Localize"? A call for better crosstalk between auditory and visual communication systems researchers: From meerkats to humans. In Abry, C., Vilain, A. & Schwartz, J. L. (Eds.) *Special issue: Vocalize to Localize, Interaction Studies, 5 (3)*, 313–325.

Arbib, M. A. (2005). Interweaving protosign and protospeech. Further development beyond the mirror. In Abry, C., Vilain, A. & Schwartz, J. L. (Eds.) *Special issue: Vocalize to Localize II, Interaction Studies, 6 (2)*, 147–171.

Baron-Cohen, S. (1995). *Mindblindness: An essay on autism and theory of mind,* Cambridge, MA: MIT Press.

Bates, E. & Dick, F. (2002). Language, gesture and the developing brain. In B. J. Casey & Y. Munakata (Eds.) *Special issue: Converging method approach to the study of developmental science. Developmental Psychobiology, 40(3)*, 293–310.

Bickley, C., Lindblom, B. & Roug, L. (1986). Acoustic measures of rhythm in infants' babbling, or "All God's children got rhythm," *Proceedings of the 12th International Congress of Acoustics (Toronto)*, A6–4.

Bonvillian, J. D., Orlansky, M. D. & Novak, L.L. (1985). Early sign language acquisition and its relationship to cognition and motor development. In J. Kyle & B. Woll (Eds.) *Language in sign: An international perspective on sign language,* London: Croom Helm.

Boysson-Bardies, B. De, Bacri, N., Sagart, L. & Poizat, M. (1981). Timing in late babbling. *Journal of Child Language, 8*, 525–539.

Butterworth, G. (2003). Pointing is the royal road to language for babies. In S. Kita (Ed.) *Pointing. When language, culture, and cognition meet* (pp. 9–33). London: Erlbaum.

Code, C. (2005a). Syllables in the brain: Evidence from brain damage. In R. J. Hartsuiker, R. Bastiaanse, A. Postma & F. Wijnen (Eds.) *Phonological Encoding and Monitoring in Normal and Pathological Speech* (pp. 119–136). Hove, Sussex: Psychology Press.

Code, C. (2005b). First in, last out: The evolution of aphasic lexical speech automatisms to agrammatism and the evolution of human communication. In Abry, C., Vilain, A. & Schwartz, J. L. (Eds.) *Special issue: Vocalize to Localize II. Interaction Studies, 6 (2)*, 311–334.

Davis, B. L., MacNeilage, P. F. & Matyear, C. (2002). Acquisition of serial complexity in speech production: A comparison of Phonetic and Phonological Approaches to First Word Production. *Phonetica, 59*, 75–107.

Den Os, E. A. (1990). Development of temporal properties in the speech of one child between one and three years of age. *Proceedings of the Institute of Phonetic Sciences of Amsterdam, 14*, 39–52.

Diessel, H. (1999). *Demonstratives: Form, function, and grammaticalization.* Amsterdam: Benjamins.

Gerken, L. (1994). A metrical template account of children's weak syllable omission from multisyllabic words. *Journal of Child Language, 21*, 565–584.

Green, J. R., Moore, C. A. & Reilly, K. J. (2002). The sequential development of jaw and lip control for speech. *Journal of Speech, Language, and Hearing Research, 45(2)*, 66–79.

Hilaire-Debove, G. & Demuth, K. (2005). Troncation de mot chez l'enfant francophone. *ELA: Emergence of Language Abilities: Ontogeny and Phylogeny, (Lyon 8 –10 dec.)* (A).

Indefrey, P. & Levelt, W. J. M. (2004). The spatial and temporal signatures of word production components. *Cognition, 92*, 101–144.

Iverson, J. M. & Goldin-Meadow, S. (1998). Why people gesture when they speak. *Nature, 396*, 228.

Kennerly, S.W., Sakai, K. & Rushworth, M.F.S. (2004). The organization of action sequences and the role of the pre-SMA. *Journal of Neurophysiology, 91*, 978–993.

Konopczynski, G. (1998). Interactive Developmental Intonology (IDI): Theory and application to French. *Revue Parole, 7–8*, 177–201.

Koopmans-van Beinum, F. J. (1992). The role of focus words in natural and in synthetic continuous speech: Acoustic aspects. *Speech Communication, 11*, 439–452.

Koopmans-van Beinum, F. J. (1993). Cyclic effects of infant speech: Perception, early sound production, and maternal speech. *Proceedings of the Institute of Phonetic Sciences of Amsterdam, 14*, 65–78.

Koopmans-van Beinum, F. J. & van der Stelt, J. (1985). Early stages in the development of speech movements. In B. Lindblom & R. Zetterström (Eds.) *Precursors of Early Speech* (pp. 37–50). New York: Stockton.

Landauer, T. K. (1962). Rate of implicit speech. *Perceptual and Motor Skills, 15*, 646.

Leavens, D. A. (2004). Manual deixis in apes and humans. In C. Abry, A. Vilain & Schwartz, J. L.(Eds.) *Special issue: Vocalize to Localize I, Interaction Studies, 5 (3)*, 387–408.

Leslie, A. M., Xu, F., Tremoulet, P. & Scholl, B. (1998). Indexing and the object concept: Developing "What" and "Where" systems. *Trends in Cognitive Sciences, 2(1)*, 10–18.

Levelt, W. J. M., Richardson, G. & La Heij, W. (1985). Pointing and voicing in deictic expressions. *Journal of Memory and Language, 24*, 133–164.

Locke, J. L. (1997). A theory of neurolinguistic development. *Brain and Language, 58*, 265–326.

MacNeilage, P. F. (1998). The Frame/Content theory of evolution of speech production. *Behavioral and Brain Sciences, 21*, 499–546.

MacNeilage, P. F. & Davis, B. L. (2001). Motor mechanisms in speech ontogeny: Phylogenetic, neurobiological and linguistic implications. *Current Opinion in Neurobiology, 11*, 696–700.

MacNeilage, P. F. & Davis, B. L. (2005). The frame/content theory of evolution of speech: A comparison with a gestural-origins alternative. In Abry, C., Vilain, A. & Schwartz, J. L. (Eds.) *Special issue: Vocalize to Localize II, Interaction Studies, 6 (2)*, 173–199.

McCune, L., Greenwood, A. & Lennon, E. (2003). *Gestures, grunts, and words: The transition to communicative competence*, Tampa, FL: SRCD.

McCune, L. & Vihman, M. M. (2001). Early phonetic and lexical development: A productivity approach. *Journal of Speech, Language, and Hearing Research, 44*, 670–684.

Munhall, K. G. & Jones, J. A. (1998). Articulatory evidence for syllabic structure. *Behavioral and Brain Sciences, 21(4)*, 524–525.

Oller, D. K. (2000). *The emergence of the speech capacity*. Mahwah, N.J.: Erlbaum.

Petitto, L. A., Holowka, S., Sergio, L.E. & Ostry D. (2001). Language rhythms in baby hand movement, *Nature, 413*, 35–36.

Petitto, L. A., Holowka, S., Sergio, L.E., Levy, B. & Ostry D.J. (2004). Baby hands that move to the rhythm of language: Hearing babies acquiring sign languages babble silently on the hands. *Cognition, 93*, 43–73.

Pizzuto, E., Capobianco, M. & Devescovi, A. (2005). Gestural-vocal deixis and representational skills in early language development. In Abry, C., Vilain, A. & Schwartz, J. L. (Eds.) *Special issue: Vocalize to Localize II, Interaction Studies, 6 (2)*, 223–252.

Pylyshyn, Z. (2000). Situating vision in the world. *Trends in Cognitive Sciences, 4(5)*, 197–207.

Schaal. S., Sternad, D., Osu, R. & Kawato, M. (2004). Rhythmic arm movement is not discrete. *Nature Neuroscience, 7 (10)*, 1137–1144.

Slocombe, K. E. & Zuberbühler, K. (2005). Agonistic screams in wild chimpanzees (*Pan troglodytes schweinfurthii*) vary as a function of social role. *Journal of Comparative Psychology, 119 (1)*, 67–77.

Sorokin, V.N, Gay, T. & Ewan, W.G (1980). Some biomechanical correlates of the jaw movements. *Journal of the Acoustical Society of America*, Suppl. 1, 68, S32.

Thelen, E. (1981). Rhythmical behavior in infancy: an ethological perspective. *Developmental Psychology, 17*, 237–257.

Tomasello, M. (2003a). *Constructing a language. A usage-based theory of language acquisition.* Cambridge, MA: Harvard University Press.

Tomasello, M., Carpenter, M., Call, J., Behne, T. & Moll, H. (in press). Understanding and sharing intentions: The origins of cultural cognition. *Behavioral and Brain Sciences.*

Vihman, M. M. (1999). The transition to grammar in a bilingual child: Positional patterns, model learning, and relational words. *Journal of Bilingualism, 3(2)*, 267–301.

Vihman, M., DePaolis, R., Nakai, S. & Hallé, P. (2004). The role of accentual pattern in early lexical representation. *Journal of Memory and Language 50*, 336–353.

Vihman, M. M. & McCune, L. (1994). When a word is a word? *Journal of Child Language, 21*, 517–542.

Volterra, V., Caselli, M.C., Capirci, O. & Pizzuto, E. (2004). Gesture and the emergence and development of language. In M. Tomasello & D. Slobin (Eds.) *Beyond Nature-Nurture. Essays in Honor of Elizabeth Bates* (pp. 3–40). London: Erlbaum.

Ziegler, W., Kilian, B. & Deger, K. (1997). The role of the left mesial frontal cortex in fluent speech: Evidence from a case of left supplementary motor area hemorrhage. *Neuropsychologia, 35 (9)*, 1197–1208.

Author Index

A

Abbs, 232
Abler, 331
Aboitiz, 19
Abry, 31, 86, 409, 410, 411
Aichert, 161
Ainsworth, 48
Aitchison, 76, 77
Als, 38
Amundin, 54
Anderson, 338
Andrew, 31, 41, 54, 111
Anthoney, 112, 113
Arbib, 17, 114, 117, 124, 133, 140, 147, 411
Arcadi, 146
Armstrong, 133
Ashby, 163, 164
Aureli, 116

Aurelius, 37
Austin, 47

B

Baayen, 159, 200
babbling \f, 41
Bagemihl, 156
Bailey, 143
Balcomb, 51
Baptista, 51
Barker, 205
Barnes, 118
Baron-Cohen, 422
Basinger, 37, 123
Bates, 295
Bauer, 277, 278
Baumann, 165
Beaumont, 123
Bekken, 117
Bell, A., 15, 155, 357

Subject Index

A

acoustic modulations, 182
age of implantation, 207, 222
altriciality, 44, 52, 53
ambient input, 335, 342
amplification, 207
AMSTIVOC, 234, 236, 239, 418
arcuate fasciculus, 19
articulation, 7, 10, 34, 35, 36, 38,
   39, 40, 43, 45, 85, 94, 103, 107,
   160, 169, 182, 194, 195, 196,
   197, 211, 226, 227, 229, 230,
   231, 235, 236, 237, 238, 239,
   247, 248, 255, 260, 261, 262,
   264, 266, 267, 275, 278, 279,
   280, 281, 284, 285, 286, 287,
   295, 297, 298, 299, 307, 308,
   309, 318, 327, 332, 333, 336,
   337, 338, 339, 340, 341, 343,
   345, 346, 347, 355, 356, 357,
   358, 360, 361, 362, 363, 364,
   365, 366, 367, 368, 370, 371,
   373, 374, 383, 384, 393, 394,
   397, 399, 418, 419
articulators, 8, 248, 252, 273, 274,
   275, 277, 278, 346, 393
articulators ease, 338
articulatory ease, 347
articulatory gestures, 157, 182
articulatory phonetics, 357, 358
articulatory phonology, 330
Articulatory preference scores, 343
articulatory transition, 37
auditory feedback, 238, 239
auditory-oral language, 207

B

babbling, 6, 7, 8, 11, 13, 18, 39, 42,
   44, 52, 93, 94, 108, 112, 121,
   122, 123, 124, 187, 188, 189,
   190, 191, 194, 195, 197, 199,
   201, 202, 211, 212, 225, 226,
   230, 233, 236, 237, 238, 239,

phonetic learning, 335, 349
phonological encoding, 156, 157, 161, 165, 168, 170, 172
phonological equivalence, 81, 83, 86, 167
phonological shapes, 71, 73, 75, 81, 82, 83, 86
phonological system, 84, 85, 94, 103, 331, 380
phonological word, 157, 158, 159, 160, 168, 393
phonology, 15, 84, 163, 281, 295, 310, 347, 380, 382, 383, 384, 386, 393, 395, 398, 399, 400, 401, 403, 411, 422, 423
phylogeny, 6, 22, 95, 97, 98, 107, 108, 355
pinnipeds, 51
pointing, 134, 411, 412, 413, 414, 415, 417, 418, 419, 421, 422
premotor programming, 107
preparation paradigm, 168
production constraints, 275, 276
profound deafness, 207, 223
proprioception, 250
proto-language, 64, 69, 86
pure frame, 8, 11, 107, 206, 275, 278, 346

Q

quasivowel, 37, 43

R

recalibration, 345, 347
respiration, 95, 96, 227, 231, 236, 237, 239, 246, 247, 249, 250
re-use, 335, 344, 345, 346, 347, 348
ritualization, 48, 119, 142
secondary handicapping conditions, 208

S

segment sequencing, 357, 358
segmental independence, 328, 330, 335, 346, 349
segmental overlap effect, 165, 167
semantic equivalence, 70, 71, 81
sensori-motor system, 226
serial order problem, 355
sign, 379, 380, 381, 382, 383, 384, 385, 386, 387, 388, 389, 390, 391, 392, 393, 395, 396, 397, 398, 399, 400, 401, 403, 404, 412, 418
sign supported speech, 208
size principle, 12, 348
social display, 115
sonority, 183, 184, 356, 357, 374, 392, 396
sound production, 36, 39, 54, 93, 142, 226, 227, 228, 231, 234, 236, 237, 238, 239, 245, 246, 247, 248, 249, 250, 253, 254, 256, 257, 259, 260, 262, 263, 264, 265, 266, 267, 289
source-filter system, 228, 231
spatial targets, 19, 327
speech apparatus, 249, 250
speech development, 10, 207, 220, 226, 227, 228, 229, 230, 235, 238, 239, 246, 253
speech errors, 5, 18, 156, 308
speech motor milestones, 247, 249, 254
speech perception, 165, 209, 329
speech production, 10, 18, 20, 64, 84, 93, 108, 117, 143, 156, 158, 159, 160, 161, 162, 164, 168, 172, 206, 221, 222, 223, 225, 226, 227, 228, 231, 232, 234, 235, 238, 245, 246, 247, 250, 251, 265, 327, 329, 334, 355, 356, 374
supplementary motor area, 17, 20, 410